AF607953

PROPAGANDA IN REVOLUTIONARY UKRAINE

Leaflets, Pamphlets, and Cartoons, 1917–1922

STEPHEN VELYCHENKO

Propaganda in Revolutionary Ukraine

Leaflets, Pamphlets, and Cartoons, 1917–1922

UNIVERSITY OF TORONTO PRESS
Toronto Buffalo London

Toronto Buffalo London
utorontopress.com

ISBN 978-1-4875-0468-7 (cloth)

Library and Archives Canada Cataloguing in Publication

Title: Propaganda in revolutionary Ukraine: Leaflets, pamphlets, and cartoons, 1917–1922 / Stephen Velychenko.

Names: Velychenko, Stephen, author.

Description: Includes bibliographical references and index.

Identifiers: Canadiana 20190153830 | ISBN 9781487504687 (hardcover)

Subjects: LCSH: Ukraine – History – Revolution, 1917–1921 – Propaganda. | LCSH: Ukraine – History – Revolution, 1917–1921 – Caricatures and cartoons. | LCSH: Ukraine – History – Revolution, 1917– 1921 – Public opinion. | LCSH: Propaganda, Ukrainian – History – 20th century. | LCSH: Propaganda – Ukraine – History – 20th century. | LCSH: Ukraine – History – Revolution, 1917–1921.

Classification: LCC DK265.8.U4 V45 2019 | DDC 947.708/41–dc23

This book has been published with the help of a grant from the Federation for the Humanities and Social Sciences, through the Awards to Scholarly Publications Program, using funds provided by the Social Sciences and Humanities Research Council of Canada.

University of Toronto Press acknowledges the financial assistance to its publishing program of the Canada Council for the Arts and the Ontario Arts Council, an agency of the Government of Ontario.

Canada Council for the Arts | Conseil des Arts du Canada

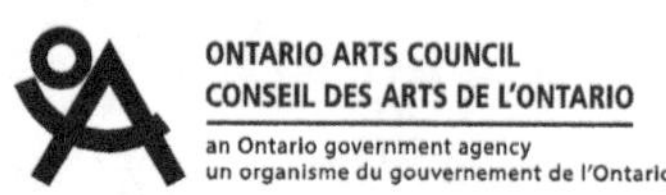

Funded by the Government of Canada | Financé par le gouvernement du Canada | Canada

Contents

Online Documents and Illustrations for *Propaganda in Revolutionary Ukraine: Leaflets, Pamphlets, and Cartoons, 1917–1922*

Access: https://utorontopress.com/pru-pdf

Documents: Leaflets

Illustrations: Cartoons and Postcards

Note on online documents and illustrations: There are references throughout the book to both the figures and documents found in this book and also online. Illustrations 1 to 43 will be found at the end of the chapters as indicated in the table of contents. Illustrations 44 to 96 and documents 1 to 357 are online as indicated above.

PROPAGANDA IN REVOLUTIONARY UKRAINE

Leaflets Pamphlets and Cartoons 1917–1922

Introduction

> The peasants listened very carefully to my speech and afterwards leaflets and announcements were distributed to the audience, [copies] of the Pereiaslav Treaty were sold and immediately bought-up.
>
> Petro Solukha, Central Rada agitator, Baturyn, May 1917.[1]

This book is a survey of domestic governmental and party printed-text propaganda in revolutionary Ukraine. It summarizes and analyses an illustrative sample of leaflets, pamphlets, and cartoons published under and/or by the Central Rada, the Ukrainian State, the Ukrainian National Republic (UNR/Directory), the left wing of the Ukrainian Socialist Revolutionary Party (*Borotbist*), the Ukrainian Social Democratic and Labour Party (Independentists and Ukrainian Communist Party – UCP), Ukraine's Bolsheviks (Communist Party of Ukraine – CPU), and anti-Bolshevik warlords (*otaman*). Some publications by unions, cooperatives, *zemstvos*, and Provincial Information Bureaux are included. It also describes the organizational infrastructure that underlay the production and dissemination of those texts. Most of the reviewed leaflets and pamphlets have long been forgotten, yet their contents offer information that historians should incorporate into the historiography of Ukraine's revolutions.

After the war, the propaganda of the major protagonists began to be studied, and since then, many publications have reproduced posters, proclamations, caricatures, and leaflets from that war.[2] English-language works on Bolshevik propaganda normally focus on Russia.[3] Ukrainian propaganda has been little studied.[4]

The reproduced materials are grouped chronologically and analysed in the text by subject matter. Most are summarized in English for those who do not know Ukrainian or Russian but who are interested either in Ukrainian-Russian issues specifically or in revolution and media in general. The book includes statistics with the proviso that the deceptively precise figures that are available for the years 1917 to 1923 are almost exclusively from the Bolshevik side and should be regarded as only an approximate guide. The book is not a history of propaganda during the years in question – that remains to be written.[5] It does not cover the West Ukrainian National Republic,[6] the restorationist White movement,[7] or Nestor Makhno's anarchists.[8] Nor does it review materials issued by Russian Mensheviks and Socialist Revolutionaries in Ukraine (Illus. 7). All of these cannot be adequately covered in a single volume, and each deserves a separate monograph.[9] Newspapers were used only as sources for press runs to ascertain publishing potentials and average per capita distribution.

Propaganda in Revolutionary Ukraine is divided into five chapters, with accompanying documents and illustrations presented in chronological order, which can only be approximate, because many leaflets and pamphlets are undated. Political, theatrical-cultural, and health and sanitation texts are grouped separately. Chapter 1 reviews how propaganda was understood at the time and describes the pre-revolutionary publishing and transportation networks in tsarist Ukraine that underlay the production and distribution of printed materials. It includes estimated totals for the number, location, and type of presses, as well as the number of paper mills, printers, and typesetters, and estimates the density of the communications and transportation systems. Where possible, it indicates newspaper totals, press runs, and approximate per capita distribution. Two chapters survey and summarize materials published by three of Ukraine's governments, the two largest Ukrainian political parties, and the anti-Bolshevik warlords. Chapter 4 covers Ukraine's Bolsheviks. Each chapter examines the publishing and distribution networks in the territories the given party or government controlled. It then reviews and summarizes the messages each government or party disseminated thematically. The chapter on Bolshevik propaganda is the most detailed because their Agitation and Propaganda Department records are the best preserved. These include data on paper production, printing, and distribution. In some cases, these data permit estimates of per capita distribution at the village level. The chapters on Ukrainian governments and movements are less comprehensive. The records still extant of the information and press agencies of the Central Rada and the Ukrainian National Republic, compared to those of the Bolsheviks, are fewer and more fragmentary. The Hetman State had no information ministry and did not engage in mass propaganda except during the last weeks of its existence. Extant documents of the left-wing factions of the two major Ukrainian socialist parties, the Social Democrats and the Socialist Revolutionaries, and the warlords, contain little material related specifically to the technical details of propaganda.

The conclusion reviews the principal ideas found in the sample and contemporaries' assessments of the impact of printed propaganda. It suggests that in the war of words neither Ukrainian failures nor Bolshevik success should be exaggerated, for each side managed to sway opinion in its favour in specific places at specific times. The Bolsheviks had more paper, ink, presses, printers, and probably typewriters, than did the Ukrainian government parties and warlords. But because during the period in question no one side controlled the production and distribution of all printed text messages in the territories it claimed, it could not isolate its audience from rival sources of information. Although the Bolsheviks had obviously won the war of weapons by 1923, both Ukrainian national and Bolshevik Russian situation reports indicate it was not so obvious that they had won the war of words. Bolshevik reality, there as in Russia, nullified official propaganda.[10] In Ukraine that reality lent credence to the ideas of the defeated national movement, which, irrespective of the Bolshevik's control over the media, circulated in text and oral form into the 1930s.

Since not all leaflets and political pamphlets from the period have been located or catalogued, this book is necessarily based on an illustrative and not representative sample and should be regarded as an initial survey of the subject.[11] The sample consists of 90 party and governmental pamphlets (30 Bolshevik), and approximately 1,000 leaflets, of which 357 are in a supplement that, due to costs, has been exiled to Cyberia: https://utorontopress.com/pru-pdf.[12] Because the Ukrainian government-in-exile and anti-Bolshevik partisans rarely had access to presses in Ukraine after 1920, the sample includes summaries of original, sometimes handwritten messages, as well as copies made by Bolshevik secretaries during and after that year, of leaflets that probably no longer exist.

Picture postcards were the period's equivalent of bumper stickers and played a role in popular mobilization alongside other published materials. In tsarist Ukraine private publishers were allowed to print postcards after 1896. After censorship was eased in 1905, activists used postcards to popularize a patriotic notion of "Ukraine" as a place and to disseminate images of "Ukrainians," national heroes, poets, and sympathetic national stereotypes. The best known today are those by Vasyl Hulak, although there is no indication of how popular they were at the time they appeared (Illus. 1–6).[13] Ukrainian governments apparently did not issue patriotic picture postcards, which appear to have been published only by private publishers. How many such postcards were published during the revolutionary years, and whether these included reproductions of posters, is unknown.[14] The online supplement to this book includes a selection of non-governmental postcards and caricatures, among which are rare satirical cartoons from three Ukrainian satirical journals, *Repiakhy*, *Budiak*, and *Gedz*. Published in Kyiv, these were socialist in orientation and had ceased publishing by 1919.[15] Some White cartoons are included because they comment on issues not encountered in Ukrainian or Bolshevik materials.[16] The book does not include Bolshevik caricatures, many of which were reproduced before 1991.

Leaflets and pamphlets deserve attention because they were an efficient means of imparting information to a mass audience, alongside posters and speeches. They made effective use of space when paper, ink, presses, type, transportation, cinemas, and film were in short supply, almost no one had a radio, and mail was irregular.[17] Leaflets and pamphlets, unlike newspapers, could be printed, distributed, posted quickly, dropped from planes, shot from guns, and hidden when necessary. They could not be traced to sources if they did not include publishing details. As such, they could be more effective in the war of words than books, newspapers, or journals. Most propaganda was disseminated in cities, but all sides attempted to reach villages with travelling agitators – with varying success. Unlike prewar commercial advertising, which was posted primarily in cities in regulated commercial spaces and which used slogans aimed at shoppers, and unlike public messages, which were restricted to government notice boards, wartime leaflets, pamphlets, and political posters were intended for all and appeared in all public spaces if not all vertical surfaces. Before the war, critics and concerned citizens complained about sweeping vistas of vulgar advertising that defaced buildings and overwhelmed the cityscape. Commercial materials gave way to political ones after 1914, but the former remained. Under Bolshevik rule, the loyal citizen would protest the persistence of commercial advertisements for worldly things such as all-night dancehalls, exhibited on "proletarian streets" alongside posters celebrating the Red Army and the Bolshevik cause.[18]

While images and the spoken word can be understood by all, the impact of printed text on mobilizing, democratizing, socializing, and nationalizing populations should not be underestimated in societies in which few people had a telephone or a radio or a daily newspaper. Illiteracy was not an insurmountable barrier to the dissemination of ideas in print. Meetings as well as collective readings, where the knowledgeable presented and elucidated a text, created a collective aural experience. The literate read to the illiterate. Posters urged all to learn to read (Illus. 8–9). Public readings and speeches transmitted messages to the illiterate, and public posting ensured that single copies had multiple readers. In 1905 a literate peasant writing to the Ukrainian-language paper *Rada* described what was probably a typical situation. He could not afford to subscribe, he wrote, but he would read the paper at the houses of friends, where as many as thirty would gather when an issue arrived and listen while someone read the text.[19]

The printed materials discussed in this book offer insight into how elites simplified issues of high politics for the masses during Ukraine's revolutions. All sides produced pamphlets and leaflets, which were intrinsic to the visual landscape of the time along with posters. The result was a landscape dominated by political rather than commercial advertising. One historian has estimated that on all of Ukraine's fronts during 1919, all of the rival powers together produced more than 2 million leaflets – an approximate average for that year of one for every fifteen people. In 1920 the Bolsheviks alone released in Ukraine the same number of copies of 142 leaflets.[20] These ratios, like most of those given in the text, are calculated on the basis of the estimated total population in 1917 of 30 million. The number of readers per leaflet, pamphlet, or newspaper would be much lower if we divided copies only among the urban literate. At times there were multiple copies for single urban readers.

These forgotten mass-produced pamphlets and leaflets were what people would have seen and heard discussed in their daily lives. They show the brief, condensed form that central elites used to impart ideas and which ideas they deemed vital. The best pamphlets and leaflets delivered simple, concise messages cheaply and quickly. Leaflets in particular – a "literature of the instant" – provide an important view of the moment they were issued. They offer insight into the prosaic details of daily life and the communicative culture of the time. As sheets of paper with texts designed to be seen or read in public places, leaflets and pamphlets informed, instructed, or ordered. Some demonized the enemy. Examining these materials reveals which ideas – be they rational or emotional – the mobilized elites thought they should disseminate to populations in order to win their loyalty and influence them to understand events according to those ideas. The explosion of texts and pictorial images in the public sphere after 1917 amounted to a democratization of, and revolution in, mass communication. That explosion accompanied the social and national revolutions that broke out that year. The centralized simultaneous mass distribution of single messages in different places within a definite territory to create a sense of national belonging among people who had never seen one another was, of course, central to state and nation building.[21]

Although this book focuses on materials related to the momentous, it must be remembered that propaganda also addressed the mundane.

Leaflets instructed people to wash their hands, clean their dwellings, and take baths in the interest of public health, as well as how to read books (Illus. 9–12). Sometimes messages contradicted each other – for example, when the health ministry issued warnings not to smoke even while the state Tobacco Trust urged people to smoke (Illus. 13, 14). Materials such as these, like the cartoons of the time reproduced in the supplement (Illus. 44–96), remind us that life went on in the shadow of the great events. On 7 November 1917, Ukraine's Bolshevik papers printed Lenin's "Declaration of the Right of the Nations of Russia" and Mykhailo Hrushevsky in the Rada declared it was time to proclaim the Ukrainian National Republic and read the Third Universal. That same day, in the town of Tarashcha near Kyiv, theatre advertisements warned those with weak nerves not to attend that evening's performance of Jacob Gordin's *Di Shkihte* (The Slaughterer) – a play attacking arranged marriages (Illus. 15).

Unlike books, leaflets and pamphlets were ephemeral in the long run because they were either thrown away or used for other purposes after being read. All sides experienced a paper shortage. Bolshevik posters included warnings that those caught destroying them would be punished (Illus. 16). In the short term, however, they were listened to and read by many more people than were books or newspapers. Pamphlets and leaflets were short, topical, narrowly focused on a crucial issue of the day, and usually simply written, and their press runs eclipsed those of books. Accordingly, a review of these once omnipresent but now rare items, of their idioms and arguments, provides insight into aspects of the revolution omitted or noted only superficially by those who work with less ephemeral printed forms such as memoirs, historical accounts, and government documents.[22]

This study is based on the holdings of the Central State Archive of the Higher Organs of Ukraine (*Tsentralnyi derzhavnyi arkhiv vyshchykh orhaniv vlady* –TsDAVO) and the Central State Archive of Civil Organizations of Ukraine (*Tsentralnyi derzhavnyi arkhiv hromadskykh obiednan* - TsDAHO). Fond 57 op. 2 of the latter contains nineteen volumes with hundreds of transcribed leaflets dated 1919, collected from provincial branches in 1949 for deposit in the central archive. These archives also contain reports on the public mood and the impact of propaganda sent by local officials and/or agitators/instructors to their respective central ministries/commissariats of internal affairs, or agitation and propaganda departments. The original items reproduced in this book are primarily from the Ukrainian State Archival Academic Library (*Derzhavna naukova arkhivna biblioteka* – DNAB), the State Print Archive (*Arkhiv Druku*), Ukraine's Central Academic Library (*Tsentralna Naukova*

Biblioteka im. Vernadskoho – TsNB), its former KGB archive (*Tsentralnyi Derzhavnyi Arkhiv Sluzhby Bezpeky Ukrainy* – TsDASBU), and the Ukrainian National Museum (*Natsionalny Muzei Istorii Ukrainy* – NMIU).[23] Any comprehensive and definitive study of propaganda during the revolutionary years would have not only to collate Ukrainian central and provincial archive collections but also collections abroad.[24]

In Ukraine, five thousand Bolshevik leaflets issued between 1917 and 1920 were located and catalogued as of 1980. Some of them, and a considerable number of Bolshevik posters, have been reproduced.[25] Many pamphlets have survived, but no one has yet determined how many were published, nor have they all been catalogued into a single bibliography. The leaflets, caricatures, pamphlets, and satirical prints of the Ukrainian national governments, anti-Bolshevik warlords/partisans, and anti-Bolshevik socialists remain little known.[26] Some still lay unopened and uncatalogued as of 2016. The substantial collection of leaflets and posters in the State Academic Archival Library in Kyiv was not fully catalogued and accessible until 2010. Ukrainian national government posters and cartoons are very rare. Historians don't know whether this is because they were not produced, or whether Bolshevik commissars, aware of the power of graphic satire and pictures of idealized heroics, destroyed them when they found them. The times were not conducive for collecting, as those found in possession of non-Bolshevik materials could well face arrest or death.

In August 1919 when the Whites controlled parts of Ukraine, they issued a secret circular to "destroy all anti-state literature." According to a report from Kyiv, local officials chose only Ukrainian-language materials.[27] Although the substantial number of surviving Ukrainian governmental, party, and partisan/warlord leaflets suggests that Bolshevik leaders decided not to destroy them, it cannot be ruled out that they did destroy many, along with pamphlets and posters.[28] Nor were national issues the only criteria of exclusion. Among the hundreds of leaflets and pamphlets in the four Kyiv collections noted above reviewed for this book, for instance, there were none dealing with syphilis, which at the time was as widespread as typhus. I found only one example, by chance, in a bound volume of documents of a Bolshevik public health agency. Bolsheviks began destroying library holdings in Ukraine in 1920.

After 1921 they began sending to libraries non-Bolshevik materials they had not immediately destroyed when found. In 1922 they established the Central Commission for the Elimination of Hostile Literature (*tsentralnaia komissiia po iskliuchennia vrednoi literatury*) within the Press Department, whose personnel conducted a systematic removal from libraries of all materials considered harmful. A series of decrees between

1923 and 1925 emptied libraries of publications deemed anti-Bolshevik. Specific orders to retain at least two copies of all proscribed items and to establish closed collections (*spetsfond*) to hold them were issued in 1923. All other copies were destroyed. As much as 70 per cent of Ukrainian pre-1921 library holdings had been removed by 1929. In the city of Vinnytsia and its environs, for example, in 1923 alone, local Bolsheviks destroyed 10 poods (160 kilos/360 lbs) of "Petliurite literature." In 1934 a special secret subsection was established in Ukraine's Book Palace (*palats knyhy*) to collect all remaining publications from the revolutionary period. The destruction was halted the following year when officials judged it was becoming too indiscriminate. Destruction occurred again in 1941 before the arrival of German troops, and was resumed after 1947 when a series of sweeps removed undesirable literature from second-hand bookshops and museums.[29] During the Second World War the Vernadsky Library in Kyiv lost approximately 360 000 leaflets or the equivalent of 98 per cent of its pre-war collection.[30]

Very few of the leaflets and pamphlets in the illustrative sample have been republished or reproduced since they first appeared.[31] None have been translated. Two categories of leaflets and pamphlets were excluded from the sample because they have been republished and translated and are well known to historians. These are, first, key policy statements published in leaflet form such as the "Universals" of the Central Rada, the declarations of the warlord Hryhoriev, and the Bolshevik "decrees" on land, peace, and self-determination. Second, the sample excludes published statements by prominent leaders like Lenin, Trotsky, Mykhailo Hrushevsky, and Simon Petliura, which were disseminated *en masse*.[32]

There exists a fashion of late for authors to compile extremely long lists of acknowledgments, extended by some to include unborn children and pet cats. This diluted version of *argumentum ad verecundiam* is presumably intended to show that the author is a fine fellow and decent chap – or bonnie lass. Like name-dropping at soirées, it is presumably intended to lend authority – a kind of spurious supplement to the footnotes. I am not a dedicated follower of this fashion. But I am grateful to my editors who bear with me and to my anonymous reviewers. Their long, detailed comments ensured that this book became better than it would have been otherwise.

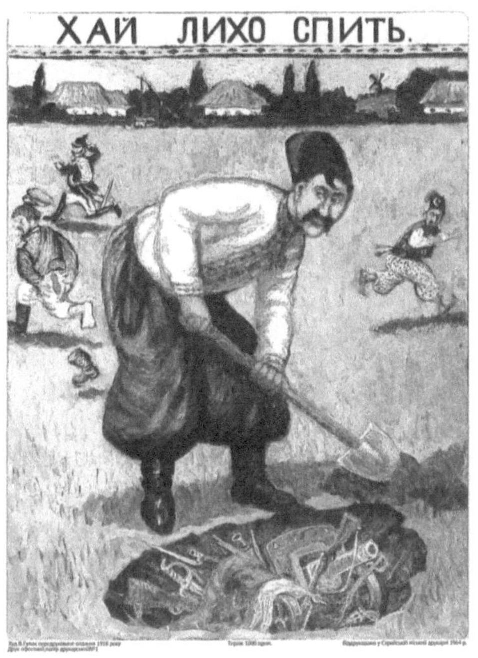

1 Postcard (1918?). Vasyl Hulak: "Good riddance to bad rubbish." Presumably a comment on Petliura's overthrow of Hetman Skoropadsky in November 1918, it depicts a Ukrainian burying a Russian flag while Germany, Turkey, and Russia flee in the background. https://gorbutovich.livejournal.com/64570.html

2 Postcard (1918?). Vasyl Hulak: "Do not forget your native Ukraine"

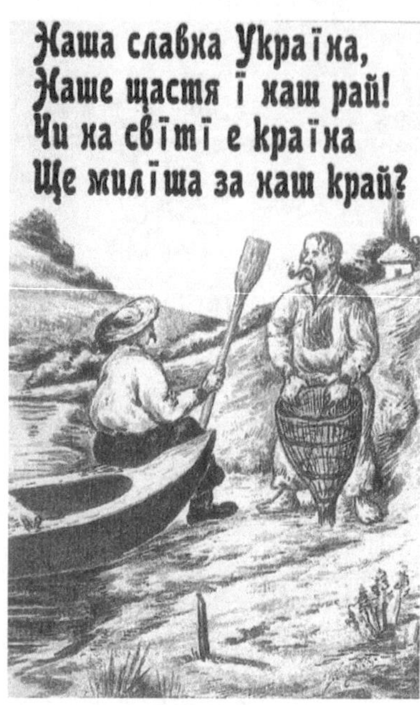

3 Postcard (1918?). Vasyl Hulak: "Our glorious Ukraine ... Is there a country more dear in the world?"

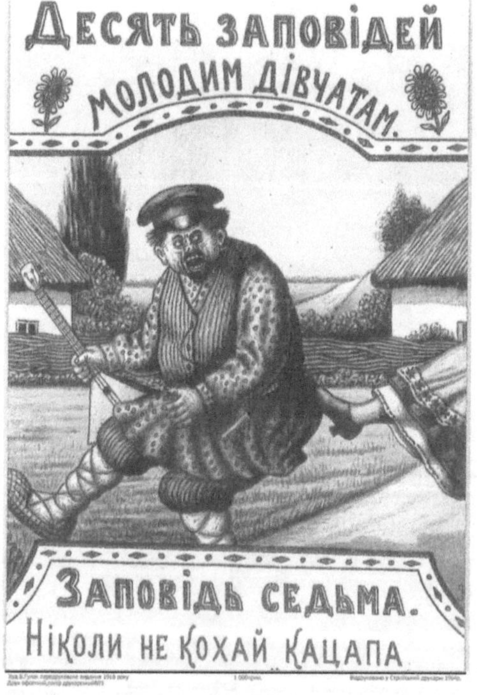

4 Postcard (1918?). Vasyl Hulak: "Ten Commandments for young girls. Commandment seven. Never love a Russkie." https://gorbutovich.livejournal.com/63808.html

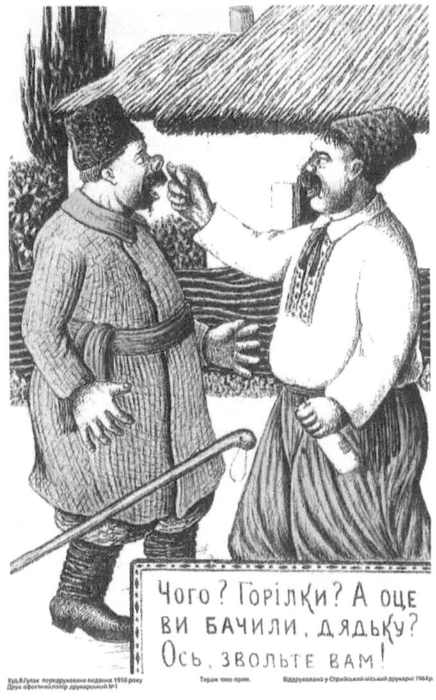

5 Postcard (1918?). Vasyl Hulak: Ukrainian tells Russian: "What? You want whiskey? See this old man?" https://kaktus-okamenel.livejournal.com/1105607.html

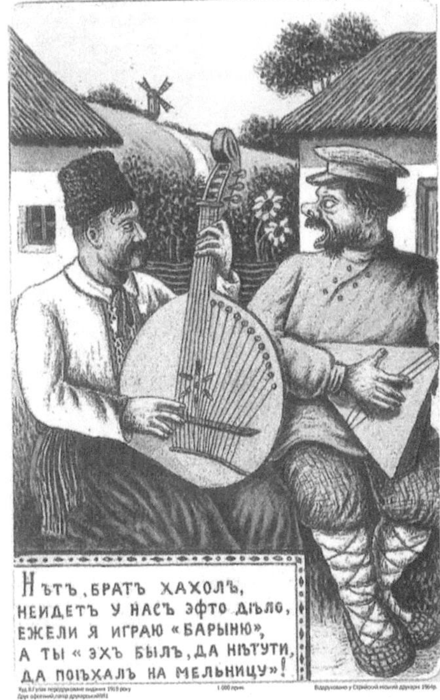

6 Postcard (1918?). Vasyl Hulak: "No brother *khokhol*, it's not working." The caption makes the point that a Ukrainian and Russian, each with different instruments, cannot play the same tune. https://gorbutovich.livejournal.com/64197.html

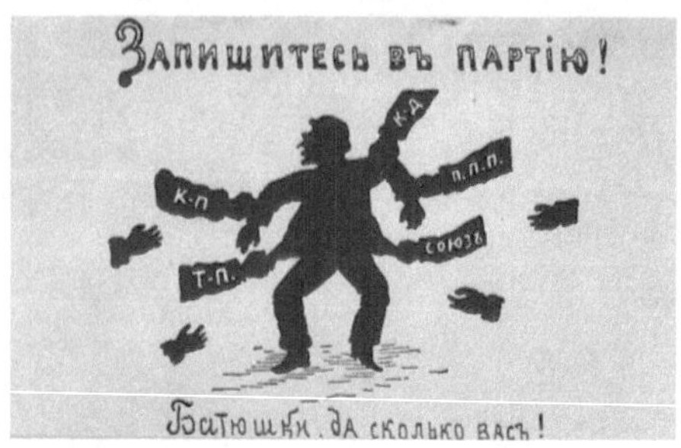

7 Postcard (1917?). Vasyl Hulak: "Join the party. Oh my little fathers how many of you there are." This is a comment on the sudden increase in numbers of political parties in 1917.
https://gorbutovich.livejournal.com/64570.html

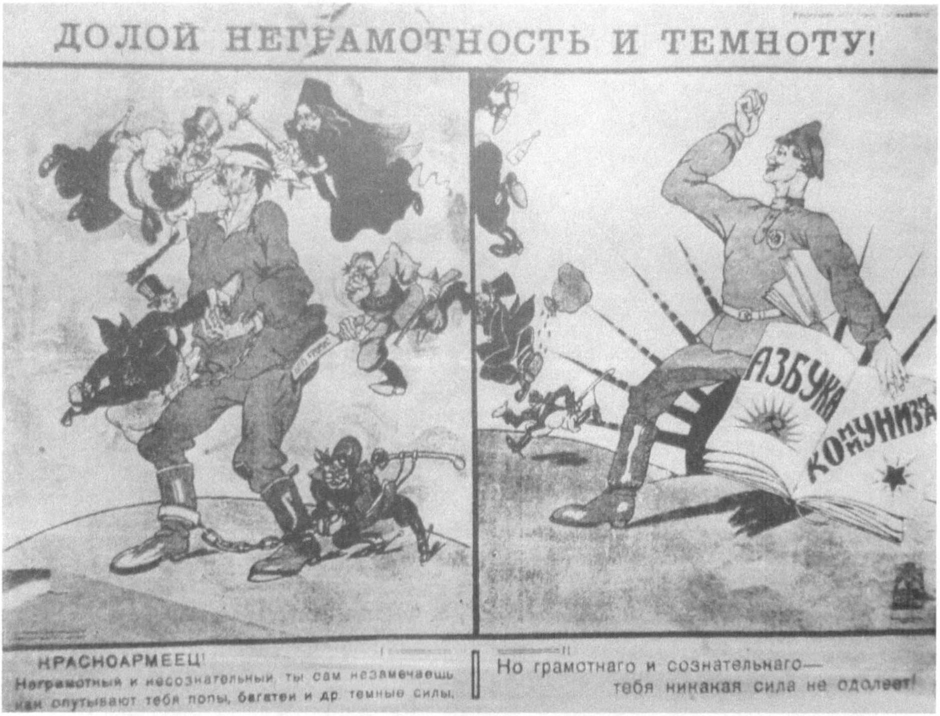

8 Poster (Russ.; 1920?). "Down with illiteracy and darkness."
S. Tomakh, Ie. Holostenko, *Ukrainsky revoliutsiiny plakat* (Kharkiv, 1932).

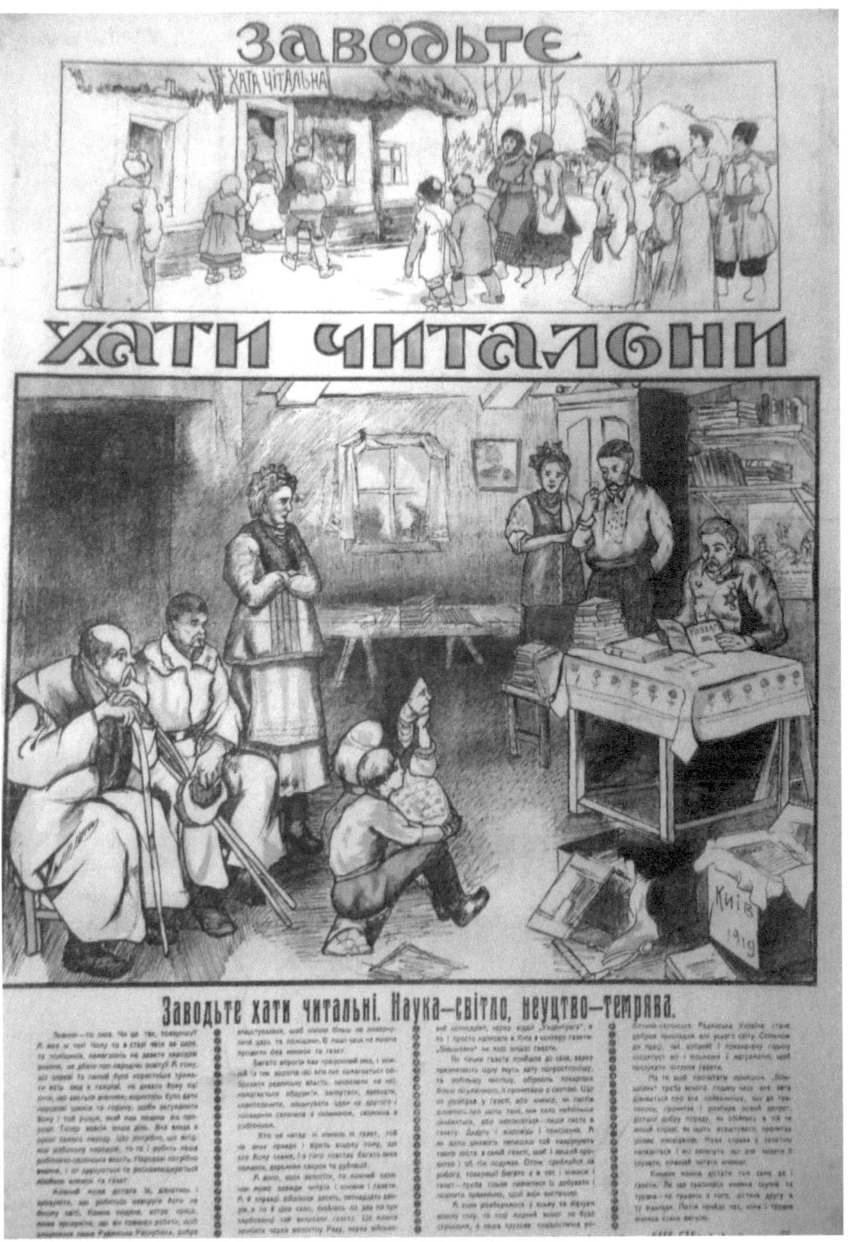

9 Poster (1919). "Form reading houses. Learning is light, ignorance is darkness." National Art Museum of Ukraine. For a Russianized version of this poster see Kenez, *The Birth of the Propaganda State*, 80.

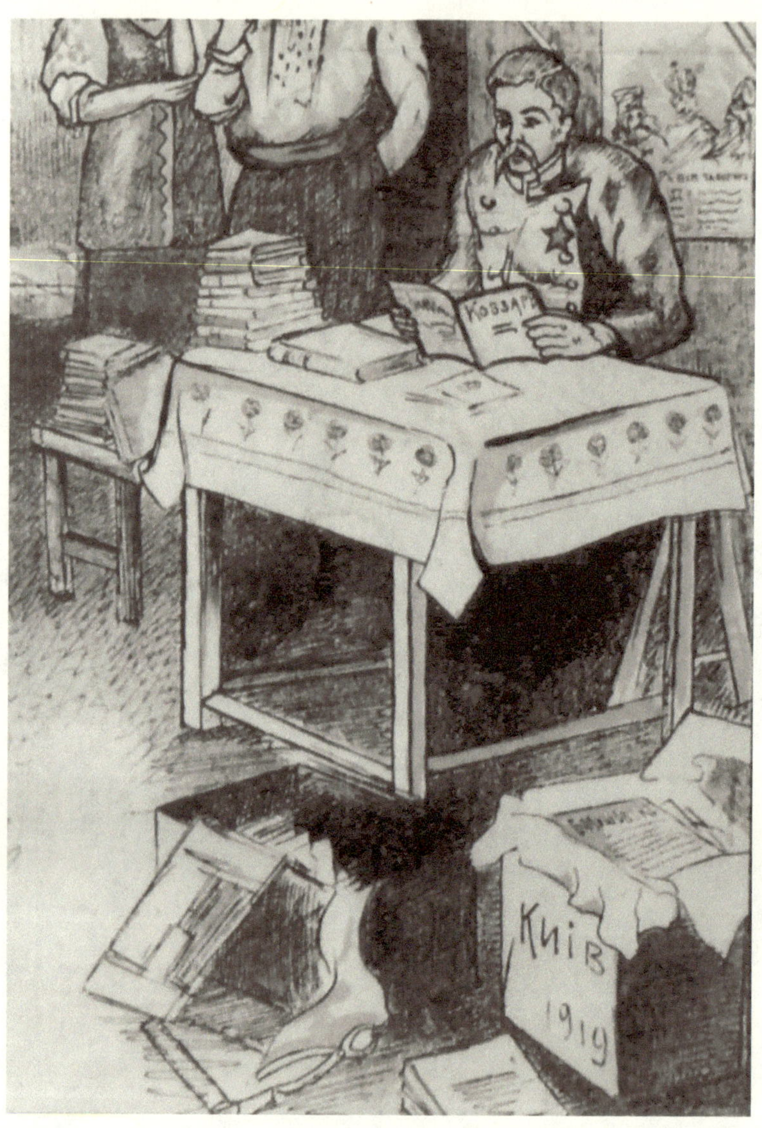

9 (detail).

аука—світло, неуцтво—темрява.

вий комисаріят, через відділ „Укцентрага", а то і просто написати в Київ в контору газети: „Більшовик" чи якої иншої газети.

Як тільки газета прийшла до села, зараз призначають одну якусь хату попросторнішу, та побільшу чистішу, обірають товариша більш письменного, її прочитаєш з охотою. Що не розібрав у газеті, або книжці, чи схотів дізнатись про щось таке, чим село найбільше цікавиться, або непокоїться—пиши листа в газету. Дадуть і відповідь і пояснення. А як щось цікавого напишеш той надрукують твого листа в самій газеті, щоб і инший прочитав і об тім подумав. Отож приймайся за роботу, товариші! Багато є в нас і книжок і газет—треба тільки навчитися їх добувати і поділяти правильно, щоб всім вистачило.

А коли розберемося у всьму та відчуєм власну силу, то тоді марний ворог не буде страшним, а наша трудова соціалістична робітничо-селянська Радянська Україна стане добрим прикладом для усього світу. Спільнож до праці, час добрий! І призначену годину сходяться всі і письменні і неграмотні, щоб послухати читання газети.

На те щоб прочитати примірок „Більшовик" треба всього годину часу але зате дізнається про все найважніше, що де трапилось, прочитає і розбере новий декрет, дістане добру пораду, як обійтися в тій чи иншій справі, як щось влаштувати, прочитає цікаве оповідання. Коли справа з газетою наладиться і всі звикнуть що дня ходити її слухати, починай читати книжки.

Книжки можна дістати там само де і газети. Як що трапилася книжка скучна та трудна—не гризись з того, дістань другу а ту відклади. Потім прийде час, коли і трудна книжка стане легкою.

Відділ розповсюдження та постачання літератури Всеукраїнського Видавничого Комітету при ЦВКР і СДУ [illegible] 39

9 (detail) Text explaining that people should collectively subscribe, organize reading sessions, and write to the newspaper with questions, and that reading a newspaper and learning about events, laws, and how to do things only takes one hour.

ГРЯЗЬ-главная причина заразных болезней. Чтобы избавиться от этой ГРЯЗИ в городе Кременчуге устраивается

„Неделя ЧИСТОТЫ"

В эту неделю каждый должен хорошенько вычистить, убрать и вымыть помещение в котором живет, а также почиститься и вымыться сам.

10 Leaflet (1920?). Dirt is the main cause of infectious diseases. Public Sanitation Week. Arkhiv druku.

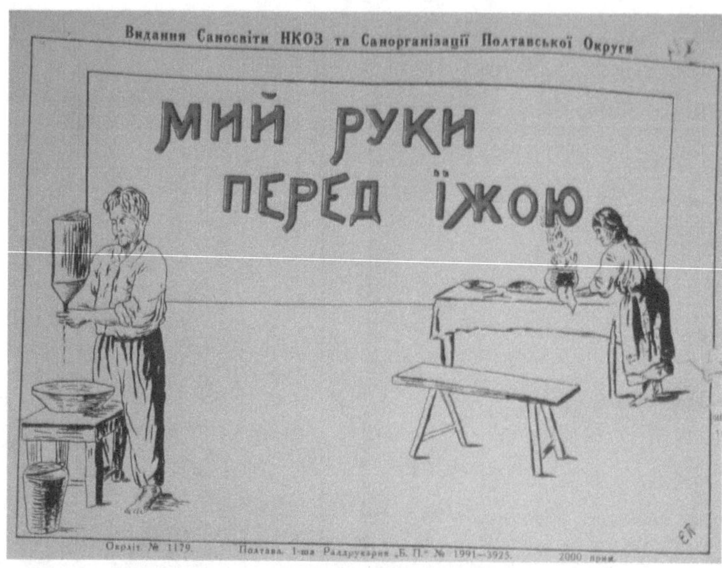

11 Poster (1920?). Wash your hands before meals. Arkhiv druku.

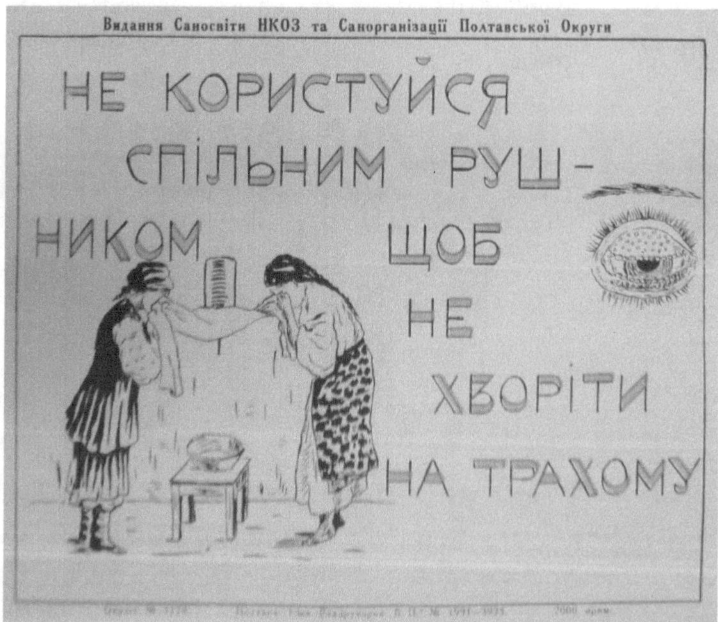

12 Poster (1920?). Don't share a common towel so as not to get trachoma. Arkhiv druku.

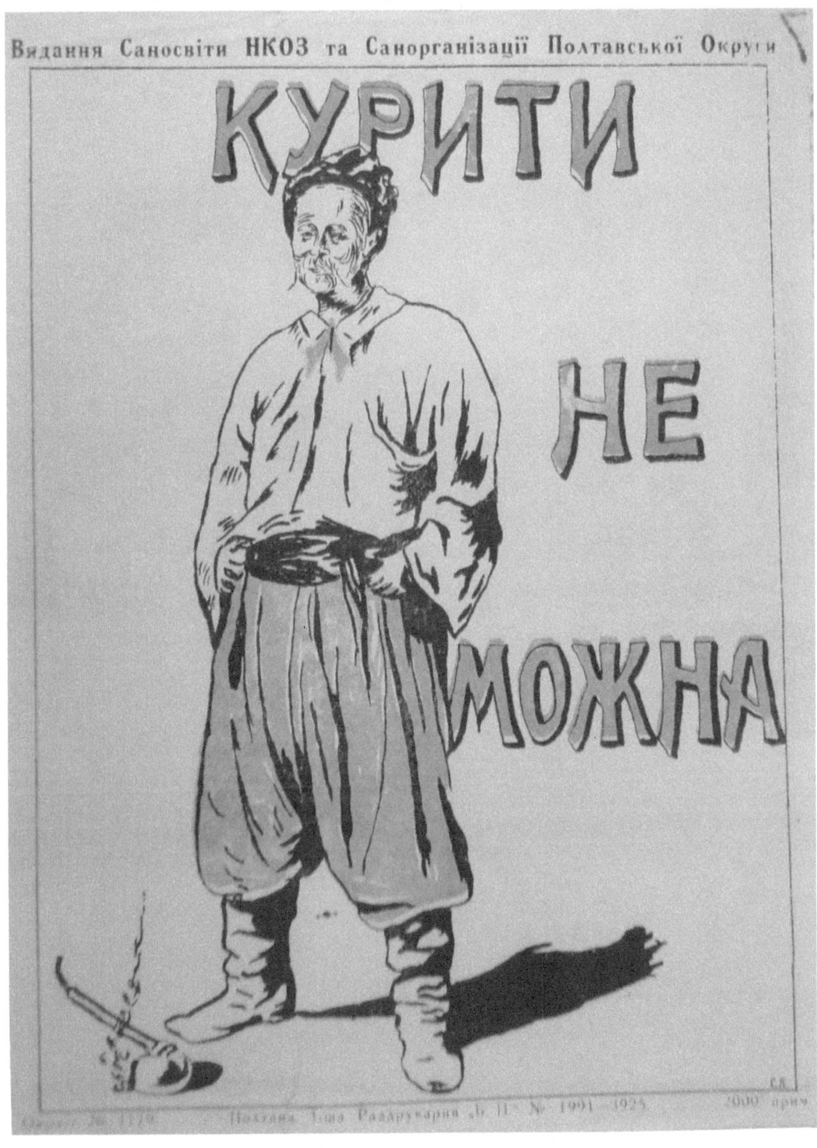

13 Poster (1920?). Don't smoke.
Arkhiv druku.

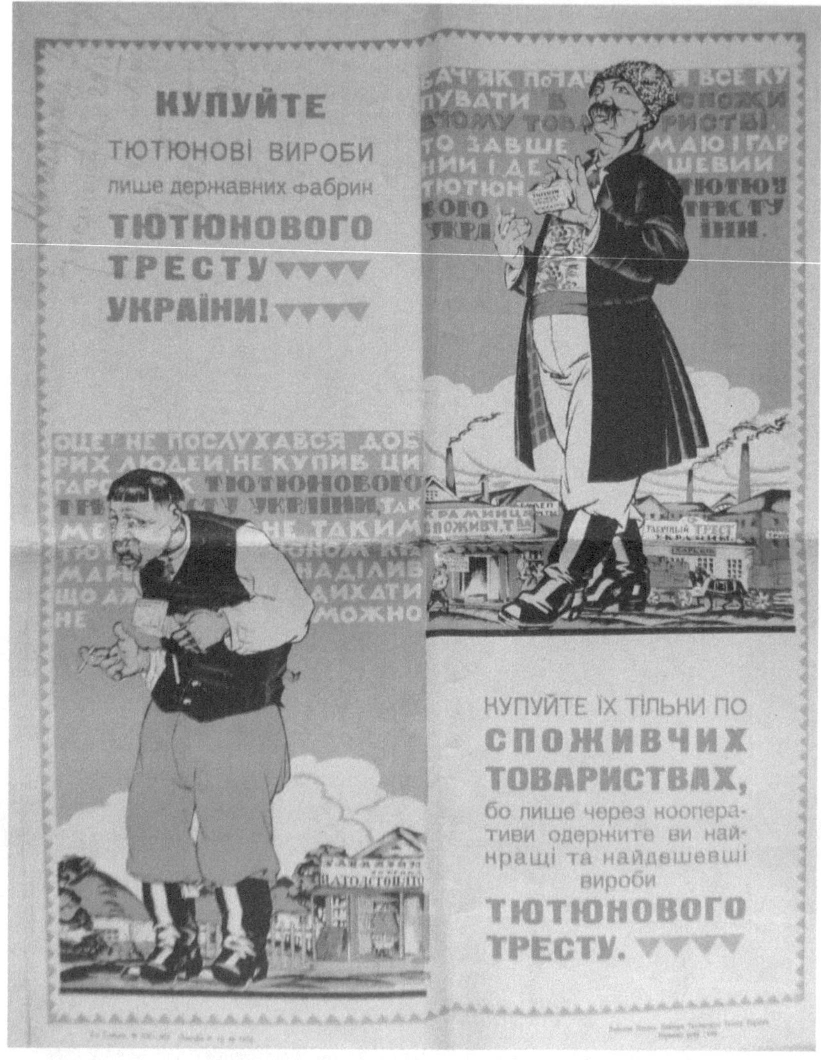

14 Poster (1921?) [Ukr.]. BUY tobacco products only at the state factories of Ukraine's Tobacco Trust.
Arkhiv druku.

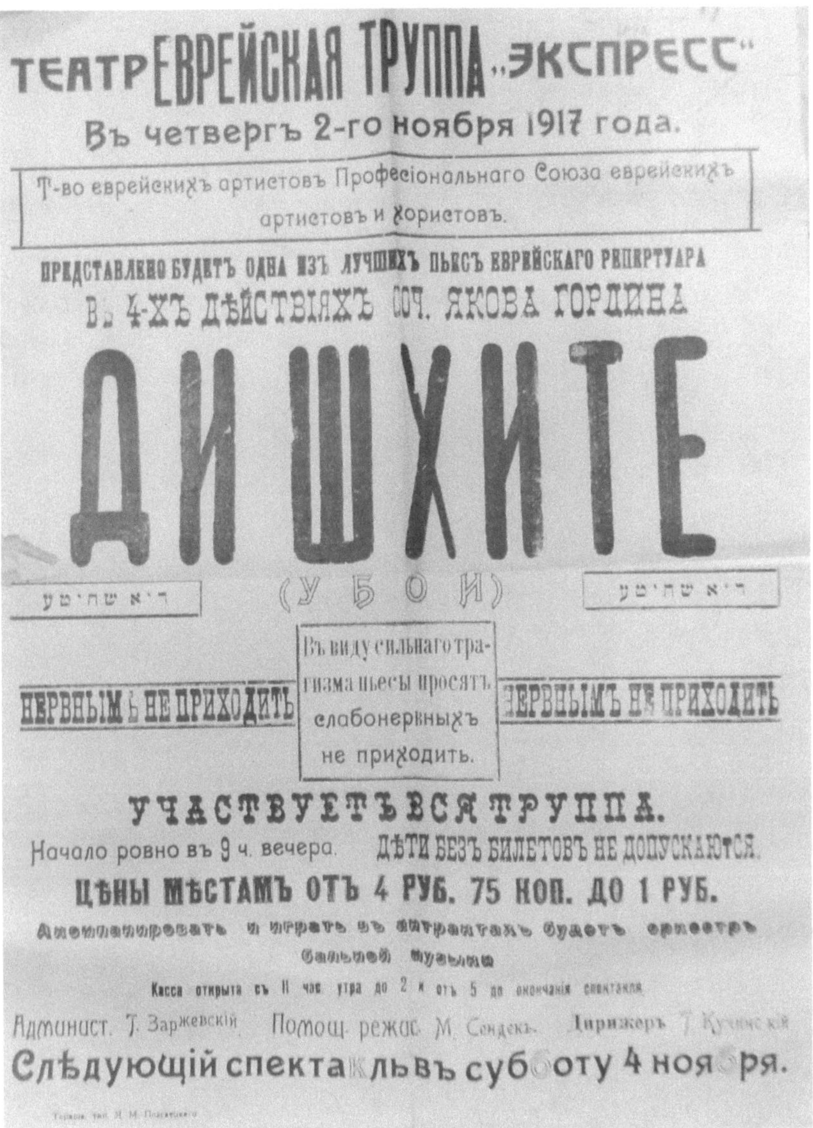

15 Poster (Russ.; 1917). Theatrical announcement for a Yiddish play. Arkhiv druku.

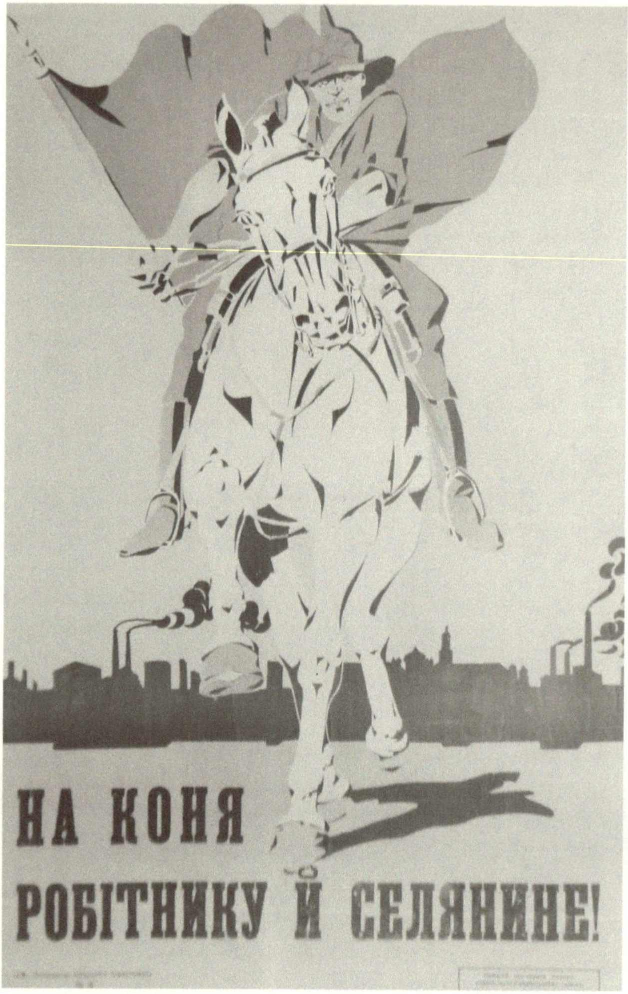

16 Recruiting poster (1920?).
National Art Museum of Ukraine.

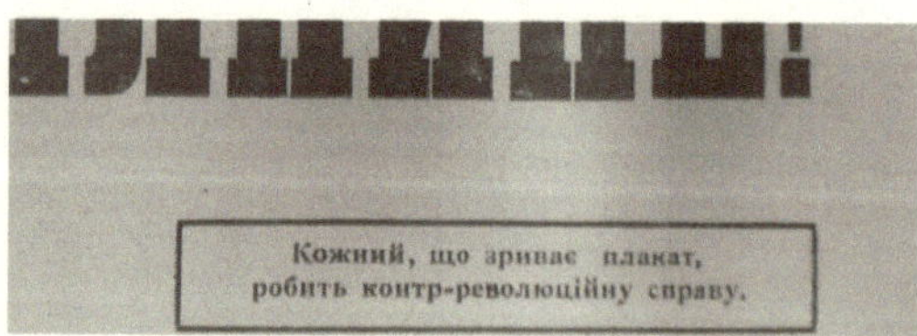

16 (detail) "Whoever tears down posters commits a counter-revolutionary act."

Chapter One

Message and Medium

Propaganda and War

Elites have always manipulated information, resorting to deception, omission, distortion, manipulation, broad humour, and lies to serve their own purposes.[1] Speakers have used sophistry and rhetoric to convince since the time of the ancient Greeks. The word "propaganda" was coined in the 1600s and originally referred to organizations established to spread the Catholic faith. By the 1790s it encompassed the means used to disseminate *any* beliefs or ideas. Between 1814 and 1914, the word was rarely encountered in Europe. Until the First World War, there was little discussion of propaganda techniques or uses beyond the realm of advertising. The word did not appear in prewar French encyclopedias. Germany's *Brockhaus Enzyklopadie* defined its principal meaning as the dissemination of Catholic and French revolutionary ideas. The entry's last sentence noted that it also could refer to an activity intended to win followers for individuals or associations. Brokhauz and Iefrom's *Entsiklopedicheskii slovar* (1890–1907) defined propaganda as something conducted by Catholics and revolutionaries. Dal's Russian etymological dictionary (1880–3) also defined it as the dissemination of ideas. Iuzhakov's *Bolshaia entsiklopediia* (1900–9) reprinted Meyer's *Konversationlexikon* definition of the term as the dissemination of ideas to win adherents. Samuel Orgelbrand's *Encyklopedja Powszechna* (1902) defined propaganda as primarily a Catholic phenomenon alongside mention of it as simply the spreading of an opinion. The word did not appear in Hrinchenko's Ukrainian dictionary (1908), nor in the prewar *Encyclopedia Britannica.* In his 1908 book *Human Nature in Politics,* the Fabian socialist Graham Wallas spoke of "manipulation of popular impulse," instead of propaganda, and "professional controller of public opinion," instead of propagandist. Sergii Shchegolev did use the word in the title of chapter XII of his 1910 analysis of the Ukrainian movement *Ukrainskoe dvizhenie kak soveremnyi etap Iuzhnorusskoho separatizma*: "Propaganda Ukrainstvo v Rossii." In the 3rd edition of Viktor Dubrovsky's *Slovnyk moskovsko-ukrainskyi* (1918), it was defined simply as propagation.

During the First World War, mass warfare, mass literacy, and mass commercial advertising appealling to emotion rather than thought coincided for the first time in history. All governments realized that the dissemination of information supporting the war effort could not be left to voluntary patriotic organizations, newspaper owners, and ad hoc bureaux alone. As part of the war effort they progressively centralized, or coordinated, propaganda and assigned personnel to do it – something the Bolsheviks did as soon as they took power. "The conscious and intelligent manipulation of the organized habits and opinions of the masses is an important element in democratic society. Those who manipulate this unseen mechanism of society constitute an invisible government which is the true ruling power of our country." These were not Lenin's words. They were written by an American, Edward Bernays, in the opening sentence of his book *Propaganda* (1928). Much influenced by his uncle Sigmund Freud, Bernay realized that advertisers could exploit the unconscious to influence opinion and behaviour. During the war, he had been in charge of the Export Service of America's Committee on Public Information, formed in April 1917. In 1918 the British and the French centralized their information administrations. That August, in London, the Entente leaders held the world's first Conference on Propaganda, which led to the founding of a committee to coordinate the messages the Allied governments were disseminating to enemy and friendly peoples. All of these agencies were shut down a few months after the war. The British destroyed almost all the records of their propaganda agencies.

In 1914 in Britain there existed a number of separate organizations, governmental and private, that published materials intended to influence public opinion. Among these was the secret War Propaganda Bureau, headed by John Masterman, a Christian socialist cabinet minister, who declared that his bureau would disseminate only reports that could be substantiated. George Creel, the head of the Americans' Committee on Public Information, refused to use the word propaganda for his committee's activities because "that word, in German hands, had come to be associated with deceit and corruption." What his committee did was provide a torrent of vetted information to all kinds of media in the form of rational argument made powerful through its volume, repetition, and ubiquity.[2] As the war dragged on, people increasingly began to distinguish propaganda from information, although they still used those two terms interchangeably to refer to the spreading of ideas in order to inform, enlighten, and persuade – ends not necessarily dishonourable or dishonest. Persuasion, defined as the provision of information through rhetorical techniques and arguments in order to illuminate, edify, and explain, was not yet completely dissociated from propaganda. The term propaganda in this book's title, which in the Bolshevik lexicon, as noted below, meant "agitation," should be understood in this prewar sense. That usage encompassed the rational elaboration of information containing little or nothing particularly mendacious or emotive, – for instance, texts related to public health and sanitation. The prewar standard notion of propaganda included texts by authors who applied classical rhetorical techniques of persuasion: argument, the contrasting of options, the refutation of opposing positions, and metaphor.[3] Only after the war was propaganda associated solely with the intentional and sometimes covert dissemination of lies and half-truths, usually by governments, and with the manipulation of emotions and prejudices by devious and cynical demagogues using techniques of experimental psychology. Central to the demise of propaganda's neutral connotations was Arthur Ponsonby's book *Falsehood in Wartime* (1928), although ironically, the author himself, a Germanophile, had thought up some of the atrocities he described. In any case, Masterman had refused to disseminate unsubstantiated stories through his bureau during the war.[4] In this context, some of the materials in this book can be categorized as information rather than as propaganda, for they consist of extended texts with verifiable propositions rather than unverifiable assertions, and of arguments appealing to reason rather than slogans appealing to the emotions.

In the early months of the war, while American propagandists were admitting to "manipulation," their British counterparts continued to insist that "the first of all axioms of propaganda is that only truthful statements be made."[5] However, Masterman's axiom fell by the wayside as British officials, like those of every other government, launched campaigns using lies, rumours, half-truths, and fabrications intended to alarm and confuse the enemy, demonize him among the populace, and rouse support for the war effort. The best-known example of a successful plausible lie in propaganda that could not be completely refuted is found in Britain's Bryce Report of 1915, which was published in thirty languages. It included the story that the Germans were sending their soldiers' corpses to soap factories (the British also circulated this lie as a separate leaflet).[6] In 1920 during the Polish–Russian War, Polish intelligence circulated an anti-Bolshevik Russian-language newspaper among the Red troops called *The Latest Truth* (*Poslednaia Pravda*), complete with the slogan "Workers of the World Unite."[7]

When it became obvious that the war would not be over by Christmas, governments realized they were going to have to mobilize their populations, but none yet had what is today called a centralized national media strategy. Their early initiatives involving the press and popular opinion were limited to issuing military bulletins about battles, classifying some information as secret, and relying on voluntary patriotic associations to muster popular support. Techniques for mass mobilization of public opinion did exist, however. Some had been developed by mass political party leaders, who, in the second half of the nineteenth century, began to mass-produce handbills and posters, or bought newspaper space for advertisements, to appeal to voters. In the United States, the massive increase in cheap commodities at the end of the century was accompanied by the emergence of advertising agencies, whose personnel used psychological techniques that appealed to passions and feelings rather than to reason to sell those commodities. They came to understand, for instance, that effective advertising had to be created with specific groups in mind and that ads had to carefully align text and image. Consequently, by 1914, alongside political party activists and journalists who spent their careers telling vivid stories to the average person with no particular concern for accuracy, there had emerged a group of advertising specialists paid to exploit prejudices, fears, desires, and enthusiasms for the profit of their employers.

Europe was a pre-electronic society at the turn of the century. Mass printed texts still dominated the public sphere as the major source of information. These texts were only beginning to be displaced by images. Because public discourse was still dominated by the printed and spoken word, words had to have meaning. Only urban advertisers could risk making vacuous assertions ("Coke is it") that left any thinking person wondering just what "it" was. Accordingly, public discourse back then was arguably more serious and rational than it is now. And the farther removed a territory was from an urban metropolis, where images were beginning to invade the streetscape, the more influential the printed text was in the public sphere – particularly in light of rising literacy rates. This had social consequences because printed text, unlike images, conveyed meaningful propositions that could be argued, contradicted, proven, or disproved. As thinkers of the time realized – among whom French sociologist Gustave LeBon was particularly influential – text, unlike images, still involved rational argument, counter-argument, classification, exposition, scrutiny of assumptions, comparison, debunking, and deduction. Where print text dominated the public sphere, reading about and listening to political messages in particular, was more serious than where images dominated. Reading demanded more time, concentration, scrutiny, and analysis than did looking at a picture.[8] With communications still dominated by print, public figures were better known by their written words than by sight. Their credibility thus depended more on their past record for saying the truth than it did on artifice, phony sincerity, or physical attractiveness.

When the war began, officials in all countries still considered journalism and commercial advertising separate from official governmental announcements, both conceptually and spatially. Nonetheless, that distinction was already slowly fading, for governments were drawing revenue from selling public space for commercial ads, which progressively encroached on that public space as revenue needs grew. With the outbreak of the war, the public demand for news and the need for men and materials, as well as the need to counter rumours and to foment hatred for the enemy (and love for allies), finally broke that conceptual and spatial barrier between the public-governmental and the private-commercial. It did so more completely among the Entente than among the Central Powers. American, British, and French officials, sooner than their German and Russian counterparts, realized they would have to use the knowledge and methods of advertising agencies and newspaper publishers to disseminate to maximum effect governmental messages to fight, to hate, to work, to give, and to sacrifice.[9] In short, the Great War marked the first time that government information merged with mass media and commercial advertising. War, patriotism, and nationalism began to be advertised to mass audiences in public spaces as if they were commodities. This governmental exploitation of commercial advertising techniques during the war was as important as universal suffrage, conscription, and trade unions for drawing populations into national political life.

Governments began hiring and consulting with ad men and publishers, who adapted their commercial techniques and strategies developed to persuade consumers to buy, for the purposes of demoralizing the enemy abroad and mobilizing political support for war at home.[10] Government messages, like those created by private organizations or individuals, were presented simply and with little nuance. They were crafted to appeal to emotion rather than reason, and designed to work within specific sets of values. There were no "good Britons" in German propaganda, nor were there "good Germans" in British or French propaganda. British ministers soon realized it was better to use Irish than English symbols for recruiting posters in Ireland, and to use Welsh in Wales. Because civilian experts in publicity and marketing, rather than military censors or government bureaucrats, controlled propaganda in the United States, Britain, and (to a lesser degree) France, these countries' campaigns expressed a distinct populism in terms of verbal and visual style that linked the official and the national with individual self-interest. German and Austrian propaganda, dominated by generals, did this to a lesser degree; it focused on Nordic myth, defence of the nation, and sacrifice. The German army had formed a War Press Office in 1915, located within its intelligence unit, that supplied controlled information to the press, but there was no German propaganda ministry per se until February 1918. In October 1917 the German chancellor refused outright to create such a ministry, fearing that it would further weaken civilian influence in the government. German generals did not think war a suitable subject for commercialization, humour, or satire. Such things might appear on postcards, but not on posters. Conservative commentators agreed: "Should an army be raised by the same means as customers for jam?"[11]

Wilhelm Wundt in Germany in the 1870s established experimental psychology as an academic discipline. On the eve of the war he and his students were pointing out that most people were less persuaded by rational argument than by suggestion and circumstances. Freud was writing on the role on the unconscious.[12] By the outbreak of the war, ad men using psychological theory were already producing mass advertisements for commodities using suggestion and repetition rather than rational argumentation to persuade. The impact of their findings may be illustrated by the publishing history of Marx's *Capital.* From its first appearance in 1867 it had slow sales among intellectuals. No English publisher was interested in it during his lifetime, and the 1887 English-language edition of volume 1 sold badly. It took two years to sell the 1,000 copies of the 1906 American edition of volume 2. In 1890 a wit in New York's left-wing Humboldt Publishing Company decided to advertise their illegal reprint of the 1887 edition of volume 1 among bankers with the claim it would explain "how to accumulate capital." The 5,000 copies soldout in a few days.[13]

Wundt and Freud were known to Russians, and two of Wundt's books had been translated into Russian before the war. Whether those Bolsheviks involved with propaganda during the Revolution were influenced by their ideas is unstudied.[14] Many among the educated had read LeBon, including Lenin. They knew his argument about using assertion and repetition to influence behaviour and that feelings and emotions rather than reason underpinned the spread of opinions and beliefs within crowds. Influential among prewar Russian Social Democrats was *Ob agitatsii* (Geneva, 1897) by the Bundist Aron Kremer. He observed that the best way to win workers to the cause was not in small study groups, which tend to isolate theoreticians from other workers, but to address large groups using texts specially written for the purpose. He stressed that good propagandists had to know intimately not only their subject but also their audience. Julius Martov, then Lenin's associate, had worked with Kremer on the pamphlet and acquainted Lenin with it in Saint Petersburg.[15] Lenin regarded propaganda and education as methods of convincing workers that the Bolsheviks were explaining the world to them as it actually existed. In *What Is to Be Done?* (1902), he repeated a distinction taken from Georgii Plekhanov that did not exist in western Europe or the United States, namely, the idea that propaganda, ideas expressed in print for the few, should use primarily rational argument to explain the causes of social inequities such as unemployment. Agitation, words, and text addressed to the many had to appeal to emotion to persuade by repeating slogans capable of arousing and mobilizing the audience. In a party circular that same year he stipulated that propaganda had to be strictly centralized and agitators had to know their subjects.[16] In April 1918, he added that "the fight against this element [petty-bourgeois anarchy] cannot be waged solely with propaganda and agitation ... The struggle must also be waged with coercion." Karl Radek, Lenin's Deputy Commissar for Foreign Affairs in 1918, wrote: "It is necessary to proceed in two ways against an enemy army: by word, which demoralizes, and by force that breaks the enemy's power."[17] A 1919 leaflet explained that workers and peasants fought in non-Bolshevik armies because they had succumbed to false slogans of patriotism, nationalism, freedom, law, order, and peace, and that it was the Bolsheviks' duty to make them see the socialist truth. "Books pamphlets and leaflets are our bullets that will give us victory. Even such disciplined armies like the Czechoslovak and German could not stand against such bullets."[18] In 1920, summarizing his party's experience, Lenin declared in *Left-Wing Communism: An Infantile Disorder* that propaganda had to exploit "thoroughly, carefully, attentively, and skilfully ... every, even the smallest, 'fissure' among the enemies, every antagonism of interest."

The Bolsheviks centralized more than propaganda. After taking power, they also centralized all publishing, paper production, and distribution. As of July 1919, for instance, only one of their radio stations in Ukraine was allowed to receive foreign broadcasts, and all incoming message transcripts had to be submitted immediately to the foreign and military commissariats.[19] Before expropriating all presses on their territory in 1921, they decreed that private and co-op presses had to register, provide inventories, and submit publication plans for approval; furthermore, they could not accept orders without prior government approval. Anything published on Bolshevik territory that did not reflect government opinion was declared illegal. By August 1921, just after the introduction of the New Economic Plan (NEP), the few private presses remaining had access to government paper stocks only if they had government contracts. What paper was available on the market was very expensive.[20]

Material and Machines

By 1914, Ukraine's principal cities were linked with Saint Petersburg by rail, telegraph, and telephone. By then, there were an estimated 17,400 telephones in Ukraine (compared to almost 600,000 in Germany and 700,000 in Britain).[21] Ukraine's 99 district (*povit/uezd*) and 1,811 county (*volost*) capitals were all linked by phone and telegraph, and lines were beginning to be extended to villages. Letters normally took twenty-four hours to travel from one post office to another.[22] Manual typewriters had become common in offices in the 1890s. Telegraph machines transmitted between thirty and seventy words per minute, their speed dependent on the capacity of exchanges. In 1914, two of the empire's three largest telegraph exchanges were in Zhytomir and Mykolaiiv. Kharkiv province's exchange in 1920 could handle 28,500 words every twenty-four hours (Illus. 31–3).[23]

The Ukrainian provinces had 9,000 kilometres of train track. That was less track per square kilometre than France or Germany, but more than central Russia. Katerynoslav province (33 metres per square kilometre) had the densest network; Volyn province (12) had the least dense. Kyiv, Chernihiv, Kharkiv, Podillia, and Katerynoslav provinces averaged 20 metres or more track per square kilometre. Kherson, Poltava, Taurida, and Volyn provinces averaged 17 metres or less. A distorted wartime railway system brought trains to the front but returned few of them to their points of origin; by 1916 this had resulted in a glut of rolling stock west of the Dnipro.

Given the importance of railways for the bulk distribution of printed matter, it is worth noting that the amount of functional rolling stock declined during the years of revolution. In 1914 the Ukrainian provinces had 132,041 freight wagons, 6,241 passenger wagons, and 4,983 locomotives. In terms of rolling stock per 100 kilometres of track, Ukraine had more freight wagons but slightly fewer locomotives than Russia itself. By 1920 the number of functional units in Bolshevik-controlled Ukraine had dropped to 1,200 locomotives and 50,000 to 60,000 wagons.[24]

Besides rail transportation, printed text required paper, in which Ukraine was not self-sufficient. As of 1914 the Ukrainian provinces annually used an average of 6 million poods (110,000 tons) of paper, of which 45,000 tons was produced locally. The remainder was imported, as was 90 per cent of all printing and writing paper. This presumably included the huge rolls of newsprint that could withstand the high speeds of the new rotary presses and be printed on both sides. In one year the city of Kyiv alone imported 686 tons from various northern sources. The Ukrainian provinces had twenty-four pulp mills, seventeen of which were in Kyiv, Volyn, and Podillia provinces. These latter produced roughly three-quarters of all paper produced in the Ukrainian provinces on the eve of the war. Only two mills, in Chernihiv and Kharkiv, produced writing- and printing-quality paper. All three mills in Kyiv province produced cigarette paper. In the summer of 1919, four functioning mills, none of them at more than 70 per cent capacity, produced 180 tons of paper.[25]

Before the war, paper cost between 8 and 20 kopeks per pound, depending on quality. By 1917 that had risen to 1 to 3 roubles. Press runs were restricted by paper shortages and rising prices and also by the unavailability of parts, print, ink, type, and electrical power, not to mention a shortage of printers. By mid-1917, in Kyiv province, "with each passing day there is less paper on the market ... It is impossible to place an order at printing shops most of whose workers have left [and,] it is impossible to obtain the insanely expensive publishing materials [*nema zasobiv na bozhevilnoi zdorozhnilyi vydavnychyi material*]." Strangely, although prices of materials had gone up as much as twenty times from prewar averages, book and pamphlet prices as of 1918 had at most only tripled, because publishers were using cheaper-quality paper and could count on press runs in the tens of thousands thanks to the soaring demand for information. High press runs continued in 1918.[26]

The records of a paper mill in Volyn provide an example of decline in productive capacity. Before the war, with four machines and 1,000 employees, this mill could produce 8,126 tons of writing/printing paper and tens of thousands of tons of other sorts of paper. Between 1918 and 1920, with only one machine and some 400 employees, it could produce 5.4 tons of writing/printing and 29 tons of cigarette paper daily – when fuel and timber were available.[27]

Turning now to presses, there were approximately 2,668 printing shops and 7,000 printing presses of various kinds in the Russian empire in 1914. Moscow and Saint Petersburg had the largest printing establishments, which accounted for roughly 70 per cent of imperial book production. Almost all machinery and equipment was imported from Germany. By 1921 the number of working presses on Bolshevik territories had fallen to about 4,000. Total paper production had fallen from an imperial prewar total of 234 million tons to 40 million tons. By the same year, 2,230 of the former empire's 2,668 printing establishments had been nationalized, but only 1,839 of these now state-owned enterprises were still functioning. Total production of printed materials on the former imperial lands had fallen to an estimated 30 per cent of its prewar total. Ninety per cent of the most up-to-date rotary presses and typesetting machines after 1917 were in Moscow and Saint Petersburg.[28]

The war changed the nature of publishing in Ukraine, as it did in the empire as a whole. With the tsar's abdication, the collapse of censorship, and the participation of the masses in political affairs, the printing business shifted from providing thick publications for the educated elites to printing short, didactic works. The latter were aimed at the new reading public born of the prewar surge in primary education. These new publications in the vernacular for the newly literate in the non-Russian provinces were vital to what is now called nation-building. Frequently distributed free by political parties, civilian organizations, and governments in order to mobilize supporters, these mass publications incorporated people into public debates beyond their own towns and villages.

As far as is known, between 1917 and 1920 the number of printing shops on Ukrainian territory increased from 620 to 1,036. All but the tiniest shops had least two presses. In provincial towns, shops averaged between three and five presses. These were hand-operated in towns without electricity. Some universities and monasteries also had presses. By 1910, there were 86 printing shops and 187 presses in Kyiv, and all of Podillia province had 41 presses, with the most in Vinnytsia (10).[29] By one count, there were at least nine hundred presses of various sorts in the Ukrainian provinces at the beginning of the war. However, information on how many working presses, typesetting machines, and lithograph presses were controlled by each side between 1917 and 1920 is scanty and contradictory.[30] Of the 808 shops in Ukraine that functioned between 1917 and 1921, around 45 per cent (351) were in three cities: Kyiv (186), Kharkiv (134), and Katernynoslav (41).[31] During power failures, printing could only be done on hand-operated presses.

Figures on the total number of presses during the revolutionary years vary. The only thing we can know for certain today is that the number of functioning presses in each shop changed with circumstances and available supplies. After six months of relative peace, in November 1918 a government survey found 89 printing shops in Kharkiv province (55 in the capital) and 99 in Katerynoslav province (30 in the capital). That December there were 112 shops in Kyiv.[32] In May 1920, Poltava province had 60 presses (38 in the capital). That July, Kyiv had 152 printing shops and 392 presses.[33] A survey conducted in December 1920 gives the total number of shops in Ukraine as 147. Yet another survey from March 1921 listed 248 printing shops in the entire country.[34] A detailed inventory of Kyiv province taken the following year, which included the names of the original owners, revealed that only 20 of the city's original 161 shops were still operating as state-owned enterprises, alongside another 23 in the rest of the province.[35] Kremenchuh in June 1919 had 7 shops with 29 presses, while Odesa had 109 shops with 459 presses, of which 6 were rotary. Of the 459, apparently only 106 still functioned.

At the time, the most advanced type of press was the electric rotary press. Using rolls of newsprint, they could to print 200,000 *arkush* (16 printed pages) or more in one hour – 90,000 copies of a four-page newspaper. The Ukrainian provinces after 1896 had some of the empire's 182 modern electric rotary presses. Twelve were in Kyiv. Serhyi Kulzhenko, one of the city's biggest publishers and a supporter of the Ukrainian movement, owned such a machine. Thus, Ukrainian organizations and the Ukrainian governments, although not necessarily every Ukrainian newspaper, would have had access to a rotary press whenever they controlled Kyiv. Saint Petersburg and Moscow together had 476 printing shops. In 1920 they had 72 per cent of the 174 rotary presses on Bolshevik territories. As of January 1921, Ukraine had 25 rotary presses (including 13 in Kyiv and 6 in Odesa).[36] Access to rotary presses was obviously important to governments. The Ukrainian national government and Ukrainian political parties, accordingly, printed fewer publications and reached fewer readers than the Bolsheviks, because they were not in constant control of at least one city with a working rotary press. The Bolsheviks, in control of central Russia, had permanent access to working machines, which they could use without interruption, subject only to the availability of workers and materials. Ukrainian governments and organizations most often had access to the older flatbed presses, which printed only 1,000 to 1,200 pages per hour. Under normal conditions, editors with flatbed presses had to have copy ready by eight p.m. in order to have newspapers out for sale by the next evening, because it took two machines sixteen hours to print 20,000 copies. With rotary machines, copy that was in by three a.m. normally could be printed in just as many copies, if not more, and be on the streets by morning.

Besides the rotary press, the other prewar invention that vastly increased output during the prewar years was the typesetting machine. The first such machine in Russia arrived in Moscow in 1903, and by 1914 there were 560 in the empire. Kyiv saw its first such machine in 1907. It is not known which Ukrainian cities outside Kyiv had these machines by 1914. We know that as of January 1921, Bolshevik Ukraine had 43 (15 in Kyiv, 12 in Katerynoslav, 10 in Kharkiv, 6 in Odesa).[37] But we do not know whether any Ukrainian party or government had access to one between 1917 and 1920. Nor do we know how many teleprinters, which were faster than telegraph machines and did not require knowledge of Morse code, were in Ukrainian lands before 1914, nor which Ukrainian governments might have had one. Duplicating machines, called mimeographs or Roneo duplicators, were invented in 1891 and were in general use in western Europe by 1914. How many were in Ukraine, and where, is unknown.

Until the beginning of the twentieth century, only government publications were distributed systematically throughout the empire via a centralized system. There was limited mass distribution of commercial publications separate from publishers outside the big cities. Beyond, publications were distributed in railway stations, *zemstva*, schools, churches, local reading clubs, and co-ops, or by peddlers. The government controlled printed text and issued permission to distribute it – even lowly peddlers required a permit. Police supervised those involved.[38] The high cost of postage limited the number of subscribers. By 1914, on average, all rural districts were getting at least one postal delivery weekly. The empire's first centralized commercial press distribution system was established by the private publisher Alexei Suvorin. By 1911 his organization had become the empire's biggest single commercial distributor. It centrally organized printed-text distribution through 1,600 newspaper kiosks, 600 of them at train stations. With almost 20,000 employees, it had representatives in each district capital in every province, and another 2,000 in county capitals. By 1916 it was distributing an average of 56,000 newspapers each day, as well as 310,000 journals each week. By early 1917 those totals had risen to 140,000 (daily) and 450,000 (weekly). The Bolsheviks expropriated what by 1917 was called the Suvorin–Efimov network the day after they took power and placed it in the control of their Central Printers Agency (*Tsentropechat*). A few weeks later they took the novel step of resorting to the postal system to distribute all government publications.[39]

Some idea of prewar printed-text distribution in tsarist Ukrainian provinces can be gleaned from figures for cheap pocket books (*lubok*) and newspapers. Out of 2,915 titles (1,053 legal newspapers and 1,862 periodicals) published in the empire in 1913, approximately 30 per cent were produced in Saint Petersburg (628) and Moscow (297). The Ukrainian provinces published 857. Of these latter, 229 were published in the three biggest cities (95 in Kyiv, 80 in Odessa, 95 in Kharkiv). As of 1915, 54 of imperial Russia's then 859 newspapers were being published in the Ukrainian provinces, 31 of them in Kyiv, Kharkiv, Katerynoslav, or Odessa.[40] The biggest Saint Petersburg papers had daily press runs between 80,000 and 250,000. The biggest of those, by 1914, was printing 500,000 copies daily. During the war the popular newspaper *Gazeta kopeika* saw one million copies daily.[41] Pre-war papers in Kyiv and Odessa printed between 12,000 and 40,000 copies; smaller provincial papers, between 1,000 and 3,000. The average press run of the nine legal pre-1917 Ukrainian-language newspapers and journals was 1,000 copies each.[42] Illegal Ukrainian-language materials, printed abroad and on secret presses domestically, had bigger runs. Between 1900 and 1904 the first Ukrainian political party, the Revolutionary Ukrainian Party, printed and distributed thirty-eight titles, including pamphlets, leaflets, and newspapers – a total of 144,000 copies. The Russian Social Democrats were printing nothing in Ukrainian yet.[43] There was a marked expansion of publishing despite repression in the Ukrainian provinces before the war as more titles began to reach small towns and villages within two or three days. The biggest Russian-language daily newspaper east of the Dnipro was the Kharkiv-based *Iuzhnyi Krai* (30,000 copies).[44]

The combined total daily press run of all of the empire's legal newspapers in 1913 was 3.3 million. There are no figures on the total press run of all of Ukraine's pre-1917 newspapers, but like the imperial total, it was much less than the press runs in northwestern European countries. British and German newspapers averaged a total of 10 million copies per day in 1890.[45] Ireland in 1914 had 289 newspapers (1:13,800), of which more than 150 were politically nationalist.[46] Ukraine's press runs in tsarist times might best be compared to those in Spain, where the biggest paper in 1914 published 17,000 copies. Periodical totals from 1912 show that tsarist Ukraine had a smaller network than did Habsburg eastern Galicia (western Ukraine). In six tsarist Ukrainian provinces that year, with an approximate population of 20 million, 223 periodical titles were being published in all languages, but primarily in Russian – an average of 1 per 90,000 people. Total press runs for the Ukrainian provinces only are unknown. That same year in Habsburg Galicia, the legal 45 Ukrainian-language newspapers and periodicals published for the province's 3.5 million Ukrainians amounted to one per 80,000 people.[47] In Podillia, the poorest Ukrainian province, before the war 63 periodicals and newspapers were published. Using 1897 census totals, that meant an average of one journal or newspaper for every 48,000 people; for urban dwellers, one for every 3,250.[48]

By mid-1917 there were some seven hundred newspapers and journals in the eight Ukrainian provinces (an average of one title per 43,000 people). Of these, 106 were in Ukrainian. Between October of that year and March 1918, when they were driven out by the Germans, the

Bolsheviks published a total of 67 newspapers in almost 400,000 copies with an average daily run of 10,000 to 15,000 copies.[49]

Besides newspapers, cheap paperbacks in Russian (and, after 1881, in Ukrainian) on Ukrainian subjects had significant circulation figures. Distributed by bookshops, reading clubs (*prosvita*), Ukrainian co-ops, and the big Russian publisher-distribution companies, as well as by peddlers at Ukraine's more than four thousand fairs and markets, these paperbacks averaged 10,000 copies each. Taras Shevchenko's *Kobzar* had runs of 20,000. Runs would sell out in a few weeks. Between 1906 and 1914 around one million copies of 350 cheap Ukrainian-language paperbacks alone had been printed out of a total of 4 million copies of 1,563 Ukrainian-language books. This averaged out to 6 titles for every 10 literate Ukrainians.[50]

Total production in Ukraine after 1917 was seriously reduced by widespread destruction that had not affected Moscow and Petrograd, where the only problem was shortages. In Ukraine, almost half the available type had been ruined by 1920. This exacerbated shortages resulting from closed borders because before the war all printing materials had been imported. Machines were run down and were often damaged when they were evacuated on wagons. Also, machines in printing shops were slowed down by the winter cold, which made all fluids viscous (including ink). The poor quality of paper, which by that year was being manufactured mainly from recycled archival documents, slowed down press speeds. In addition, printing shop staffs were often hungry, sick, and cold. In Mykolaiv, in a print shop with 197 staff, 54 could not work due to illness, and most of the others showed up only because doctors were forbidden to excuse anyone who could walk.[51] The total number of journals and newspapers published in Ukraine fell from 857 in 1917 to 224 in 1920.[52] With each passing month the shortages of parts, ink, paper, and printers grew worse. The poorly functioning transportation network impeded distribution of printed materials. Limited access to the latest printing technology (or none at all), alongside the broader problem of shortages and breakdowns that plagued all sides, limited the amount of printed materials that political leaders and governments could disseminate among the populace.

The People

In the Russian empire a mass urban consumer market was only just emerging at the turn of the last century. Merchants and manufacturers generally still produced their own advertisements, with larger enterprises hiring their own artists and writers. In the decades before the war, however, specialized advertising agencies (*kontory obiavlennii*), with staffs of what are now called ad men, existed alongside information offices (*kontory spravochnye*) duly listed in city and provincial directories. Sophisticated manuals explaining psychological based advertising techniques that included instructions on efficient distribution were also being published. In his *Russkaia reklama* (1898), Aleksii Verigin discussed these techniques as a social phenomenon that, in Russia, should take the "national soul" into consideration to have maxmum effect. Odesa as of 1902 had a specialist journal for ad men *Reklamist*, and in 1911 saw the publication of the detailed manual *Rukovodstvo reklamirovat*. Three other such manuals were published in the Ukrainian provinces before the war – in Volodymyr-Volynskyi, Poltava, and Kyiv.[53] By 1914 there were sixty-seven ad agencies in Moscow and Saint Petersburg and Russian and Russian advertising was on par with the best in Europe. The biggest agency, Metzl Brothers, founded in 1878, controlled 80 per cent of the empire's agencies when the Bolsheviks closed it in 1917. An unknown number of these agencies probably had affiliates in prewar Ukrainian territories. In 1913, for all of Volyn, Podillia, and Kyiv provinces, there were four separate agencies in Kyiv.[54] It is not known what these generators of consumer advertising did after the Bolsheviks abolished private commercial advertising. Those who took up government propaganda work, whether out of sympathy for one or other cause, or simply to earn a living, would have applied their expertise to make printed materials more effective than they might have been otherwise. How many such advertising professionals in Ukrainian cities sympathized with the national movement and worked for the Ukrainian governments or parties or co-ops is unknown.[55]

Journalists were another group skilled at manipulating texts, symbols, and pictures vital to government and party propaganda efforts. There was an identifiable group of professional journalists by the turn of the century, but the 1897 imperial census did not record them. All Ukrainian newspapers were closed down in 1914, but even before, they could not sell enough copies or subscriptions to finance themselves. In part this was due to a well-intentioned but commercially dubious policy of free distribution to Ukrainian institutions. Most depended on patrons, and staff often worked without pay. In Ukraine, professional Ukrainian-born journalists undoubtedly worked for Russian papers, and some Russian papers printed stories by Ukrainians. Leading intellectuals wrote articles for the press; however, there seem to have been few if any professional journalists working for Ukrainian newspapers. In a critical review of the Ukrainian press in 1910, one editor bemoaned the low status, low pay, and low qualifications of those who did write for the Ukrainian press – most of them were unemployed, ex-students, ex-village teachers, dilettantes, or "failures." "And it often occurs: today – he is a man off the street, tomorrow – a Ukrainian journalist." This, he added, did not help attract readers. Editors and staff spent more time at secret police offices, answering questions, or in prison, than they did in newsrooms. The very few Ukrainians who did set out to become journalists for Ukrainian publications knowingly "committed themselves to a hungry existence."[56]

The 1897 census registered nearly 72,000 men and women printers and print shop workers. Almost half of them were to be found in Saint Petersburg and Moscow. These numbered almost four times more than the total number in the eight Ukrainian provinces, where just under 15 per cent of them declared their native language as Ukrainian. Almost half of Ukraine's printers worked in Kyiv. As of 1911 the two major publishing centres in Ukraine were Kyiv and Odesa.[57] In Petrograd and Moscow between 1917 and 1922, production plummeted not only because of the circumstances noted above, but also because printers were spending their time foraging for basics, staging work stoppages, or going on strike. Until 1920, the Mensheviks dominated the printers' unions, and printers were in a position not to print what they disagreed with. I have found only one example of such an action in Ukraine. Under the Rada in April 1918, the novelist Hryhory Kovalenko prepared a booklet complaining that, despite the liberties the Ukrainian government had given them, pro-Bolshevik Jewish youth and Bolshevik Jewish workers were strongly anti-Ukrainian. He described how they had wantonly killed Ukrainians during the Bolshevik occupation that January and had then condemned the Ukrainians who lynched Jews afterwards. When he submitted his article to the Ukrainian SD party newspaper, the editors rejected it. Then Kyivan printers, whom he did not identify by political affiliation or nationality, refused to print it as a pamphlet. Concluding that nothing could be printed about Jews in Ukraine unless it was good, he published his work in Lviv and shipped the consignment to Kyiv.[58]

Working conditions in print shops were dangerous and unhealthy. In Kremenchuh, such shops were commonly called "death boxes." The average annual death rate among printers was 10 per cent.[59] During the war years, all sides considered printing shops strategically important, alongside telegraph and telephone exchanges. Incoming forces tried to occupy all of these as quickly as possible to ensure that the opposing side took as little as possible of the machinery and materials with them as they fled. Some printing presses were set up on trains, where working conditions were usually as bad as in the shops, if not worse, because the personnel literally lived on the presses, which were hand-operated.[60]

Table 1 Total print workers by province and language in 1897

Province	Ukrainian	Russian	Jewish	All
Kyiv	455	1,064	982	2,689
Volyn	63	33	667	818
Podillia	49	32	562	680
Chernihiv	140	97	338	588
Poltava	203	34	674	968
Kharkiv	401	679	285	1,408
Katerynoslav	56	212	486	775
Kherson	84	944	1,494	2,690
Total Ukraine	1,451	3,095	5,488	**10,616 (9,811)**
Moscow				20,163 (16,735)
Saint Petersburg				16,393 (13,606)
Total Empire				**82,397 (71,500)**

Source: See note 57 on page 232.

All governments had couriers and agitators, who carried, displayed, and (usually) explained texts to audiences. As of mid-1918, only the Bolsheviks had organized schools and courses for their personnel within various commissariats and at all levels – an intiative that might be compared to America's "Four Minute Men." These included special courses for women agitators. By 1920 the political section of the Revolutionary Military Council (*Revoensovet*) alone controlled 14,659 agitators. Bolshevik leaders attached departments of supply and distribution responsible for dissemination to the provincial sections of their press and propaganda offices. They created special subsections centrally and locally, and within various commissariats, to deal specifically with dissemination. They specifically ordered city party officials to provide printed literature to all those travelling to outlying regions on whatever business.[61] The Bolsheviks' organizational efforts extended to foreign lands. Thus in October 1918 they created the All Russian Conference of Communist Organizations in Occupied Territories, whose targets were initially the soldiers of opposing armies.

Agents on both sides made efforts to distribute literature in public places. By 1919, however, they were reporting that walls were often bare because the locals were taking the paper to wrap food, roll cigarettes, and wipe their backsides. The Bolsheviks threatened to court-martial those caught tearing down posters and leaflets (Illus. 16, 41, 42). Also, shortages of firewood were causing people to tear down fences and wall boards, which meant less space for posting messages. By 1919, couriers, lecturers, and activists were making a point of disseminating their materials in public places rather than placing them in private hands.

Literacy and Comprehension

Literacy levels in Ukraine were higher in 1917 than in 1897. In the intervening twenty years more peasants learned to read at the growing number of rural schools, and millions more learned in the army. Military service was the main reason for the increase. In 1904, 52 per cent of recruits from the eight Ukrainian provinces could read – an increase of 20 per cent from 1894. By 1916 almost 75 per cent of soldiers were partly literate.[62] Seventeen-year-old literate soldier Andryi Rubel from central Ukraine, for instance, wrote home in 1915 in a mixture of Russian and Ukrainian urging his friends and brothers to do like him and learn how to read. Another Ukrainian soldier wrote in his memoirs that interest in the war and the wish to write to menfolk in the army had led to increasing literacy among peasants. Schools were full, he recounted, around his native town of Hlodosy, fifty miles southwest of Cherkassy.[63] Schools that continued to function during the revolutionary years also contributed to increased literacy rates. In the wake of the Hetman's demise in December 1918, Ukraine had 1,193 primary schools attended by almost 2 million of its 3 million school-aged children. As of April 1919, allegedly all children in Katerynoslav, and as many as 80 per cent in Poltava and Chernihiv provinces, were attending schools.[64] In Bolshevik-controlled Ukraine in 1919, an unknown number of primary schools and 1,071 secondary schools functioned. Of the latter, 950 used Russian and 121 Ukrainian as the language of instruction.[65]

Surveys conducted during the revolutionary years illustrate the increases in literacy. The incomplete 1920 census indicates that the total number of literate in Ukraine had risen to roughly 13 million from the 1897 total of 3.5 million. The number of literate Ukrainians was almost 9 million, nearly five times the 1897 total of just over 2 million.[66] Local reviews provide additional detail. A 1919 Kyiv city census indicated that 20 per cent of the 544,369 counted could read and write in two languages and that 46 per cent could read and write in one language. Another 9,300 could only read.[67] In Kharkiv province the number of literate males had risen from 26 per cent in 1897 to 42 per cent in 1920, and the number of literate females from 8 to 24 per cent. For "self-identifying" Ukrainian men the figures for those same years were 23 and 39 per cent, and for women 4 and 19 per cent. In Kharkiv city between those two years the percentages rose from 62 to 74 for men, and from 42 to 63 per cent for women. A 1923 survey of 263,564 rural inhabitants in all Ukraine found a rural literacy rate between 1920 and 1923 that averaged

41 per cent for males and 17 per cent for females, with highest rates in Poltava province and the lowest in Podillia province.[68]

While the number of literate had increased since 1897, not all of the literate necessarily comprehended messages as authors intended. An Englishman present in Petrograd in 1917, for example, passed a meeting where an agitator was explaining peace without annexations and contributions. At the time, the Russian words *aneksiia* and *kontributsiia* were recent neologisms not understood by the average literate, let alone illiterate, person. His audience concluded that the agitator had said the tsar's daughter, Aneksiia, should not be allowed on the throne, and that the town Kontributisiia could not be left in the hands of the English who had seized it. Surveys taken by officials in Russia indicated that common people did not understand words like *imperializm, sotsialism, buidzhet*, or *demokratiia*.[69] In Siberia the Russian writer Stepan Chardymskii observed that for the common people "the newspaper language is not accessible. The general idea is never grasped." Except for very simple jingoistic pieces, people only recognized individual phrases. They then jumbled these together with rumours, an occasional poster or leaflet, legends, local lore, and superstitions to create an distinctly idiosyncratic understanding of what was happening around them.[70] An analogous situation probably existed in Ukraine.

While some words meant nothing to many people, other words changed their meanings. For instance, the words *burzhui, kulak-kurkul*, and *nezamozhnyi* came to denote political loyalty or an ideological attiude rather than a social position. Moreover, inasmuch as these terms either were not used at all before 1917 or had different meanings before that year than they did in Bolshevik propaganda, whether peasants in particular understood them as the Bolsheviks intended remains an open question. A *kurkul* before the war was not a rich exploiter, but an outsider settled in the village. After 1917, propaganda presented a village divided into a "bad" rich group (*kurkul* or *kulak*), and a "good" middle (*seredniak*) and poor group. But inhabitants divided themselves into "honest yeoman farmers" (*hospodar-khazaiin*), and the poor (*bidniak, bidak*), and more specifically, into one of more than eight legal-social groups such as *kozak* or *kolonist*.[71] Those who were poor as result of misfortune had the sympathy and support of family and neighbours – an element of a common European rural "moral economy," in which clan/kin trumped class. Those who were poor because of faulty character were tolerated but scorned. In Hrinchenko's dictionary (1908), "seredniak" was defined as horn-pith, not "middle peasant." The term did not appear at all in Dubrovsky's dictionary (1918), which defined "burzhui" as urban dweller.[72] Borys Martos remarked in 1917 that peasants understood socialism to mean only the transfer of property from landowners to themselves. By the end of that year in cities a "bourgeois" (*burzhui*) was anyone more or less well dressed and with an intelligent face. To avoid the risk and opprobrium of the label, people took to wearing hand-me downs or old army uniforms, and army forage caps instead of hats.[73]

A report from Kremenchuh in central Ukraine from December 1918 noted that the town secretary dutifully pasted up leaflets. However, he had no idea what they were about, nor did the public, who would read them, then leave. If there happened to be present someone who read and then explained the contents to the assembled, they would all nod and say, "May God grant it be so." The author concluded that agitators should not simply paste their notices and then leave, but be sure first to explain their contents to the local dignitaries.[74] Borys Antonenko-Davydovych related that in 1920, while with a local partisan leader, he addressed a leaflet he wrote for him "Undefeated Ukrainians" (*neskoreni Ukraintsi*) that was duly posted in surrounding villages. Meeting a peasant some days later and asking him what was new, he was told that "little papers" (*bomazhki*[*sic*]) had appeared by the store that told people to wait until the spring. When asked what it was that people were supposed to wait for, the peasant replied: "Some sort of rebellious [*nepokorni*] Ukrainians – seems a new party has appeared." In June 1919 villagers near Zhytomir, only recently occupied by Bolsheviks, held a mass to celebrate their liberation from capitalism.[75] That same month in Podillia province a Ukrainian agitator related how in a village he visited after the Bolsheviks had fled one of the inhabitants told him that the "bichevnyky" had brought so much of "those papers [leaflets and pamphlets] with them," that "even now my wife still has more than she needs to fire the stove." They asked him: "do those papers that you have brought say the same thing as they [the Bolsheviks] did?"[76]

There are reports of postmen who could not deliver items because they could not read, and of village clerks semi-literate in Russian who could not always understand written Ukrainian. Thus in Podillia in 1919 an inspector reported how, when a local clerk got a telegram in Ukrainian requesting horses and clothing from villagers for the army, he read out the words including the punctuation as part of the text. Neither he nor the assembled could understand the telegram. They all had a good laugh, and the clerk excused his ignorance by saying he had never read a telegram "so sternly written" (*kruto napysano*) as that before. As a result, the inspector continued, the army went without, and furthermore, the peasants concluded that the government was not using Ukrainian, but "something from Galicia," and thus were alienated both from the UNR and Ukrainians. He concluded his report by noting the urgent need for courses for village clerks, where they would learn punctuation and short forms, among other things.[77]

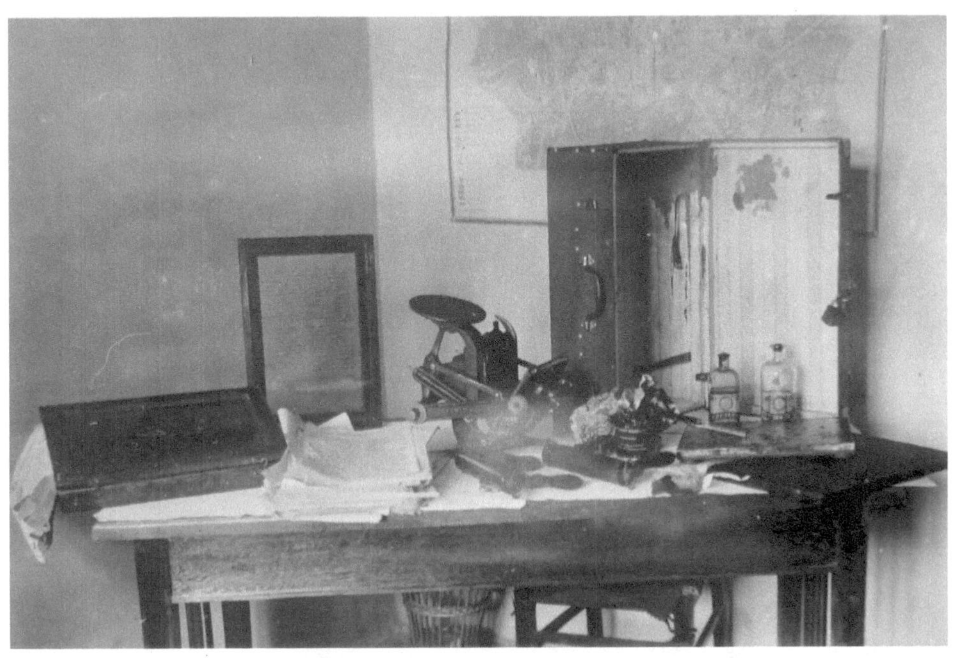

17 Portable hand printing press confiscated in 1929 from an opposition group. Typical of many used during the revolution.
TsDASBU.

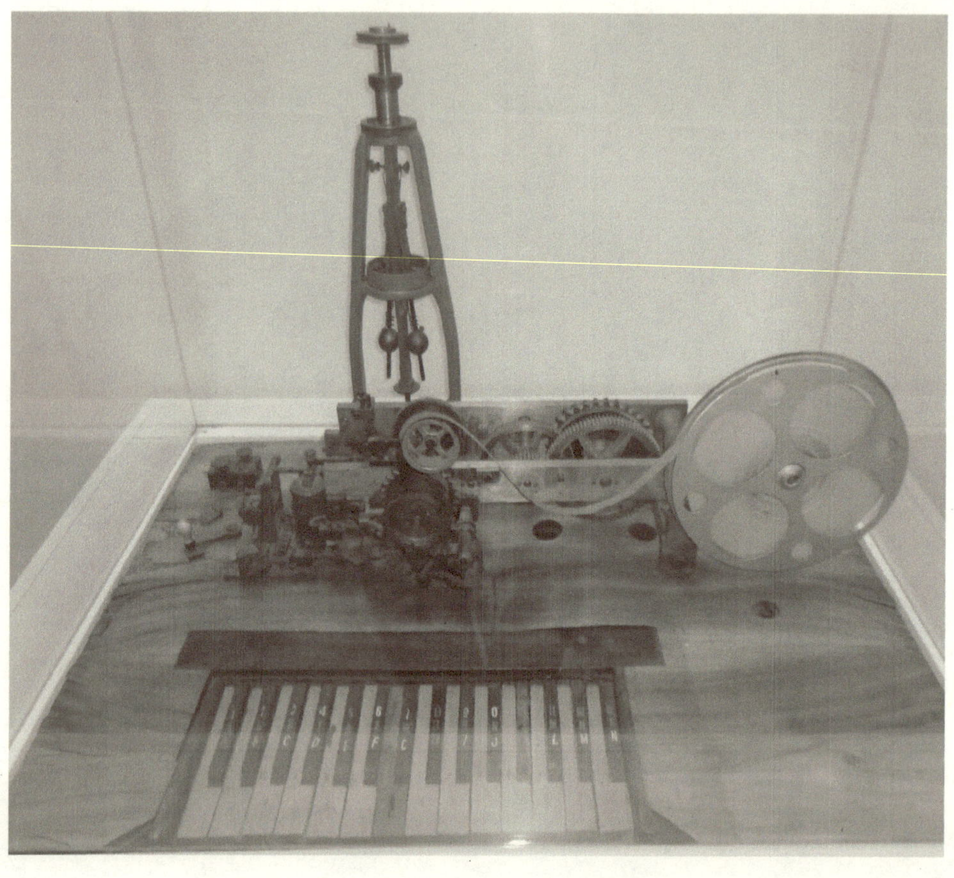

18 Early-twentieth-century Hughes teleprinter with keyboard. This machine had Cyrillic and Latin letters. Operators did not have to know Morse. NMIU.

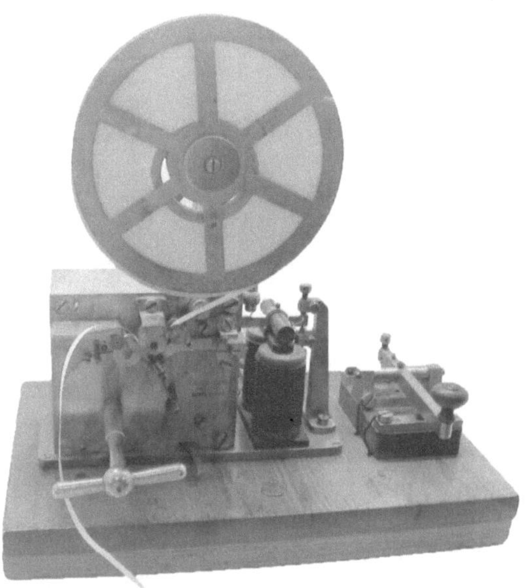

19 Standard early-twentieth-century telegraph machine with key that required the operator to know Morse.
Aalborg Maritime Museum, Denmark. Photograph at Wikimedia Commons © 2006 by Tomasz Sienicki. Used under the CC BY 2.5 license / Background removed.

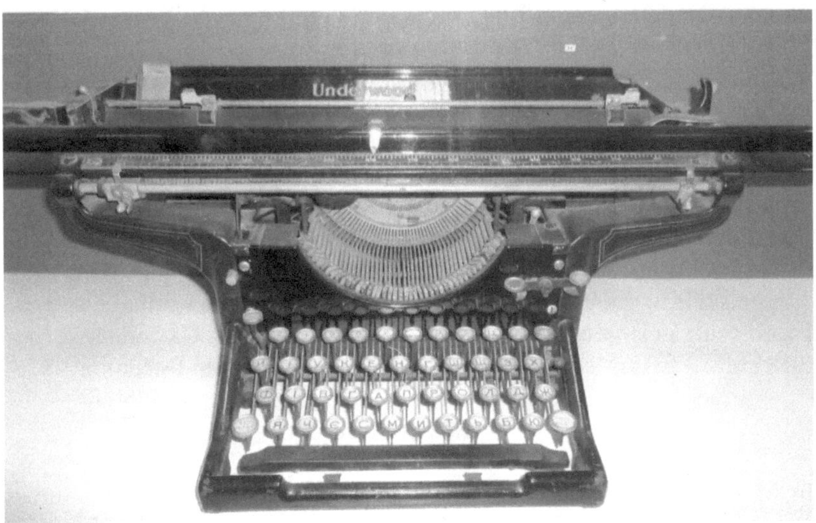

20 Typical early-twentieth-century typewriter with Ukrainian letters.
NMIU.

Chapter Two

The Central Rada and the Ukrainian State

Ukrainian leaders in Kyiv created the Central Rada in March 1917 and that November proclaimed the Ukrainian National Republic (UNR) (Illus. 22). The Rada claimed authority over the Ukrainian provinces of the Russian empire, excluding the Crimea. After the summer of 1917, the Rada was one of six organizations nominally responsible for administering the empire alongside commissars appointed by the Provisional Government, the central government ministries, the army general staff, the newly elected city *dumas*, and provincial rural government councils (*zemstva*). During the Russian Bolshevik invasion in January 1918, it was forced to flee Kyiv, but it returned that March, allied with Germany. On 29 April 1918 the Ukrainian-born former tsarist general Pavlo Skoropadsky overthrew the Rada with the support of the Central Powers. Backed by the Association of Landowners, the Manufacturers and Business Association (PROTOFIS), and the wealthy farmers of the Ukrainian Democratic Farmers Party (UDKhP), he ruled Ukraine until December. He established a neo-monarchist regime called the Ukrainian State (*Ukrainska Derzhava*) with himself, as Hetman, at its head. Skoropadsky was a conservative noble Ukrainophile. He was disliked by Ukrainian socialists, who boycotted his government. This left him little choice but to appoint as ministers former tsarist officials, who were sympathetic to the Whites and sometimes hostile to Ukrainian interests. Faced with Germany's defeat, Skoropadsky declared Ukraine incorporated into a federated Russia as an autonomous unit in December 1918.

The Medium

In March 1917 the Central Rada established an "Agitation Commission" (separate from the Press Bureau) under Serhiy Veselovsky, with offices in Kyiv's Pedagogical Museum. Like other political leaders in other countries with high percentages of rural dwellers, the commission faced the task of sending approved information in large amounts of printed text to families not always near railways and post offices. Few such people would have seen paved roads, and their nearest town may or may not have published a newspaper. The commission began collecting printed materials; it also organized travelling lecturers, called agitators or instructors, and briefed them before their departure regarding what they were to tell audiences (Illus. 23–5). In June the commissioners decided to increase the number of agitators, centralize all propaganda work, and coordinate that work with local *zemstva* – renamed that summer "popular councils" (*narodna uprava*). The aim was to develop a nationwide hierarchy of elected pro-Rada committees. The commission itself was reorganized, and party representatives were replaced by representatives from the *soviets*, which were not yet all controlled by the Bolsheviks. That November the Rada replaced the commission with an information bureau subordinated to the Interior Ministry.[1] By July 1917 the Ukrainian General Military Committee had established an Agitation-Educational Section to disseminate propaganda among Ukrainian soldiers. Meanwhile, local party and non-party national activists formed ad hoc provincial "agitation sections" attached to local "enlightenment societies" (*prosvita*), co-ops, and Peasant Union organizations. They also established small libraries and reading rooms. It seems that none of these local groups used the word propaganda in their name. It is unknown how many villages were visited by Ukrainian agitators with their leaflets in 1917. The situation in Poltava province was perhaps typical. After travelling the region that autumn, Central Rada member Serhyi Iefremov reported that some villages there had been visited by agitators and pasted with literature, while others had been completely bypassed.[2] In the last week of December the Rada set the terms according to which it would take over the Ukrainian section of the Suvorin distribution network. In March it decided to annul that agreement and hand the network to the Ministry of Highways.[3]

By April, hundreds of Ukrainian volunteer agitators were roving the country, addressing audiences in competition with rivals from Russian parties. Surviving Ukrainian reports reveal villagers' attitudes towards them as well as where they developed support. Some reported encountering suspicion and hostility, including catcalling, as well as indifference to politics. Agitators noted that local government officials, many of whom belonged to non-Ukrainian parties, refused to assist them; also, difficulty with transport and communications left them without instructions or materials and ignorant of events beyond their regions. Others reported a demand for Ukrainian materials. In the town of Vovchansk in

Kharkiv province in November 1917, the Rada agitator reported: "There is a copy of the Third Universal in every house. The Ukrainian bookstore is filled with peasants all day. The demand for Ukrainian books is phenomenal."[4] As of the fall of 1917, local co-ops and party organizations and the education societies were the main disseminators of Ukrainian printed texts. The reports suggest that timing and personnel could be as crucial as programs and policies in establishing loyalties. Whose representatives arrived first, how many of them there were, and how competent they were as speakers and organizers often had a decisive impact on opinion. Where possible, Ukrainian leaders preferred to send soldiers rather than intellectuals as agitators because peasants more readily trusted the former. For lack of funds, the Rada was short of agitators. Kharkiv province had only ten in 1917. Agitators who consequently decided to focus their efforts on villages left their Russian rivals unchallenged in towns.[5]

Ukrainian leaders issued instructional materials to their agitators. A three-page pamphlet the Rada issued to army agitators instructed them to inform soldiers about the Rada and its social policies, to report by telegraph as often as possible about the resolutions of local military committees and the strength of the national movement among Ukrainian troops, and to help promote the Rada by linking Ukrainian soldiers with one another and with Kyiv. Instructors were expected to help form separate Ukrainian units and to remind Ukrainian soldiers to maintain exemplary discipline among themselves based on mutual respect and comradeship.[6] A more detailed set of instructions (Illus. 23–4) specified that peasants were to be told that the Rada would represent their interests effectively and that they should keep the peace, for the upcoming Constituent Assembly would defend their social and national interests; also, they should keep the army supplied. Instructors were to explain what the assembly would do, that land issues could only be resolved within an autonomous Ukraine, and that under the new regime, educational, church, and administrative affairs would be conducted in Ukrainian. Instructors were to avoid Jewish-related issues, and if those emerged, they were to state that all nationalities were equal. They were to stress the importance of co-ops, explain the need for local elections and for the creation of local councils to take over all functions from tsarist officials, and underscore the importance of voting not by shouts but rather by a public count of hands. They also were to emphasize the importance of organizing reading clubs and cultural centres. The instructions noted that all tsarist officials had to be replaced and that it was necessary to cooperate with local teachers and priests; they then concluded that agitators should not waste too much time with "the intelligentsia" because "the people did not trust them."

In 1917, activists rented presses if they did not own any. Ukrainian organizations in Moscow, Petrograd, and Finland published in those places, as indicated on some leaflets, and then shipped materials to Kyiv. The Rada established its own press section within the General Secretariat and later the Military Secretariat. It also funded private presses with interest-free loans to produce Ukrainian-language materials.[7] As of January 1918, there were an estimated 111 print shops in Kyiv, 6 of which were government-operated. More than half were owned by Jews. Almost all were in the city centre. The publishing firm Vernyhora under Valentyn Otamanovsky was perhaps the most important publisher of Ukrainian governmental materials.

In the spring of 1917, typesetters were apparently in high demand and could set their own wages and working conditions. Editors would lure them away from rivals with promises of higher wages and various perks, such as self-service office samovars. Kyiv had plenty of presses, including modern rotary presses, but not all of them were owned by or at the disposal of Ukrainian parties or organizations, whose printers and publishers used whatever presses they could find. The editors of *Nova Rada*, for example, ordered a rotary press from the United States in 1917 that was never shipped. They finally managed to purchase one in Odesa. Someone in Kyiv supposedly ignored an opportunity to buy a rotary press for the Central Rada in August direct from the American manufacturer in Petrograd.[8] One group of activists heard that Kyiv's *soviet* had confiscated the presses of a Russian extremist newspaper. Collecting their last capital, the group purchased it and then used it to publish Rada materials. In another instance, Ukrainian soldiers located the press of the Caves Monastery, which had been evacuated to an outlying village during the war. They confiscated it, transported it to Kyiv, and placed it at the disposal of the Central Rada. Ukrainians in Petrograd also managed to ship a press to the Rada. The Berdychiv region *zemstvo* requisitioned the presses of the Pochaiv Monastary and placed them at the disposal of the Rada. Over the course of the summer, local Rada supporters took over provincial *zemstvo* presses.[9]

A relaxation of censorship after 1905 allowed Ukrainian-language published texts to reach a wider readership than previously. By 1913, 1,563 Ukrainian-language books had been published in a total of 4.1 million copies. During the first six months of 1911 more than 514,000 copies of 164 Ukrainian-language books were published – an unprecedented number. Wartime censorship destroyed this nascent publishing industry. It revived dramatically after the tsar abdicated, limited only by shortages of paper, ink, and qualified workers as well as by high costs. Of approximately 800 titles published in Ukraine in 1917, 106 were in Ukrainian.[10]

A shortage of data on Ukrainian publishing prohibits reaching definitive conclusions about media saturation; however, figures from Kyiv's printing shops in 1917 offer some sense of scale. Available figures for the last five months of the year from the Vernyhora publishers indicate that it published 350,000 leaflets and posters.[11] Some Ukrainian school texts were published in runs of 100,000. The most heavily published author was the writer and national activist Borys Hrinchenko, whose works that year totalled almost 400,000 copies; he was followed by historian and then Rada chairman Mykhailo Hrushevsky, at approximately 300,000 copies. Each of these men ran his own publishing firm. The Ukrainian book with the highest total press run in 1917 was apparently the *Katekhizm Ukraintsa* by Bohdan Zaklynsky. Since its appearance in 1911 it had gone through seven editions totalling more than 160,000 copies. As of December 1917, Ukrainian leaflets and pamphlets published in Kyiv had press runs of between 10,000 and 100,000. As costs rose, so did prices, which in turn reduced the number of buyers. The editor of the centrist paper *Nova Rada* complained that spring about a threefold increase in the price of paper and a fourfold increase in postage, which together resulted in a threefold increase in the publishing cost of one issue.[12]

By the end of 1917 there were eighty Ukrainian-language or bilingual newspapers on former tsarist Ukrainian territory; about half of these were published in Kyiv province. That worked out to roughly one title per 325,000 people. Including Russian newspapers and the urban-literate population only would lower the number of readers per title.[13] How many copies of these newspapers got beyond city limits is unknown. In prewar eastern Galicia the ratio was one newspaper per 70,000 people – assuming dissemination. There is no record of total press runs for all Ukrainian papers. One paper for which there are figures, *Nova Rada*, increased its run from 15,000 copies in March to 20,000 in September – and it was in debt.[14] The Ukrainian SR newspaper *Narodna volia*, at its maximum in 1917, published 200,000 copies.

The city of Kyiv was home to twenty of Ukraine's thirty-eight Ukrainian publishing companies and accounted for almost 75 per cent of all Ukrainian books and pamphlets published in 1917.[15] Publishing in provincial capitals beyond Kyiv probably declined after 1917, but this matter has not been studied. In Cherkassy, for instance, only three or four firms instead of a pre-revolutionary dozen were still in business in 1918. For the next two years they continued to publish books, but their focus was on leaflets and decrees in runs of a few hundred.[16] To meet the demand for Ukrainian materials, the Rada set up "book wagons" on the rail system to distribute publications outside the capital. As of May 1918, after the Bolsheviks had been chased from Ukraine, the Kherson provincial governor reported that sellers in Odessa, exploiting the huge demand and small supply of Ukrainian books, had doubled prices. He requested that the book wagon program be renewed.[17]

For most of 1918, relative internal stability and trade with Germany made it possible to restore and repair presses. The paper shortage had become so acute, however, that the Hetman's government imposed rationing. In the central offices of the Health Ministry, a circular posted in August 1918 instructed employees not to tear pages out of the regulations and procedures book to use for wrapping and other purposes.[18] The government signed a trade agreement with Finland for a shipment of paper in return for sugar; the paper duly arrived in Riga and was loaded onto a train. But it was never shipped. Local Ukrainian officials later sold it. Another trade agreement with Finland, signed in September – this time, a barter deal that exchanged paper for grain – was never implemented. An attempt to establish a government press came to nothing. Apparently, a rotary press was found and prepared for shipping, but it fell off its wagon onto the rails while being transported, and there it remained until someone from PROTOFIS took it away and set it up to publish that group's own newspaper.[19]

The Hetman had a press secretary, Russian journalist Aleksandr Maliarevskii, but no propaganda ministry. Individual ministries had information sections, as did the Hetman's personal staff (*Shtab Hetmana*). Some ministers developed plans to subsidize "brochures and leaflets properly describing government activities" but did little besides establish an official newspaper. Propaganda activities were allotted to a Press Department subordinated to the Interior Ministry, while some local officials on their own initiatives published their own materials reflecting their own ideas, free of any central guidelines or supervision. A thirty-page popular, sympathetic biography of the Hetman was written and supposedly published in one million copies – but never distributed.[20] The Ukrainian Telegraph Agency was part of the Press Department. Before conservative Ukrainian writer Dmytro Dontsov took it over in May 1918, it was run by three anti-Ukrainian activists – Dyvyina, Labensky, and Didukh. Skoropadsky thought Dontsov did little at his post.[21]

The Hetman's government produced almost no printed propaganda, either domestically or abroad. Funds were allotted for a "cheap popular organ for peasants," but it does not seem to have appeared. As noted, Maliarevskii's Russian pamphlet, also aimed at a mass audience, was apparently published but not circulated.[22] This neglect might be related to the social origins of Skoropadsky's ministers.

Like their prewar counterparts throughout Europe, these were conservative landowners, officers, administrators, or businessmen, with imperial loyalist convictions, sometimes tempered by cultural Ukrainophilism. As such, they spent their working days giving orders, on the presumption that they should command and others obey. The notion that they should mobilize agitators to win the hearts and minds of their inferiors via mass propaganda of any kind was alien to them.[23] Obviously, sponsoring Ukrainian national propaganda held no appeal for White tsarist loyalists. In this regard they were the opposite of the nationalists, socialists, and anarchists, who were of lower status and whose beliefs obliged them to win public support through the printed and spoken word. While war had forced their upper-class European and imperial Petersburg counterparts to resort to mass public persuasion, it did not have the same effect on the Hetman's officials. Another reason for this lack of official interest in propaganda was that Ukraine was formally neutral and at peace until the last weeks of 1918, which meant there was no pressing need to mobilize the population. Skoropadsky admitted that his officials paid little attention to propaganda. He blamed, in particular, his interior and finance ministers, who were reluctant fund it. Ironically, Germany's Ukrainian ally was awash with anti-Ukrainian propaganda produced and illegally disseminated *en masse* by its other ally, Bolshevik Russia, thanks in part to German funding.[24]

The only national propaganda initiative that was undertaken under the Hetman's government was by the roads minister, Borys Butenko, a non-party engineer. He assigned this task to his ministry's School and Enlightenment Division (*shkilna – prosvitna uprava*). When the Hetman took power, the Suvorin network was still functioning as a private agency, but business was slow. In June 1918 the Polissia regional rail chief reported that no one knew who was in charge in his region and that no Ukrainian materials were on sale.[25] That May, an Ivan Sukhotin, Suvorin's representative in Ukraine, had approached the Hetman about running the system. The head of the government's Culture and Education Section heard about this and wrote the Hetman that he had rejected an earlier similar request because Sukhotin was a boor and unprincipled trader. He treated books as mere commodities and was fit only "to sell kvas and donuts in the market." Butenko, meanwhile, was of the opinion that concessions to private owners could not be given for books, as they were for forests or coal, because education should not be a source of profit. He wrote the Hetman that his ministry had the necessary personnel and resources to disseminate publications, and, unlike Sukhotin, it would not sell "literary garbage, pornography, pinkerton novels, and penny-dreadfuls about various gangsters, that will do nothing but incline the dark masses to crime."[26]

The government nationalized the system because Sukhotin had contrived the terms of his contract. But the takeover proceeded very slowly and was still going on in 1919. The agency, now under government control, was supposed to distribute Ukrainian-language publications and "artistic leaflets drawings and portraits of important activists which were not produced in Ukraine because of the upheavals of the last years, price rises and lack of materials." It planned to obtain these materials from Austria via western Ukraine, to which end Butenko removed the import tax on them.[27] The organization planned to cooperate with local Ukrainian organizations and would hire crippled veterans and war widows to run the kiosks.[28] Agents would take one or two wagonloads of materials and distribute them to district station kiosks over the course of a few weeks. A report from October 1918 illustrates some of the problems involved in the mass dissemination of printed text. Of six stations on a route, four were either closed or so badly run that they sold nothing and were so stacked with unsold materials that they could not accept new shipments. At one of these stations, a full storage shack was rented from the stationmaster, who told the agent if he did not remove the materials in ten days he would throw them all out. Some sense of the size of the various stores of materials may be gauged from a 27 January 1919 report, written on the eve of the Bolshevik occupation of the city. It reported twelve tons of unsold newspapers and journals sitting on Kyiv station platforms, presumably not shipped because of the anti-Hetman uprisings.[29]

The Message: The Central Rada

The first messages issued after the tsar's abdication by the Central Rada, Ukrainian political parties, non-Bolshevik-dominated *soviets*, and various Ukrainian groups dealt with national and practical-governmental issues. Leaflets referred to "the nation rising" to freedom after 250 years of oppression and urged people to keep order, to await the elections for the Constituent Assembly, and, in the meantime, to organize, vote, donate to Ukrainian institutions, participate in civic life, and introduce Ukrainian and Ukrainians into all public institutions (Doc. 1–14).[30] One leaflet, written in Petrograd, printed in Finland, then distributed in Ukraine, called on Ukrainians to use their new freedom to create a new national life after waking from a long sleep (Doc. 9).[31]

National issues were muted. Probably typical of those early days was a notice from activists in Kharkiv addressed to the "respected Ukrainian citizen" and greeting them on the occasion of the rebirth of their nation "without noisy words and phrases" (Doc. 11).[32] "We [nationally] conscious must open the eyes of the unconscious." This notice explained that while the old regime had oppressed the Russians in some matters, they had not known national oppression. With regard to Ukrainians, however, it had "gnawed out [*vyhryzlo*] our very soul." Forbidden everything, including the opportunity to speak their own language, Ukrainians had to "start everything from the beginning." Thus, no one could blame them for being disorganized. "So we call upon you, Ukrainian citizen, to work to establish that all-Ukrainian organization. Do what you can ... or at least financially support those who do." Ukrainian co-ops established the first Ukrainian National Cooperative Bank, which urged all citizens in Ukraine to deposit money, stressing that it would serve all of Ukraine's population and had no "chauvinist tasks." Ukraine's manufacturing and agricultural workers, it explained, would no longer be financially dependent on big (i.e., central Russian) capital and industrialists.[33] Particularly significant in these early materials was their frequent use of "Ukrainian" as both an adjective and a noun in reference to the majority population of present-day Ukraine. While the literate and educated were familiar with that term and had used it before 1917, from that year on it was disseminated among the population at large in mass publications. The Ukrainian faction of the Kyiv Military District *soviet* issued a leaflet condemning the wealthy. It included an explanation of what Ukraine and Ukrainians were. "Little Russians," it noted, was a term invented by foreigners and had been used by the tsar's wealthy henchmen to deny the people, "Ukrainians," their land and historic rights (Doc. 2, 3).[34]

Activists called on people to form groups, and the groups issued leaflets. In April, Hrushevsky published a personal appeal to all university faculty calling on them to attend a general meeting in Kyiv to discuss de-Russifying the education system (Doc. 7).[35] A Central Ukrainian Student Council called on "comrade students" to "go to the people," prepare them for the elections, and explain the importance of federalism to them, and pointed to the need to unite with non-Ukrainians, for "we must live alongside them" (Doc. 6).[36] The Rada's Education Commissar in Poltava province congratulated local teachers, "Mr. Comrades [*panove tovaryshi*]," for their achievements in establishing Ukrainian schools during the previous five months and urged them to continue their efforts. Another leaflet explained that education in the native language led to people demanding better conditions. It asked: "Is our Ukrainian language worse than Russian, Polish or any other?" (Doc. 4).[37] "In no other states [than Ukraine] is there such a thing as the 'peasant's language' and the 'lord's language' but there is only one national [language]." "Comrades – teachers Ukrainian and non-Ukrainian throughout Ukraine! Ukrainian children Ukrainian parents and the entire Ukrainian nation await your work, joy and advice." The educated were called to "do their duty," organize the nation, and show the provisional government that there really did exist a mass movement for autonomy. Notices from Poltava, Kharkiv, and Chernihiv emphasized the importance of peasant unions and reading clubs at all levels of society. They complained that too many local people were either doing nothing politically or limiting their efforts to their own villages. One anonymous leaflet urged people at all levels to establish and attend "information bureaus," to encourage and engage in activism (Doc. 8, 10, 11, 12).[38] Many *soviets* supported the Rada.

Workers organized unions and printed announcements. Kyiv officials founded a branch of the central Russian administrators' union. An organizing committee of the city's post and telegraph workers called for a national conference to show support for the Rada. In June, the Ukrainian council of the Southern Rail Union reminded its members: "We request brother Ukrainians and comrade Russians to distribute and exhibit this leaflet everywhere remembering that without a strong free Ukraine, that the Russian nation always loved and supported, there will be no strong free Russia." Accept non-Ukrainians "whose soul is with you and want in the future to live and remain a native son of Ukraine," Ukrainians were told (Doc. 13, 14, 15).[39] Co-op and party organizers maintained that social reforms would be easier to implement once national rights had been secured through political autonomy, and that Ukrainians faced a hard struggle because, unlike the Russians, who suffered only social oppression, they had also suffered national oppression. Among the many groups appearing and disappearing in 1917 was an executive committee of students who wanted to unite all Ukrainian left-wing currents. In a leaflet, they explained that the Bolsheviks had provoked anarchy and useless sacrifices while the Rada was too moderate and "bourgeois." "We want to go along a clearly demarcated path of struggle, including Bolshevism, but not along the same path as the Russian Bolsheviks" (Doc. 16).[40]

During and after the Bolshevik invasion, leaflets condemned "Russian Bolsheviks" or "pogromists" as the enemy, not Russians. As Hrushevsky noted in 1918, that January's declaration of statehood meant that in their publications, Ukrainian leaders could present the fight against the Russian Bolsheviks as more than a political struggle against a party. The fight was to prevent Russia from destroying Ukraine and its independence.[41] A "group of independent Ukrainian socialists" voiced support for the Rada and called on it to do more to halt that invasion in January 1918. Their leaflet listed a number of incidents during which Ukrainians had been murdered and national symbols desecrated. "Ukrainians were not the first to spill your blood. So when you [Bolsheviks–SV] began to kill shoot and desecrate the bodies of our dead brothers – you will pay. The blood you shed is dear to us and Ukrainians will not rest until they sweep you away from our land like filthy garbage." While this group identified Bolsheviks as the enemy, a group calling itself the Young Ukrainian Association specified that the enemy was *Russian* Bolsheviks. The leaflet explained that the group shared their aims but not their methods (Doc. 16, 17).[42] Ukrainian social democrats produced Ukrainian-language leaflets both with and without national motives. A party recruiting leaflet issued during the invasion, for instance, urged workers to join the "proletarian free Cossacks" (Doc. 18).[43]

Texts often focused on specific political and historical issues (Doc. 2, 21–4).[44] These informed people that the term "Little Russian" had been invented by supporters of the old regime to confuse them so that they would not remember their ancient rights to their land. Leaflets reproduced the terms of the Pereiaslav Treaty of 1654, to remind readers that it had allowed Cossack Ukraine its own army and foreign policy. They called on Ukrainians to "return [to] our illegally abolished rights and privileges." They explained what terms like republic meant and what the Central Rada was. In response to Bolshevik claims that the Rada was "bourgeois" and did not represent Ukrainians, Rada leaders replied that the Bolsheviks were a distinctly Russian party waging a war against the liberation struggle of Ukrainian soldiers, peasants, and workers, whose goal was a free and democratic society. One such leaflet included a chart listing the number of non-Ukrainian representatives in the Rada (Doc. 23).[45] During the Bolshevik invasion of January 1918 the All-Ukrainian Council of Soldiers Deputies issued an information sheet that explained that the Bolsheviks were a purely Russian party totally ignorant of Ukraine that sought to control the country through its Russian-dominated *soviets*, which all anti-Ukrainian elements were joining. The party wanted "to drown the Ukrainian National Republic, the riches of our land and our freedom in a sea of blood." A joint statement by Russian, Ukrainian, and Jewish socialist parties issued during the Bolshevik invasion declared the Bolsheviks liars. Under the guise of *soviets* they were bringing with them disorder, terror, and worthless declarations. The Rada, as the elected body of Ukraine's *soviets* dominated by socialists, called on workers to end their strike and support it (Doc. 25).[46] A summary of recent events issued in early January 1918 declared that the pro-Bolshevik *soviets* knew nothing about Ukrainian history (Doc. 24).[47] They could not even speak Ukrainian, yet they wanted the Russians to rule Ukraine. All enemies of the national will, equality, and fraternity who wanted to kill national self-determination and drown the Ukrainian National Republic in blood, it continued, joined the Bolshevik party, alongside ex-policemen and common criminals. Like the tsar, Lenin and Trotsky claimed they knew what was best for the people. They had dissolved the Constituent Assembly and branded as bourgeois all peasants and those who loved their nation. While fighting the Bolshevik invasion, the Rada had had no choice but to sign a treaty with Germany, it explained, because otherwise all the achievements of the revolution would have been threatened. Among those publicly expressing their positions were Orthodox Ukrainians (Doc. 27).[48] They explained that they wanted to conduct services in Ukrainian in an autocephalous church, independent and equal to all the other Orthodox churches. As per tradition, laymen would have considerable say in church affairs, including the election of bishops.

In the days following the attempted Bolshevik coup in Kyiv in December 1917 and prior to the invasion, the Rada informed the population that the Black Hundreds had been involved alongside the Bolsheviks. The leaflet added that the Rada would meet workers' demands, implement land reform, and help the unemployed and their families (Doc. 26).[49] Prior to the invasion, Ukrainian texts tended to identify the Russian and Russified upper classes as enemies. Now, Russian Bolsheviks were added to the list.

Governmental and party announcements and appeals were normally plain, simple, printed texts with highlighted headings. Some included personal observations made by the issuing official. In 1917, when the tsarist dry law was still in effect, the local official in Balta district (*povit/uezd*) declared that the penalty for public drunkenness would be two to eighteen months imprisonment or a 300 rouble fine. He included in his message that he had decided to issue the ordinance when he noticed on his rounds "a large number, not totally drunk, yet not totally sober citizens" (Doc. 19).[50] That December, on a more serious note, the government warned of impending hunger in cities and in the army. It appealed to producers to sell to government agencies and warned that speculators would face "measures" (Doc. 20).[51]

A large number of leaflets in the sample provided information on the imperial and later Ukrainian constitutional assembly elections. Unlike those noted above, many of electoral items resembled theatrical announcements (Doc. 53–4).[52] They were designed to catch the eye, had mixed fonts, slogans in very large, heavy fonts, and were often bilingual or trilingual (with Hebrew as the third language). Besides the expected political messages, such as: "Out with Russian Disorder," lists of claims, or entreaties to vote, some election materials listed who *not* to vote for and why (Doc. 32, 34, 38).[53] One explained: "The Black Hundreds, no. 3 [on the voting list], want the tsarist whip on the Ukrainian spine! Ukrainians, as one, vote for no. 12." The Socialist Bloc warned people not to vote for the Bolsheviks, who ignored the *soviets* and had started a bloody war against Ukraine; for Ukrainian or Polish "bourgeois" parties, who were concerned only with their own people; or for the parties of wealthy Jews (Doc. 31, 37).[54] Women were warned that if they wanted war and more bloodshed, they should vote for the Constitutional Democrats (Kadets), the party of the rich, and that if they wanted to see their menfolk again, they should vote for the Peasant Union (Doc. 30).[55] Not one vote, warned the Ukrainian Social Democrats, for the Bolsheviks, Kadets, or Black Hundreds, who were "the enemies of liberty equality and national fraternity who want to destroy at the root national self-determination, drown the Ukrainian National Republic in blood, steal the wealth of your land and the peoples' freedom." The Ukrainian SDs assured all that they were the only true socialist party. They claimed to represent peasants and workers and provided a list of parties and platforms for voters, warning that not all parties called socialist were really socialist. In Ukraine, power belonged to all the working people and not just to the Bolshevik party, declared the Ukrainian Army *soviet* (Doc. 28, 31, 35, 39).[56] Texts sometimes included what now sound like melodramatic appeals (Doc. 33): "I [agitator Iachnyk] beseech you, and you are called from their graves by our glorious ancestors who defended Ukraine's freedom ... Go into every house and tell them to vote only for list no. 10 [the Peasant Union]."[57] Slogans included: "Now every peasant will be his own lord," or: "If you want BREAD in Konotop [a town] vote for no. 2 [Peasant Union]," or: "Whoever does not vote for no. 10 [Ukrainian SRs] is an enemy to himself and the nation."

After the Rada returned to Kyiv in March 1918, its messages associated Ukrainian rule with the return of stability for all. They appealed for order and called for vigilance. Local officials reassured the people that the Third and Fourth Universals, which had declared political autonomy and then independence, had not been rescinded and that land redistribution without compensation would continue. Leaflets instructed people to sow their fields, urged them to pay taxes if they expected services, and stated that non-compliance would be met with court action but no more (Doc. 40, 42, 44).[58] That month the Ukrainian members of the Kyiv City Council issued a leaflet that greeted the Ukrainian troops after they had expelled the Bolsheviks, noting that all inhabitants of the city, not just Ukrainians, had suffered. It reminded them that they were fighting "the Bolshevism brought to us from the north on the points of bayonets," and not the nations inhabiting Ukraine, whom they now had to protect (Doc. 41).[59] A leaflet dated April 1918 from Kyiv warned "Ukrainian Patriots" about spies and saboteurs, even among officials, and gave an address where people could report them. It included the admonition, "Hang This on Walls," but no issuing body. It specified that all reports were to be in writing and accompanied by evidence (Doc. 45).[60]

Ukrainian units entering other liberated towns that March issued leaflets instructing the local inhabitants to ignore "bourgeois Russian" lies, and promising them that order would prevail and that they would be protected (Doc. 43, 44, 46).[61] A Ukrainian army regiment comprised of former POWs informed the inhabitants of Chernihiv when they arrived that they were not hired tsarist gendarmes but patriots, who instead of returning to their homes had come to free Ukraine from 250 years of Russian slavery. They would keep order and ensure that the Universals were implemented. Some units made public their disciplinary codes, which included stipulations against pillaging, the use of force against prisoners or civilians, and the instigation of pogroms (Doc. 47–8).[62] When Ukrainian officials first re-entered towns, not all had access to paper and presses. Thus, some of the posted routine ordinances, such as calls to surrender arms or to cease illegal logging, were typed on notebook paper or even written by hand – although these latter might have been originals for submission to typists or printers (Doc. 50–2).[63] Two theatre bills indicate that life went on despite the troubled times (Doc. 53–4).[64]

In November 1918, Ukrainian socialists from the Rada who had opposed the Hetman formed the Directory. After Skoropadsky's fall and before their entry into Kyiv, they issued a mobilization decree that gives an idea of the circumstances at the time. It told men to appear with a good pair of shoes or boots, seven days' food, and uniforms and weapons if they had them. Peasants were "called upon" to send one wagon for every three men, with food and fodder for seven days. Training was to begin immediately, and conscripts were told they would serve only until a regular force could be organized. In another decree, "citizens of Ukraine" were told that "the lords have sold us to the Russians and the Don [Cossack] officers known for their oppression of the working people." Germans were to be treated politely, and "true Ukrainians" were to volunteer (Doc. 55).[65]

Ukrainian parties and the Rada apparently issued very few posters or postcards. The posters in the sample were not government-issue. These consisted not of a single large image with some text, but rather of text with some small pictures inserted. One from November 1917 titled "Life or Death for Ukraine?" condemned the Bolsheviks as German agents who aimed to overthrow the Central Rada, which was then still loyal to the provisional government. It described Ukraine's Bolshevik leader Georgii Piatakov as a "millionaire" whom the Germans had placed in power in Ukraine in order to establish Bolshevism, with its hunger, mass arrests, and anarchy.[66] Two posters provided summaries of Ukrainian history (Illus. 26–7). "Can Ukraine Coexist with Russia?" probably dates from January 1918. It is noteworthy because it includes the first mass-reproduced map of Ukraine indicating ethnographic borders, along with statistical charts demonstrating that Russia had long exploited the Ukrainian provinces by extracting more in taxes than it invested. It declared that independence was the only way to ensure prosperity because then all taxes would be spent only in Ukraine. The other, "How the Ukrainian Nation Lived," likely appeared in March–April 1918. It provided readers with a patriotic summary of a national history "as glorious as that of [any] other nation in the world." Ukrainians from time immemorial always had to defend their lands because of their rich resources. The anonymous author explained that Ukraine's worst oppressors were the Muscovites. The Russians and the Jews, as soon as they saw they were losing the rich lands of Ukraine, had established the "Central Committee of Soviets," invaded, and begun to devastate the country. A section at the bottom of this poster titled "What Does History Teach Us?" explained that treacherous Muscovy and Poland had long been and still were Ukraine's worst enemies. The Ukrainian nation was the only legitimate master of its land, which it should not share with anyone: "Our nation suffered greatly under foreign yokes and that is why we must defend with all our strength our state – the sovereign Ukrainian National Republic." The Jews were "always our enemies and will betray our state at the earliest opportunity." The text above the top margin declared: "If you are Ukrainian, then for the benefit of your unenlightened brothers you should hang this poster in your office." Beside this was an advisory: "ATTENTION: This poster should hang on the wall of every train station and all governmental and civic institutions."

This is first Ukrainian text in the sample that identifies all Jews as enemies.[67] Soon after it was posted, Serhyii Iefremov, a moderate member of the Central Rada, condemned the poster as inflammatory and extremist.[68] In October the Rada established a commission to counter pogroms and listed a number of preventative initiatives, including the publication of a statement condemning them. The draft included these words: "We [Ukrainians] were oppressed, but we should not oppress anyone because we know how hard it is to live under a yoke." The item was published and disseminated as a circular. That November Petliura, as Minister of War, issued another circular condemning pogroms[69] It should be noted here that mere use of the word "Zhyd" in printed texts did not imply anti-Semitism or an anti-Jewish attitude. "Jew" in Ukrainian as in Polish, is "Zhyd." The word has no pejorative connation in either language. It does have derogatory intent in its diminutive forms; thus, "yid" or "kike" or hebe," would be "*zhydiuga*" or "*zhydok*" or "*zhydovukha*" or "*zhydochok*." This is not obvious to those ignorant of Ukrainian and Polish. In Russian, though, Jew is "Evrei," and "Zhid" does have pejorative connations.

A number of pamphlets released by the Rada in 1917 elaborated on historical and political issues mentioned in leaflets. Some incorporated economic arguments to highlight Ukraine's sorry predicament within the Russian empire. Petro Maltsiv labelled Russia a "state" rather than an empire and attributed Ukraine's unfavourable position to excessive centralization rather than to imperialism or colonialism. His detailed statistical analysis illustrated that Ukraine was an exploited colony. It showed that between 1900 and 1914, the Ukrainian provinces had consistently paid more into the state budget than they received from it, and that during those years, the amounts they paid rose faster than what they received in investments. Saint Petersburg and Russian culture, he continued, were living off "the countries enslaved by Russia." He concluded with an examination of tariff policy showing that the Ukrainian provinces paid high prices for agricultural machinery manufactured in central Russia while being paid low prices for their grain – all to the benefit of central Russia. Maltsiv did not advocate secession. Rather, what Ukraine needed was its own budget: the centralized empire had to become a federal "United States of Russia." Stepan Kulyk estimated that taxation, central bank interest income, foreign capitalist profits, and landowner spending in the imperial capital annually drained 312 million roubles from the Ukrainian provinces. Also in 1917, in what was perhaps the first use of the term, the Ukrainian SR Joseph Maievsky published a pamphlet titled "Red Imperialism." The Great Powers, he wrote, had promised self-determination to colonized peoples like the Ukrainians, Irish, Indians, and Vietnamese, only because they needed them for their war efforts, but those promises were empty. In the Russian empire in 1917, "[i]mperialism merely changed its tricolour flag into a red one."[70] Two pamphlets in 1917 linked land reform in

Ukraine with political autonomy. One pointed out that Ukrainians had more good land, both fields and forests, than the Russians, which they farmed well because of private ownership, in contrast to the Russians, who had less land and who practised land repartition. Also, Ukrainians wanted high grain prices, while Russians wanted them low. The author wrote that if Ukraine did not achieve and keep its autonomy, Russian migrants would take its land. The case against socialization without compensation was put by M. Baier. He claimed that Ukrainians, unlike Russians, had developed a sense of private property and would oppose any such measure. [71]

Central Rada member Fedir Kolomeichenko demonstrated that over the preceding decade, total Russian grain exports had declined, as had French, English, and German imports of Russian grain, while Argentinean, Canadian, and Australian exports had increased. He then noted that fourteen European countries had higher grain yields than Russia. All of this demonstrated that Ukraine was being held in the claws of a primitive country. The revolution had allowed Ukraine to be master on its own land and Ukrainians to raise themselves to the level of other civilized nations. Russians, he continued, opposed Ukrainian autonomy and feared the Ukrainian army because Ukraine produced more coal and metals than any other part of the empire. Rada member Aristarkh Ternychenko pointed out that despite being rich in grain, Ukrainian yields were low, and that its agriculture had failed to develop because of illiteracy, Russification, and a "yoke of slavery."[72] As a consequence, eastern Ukrainians were culturally far behind the Danes, the Germans, and western Ukrainians. "The masters of our land," meanwhile, lost no opportunity to take over that land as if it were the property of the Muscovite tsarist government. He blamed officials, "our protectors," for arranging the economy so as to further their own interests. Besides paying more into the state budget than it received, Ukraine was subject to unfavourable tariffs as well as to policies that favoured Russian settlers and merchants, directed exports north, and forced producers to buy low-quality machinery manufactured in central Russia. This impeded broader economic development in Ukraine, as did artificially low food export prices and the lack of grain elevators. As a result, Ukrainian producers remained poor and exploited. The Russian people, he added, did not benefit from those policies. The Stolypin reforms had benefited only the rich, who could take advantage of them. Those who started private farmsteads only weakened the nearby villages by isolating themselves from them. Insofar as the government also sponsored Russian settlers, who took Ukrainian lands, and then could not finance them, it was producing an underclass of dissatisfied and potentially violent peasants in Ukraine. Russification, anti-Ukrainian legislation, and Russian co-ops that undermined or destroyed Ukrainian co-ops all compounded Ukraine's problems; indeed, some Russians treated Ukraine as if it were an African colony. The solution these problems was an autonomous Ukraine within a democratic Russian federal republic. To the extent that Ukrainians were responsible for their plight because of their pre-1917 ignorance, disorganization, and backwardness, they could now begin to overcome these things.

Another group of pamphlets might be classified as self-help materials. Mykhailo Hrushevsky published short popular histories of Ukraine.[73] He and others also wrote pamphlets explaining basic concepts such as autonomy, nation, and identity in their nineteenth-century Mazzinian liberal form. Bohdan Zaklynsky's widely disseminated *Katekhizm Ukraintsa* was a forty-page booklet in question–answer format containing elementary information about all aspects of Ukraine. It expressed his own opinions and was not a government publication. He defined Ukrainians in terms of language rather than heredity, and Ukraine in terms of its ethnographic territory, and he explained that all nations aspire to independence. The author condemned as traitors Ukrainians who had assimilated, and he contended that national liberation required the use of force; but he made no hostile or denigrating comments about other nationalities. A similar introduction to Ukrainian issues was a sixty-two-page booklet in Russian for soldiers by Oleksandr Pylkevych, who was in charge of military propaganda under the Rada. The author explained who Ukrainians were via a brief summary of their history. Writing before the Bolshevik takeover, he explained that Russians, who had never experienced national oppression, had to understand that meeting nationalists' demands and decentralizing administration were revolutionary proposals and that democratic measures would save the revolution and the provisional government. Any blows delivered against Ukrainian interests would be blows against the Russian Revolution.[74]

Other pamphlets defined terms and concepts such as *autocracy* and *republic*, discussed how to organize locally, explained what political parties were and why nations should have states, and delineated role of law and voting in liberal democracies. Some of these works discussed the finer points of democratic administration and constitutional law. They explained that bureaucrats should not be parliamentary representatives and that the best and most prosperous countries were federal democracies (often pointing to the United States and Switzerland as models).[75] A 1917 publication cited leading western European thinkers. It repeated Lenin's idea that high wages in the imperial states were possible only because of the excessive profits generated in their colonies, and it pointed out that nationalism and socialism were compatible. It explained that nations were divided between the rulers and the ruled and that their proletariats all shared the same socio-economic interests. However, their national interests differed because in ruling nations, higher wages depended on the continued exploitation of the ruled proletariat. The solution was national autonomy for territorial nations and national rights for colonies. That way, no working class would have to depend on surpluses generated by ruled nations. Education had a crucial role to play in countering ignorance, which in Ukraine was born of low literacy, the persistence of superstition, and the lack of an intellectual tradition. Because of the resulting backwardness, others had long treated Ukrainians as an ethnographic mass suited for nothing but Russification.[76] The country lacked a strong intellectual and educational tradition, and what it did have had been destroyed by centuries of Russian centralist rule and by intellectuals who had betrayed their people in order to advance imperial careers. It called on the current generation of educated Ukrainians and non-Ukrainians to expiate their fathers' sins, follow the path of other nations, and educate their own people in their own language so as to bring them into the modern world. The author included a comparison of Bolshevik and Austrian Marxist theories on nationality.[77]

The Message: The Ukrainian State

The Hetman understood the significance of propaganda and claimed to have considered a campaign based on national and Cossack themes. In July he drew the attention of his ministers to their failure to spread information about the government and to counter propaganda against it. On 26 August, ministers passed a resolution providing for the mass dissemination of popular literature, pictures, books, and films about Ukrainian history and culture. The head of the secret police that month noted how the Bolsheviks' expert use of propaganda had had a profound influence on the "unsophisticated Russian worker and peasant masses," and recommended that the interior minister similarly exploit the printed word in the government's interest and establish schools to train agitators. Many unemployed intellectuals, he added, would readily enter such schools and do the job.

The Hetman's ministers never implemented this recommendation, nor did they envisage a mass popular-history publication campaign.[78] With one exception, central officials limited their mass-dissemination materials to official notices. These advised people to keep the peace, ignore rabble rousers, and respect property (Doc. 56–8).[79] The exception occurred in September while Skoropadsky was in Berlin. Two senior officials submitted memoranda to the Senate and Fedir Lyzohub, the interior minister, calling for Russian to be given official status as a state language. He agreed, and there followed a massive press campaign against not only the Ukrainian language but also Ukrainian independence.[80] The Hetman's government did not undertake a massive campaign to identify itself as a national Ukrainian state. However, it indirectly identified itself as such in its decrees rescinding land reforms. These, paradoxically, undermined the appeal of Ukrainian independence to peasants because they linked it to estate restoration and the return of landlords. In Volyn and Podillia provinces those landlords were primarily Polish and their local punishment units brutally enforced the restoration of property seized in 1917. In eastern Ukraine, those who had suffered in the wake of the Stolypin reforms were inclined to such an opinion and to believe Bolshevik propaganda about Ukraine being an invention of the rich – particularly where those who had benefited from the reforms were activists in the national movement.[81]

Although Ukrainian conservatives, like their Russian counterparts, who had initially backed the Hetman considered all Jews to be enemies and undesirables, his government did not sponsor anti-Semitic campaigns. Articles condemning all Jews as enemies of Ukraine appeared in *Vidrodzhennia*, but it is unclear whether, at the time, this was a private or an official newspaper.[82]

The 2,000-strong western Ukrainian Sich Riflemen Legion had a press office active in Volyn province during the summer of 1918. Formally part of the Austro-German army backing the Hetman, the unit was commanded by the politically Ukrainophile but anti-Skoropadsky Austrian Archduke Wilhelm. With his consent, the unit disseminated the Ukrainian national message among the Hetman's subjects in Volyn, and later, in Kherson and Katerynoslav provinces. The unit did not conduct requisitioning or punitive operations; also, it protected local anti-Hetman partisans, including Makhno, killed Bolshevik agitators, and enjoyed the widespread support of the local population.[83]

A report on sales from a three-day period compiled by the Kyiv station kiosk in October 1918 gives insight into what travellers were reading that autumn on the eve of the Hetman's collapse in the capital region. The most popular newspapers were the liberal Russian *Kievskaia mysl* and *Posledniye novosti*, which averaged 400 copies daily. The least popular was the Black Hundred *Russkii golos*, which averaged 25 daily. The three major Ukrainian papers *Nova Rada, Vidrozennia*, and *Robitnycha hazeta* averaged 40 to 50 sold issues each. The books most in demand were by

Hrushevsky, Taras Shevchenko, and Ivan Franko, together with Ukrainian dictionaries and grammars and the Ukrainian journal published in Lviv, *Literaturnyi Naukovy vistnyk*. Also in demand was the Russian satirical journal *Kryvoe zerkalo* and picture postcards of landscapes.[84]

By 11 November, the day Germany surrendered, one month of negotiations between Ukrainian parties and the White Loyalist Russophiles who dominated the government had left the latter still in control. On 13 November they proclaimed martial law; two days later the Hetman declared that Ukraine would reincorporate itself within a restored Russian empire as a federal unit. Shortly afterwards the new Russophile ministers began issuing propaganda leaflets.[85] Their message was based on the idea that, with Entente military aid arriving via the Black Sea, their "Ukrainian" army, comprised overwhelmingly of White Russian officers, would topple the Bolsheviks and then defeat the Ukrainian forces under Simon Petliura, who had declared the UNR re-established under the Directory.[86]

It seems that these leaflets were printed and distributed in Kyiv city only. They were devoid of national content, and almost all were in Russian. The messages focused on anti-Bolshevism, the Hetman's generous land laws, calls for social order, and the prospect of peace allied with the Entente. The leaflets dismissed the anti-Hetman coalition led by Petliura as a gang of criminals allied to the Bolsheviks who threatened to destroy the stability people enjoyed under the Hetman: "Did any of you peasant-Ukrainians suffer any wrong either from the Hetman or by his order?" Only one of the sample leaflets was addressed to "Ukrainians." The rest were addressed to "Kievans," "Women," "citizens," "citizens of Ukraine," "workers," "administrators," "peasants," "brother peasants," or "brothers" (Doc. 60–72).[87] Women were urged to encourage men to enlist and to enlist themselves in order to "restore the unfortunate great motherland" and to prevent the horrors that had befallen Petrograd and Moscow from happening in Kyiv (Doc. 74).[88] Workers were asked: "Don't you understand that [Ukrainian–SV] independence is a sign of narrow national intolerance having nothing in common with the professional defense of workers interests?" (Doc. 67).[89] One leaflet carried two messages for two audiences (Doc. 59).[90] On one half of the page, a message addressed in Ukrainian to "Ukrainian Cossacks" called on them to fight for Ukraine and their Hetman. On the other half, a message in Russian told "warriors" that Ukrainian and Russian interests were now one and the same and that they should defend Ukraine, "that free part of GREAT RUSSIA [*sic*]," as an "oasis" of the future united single Russian motherland. Another equated fighting for Ukraine with the restoration of Russia (*Rossiia*) (Doc. 73).[91]

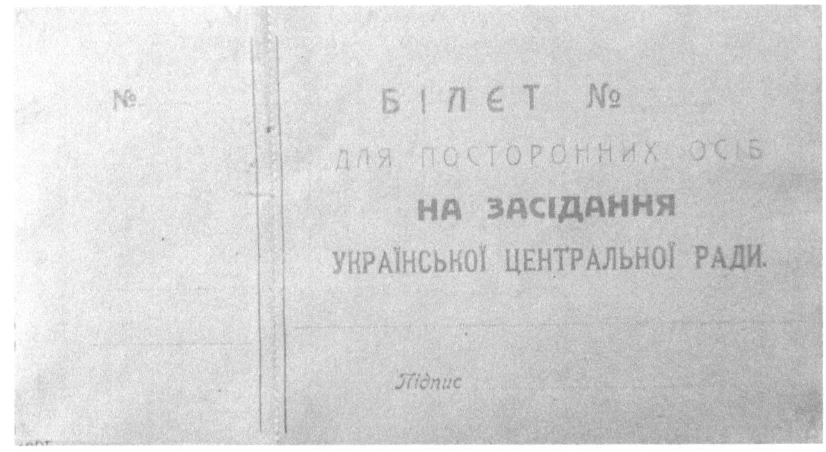

№

БІЛЕТ №

ДЛЯ ПОСТОРОННИХ ОСІБ

НА ЗАСІДАННЯ

УКРАЇНСЬКОЇ ЦЕНТРАЛЬНОЇ РАДИ.

Підпис

21 Entry-pass to visitors gallery in Central Rada.
TsDAB.

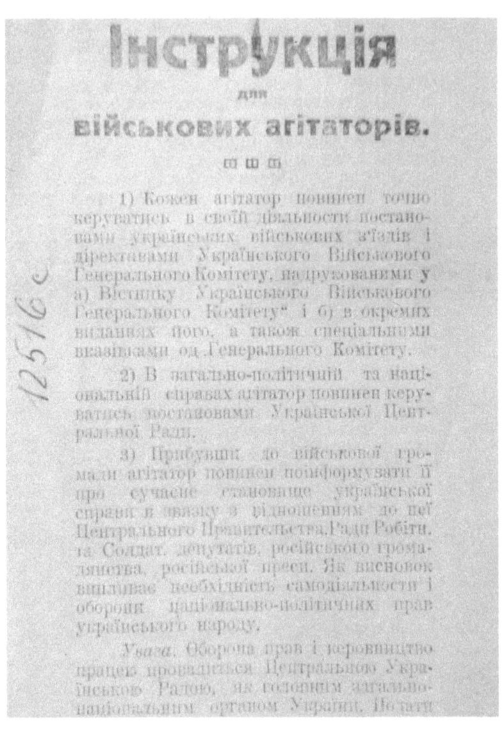

Інструкція

для

військових агітаторів.

1) Кожен агітатор повинен точно керуватись в своїй діяльности постановами українських військових з'їздів і директивами Українського Військового Генерального Комітету, надрукованими у а) Вістнику Українського Військового Генерального Комітету" і б) в окремих виданнях його, а також спеціальними вказівками од Генерального Комітету.

2) В загально-політичній та національній справах агітатор повинен керуватись постановами Української Центральної Ради.

3) Прибувши до військової громади агітатор повинен поінформувати її про сучасне становище української справи в звязку з відношенням до неї Центрального Правительства, Ради Робітн. та Солдат. депутатів, російського громадянства, російської преси. Як висновок випливає необхідність самодіяльности і оборони національно-політичних прав українського народу.

Увага. Оборона прав і керовництво працею проводиться Центральною Українською Радою, як головним загально-національним органом України. [illegible]

22 Title page of instructional pamphlet issued by Central Rada for army agitators (1917).
DNAB.

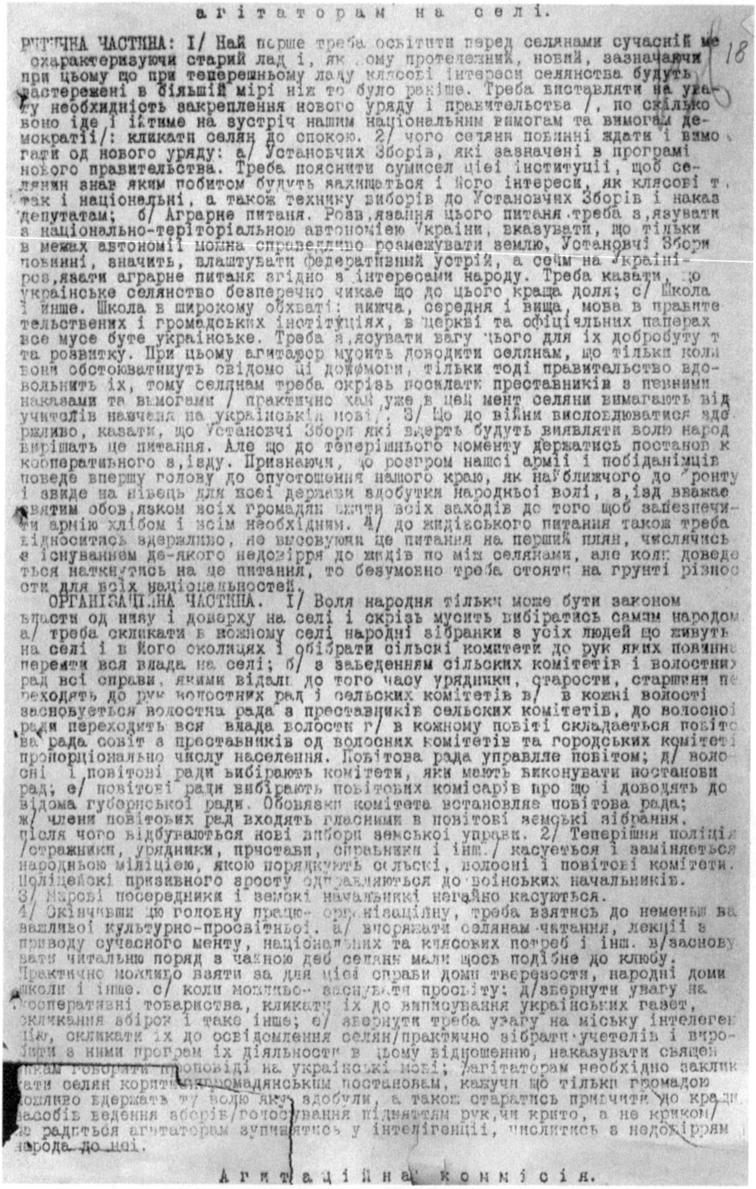

а г і т а т о р а м н а с е л і.

[illegible]ТИЧНА ЧАСТИНА: І/ Най перше треба освітити перед селянами сучасній мо[illegible] охарактеризуючи старий лад і, як [illegible]ому протележний, новий, зазначаючи при цьому що при теперешньому ладу клясові інтереси селянства будуть застережені в більшій мірі ніж то було раніше. Треба виставляти на ук[а]ру необхидність закреплення нового уряду і правительства /, по скілько воно іде і йтиме на зустріч нашим національним вимогам та вимогам демократії/: кликати селян до спокою. 2/ чого селяни повинні ждати і вимогати од нового уряду: а/ Установчих Зборів, які зазначені в програмі нового правительства. Треба пояснити сумисел цієї інституції, щоб селянин знав яким побитом будуть захищаться і його інтереси, як клясові т. так і національні, а також технику виборів до Установчих Зборів і наказ депутатам; б/ Аграрне питаня. Розв,язання цього питаня треба з,язувати з національно-теріторіальною автономією України, вказувати, що тільки в межах автономії можна справедливо розмежувати землю, Установчі Збори повинні, значить, влаштувати федеративний устрій, а сейм на Україні розв,язати аграрне питаня згідно з інтересами народу. Треба казати, що українське селянство безперечно чикае що до цього краща доля; с/ Школа і инше. Школа в широкому обхваті: нижча, середня і вища, мова в правительственних і громадських інстітуціях, в церкві та офіціяльних паперах все мусе буте українське. Треба з,ясувати вагу цього для іх добробуту т та розвитку. При цьому агитатор мусить доводити селянам, що тільки коли вони обстоюватимуть свідомо ці домогоги, тільки тоді правительство вдовольнить іх, тому селянам треба скрізь посилати преставників з певними наказами та вимогами / практично хай уже в цей мент селяни вимагають від учителів навчання на українській мові/. 3/ Що до війни висловлюватися здержливо, казати, що Установчі Збори які вдерть будуть виявляти волю народ вирішать це питання. Але що до теперішнього моменту держатись постанов к кооперативного з,іжду. Признаючи, що розгром нашої армії і побіданімців поведе вперше голову до опустошення нашого краю, як найближчого до фронту і звиде на нівець для всеї держави здобутки народньої волі, з,їзд вважае святим обов,язком всіх громадян вжити всіх заходів до того щоб запезпечити армію хлібом і всім необхідним. 4/ до жидівського питания також треба відноситись здержливо, не висовуючи це питання на перший плян, числячись з існуванням де-якого недовірря до жидів по між селянами, але коли доведеться наткнутись на це питання, то безумовно треба стоять на грунті рівности для всіх національностей.

ОРГАНІЗАЦІЙНА ЧАСТИНА. І/ Воля народня тільки може бути законом власти од низу і доверху на селі і скрізь мусить вибіратись самим народом а/ треба скликати в кожному селі народні зібранки з усіх людей що живуть на селі і в його околицях і обібрати сільскі комитети до рук яких повинна перейти вся влада на селі; б/ з заведенням сільских комітетів і волостних рад всі справи, якими відали до того часу урядники, старости, старшини переходять до рук волостних рад і сельских комітетів в/ в кожні волості засновується волостна рада з преставників сельских комітетів, до волосної ради переходить вся влада волости г/ в кожному повіті складається повітова рада совіт з преставників од волосних комітетів та городських комітеті пропорціонально числу населення. Повітова рада управляе повітом; д/ волосні і повітові ради вибірають комітети, які мають виконувати постанови рад; е/ повітові ради вибірають повітових комісарів про що і доводять до відома губерньскої ради. Обовязки комітета встановляе повітова рада; ж/ члени повітових рад входять гласними в повітові земські зібрання. після чого відбуваються нові вибори земської управи. 2/ Теперішня поліція /стражники, урядники, прчстави, справники і інш./ касуеться і заміняеться народньою міліцією, якою порядкують сельскі, волосні і повітові комітети. Поліцейскі призивного зросту одправляються до воінських начальників. 3/ Мирові посередники і земскі начальникі негайно касуються. 4/ Окінчивши цю головну працю- организацийну, треба взятись до неменьш важливої культурно-просвітньої. а/ впоряжати селянам читання, лекції з приводу сучасного менту, національних та клясових потреб і інш. в/заснову вати читальню поряд з чайною дєб селяни мали щось подібне до клюбу. Практично можливо взяти за для цієї справи доми тверезости, народні доми школи і інше. с/ коли можливо- заснувати просвіту; д/звернути увагу на кооперативні товариства, кликати іх до випмсування українських газет, скликання зіброк і таке інше; е/ звернути треба увагу на міську інтелегенцію, скликати іх до освідомлення селян/практично зібрати учетелів і виробити з ними програм іх діяльности в цьому відношенню, наказувати сьвящен[ик]ам говорити проповіді на українські мові; /агітаторам необхідно закликати селян корит[illegible]громадянським постановам, кажучи що тільки громадою можливо вдержать ту волю яку здобули, а також старатись привчити до кра[illegible] засобів ведення зборів/голосування підняттям рук,чи крито, а не криком/ не радиться агітаторам зупинятись у інтелігенції, числитись з недовіррям народа до неї.

А г и т а ц і й н а к о м м і с і я.

23 Leaflet with Rada instructions for village agitators. TsDASBU.

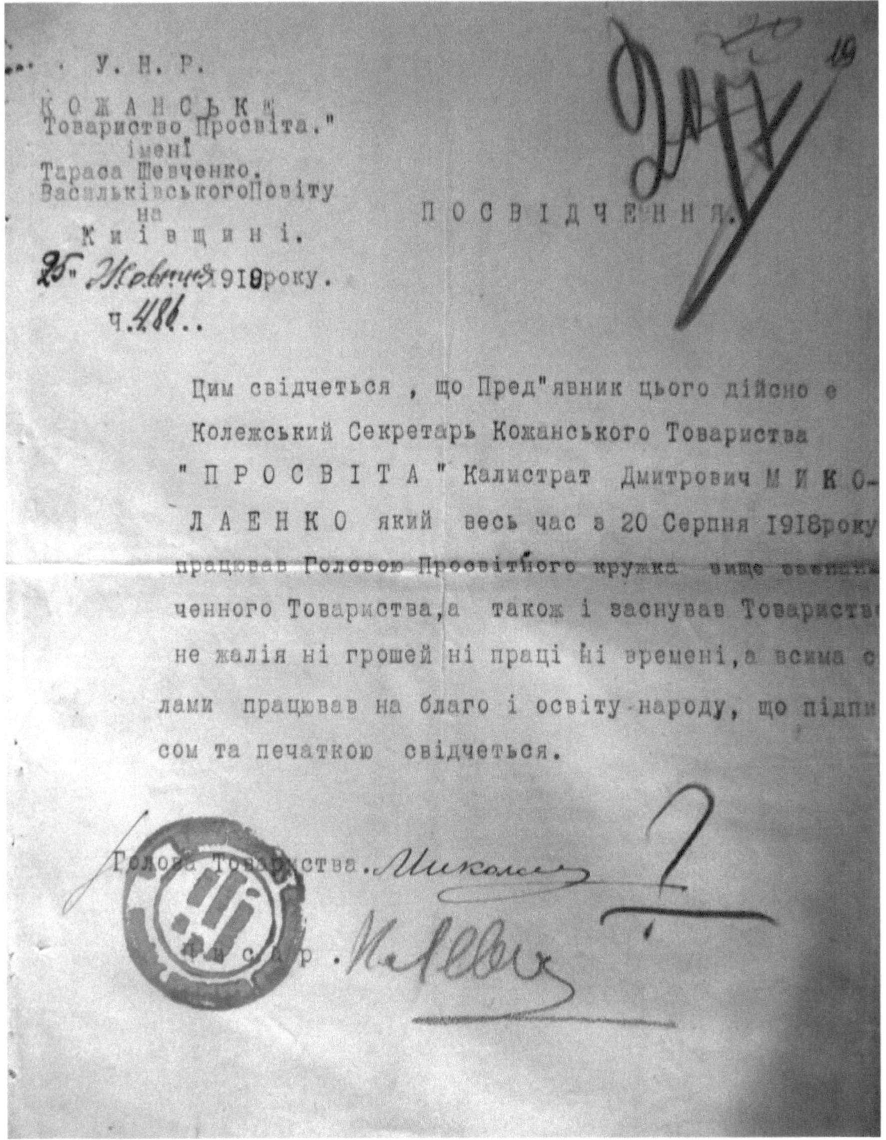

У. Н. Р.
КОЖАНСЬК"
Товариство Просвіта."
імені
Тараса Шевченко.
ВасильківськогоПовіту
на
Київщині.
25" Жовтня 1918року.
ч.486..

ПОСВІДЧЕННЯ.

Цим свідчеться , що Пред"явник цього дійсно є Колежський Секретарь Кожанського Товариства "ПРОСВІТА" Калистрат Дмитрович МИКОЛАЕНКО який весь час з 20 Серпня 1918року працював Головою Просвітнього кружка вище зазначенного Товариства,а також і заснував Товариств не жалія ні грошей ні праці ні времені,а всима силами працював на благо і освіту народу, що підписом та печаткою свідчеться.

Голова Товариства. Миколаєнко

Писар. Н. Левч

24 Document confirming that the bearer is an honourable man and secretary of the Vasylkivsky county Enlightenment Circle.
TsDASBU.

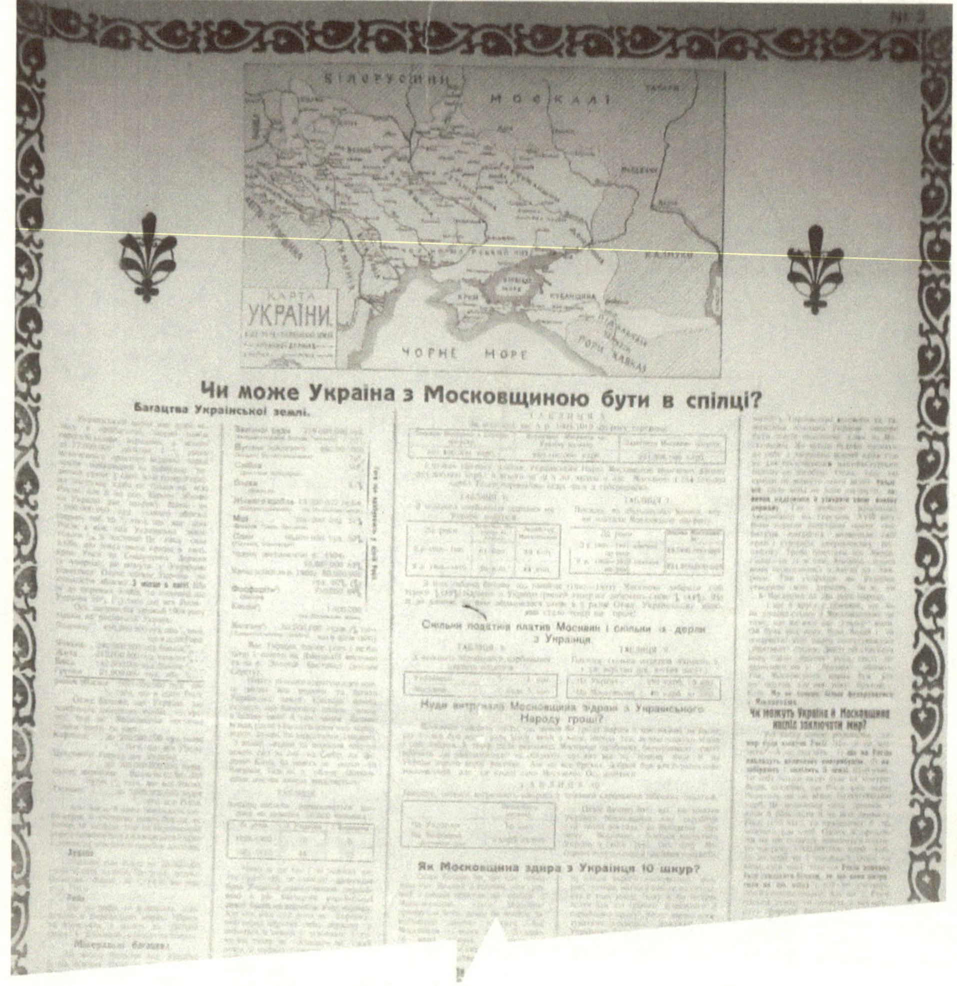

Чи може Україна з Московщиною бути в спілці?

Багацтва Української землі.

Скільки податків платив Москвин і скільки їх дерли з Українця

Куди витрачала Московщина здрані з Українського Народу гроші?

Як Московщина здира з Українця 10 шкур?

Чи можуть Україна й Московщина нас[пі]ль заключати мир?

25 "Can Ukraine coexist with Muscovy?" (top half of poster). DNAB.

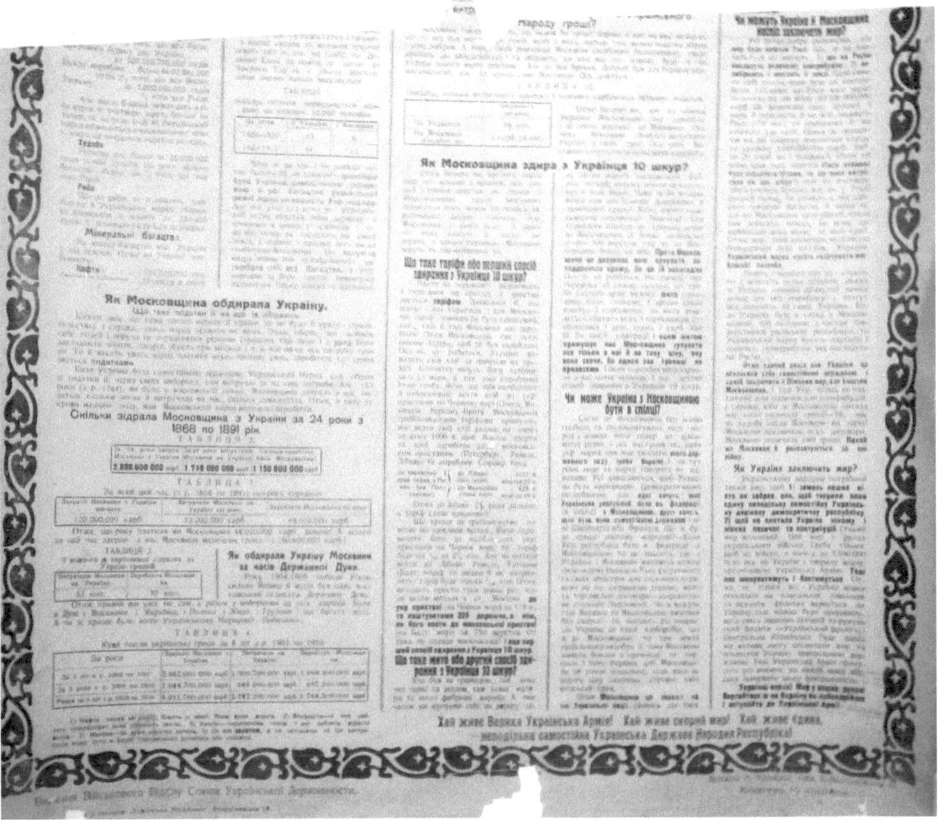

Мінеральні багацтва.

Нафта.

Як Московщина обдирала Україну.

Скільки зідрала Московщина з України за 24 роки з 1868 по 1891 рік.

Як Московщина здира з Українця 10 шкур?

Що таке тариф або перший спосіб здирання з Українця 10 шкур?

Що таке мито або другий спосіб здирання з Українця 10 шкур?

Чи може Україна з Московщиною бути в спілці?

Як Україна заключить мир?

Хай живе Велика Українська Армія! Хай живе скорий мир! Хай живе Єдина, неподільна самостійна Українська Державна Народня Республіка!

26 "Can Ukraine coexist with Muscovy?" (bottom half of poster). DNAB.

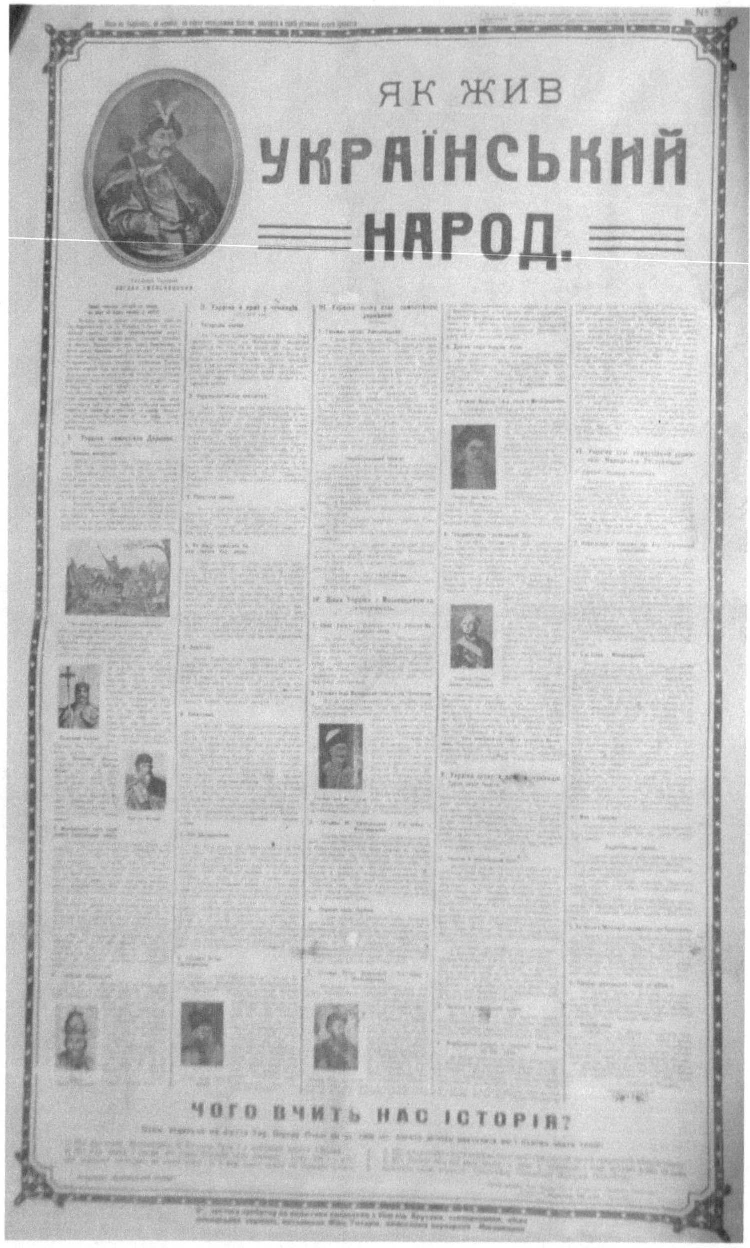

27 How the Ukrainian Nation lived: Poster containing short patriotic survey of Ukrainian history.
DNAB.

Chapter Three

The UNR, Radical Socialists, and Warlords

Pavlo Skoropadsky resigned one month after Germany's surrender in November 1918. Volodymyr Vynnychenko and Simon Petliura re-established the Ukrainian National Republic (UNR) in December 1918 and declared themselves the head of its temporary government – the Directory. The new republic fought the Bolsheviks, the Whites, and Nestor Makhno. The Ukrainian State and the Central Rada had controlled a core territory of five tsarist provinces for at least six months each; the borders of the Directory-ruled UNR fluctuated with the fortunes of war. The Directory's core territory was limited to most of Podillia province and parts of Volyn and Kyiv provinces, which it controlled for two periods of no longer than five months each – between December 1918 and April 1919, and then from August to December 1919. The total population in this area varied between three and ten million. The only territory the Directory controlled with but a few weeks' interruption was the area around the city of Kamianets-Podilskyi, when it was the capital, consisting of no more than 100 square kilometres. During 1919, as fronts moved back and forth, the size of Bolshevik and Directory-controlled regions fluctuated, with each government at different times controlling equal amounts of territory and people. In December 1919 the Directory allowed Polish troops to occupy territory as far east as the Zbruch River.

While the Ukrainian Party of Socialist Revolutionaries (SRs) and the Ukrainian Social Democratic Labour Party (SDs) dominated the Directory, their respective left wings initially opposed it and the Bolsheviks. However, by 1920 both supported Bolshevik rule. In territory east of the de facto UNR border, anti-Bolshevik warlords (*otaman*) fought Bolshevik troops to the end of 1922, as did Nestor Makhno. Some warlords were formally pro-UNR, some were connected to either the left SRs or left SDs, and some represented only themselves.[1]

The Medium

In November 1918 the leaders of the Directory established an information bureau under Nikifor Hryhoriiv. This was replaced the following month by a Directorate of Press and Information under the western Ukrainian Osyp Nazaruk. It included a department of propaganda under Lev Budai with an agent and agitators in each province, and it was intended to incorporate all other propaganda agencies. Nonetheless, the Interior Ministry also ran its own propaganda department. By January 1919 the Press Directorate had a staff of two thousand with an average of thirty people allotted to each province and seven to twelve to each district, where the local agent was supposed to work together with a council made up of local leaders. Newspaper advertisements called on students, "intelligent people," and "cultured workers with the people who feel themselves to be true democrats" to join and work as agitators for the army's Information Bureau (Illus. 28). Anyone travelling was urged to report to an office to pick up literature to take with them. Army agitators were given a one-week course. Nazaruk announced a public competition with a prize for the best pamphlets on these two subjects: "Why do we want an independent Ukrainian Republic?" and "Why the Ukrainian nation defends the independence of its state." He planned to circulate 500,000 copies of each.[2] The bureau mushroomed into numerous sections and subsections that existed alongside army information units.[3] Critics described the organization as chaotic and claimed that its publications never reached villages.[4] In March these overlapping agencies were all dissolved, and Vynnychenko, in response to critics, began organizing a single Ministry of Press and Propaganda under Ivan Lyzanivsky. After falling ill, he was replaced by Ivan Chasnyk and, later, by Teofil Cherkasky. In January 1920, propaganda was assigned to a subsection within the Interior Ministry headed by Pavlo Zaitsev. Mykola Lorchenko was in charge of the army's Culture and Education Department.

Because many experienced personnel left during the November 1918 reorganization its results were open to doubt. Leftists contended that political infighting had weakened the government's propaganda effort. They claimed that because rightists controlled the bureau, they had condemned it as Bolshevik and plotted to dissolve it, arguing that the people needed education, not information.[5] The bureau's top personnel included V. Kalynovych, I. Iushchyshyn, R. Hryzodub, and Hryhoriiv. Few of the ministry's files remain, and those of the section concerned with materials and supplies (*hospodarsky viddil*) are presumed lost.

Although by 1919 personnel in the western Ukrainian Sich Riflemen Regiment had four years' experience, they were not incorporated into the Ukrainian Galician Army Press Office or its Enlightenment Section. Between July and December 1919 this army's territory of operations included Volyn and Podillia provinces, where it worked with civilian as well as military personnel. Before it was shut down, its newspaper *Strilets* was published in press runs no higher than 16,000.[6] Some individual ministries and army units had their own press and information sections. As of February the UNR was still taking over kiosks from the Suvorin network and replacing their personnel. During the course of the year the Rail Workers co-op and local *prosvita* requested control over the system.[7]

Extant statistics on Ukrainian government publishing and distribution are few. None are as detailed as those compiled by the Bolsheviks (see Appendix) and provide only a very vague idea of dissemination and saturation. An April 1919 survey of the UNR's propaganda efforts noted that in Kyiv, the Directory's government printing office had four presses, two of which were rotary, and a good supply of paper, but lacked ink and type. The office could publish runs in the hundreds of thousands and employed fifty travelling agitators. Figures for that January show 1,375,000 published copies of thirty-six posters and leaflets. In February those totals dropped to 600,000 copies of twenty-eight titles. The army's propaganda department in Kyiv ordered leaflets in hundreds of thousands of copies in December 1918. However, as of January, it had received only 276,000 copies of eleven leaflets.[8] Ukrainian newspapers on UNR territory published a total of 45,000 copies daily. By contrast, Russian-language papers in Kyiv district alone averaged 284,000 daily.[9] Before its collapse, the Directory failed to complete its plan to consolidate all propaganda publishing activities in one ministry, and as reported at the time, few of its publications got beyond Kyiv or the other cities where it had offices. In a published report in its newspaper during the last weeks of the UNR's existence, the ministry reported that as of that October, the total number of copies for *all* its published materials was 35,000 daily.[10] The last known reference to UNR publishing activities is from the town of Uman. During the first weeks of 1920, the staff of *Ukraina* managed to print 20,000 copies of five issues of their newspaper and 200,000 copies of various leaflets, both of which circulated throughout Ukraine in the original and as reprints made by warlords.[11]

Another problem propaganda personnel faced, besides the destruction of property, was that they did not begin receiving funds until two months after their office had been formed. In addition, thousands of copies of materials sent through the post were apparently lost, and other materials never travelled farther than a government office. Some local army commanders, through negligence, left parcels unopened in their offices. When criticized for this, they claimed that they had confiscated the items because of their Bolshevik content. In other instances, local officials either sympathetic to or hired by one party would arrest the agitators of rival parties on the grounds that they were Bolsheviks and confiscate their parcels. In addition to this, local officials, conservatives, or leftover Hetman or tsarist personnel would publicly condemn all UNR agitators as Bolsheviks in order to turn the local populace against them. In one district, UNR officials arrested the local head of the Information Bureau as a Bolshevik, while the Bolsheviks arrested its secretary as a counter-revolutionary. Agitators were often ill-informed because ministers did not bother to keep their superiors at the bureau informed about government business. Peasants, for their part, sometimes chased away or even assaulted agitators who told them things they disliked hearing or who could not answer their questions. Letters from villagers complained about agitators who did arrive. One accused the man of being a spy more interested in the loyalties of the local officials than in providing information. Another complained that the agitator had no business reading government messages in church.[12] Agitators trapped behind the front and captured by the Bolsheviks were usually shot. The dangerous work alienated recruits and led others to resign.[13]

In Ukraine, most *zemstvo* presses had been nationalized by 1918 and thereafter used by whoever controlled them. Co-op and private publishers that took orders from whoever controlled their territory continued to exist until 1921. The printers' union in 1917 was controlled by the anti-Bolshevik Mensheviks. Although not opposed to the Rada, in January 1918, when Russian troops were advancing on Kyiv, the union refused night shifts to print the new, much-needed national currency, because that would have contravened its collective agreement signed the previous May with the shopowners.[14]

After it fled Kyiv, the Directory sometimes confiscated presses. Yet it continued to order brochures and pamphlets from private shops in runs of 10,000 to 30,000. Judging by the small advertising inserts sometimes found in the bottom corners of these publications, most of the shops were Jewish-owned. Figures on total copies printed and actually disseminated are rare. According to one estimate, 1,450 titles of all kinds were published on territories under the Directory's control.[15] The Directory also ordered publications from Ukrainian organizations in Germany, Poland, and Czechoslovakia, which then shipped or flew them in. Nazaruk managed to coordinate official Directory anti-pogrom propaganda in agreement with Jewish leaders, but in the absence of a single ministry and strict control over content, individuals still published what they considered appropriate. Analogously, the UNR Army Information Bureau did not control all army publications. Individual units published their own materials, as did the Ukrainian Galician Army.[16]

The UNR declared all paper a state monopoly. During the winter of 1918 the Kyivan Union of Publishers (*Drukari vlasnyky*) complained about nationalization to the Directory, explaining that it already controlled more than eighty presses and that, in any case, they were willing to cooperate.[17] Nonetheless, that June, and again in October 1919, the UNR formally nationalized all presses and declared all print and paper mill workers mobilized for government service, alongside artists and intellectuals. It is not known whether this decree was actually implemented, and if so, how. Most presses apparently remained in private hands, and there are no known data on printers.[18] Like the Bolsheviks, the Ukrainian government pulped archival holdings for paper, but the scale of this program is unknown. The general shortage of paper meant that in 1919 in Kamianets-Podilskyi and Rivne, archival documents were pulped for newsprint. As well, it was common practice for all, including merchants, to use the documents to wrap food.[19] In printing shops, wages were low, workers were few, and press runs were limited. An April 1919 editorial by the publishers of the local Ukrainian left-SD party newspaper in the central Ukrainian city of Kremenchuh, explaining why it could no longer provide daily copies, probably described a typical situation. With a press run of 1,000 copies (680 paid subscription), each issue usually cost 600 *karbovantsi*. But it often cost more to produce, which meant the paper was in debt. The editors estimated that they could break even with another two hundred subscribers. The staff worked without pay.[20]

In June 1919 the propaganda ministry created a Section for Popular Publications (*Viddil narodnykh vydan*) devoted to mass publications. It focused on posters and leaflets and released seventy-five titles in all. At the time, officials had particular need for a leaflet explaining who the western Ukrainian troops were, given that their uniforms led people to think they were Austrians or Poles. So they ordered an additional 50,000 copies printed that August, in addition to the 25,000 already circulating. The only known extant UNR political poster was released in the summer of 1919, apparently three times in a total of 60,000 copies.[21]

Situation reports from the ministry's official in Vinnytsia in the autumn of 1919 indicate that the town had eight printing shops with thirty-three presses. Its agent had arrived with one ton of paper from Kamianets-Podilsky and requisitioned three shops. With their six presses, these shops produced around 250,000 copies of four pamphlets and one leaflet over a two-week period. The agent reported that there was a great demand for the literature, that whole districts had none, but that none of his thirty couriers were going to the surrounding villages. Without couriers, agents in small towns and villages had to give speeches without literature. Not the least of problems were price rises. Between August and October of that year, the price of a pood (36 pounds) of paper rose from 900 to 1,800 *karbovantsi* – almost twice the monthly wage of a courier.[22] In August and September the Galician Army Press Office published between three hundred and five hundred copies each of three army newspapers and a total of 30,000 copies of various leaflets.[23] There are no statistics regarding distribution, but ministers and officials complained throughout 1919 that few of their materials were reaching readers.[24] One attempted alternative, announced by leaflet, involved appealing to "soldier teachers" in the army to use their time to enlighten their brother soldiers (Illus. 29). This leaflet praised the initiative of teachers, who had "led the nation against their muscovite-Bolshevik and muscovite-Denikinist oppression," and urged them to continue their work in the ranks, teaching literacy, history, and songs.

The dissemination of bulk printed materials required bulk transport, which by 1919 was in short supply. As of November 1918, after seven months of relative peace under the Hetman, Ukraine's rail system had 2,546 locomotives (1,343 functioning) and 56,285 wagons of all types (45,746 functioning). There was enough coal for no more than seven days. The Polisia region lines in the northwest had the most reserves (18 days), and the Podillia province lines the least. One month later, the rail ministry of the re-established UNR described the rail transport system on its territory as "totally catastrophic."[25] By October 1919 the firewood being used in place of coal was running out.[26] Besides staff shortages, there was sabotage, as well as a severe shortage of grease, and on top of that there were no large repair workshops on UNR territory. The army that summer controlled what rail traffic there was and had commandeered 2,032 of the available 4,976 freight wagons. With 3,176 functional wagons and 536 locomotives, the UNR during its last months of existence supposedly ran sixty-nine trains daily within its territory.[27]

Transportation was slow for other reasons besides insufficient rolling stock. They included cancelled departures, acute fuel shortages, and masses of refugees. Army officers wreaked havoc with schedules by commandeering trains, sometimes at gunpoint, and holding them for as long as they fancied. The Podillia province commissar reported in February 1919 that it was a miracle that any trains ran at all on the provincial line. Staff were indifferent, and often it was only thanks to passengers coupling cars or loading fuel that their train moved. In December 1918 the Directory had ordered free transit for government couriers, but it seems that local officials and officers were known to ignore this. Two months later, the head of the Press Ministry complained to the General Staff that his people were not being allowed on trains. The minister asked all officials to give his couriers priority, and the requisite order was duly issued, but the interference apparently continued.[28]

Two reports from September 1919 were critical of the entire propaganda effort. In one of these, the deputy director of the Press and Propaganda Agency declared that distribution was haphazard, with offices giving materials to any passersby willing to take them. Couriers, he pointed out, were an inefficient means of distribution because the more distant their destination, the later materials arrived. There was not enough money to pay for all the publications that were needed to cover UNR-controlled territory, and low pay was leading to a high turnover of couriers. A materials shortage meant that too few publications were being printed. By that August the only paper mill in UNR territory no longer had any paper, which meant that publishers had to rely solely on inventories. That same month, the UNR had retaken much of right-bank Ukraine with its paper factories, but even then, the government could not release more than 100,000 leaflets per week, 6,000 copies per day of newspapers, and 4,000 copies per week of weeklys, in its capital Kamianets-Podilsky. In early September the Kamianets region had only four couriers and not enough materials for the city population, let alone the entire region (Illus. 30). Individual couriers described other problems. Couriers had to carry as much as seven hundred pounds of materials, which led to difficulties boarding overcrowded trains. Besides that, rail personnel would refuse to help them load and unload their consignments. Those belonging to one particular party sometimes refused to allow messengers carrying materials printed by another party. Once on board, couriers had to spread their loads because of overcrowding and sometimes lost packages as a result.[29]

The second report, which focused on the activities that fall of the ministry's Kamianets field unit, noted that it had too few office staff and only fifteen agitators. Shipments of publications would arrive unannounced and irregularly and were typically dumped in any available space. Newspapers arrived as much as one week late. Pay did not arrive either, which obliged the director to use money from sales for expenses. The figures provided in this report do not differ markedly from those in the first report. Over a three-month period, the field unit distributed 4,200 copies of seven newspapers, 7,800 copies of eleven pamphlets, 20,000 to 25,000 copies of eleven announcements, and 140 copies of the "Fraternal life" poster (Illus. 96). Of that total, 75 per cent was distributed to soldiers. In addition, of 320,378 published copies of the army newspaper *Ukrainsky kozak*, 261,503 were distributed to the troops. The army also received 75,000 copies of ten leaflets and 22,000 copies of five announcements; also, 35,000 copies of four leaflets and 5,000 copies of two pamphlets were supplied as aerial propaganda to be dropped over Bolshevik territory.[30]

This critical assessment of the situation shortly before the collapse of the UNR is confirmed by two other reports. One, from the Roads Ministry sent to the Propaganda Ministry in September, complained that it was not using railway stations to distribute materials. Another, sent the following month by a local rail official to the Roads Ministry, noted that the distribution of propaganda was very poor and that some stations still had no literature at all. The second author urged his superiors to tell propaganda officials to use couriers instead of the collapsing postal system. An undated letter that autumn from the important rail junction town of Zhmyrynka described the situation there as one of total collapse, with rampant theft, no orders, and no rail movement whatsoever.[31] In his report of June 1920 to the Directory, post and telegraph minister Palyvoda concluded that its Press and Propaganda Ministry had failed miserably in its task – villages were receiving no information.[32]

The failure to provide propaganda when necessary could have profound consequences. In 1921 a former UNR employee noted that during the Polish–Ukrainian offensive of the previous year, the populace in the line of advance had remained passive and did not take up arms in a coordinated uprising. They had no idea which army was approaching them because the Ukrainians had failed to inform them earlier of their presence in the advancing army. This was exploited by the Bolsheviks, who mustered support by depicting the offensive as an exclusively Polish invasion.[33]

By 1919, instructions to agitators were much more detailed than in 1917. They now specified that agents had to serve as models of commitment. Also, they were to be thoroughly familiar with all aspects of village life. Junior agitators had to work alongside more experienced personnel to learn from them, and the same person was not to go to the same place too often. On arriving, the agent was to report to local officials and work closely with local sympathizers. They were to tell the villagers to think about what they read and to not destroy literature but circulate it. Western Ukrainians working in eastern Ukraine were instructed not to exaggerate national issues, not to parade in traditional embroidered shirts, and to avoid moralizing about national values. Instructions also provided lists of headings under which agents were to compile their reports. These included the nature of enemy "agitation," what kinds of literature were available, and what peasants did not understand.[34] By late 1919 the propaganda section of the Galician army in particular was trying to organize at the lowest levels of society in an effort analogous to that of the Bolsheviks.[35]

Pamphlets like *Pravdyve slovo pro bolshovykiv-komunistiv* (1919) often included an exhortation to conserve and circulate:

> SAVE LITERATURE, don't destroy it, don't allow it to get to stores where it is used for wrapping but pass it from house to house, hand to hand. Read carefully and don't forget THAT EVERY BROCHURE AND LEAFLET COSTS HARD CASH ... Every notice must be read by the community and posted in prominent places in villages and counties.

In September 1920 the warlord Struk ended one his leaflets: "Brother peasants. Read these pages and pass them on to other hands. Because the insurgents don't have as much money as the Jews."[36]

UNR propaganda clearly did not always reach as many people as its leaders would have liked. In September 1919 a district commissioner visiting local offices declared in a published circular that he had not seen any governmental materials whatever posted in any of them, and ordered officials to post and disseminate all such materials when they received them (Illus. 30). He also specified that, when necessary, officials were to call public meetings, read out published materials, and duly report to him reactions and attitudes. Among the problems was the collapse of the post and telegraph system – although in October 1919 the ministry claimed that the entire system in UNR territory had been restored and was functioning to county level. By the end of that year, the Directory formally controlled Ukrainian territory west of the Zbruch river. In reality, Polish troops were stationed there and it was being administered by Polish officials. The postal ministry, short of office equipment and unable to pay its staff and other costs, decided in January 1920 to close all village post offices and to distribute only to district towns. The shortage of carts and horses meant that many fewer private carters were available for hire, and those still available were charging high rates. That December an eyewitness reported that people had knocked down telegraph lines and posts for dozens of miles for wood and copper. Paper, when available, was very expensive, as was ink.[37] Nor were all personnel dedicated to their tasks. Apparently many agitators were using their travel funds to buy stylish clothes and pay for dinners in good restaurants with well-dressed women of dubious repute. Some got rid of their materials by giving them to "milk ladies," who travelled between towns and villages, in the hope that they would deliver the materials together with the milk. Some of those who did travel kept going to only one place because they had arranged warm beds and meals with a local woman, or had found quarters with a priest who had a clean house and young daughters.[38]

A rare set of figures from September 1919 illustrating per capita distribution in UNR-controlled territory has been preserved for three newspapers. These indicate that agents distributed 4,600 copies to eighteen counties (pop. 5,333,000). This would have averaged one copy of one paper per 8,000 people – assuming all copies were distributed. But distribution was allotted by group: totals included 900 for posting in public places, 1,500 to the army, 150 to three towns (Vinnytsia, Koziatyn, Berdychaiv), and 800 for the remaining counties.[39] That same month, 800 to 900 copies daily of the General Staff's newspaper (*Ukraina*) went to the army (approx. 40,000 men) – an average of one copy per 50 men. A second army newspaper (*Ukrainsky kozak*), released in 8,000 copies daily, averaged one copy for every five men. In a report from early October, the minister claimed that he could provide one to two copies of newspapers for every 100 soldiers and promised that the government newspaper *Nyvy* would soon have a maximum press run of 30,000 per day. He also complained about a lack of personnel, presses, and ink.[40] These Ukrainian figures, it must be noted, pale in comparison with Bolshevik figures. In September 1919 the First Red Cavalry Army alone (around 20,000 men) published 10,000 copies of its newspaper daily – an average of one copy for every two men.[41]

While in exile between 1920 and 1922, the UNR government tried to organize an uprising in Ukraine. To that end, it dispatched agitators with literature throughout Bolshevik Ukraine. Its agents there claimed that support remained strong.[42] Within Ukraine, various conspiratorial organizations, twenty-five in right-bank Ukraine alone, also produced propaganda.[43] One such group, the Cossack Council (*Kozacha Rada*), worked under Mykola Lozovyk, who had worked on the Rada's above-mentioned committee. In Kyiv, one-time Rada member and (later) literary scholar Serhyi Iefremov, under the pseudonym I. Ihnatenko-Kokodii, ran an organization that printed propaganda texts.[44] Some partisan units had specific individuals in charge of propaganda, printers, and small presses. In Poltava province in 1921, one such press could release 350 to 400 leaflets per day.[45] Where presses and typewriters were not available, newspapers were copied by hand. UNR agents and refugees reported that as of early 1921, this material was being widely disseminated and eagerly sought by a populace alienated by the Bolsheviks' policies. This included both printed and hand-copied materials. "Sometimes, in place of regular paper [partisans] used thousand-ruble Bolshevik bank notes [for their propaganda]."[46] Many of these materials survive only in Russian-translated transcripts (Illus. 31, 32).

In 1919, two radical Ukrainian socialist parties challenged the Directory's claim to rule the country. The first, the Ukrainian left-SRs (*Borotbisty*), formed in May 1918, existed as a separate party until March 1920, when its leaders decided to merge with Ukraine's Bolsheviks (CPU; Communist Party of Ukraine). During its independent existence, it published pamphlets, newspapers, and leaflets, but few details are available about where activists published, where they got their materials, how much they published, or how they disseminated their texts. Once they merged with the Bolsheviks, they enjoyed access to Bolshevik facilities and materials, but there is evidence that their activities were strictly controlled. In October 1919, after they had fled with the Bolsheviks, their publishing unit was located in Briansk, Russia, on a train with roughly two tons paper and one press. They could not run the press at full capacity because it was too big for their one available printer to work alone. Nor could they distribute because no Bolshevik agency was willing to cooperate. Officials also reported that without heat or light, it would soon be impossible to work in the railcars, and in any case, most of the workers had fallen ill. By November they reported that they could no longer publish, and recommended that all publishing be moved to Moscow – from where their newspaper was later published.

The second Ukrainian radical leftist group were the left-SDs, who formed the Independentists in 1919, then the Ukrainian Communist Party (UCP) in January 1920. They published anti-Bolshevik as well as anti-UNR propaganda, and they fought against Bolshevik and later UNR forces. There is no known record of where or how much they published or how they distributed their materials before they formally recognized Bolshevik rule. In 1920 the Bolsheviks allotted the left-SRs and UCP enough paper for press runs of 3,000 copies per week for whatever they wanted to publish.[47] Émigré left-SDs in Vienna in September 1919 formed an organization, renamed in March 1920 the Foreign Group of the UCP, which published a newspaper and dozens of pamphlets, including UCP materials and Ukrainian translations of western European Marxist writers. Especially important among these publications was the UCP *Memorandum to the Third Comintern Congress*. How many copies, if any, of these materials were distributed in Bolshevik Ukraine is unknown. In the summer of 1920 the head of the

Foreign Group, Volodymyr Vynnychenko, returned disillusioned from his trip to Ukraine. That autumn he began condemning the Bolshevik regime. UCP leader Iury Mazurenko then broke with the Vienna group. He explained in an open letter that the Ukrainian Party differed from the Russian one on the issue of colonialism and the organizational form of the Ukrainian revolution, and that this was a purely internal communist affair and of no concern to Vynnychenko.[48]

The Message: The UNR

Ukrainian leaders, unlike the Bolsheviks, apparently did not formulate outlines of propaganda campaigns that specified themes, political aims, approaches, audience preconceptions, and circumstances. Nor was the Ukrainian propaganda effort as centralized as the Bolshevik one, with a single government body producing and controlling all propaganda. According to one editor of the left-wing western Ukrainian newspaper *Respublikanets,* the western Ukrainian section of the UNR's Central Information Bureau, established in January 1919, was run by Bolshevik agents who "secretly conducted underground agitation."[49] One known attempt by propaganda officials to centrally coordinate text messages involved publishing slogans or entire leaflets in the newspaper *Novyny* (Kamianets-Podilskyi). These slogans, which concerned policies or the political situation, included items such as "chase deserters from your village they are traitors," "gold shoulder-board Russian generals out of Ukraine," and "establish enlightenment societies [*prosvita*]; only the conscious know who is a friend and who is the enemy." One document related to program tactics and content that has survived is a long, detailed analysis of organization, dissemination, and writing from 1919 by an officer in the western Ukrainian army's Propaganda Department. It includes a concise summary of Ukrainian themes to be exploited. Agents were to tell people they had to be personally involved in the defence of their native land against their enemies. Later, they would have schools, manufactured goods, land, and freedom. Agitators were not to idealize western Ukraine but rather to emphasize Ukrainian national unity. They were not to moralize, romanticize the peasants, urge them to wear embroidered shirts, or urge men to shave on the grounds that that Russian peasants did not. The document referred to unspecified "foreigners" and "enemies." It did not use the terms imperialism or colonialism.[50]

Materials were usually plain, typed sheets with headings and subheadings, sometimes in bold underlined or larger type. The few examples of eye-catching design in the reviewed sample are usually lecture/theatre advertisements, mobilization decrees, or appeals to specific groups to support the army, such as: "WORKERS, don't prevaricate. THE UKRAINIAN COSSACK fights for all labourers. He chases away the exploiters and oppressors of the working people. HELP him!," or "Townspeople! The national army of the Ukrainian republic freed you from the rule of Bolsheviks and Cheka [secret police] torture" (Doc. 140, 151, 152).[51] "It protects you from the pogroms of the Denikin bandits. AND WHAT HAVE YOU GIVEN TO THE ARMY?" (Doc. 139, 141–5, 148–9, 162–4).[52] One leaflet in the sample, addressed to women, also had an eye-catching format. It urged women to help the army by donating food, clothing, and hospital care: "Where are you, Pride of Ukraine?" (Doc. 130, 146).[53] Humour is rare in the sample. One leaflet warned: "Citizen! You have two pairs of boots. Give one to a Ukrainian Cossack, otherwise the commune [Bolsheviks] or Denikin will come and take both pairs" (Doc. 145).[54]

One leaflet issued during the summer of 1919 where Ukrainians in the Bolshevik and national armies faced each other on the front reproduced an exchange between the two. Each called on the other to defect in the style of the legendary "Zaporozhian Cossacks write a letter to the Sultan," immortalized in Nikolai Repnin's painting. In their reply to the Bolsheviks, the UNR Zaporozhian Division told them they weren't worthy enough even to kiss them on that part of the body "from which the legs grew," let alone write them orders. They asked their enemy why they wanted Soviet power if it was nothing more than a Jewish cabal. "If you don't believe the whole Sovnarkom is Jewish take them to the bathhouse." After refuting "the nonsense" in the Bolshevik letter, they finish by telling them in the future to send only clean untyped sheets of paper, which would be more suitable "for Cossack needs" (Doc. 153).[55] Religious themes are rare in the sample. A leaflet by army chaplains explained that God had sent the Bolsheviks to take the previous year's harvest as punishment for those who believed their lies the previous year and who did not support "their native leaders." "May God forbid you repeat the same mistake today" (Doc. 129).[56]

The sample UNR leaflets and pamphlets focus on national and social liberation. Russian Bolshevik depredations consituted a central theme of the UNR's propaganda campaign. They described Bolsheviks as a foreign Russian occupying force that included criminals, native turncoats, and tsarist-era Black Hundred supporters (Doc. 159).[57] UNR propaganda circulated throughout the 1920s in Ukraine, where dissatisfaction with Bolshevik policies ensured that it continued to influence a populace that shared a historical memory of popular uprisings and respected partisan leaders.[58] The sample indicates that one key difference between materials issued in 1917 and those issued between 1919 and 1922 was that as the scale and intensity of violence increased during those years, messages became more aggressively nationalist. Non-governmental and anonymous texts dropped an earlier distinction between Jews and Russians who were loyal to the Ukrainian cause and those who were not. They instead began to classify all Jews and Russians as enemies. Messages like "We will free Ukraine only by blood and iron," and lecture topics like "The struggle to free the Ukrainian nation from the Denikin-Muscovite yoke," did not appear in 1917 (Doc. 149, 152).[59] During the 1919 summer offensive the Directory's land minister issued a leaflet titled "Brave Cossacks." It explained that wagons with government surveyors and land markers were following in the wake of the army's artillery, ready to mark lands "cut" (*narizani*) from lord's estates and allotted to peasants. One sentence read: "Remember that the more enemies you cut [down], the more land will be cut for you and our peasants" (Doc. 147)."[60]

After arriving in Kyiv in December 1918, the UNR issued materials dealing with public administrative issues. These assured inhabitants that UNR troops were disciplined and that provisions were on their way to the city. People were warned not to believe Russian newspapers and to remember who had "marched alongside the nation and who had helped the Hetman." Army leaflets declared martial law, a curfew, and a requirement that everyone carry ID. Those arrested or charged with some offence were not threatened with execution or court martial and were instead promised access to courts and lawyers. Included in these same materials were appeals not to loot or join pogroms (Doc. 75–84).[61] Peasants were told that the "Russkie Bolsheviks" kept land in repartional communes where those who sowed died of hunger. "They make nice promises – only on paper. Will they fool us too?" Leaflets informed readers about local ordinances, as well as details of land reform and taxation, and offered assurances of due process for those arrested. They announced that possession of arms was illegal and called on people to report enemy activity.[62]

During the UNR's advance on the capital the month previous, its texts had included explanations of recent events. These related that the Rada had signed an equitable treaty with Germany, but then rich landowners had bribed the Kaiser, established a second tsar in the person of the Hetman, and set about re-establishing the old order. The uprising was directed against this oppression to restore the Rada and the Fourth Universal, not against the Germans. People were told that at a time when all the nations of the world were declaring their independence, the usurper Skoropadsky with Russian bayonets wanted to reduce their native country, again, to eternal Muscovite slavery. Once the Hetman was deposed, the UNR would establish liberty, equality, and fraternity in an independent Ukrainian republic.[63] Men who enlisted were promised land. The population was told to keep order, organize, and not to loot. Those who disclosed mobilization information were committing treason and faced the death penalty. If such persons were foreigners, their families would be deported. Agents sent ahead of the front distributed materials explaining that the Directory would soon come to power in the country, at which point those who had helped the Bolsheviks would reap their just deserts. People were told to surrender nothing to the Bolsheviks, to record the names of those who sat on Bolshevik committees, to destroy rail and communication lines, and to defend themselves from Muscovite slavery (Doc. 112).[64] A group calling itself the "Socialist independentists" explained that the Bolsheviks in Ukraine were a Russian, not a Ukrainian party, whose members refused to be Ukrainian citizens and opposed Ukrainian independence. Furthermore, their policies in Russia demonstrated they were not "real socialists." Russian Bolshevik rule in Ukraine would be horrific, but the "Bolshevik Ukrainian with sword in hand will stand in defense of the rights of the Ukrainian nation to rule its own country against the Bolshevik Russian who threatens that right" (Doc. 114).[65] The Ukrainian Peasant Union explained that Russians refused to work in their own country and preferred instead to take grain "from our land." "Besides the Red Army, 16 million [*sic*] hungry ragged people have descended on us from Muscovy, and these locust, like a cloud, covered our border regions and is moving deeper and deeper." "The butchers Lenin and Trotsky," it continued, "have decided to resettle our people in Muscovy and settle all communists in our country" (Doc. 165).[66]

Leaflets explained what the Directory was, why it opposed the Hetman, who led it, and what its policies were. They listed the names of its five members and explained that they would not, and could not, do anything without consultation among themselves and their parties. The Directory would establish peasant landownership, worker control of factories, and an eight-hour day, place a levy on big industrialists, and nationalize the sugar refineries. There would be elections to a Ukrainian constituent assembly, and democratically elected city *dumas* and *zemstva* would be re-established. Power would be in the hands of the working people. "Comrades, what more do you want?" Russian Bolshevik Soviet rule meant Russian rule and grain expropriation. The Directory would establish the Ukrainian National Workers (*trudova*) Republic. It was only just that peasants rule Ukraine, for they outnumbered non-peasants eighty to one (Doc. 76, 86, 96, 97, 108).[67] The UNR would give land and would also provide education – and, thus, knowledge of how to farm more efficiently (Doc. 115).[68]

Leaflets warned people that "Russian newspapers" only represented the upper (Russified) class and printed lies. They were told that almost all with power in Ukraine were Russians opposed to Ukrainian democracy and independence, which they falsely called bourgeois and chauvinist. A number of items in the sample focused on rebutting White claims, linking them with the Hetman, the wealthy in general, and the Bolsheviks in particular (Doc. 79).[69] Russian was the language of the bourgeoisie, while Ukrainian was the language of the peasants and the poor – "the language of the democratic nation." The wealthy and the landlords had been happy to sell out their country to maintain their privileges. They had set out to divide Ukrainian and Russian democrats in order to buttress their rule and the empire – and to steal Ukrainian resources. Texts linked the Bolsheviks and wealthy Russians, claiming that the two had been cooperating since early 1918. The Whites were using Bolshevik slogans to divide Ukrainians, separate them from their leaders, and thereby weaken them and prevent the convening of the UNR-sponsored Labour Congress in January 1919: "a congress of working peasants and workers who earn their scraps of bread with their calloused hands." Included in a leaflet issued that month was a note that the "Ukrainian Bolsheviks" – referring presumably to the Ukrainian left-SRs and -SDs – had publicly condemned the Russian Bolshevik invasion as a "crime against the proletariat," and that anyone denouncing the UNR and calling for its overthrow was a provocateur (Doc. 96, 107).[70] During the summer of 1919, one leaflet proffered rather convoluted arguments linking the Whites with the Bolsheviks. These claimed that wealthy Whites had wanted to reconquer Ukraine with the help of the French bourgeoisie, but that the French were not interested because Ukraine was a democracy. So the Whites had decided to help the Bolsheviks take over Ukraine, then use the fact of the occupation as an argument to convince the French to invade, help them topple the Bolsheviks, and re-establish the empire (Doc. 87).[71]

Leaflets directed at peasants and "the working people [*trudovyi narod*]" explained why they should support the UNR rather than the Bolsheviks, who, unlike "our Ukrainian government," promised much but gave nothing. People were urged to keep order and not be tempted to seize land illegally, for that would spark anarchy and benefit only landowners. They were told instead to record grievances for later litigation. The UNR was the peasants' government and would ensure that all received a fair portion of land. Leaflets claimed that surveyors were already at work and that notaries were already legalizing property deeds. Enemies – Whites, Reds, and Poles – wanted to overthrow the UNR and foment civil war and chaos so that they could seize Ukraine's rich land.

Only the UNR could protect that land, because it was a government of the people and not the bourgeoisie. Messages emphasized that political independence had to precede social reform and that land allotment would be just and legally confirmed. The Ukrainian government already had surveyors and notaries giving as much landowner land to people as they needed and legalizing their possession forever "with a stamped document." Protect Ukraine as you would your mother, help your army with provisions. "Because it will be the worse for you when the drunken accursed russkie-bolshevik comes! He will chase you from your own house as he chased bolshevized Ukrainians out of Kyiv" (Doc. 85, 88, 89, 91).[72] An anonymous Poltava Peasants Union member explained that Russian Bolsheviks, who called themselves "our brothers," were drafting all men for service in Russia, stripping villages of everything, shipping it all to Russia, and then reimposing the "Muscovite yoke" (Doc. 100).[73]

The centrist Ukrainian SDs, the ruling party, issued a closely typed leaflet to soldiers that summarized how 250 years of Russian rule had transformed free Cossacks into Muscovite serfs, stolen their lands, and turned "the National Cossack Ukrainian republic into a mangy Little Russia, a dispossessed ... land" where Russian tsars, nobles, and officials "sucked the tasty blood of the dumb honkies [*khakhly*]."[74] With the revolution, Ukraine had risen again. But the Bolsheviks, Russia's new autocrats, wanted to inflict on Ukrainians the same hunger that Russians suffered. Soldiers were told it was their duty to prevent that from happening. To that end, they had to maintain discipline and set an example. They had to keep order so that Ukraine could proceed with building a state. Russians, Poles French, Germans, and English took care only of themselves and mercilessly exploited Ukraine. That is why the Ukrainian nation had to take its fate into its own hands. (Doc. 90–1).[75] Army publications told workers that although most Ukrainians were peasants, their rights would be respected. Workers were promised that those among them who had been duped by Bolshevik lies would not be killed, for they had already been punished enough by the realities of Bolshevik rule. There would be no reign of terror on UNR territory. The government promised to settle land issues in the courts and instructed workers and peasants to duly record all disputes. It trusted the workers' "proletarian political sense" to ensure they would not use force to claim their rights but instead proceed peacefully through the labour ministry (Doc. 88, 126, 160).[76]

UNR leaflets did not always condemn all Russians as enemies. They pointed out that the wealthy and privileged in Ukraine, "the bourgeoisie," was overwhelmingly Russian-speaking and anti-Ukrainian and wanted Ukraine to be part of Russia. They did not want Ukrainians to rule themselves, nor did they want to be ruled by Ukrainians. "They are bourgeois and don't want a democratic nation to rule them." The Ukrainian bourgeoisie, meanwhile, was so small that it could never overcome the nation, and that was why it was pro-Russian. Most explained that Ukrainians knew their enemies were not all Russians, but Bolshevik Latvians, Chinese, and Jews who had imposed their rule on Russia by force and who had nothing in common with Russians. Bolsheviks were a reincarnation of the Muscovite autocrats, who, like them, destroyed all freedoms and liberties. "Let us not curse and slander our enemies, it is better to look at what they do and explain that to those they try to dupe with lies about our national heroes and aims of our government" (Doc. 79, 89, 90, 93).[77] "Meet the Chinese, Latvians and their agitators [in the requisition squads] with iron, swords and bullets." For every Ukrainian soldier or peasant they torture "shoot 100 of these bandits" (Doc. 101).[78] Leaflets addressed to attacking Russian troops explained: "You are not fighting Black Hundred mercenaries [as the Bolsheviks told them] but free Ukrainian workers and peasants forced to fight to defend the borders of their homeland by the politics of your new autocratic many-headed tsar under the name of the Soviet of peoples commissars – in short SOVNARKOM 1." Notions of proletarian leadership were appropriate in western Europe because the proletariat was a majority there, but not in Ukraine, where workers were not just a minority, but a largely foreign minority. Workers were assured their rights would be respected in the UNR: "Unite with the peasants and don't listen to provocateurs" (Doc. 92, 94, 120).[79]

The propaganda section of the UNR 3rd Army issued a moral appeal on plain typed paper "to all men of violence, pogromists, lovers of vice, evil, anarchy and other criminals." They were told that failure to obey government orders forbidding pillaging and arbitrary violence would be met "by the knout or a bullet in the head" and to beware because there was now a disciplined army that could punish malefactors. Anyone passing military information would be shot. "Now we must forget about that freewheeling life we [Ukrainians] enjoyed under the tsars and during all the [recent] changes in Ukraine. We must now restrain ourselves and begin to live a new truly humane honourable working life. Because it will be the worse for us if we fail to change ourselves." Otherwise, other nations would conquer and exploit Ukraine, readers were warned. "Who will win? The lords and their lackeys or 40 million workers peasants and democracy. Obviously us, but they are better organized. Organize, come to the army."[80] In a leaflet discussing Ukrainian weaknesses and strengths, the Hetman regime was presented as an example of how small minorities could rule and exploit a terrorized majority. The reasons why lay in the unity of the rulers and their willingness to spend to maintain their rule. Ukrainians were told they were behaving in the exact opposite manner and should emulate the minority oppressors. "Brothers!!! Although the enemy is powerful our perseverance will overcome him. Although he has advanced in great numbers from Moscow, our love of freedom will ensure we will undoubtedly be victorious over him" (Doc. 98, 162).[81]

In the sample, debunking of Bolshevik claims and elaboration of the gap between Bolshevik rhetoric and practice figured often. A number of leaflets explained that the Bolsheviks were failing to supply manufactured goods as they had promised and were shipping all of the goods they pillaged to Moscow, and that there was no difference between them and the Whites in that both opposed Ukrainian independence. The Bolsheviks were no more than bandits who brought disorder, hunger, and bloodshed, which in Ukraine would result in the return of landlords (Doc. 99–106, 113, 120, 128).[82] Some depicted the Bolshevik order as no order at all but a cause of *dis*order that had destroyed Russia and now was plaguing Ukraine and would result in the return of landlords. One stated that the Ukrainian army could not turn back the Whites – not, however, because it was "bourgeois," but because it had to repel the Bolshevik invasion. Some claimed that the Bolsheviks opposed Ukrainian independence because Ukrainian peasants lived better than Russian peasants. They realized that Ukrainian independence meant no Russian would ever acquire any Ukrainian land. "Conscious" Ukrainian workers supported "Our Ukrainian Bolsheviks," who would defend the rights of the Ukrainian nation against the Russian Bolsheviks. Jewish workers, this leaflet added, belonged to their own parties. Ukrainian workers, unlike non-Ukrainians, sympathized with Ukrainian Bolshevism, which had nothing in common with Russian Bolshevism because it stood for Ukrainian statehood (Doc. 107, 112).[83]

Among those leaflets explaining that Bolshevik claims were hypocritical and duplicitous was one that asked why Bolsheviks condemned the absence of *soviets* in the Ukrainian army, if the Red Army also had no *soviets*. The difference between the UNR and the Bolsheviks, it pointed out, was that the former represented real national equality because it had invaded no one, whereas the Bolsheviks merely talked about equality while wanting to rule Ukraine. The UNR supported rule by the working classes, whereas only party members ruled in the Bolshevik order (Doc. 121, 125).[84] In the wake of the Ukrainian left-SR and left-SD condemnation of the Bolshevik invasion in January 1918, a UNR leaflet announced: "Our [Ukrainian] Bolsheviks issued a manifesto protesting Piatakov's invasion of Ukraine." When in January 1919 the Russian Bolsheviks declared that their Red Army was not fighting in Ukraine, the UNR informed Ukrainians that those fighting against it under the direction of Ukraine's CPU were not "real Bolsheviks," for they were not supported by Moscow. They were only criminals and thieves bent on rapine and plunder and were to be treated as such. Having concluded within days that the Bolshevik denial was a lie, Ukrainians issued leaflets exposing it (Doc. 110–12).[85]

Rebutting the notion that Ukrainians and Russians should remain together in a single state because their soldiers had "eaten from the same pot" at the front, a leaflet statistically demonstrated that "the pot" had remained full thanks to Russian economic exploitation of Ukrainian resources. Continuing the metaphor, it explained that Ukrainians were the ones who had kept the pot filled with broth. If the Russians wanted to share a pot, they had better "listen to us now instead of as before, when we had to obey." "It is not us that must federate with them, but them with us, let our people rule and let them listen [now]" (Doc. 122).[86] Another text, issued in the summer of 1919, asked what the working people of Ukraine would eat after the Bolsheviks took the entire harvest. One leaflet warned that "Muscovite communists are already preparing sacks for the next harvest" and that they had to be repulsed before then. Leaflets explained that the UNR was indeed shipping supplies to western Ukraine, as the Bolsheviks claimed in their propaganda, but that this was only to keep them out of Bolshevik hands. Those supplies were being returned in the rear of the advancing army. People were asked how much of their looted goods the Bolsheviks had returned to Ukraine. If the Bolsheviks wanted bread, they had only to make peace and resume trade (Doc. 119, 120).[87]

As the Ukrainian–Russian war continued, propaganda became more extreme than in 1917. The Bolsheviks had promised liberation from the bourgeoisie, but instead, "brother Ruskies [*katsap*] brought our nation death, ruin and tears" (Doc. 120). Russian Bolsheviks had forced Ukrainians to meet their fire, blood, and death with iron swords and bullets: "Blood for Blood. Death for Death." The Bolshevik enemy was described in no uncertain terms as a foreigner to Ukraine cooperating with Russian Black Hundred gangs to restore the empire. When Russian Bolsheviks arrived, they pillaged and stole everything in sight, like the worst sort of imperialists – "socialist imperialists." They sent conscripts to Siberia and appointed commissars, just like the tsars. Leaflets pointed out that the UNR was socialist, not counter-revolutionary, and that none of its leaders owned capital or land or factories. It represented national independence, and it distributed church and noble land to those who worked it. One detailed text that listed Ukraine's enemies did not include entire nationalities or mention Jews. The UNR stood for workers' control, it explained, and opposed all bourgeoisie, landowners, White officers, and Bolsheviks who "want Russians to rule Ukraine," as well as "Polish bourgeoisie" (Doc. 106, 108, 137).[88]

There are no materials from 1917 in the Ukrainian sample relating specifically to Polish issues. Few leaflets in 1919 distinguished between Ukraine's Polish landlords and "Poles" in general, who were told that UNR did not oppress minorities and would not abolish Polish organizations. Invoking instances of past cooperation, bilingual leaflets noted: "Poles should remember we never opposed closer ties with them." The UNR declared that it would not oppress any nationality and indeed would require their help in the fight against the enemies of Ukrainian independence. "Those opposed will be destroyed and should best leave the country ... All sides should forget the past in the interests of neighbourly relations mutually respecting their respective borders." "The Ukrainian nation as represented by its government is not going to oppress any nationality that lives alongside it, regardless of faith, but it does require these nationalities [to] give all possible assistance in the struggle against the enemies of Ukrainian statehood" (Doc. 134–5).[89] The UNR had not invaded Russia, so why, then, had the Bolsheviks invaded Ukraine? Ukraine did not aspire to any ethnically non-Ukrainian territory, and in the interests of brotherhood, Ukrainians, Russians, and Poles had to forget their strong historical memories. The times when one nation ruled another were over. Those with anti-Ukrainian sentiments should voluntarily leave (Doc. 136).[90]

Messages invoked patriotism to attract support and volunteers, explaining that only an organized army could cast off the Bolshevik yoke. "Those who are afraid to die for their country will necessarily die [in the Red Army] in Siberia defending those who take our bread." The sooner people took up arms against the Bolsheviks, the sooner the Ukrainian government would arrive and distribute land according to the law (Doc. 115–17, 124).[91] The army assured people that its troops did not arbitrarily requisition supplies, and it told them to arrest anyone who did so without appropriate documents (Doc. 138).[92]

Few items in the reviewed sample of government propaganda categorized all Jews as enemies or Bolsheviks. Also, texts normally associated "Muscovites" and "Ruskies" (*katsap*) only with anti-Ukrainian Russian Bolsheviks. The phrase "Foreign enemies out!" that appears in one leaflet refers to foreign non-Ukrainians, not settled non-Ukrainian minorities in Ukraine: "Muscovites from Russia" (Doc. 128).[93] In direct appeals to Jews, leaflets emphasized that the UNR opposed pogroms and attributed civilian deaths to Bolshevik subterfuge that exploited the "dark instincts of the popular mass." A long message titled "About the Jews," issued in February 1919, listed four Jewish parties that had recognized Ukrainian independence and explained that Ukrainian Jews had won full and equal citizenship in the UNR. Since they shared the burden of independence, they were entitled full protection as "our friends." This included "us Ukrainians doing all in our power to stop the pogroms committed by our enemies on our territory." Ukrainians had to recognize and use the talents of a people that constituted 12 per cent of its population. Pogroms would destroy one of the foundations of independence (Doc. 131).[94] Texts issued that summer noted that "the paths of the Jewish and Ukrainian nations were closely tied due to 300 years of oppression and ill-treatment under the tsarist heel." The UNR recognized the assistance that Jews had provided to Ukrainian troops, declared that it would help and support victims of pogroms, and noted that many of those responsible for violence against Jewish lives and property had already been shot. The UNR called on the "Jewish nation" to declare its loyalty, as had western Ukrainian Jews. One leaflet expressed confidence in the loyalty of the Jewish working population, but not of the Jewish bourgeoisie "whose hostility to the Ukrainian state cannot bring anyone any good": "The hostile attitude taken by the Jewish bourgeoisie towards the Ukrainian state will not bring it any good" (Doc. 132, 133, 135–6).[95] Most often, leaflets identified the enemy as "Muscovite Bolsheviks," or they explained that Ukrainians were not fighting Russians, but only the Bolsheviks. One noted that although Bolshevik leaders had Russian names, they were really Jews – but Jews who had been condemned by their own people. "All Ukrainians know perfectly well that it is not the Great Russian nation that is waging war against them" (Doc. 94).[96]

There were exceptions. In June 1919 central leaders had ordered the publication of literature condemning pogroms. It had also instructed officials to check the contents of printed propaganda. However, implementation was not a foregone conclusion.[97] Given the failure to centralize and coordinate propaganda, it is possible that Bolshevik agents embedded themselves in press and propaganda units, where they worded texts in such a way as to discredit the UNR. Also, individual officers or officials, upon taking a town that had a press, could have as often expressed their own opinions as government positions in texts. Thus, some Army leaflets in the sample referred to all Jews as enemies. The Bolsheviks included criminals, drunks, and layabouts eager to live from others' work, as well as tsarist officers. All of them were hiding under a red flag and proclaiming socialist slogans and declarations that were all lies. "Let those who want the rule of criminals, Jews and various sinister sorts, get out of our Ukraine and go the Muscovite, soviet [*sovdepiia*] tsardom. Only honest working people can live in our Ukraine" (Doc. 123).[98] One anonymous army leaflet in the sample implying that all Russians and Jews were enemies had been printed by a Jewish-owned printing house (Doc. 99).[99]

In July 1919 the UNR's Ministry of Jewish Affairs sent to the Justice Ministry twelve leaflets that its members complained had fomented pogroms because they were anti-Jewish. The letter did not include the word anti-Semitism, referring rather to "criminal printed agitation against the Jewish population." The letter asked the minister to determine who had printed them and implied that their appearance was part of a strategy forged "according to previously determined ends." Of the twelve included items, nine did refer to all Jews as enemies, and two of these had been issued by the Press and Propaganda Ministry and a local government commissar. Three appear to have been army issue – signed cryptically "Cossacks," or "Command of the Field Army." Two had been signed by warlords. That October the justice minister, ignoring the obvious, rejected the accusations: "[the leaflets] mention that in the ranks of the Bolsheviks fight, amongst others, Jews, and that the Bolshevik regime in the commissariat of Soviet of People's Commissars is mainly made up of Jews; it is clearly underlined that only a part of the Jewish population serve the Bolsheviks, and not all Jewry, and the citizens are called upon to conduct a struggle not with all Jews in general, but only with Jewish Bolsheviks."[100]

In the second half of 1919, mobilization and other governmental decrees included pleas to the population to materially support the army. Donate before it was too late, they warned, or "our children will condemn us for our indifference and we ourselves will die in foreign chains. Who is now free, will be enslaved, those who are badly-off now will be worse-off if now in these difficult times we don't help our army." In leaflets, as well as circulars intended for public display and dissemination in newspapers, the government promised aid for widows, orphans, and veterans (Doc. 161).[101]

In early 1919 the UNR was sending supplies to the West Ukrainian National Republic (ZUNR). One leaflet explained to easterners that they had to help the poor westerners in their struggle against Polish landowners, otherwise, the triumphant Poles would ally with Russian and "our" landlords against the UNR (Doc. 118).[102] When western Ukrainian troops began fighting with UNR troops in the summer of 1919, a series of leaflets were issued explaining that the soldiers with German-style uniforms in the army were western Ukrainians.

Recruiting posters included calls for easterners to enlist in the western formation, the Ukrainian Galician Army, explaining there was no difference between east and west Ukraine. Their inhabitants, however, did have their idiosyncrasies. "Western Ukrainians are better educated than the people here [in eastern Ukraine]. They consequently cannot be as easily fooled as the locals" – which was why Russians hated them so much. When the western Ukrainian leadership and its army allied with the Whites in November 1919, UNR leaflets explained that the army remained loyal and that only the political leaders were traitors (Doc. 155, 156, 163).[103] To counter Bolshevik claims that the UNR had sold Ukraine to French capitalists, leaflets in the summer of 1919 explained that the UNR was not allied with France and was fighting the Whites. They explained that workers and peasants constituted its army, and that the government was socialist and had allotted more land to peasants than had the Bolsheviks.

On the eve of the 1920 Polish-Ukrainian offensive, Peasant Union leaflets described the Bolshevik occupation as a series of horrors committed by "16 million" diseased and hungry layabouts and criminals who preferred to loot Ukraine rather than work their own lands in Russia. Descending like a biblical plague, they had stripped Ukraine bare and shipped all its produce to Russia, where the Bolsheviks sold it abroad for luxury goods, despite claims it would go to Ukraine's workers and Red Army men. "You who not long ago fed the world with your grain," it declared, "now walk in rags and salt your food with your wife's tears." People were told not to surrender grain, to destroy it if necessary, and to do everything possible to impede collection and shipment. In the meantime, they were promised, Ukrainian leaders were preparing a general uprising (Doc. 165).[104] Leaflets addressed to Ukrainian Red Army men during the 1920 offensive asked why they were obeying Lenin and Trotsky, the "oppressors of the Russian nation." "Return to your families and don't fear the Poles," they were told. "Ukraine had signed a treaty with poor Poles like ourselves, the people, and not the landlords." That treaty specified there would be no interference in domestic affairs and that the Poles would leave once they had finished their task. One leaflet contained provisions from the Treaty of Warsaw (Doc. 173).[105] Russians were asked why they had come, under White and then Red leaders, to shoot a people with whom they had struggled together against tsarism and who only wanted to live in peace in their own state. "They tell you that you are fighting for the freedom of all nations; tell those gentlemen to be consistent and give freedom to the Ukrainians as well." Obtain products by peaceful trade, not war, Russian soldiers were told: defect or go home (Doc. 166–7).[106]

Leaflets about Ukraine's Polish alliance explained that it should surprise no one in a world that had seen so many changes over the past three years. Rivals can become allies when faced with a common evil – in this case the "Muscovite imperialism" that was re-establishing the tsarist prison of nations for all its former prisoners. "Nowhere in Europe is there such ignorance, savagery, and brutality as in the lands once ruled by Russia. Only those nations closest to European states, like Finland, Estonia and Latvia, rescued themselves. There, exists a high level of culture, order, and people are normal [*liude iak liude*]" (Doc. 168).[107] Ukraine was suffering the most because it was the most distant from the "enlightened European nations." The Poles, who were physically closer to Europe and had a longer tradition of resistance than Ukrainians, were better prepared to fight for independence and had allied with other oppressed peoples to stop the Muscovites before they reached Poland. The Poles had themselves been enslaved and had not come to conquer Ukraine. They were coming to help liberate it from black tsarist and red Bolshevik Moscow – from those who promised peace, freedom, land, bread, and manufactured goods but had instead brought war, Bolshevik secret police terror, communes, hunger, and no goods. Leaflets warned that those who talked about returning Polish landlords were lying. They instructed people to look for themselves at the returning Ukrainian troops and government they saw on the roads and in their settlements: "Our Ukrainian government signed an agreement with the Polish nation not the Polish lords" (Doc. 171–5).[108]

In ordinances and declarations the UNR presented itself as a government intent on establishing order. It forbade requisitioning and looting and stated that troops caught doing either were being punished. People were urged to report such activities if they observed them (Doc. 138).[109] In the wake of the offensive, local city officials issued leaflets addressing matters like curfews, bootlegging, and deadlines for general cleaning. They imposed fines and jail terms for failure to comply. In Kyiv a trilingual poster offered a 5,000 *karbovantsi* reward to anyone reporting Bolshevik agitators in Polish uniforms (Doc. 176–8).[110]

Pamphlets elaborated ideas in the leaflets. They exhorted Ukrainians to support the UNR and refuted Bolshevik claims.[111] They stated that Bolshevik rule meant worthless paper money, price increases, and no manufactured goods. The Bolsheviks, like the Poles and the Germans before them, would take what they wanted. Because federation with Russia meant conquest and serfdom, Ukrainians had to support independence. Some pamphlets explained that not all Bolsheviks were Russians and that what distinguished the former was their ambition for immediate changes in government and society that normally required years if not decades. Authors offered short, sympathetic accounts of revolutions and changes in western Europe. They argued that socialism was possible under proper conditions but that Lenin and his Bolsheviks refused to accept that those conditions did not yet exist in Russia's empire with its majority peasant population. By herding peasants into communes they were only provoking widespread resistance and leading people to conclude that life had been better under the tsar or the Hetman. Workers rejected Bolsheviks because they allowed only party members into *soviets*. In Ukraine, they were reimposing tsarist Russification and centralism and, like other invaders, were stealing its resources. In this way, they had transformed the 1917 revolution into a counter-revolution, which was why they had to be opposed. *Red Imperialists Out!* explained that, whatever their claims to be defenders of the working people, the Bolsheviks in practice were treating "our people" worse than counter-revolutionaries. "They are not socialists, but counter-revolutionaries and imperialists although they call themselves reds."

Pamphlets explained that the Directory and working population had overthrown the Hetman and his wealthy Russian supporters. Bolshevik rule meant disorder, no land, hunger, misery, death, and endless expropriations; Ukrainian rule would mean land for the people, no exploitation, and order. The Ukrainian army fought for the nation, not landlords; after mass desertions, only Chinese, Latvians, Hungarians, and intimidated Jews remained in the Red Army. During its July 1919 offensive, it was obvious to all that "the working population" was joining the Ukrainian national army, which was reclaiming Ukrainian lands. Included in the text was an appeal to those who were grateful to the Ukrainian army for driving out the Bolsheviks, to supply or join it. People should not hesitate and should do and give what they could for the army; otherwise, foreign troops would return and repeat the horrors of the earlier foreign occupations. UNR pamphleteers claimed that it was the wealthy and the landowners, not the Bolsheviks, who were trying to demoralize the army by spreading lies about desertion and soldier-*soviets*. Soldiers were told that real Bolsheviks had a disciplined army in which *soviets* had no say.

In early 1919, Pylkevych explained that the term bourgeoisie had been transformed from a word that referred to well-off urban dwellers into one used to describe anyone whom someone else decided was rich. The Russian Bolsheviks then extended that arbitrary usage to apply to all Ukrainians, to Ukraine and its government, as a pretext for stealing the country's wealth – having already destroyed Russia's productive capacity. Brotherhood talk was also nonsense, for what kind of brothers denied siblings the right to speak their own language, as Russia had done in Ukraine for 250 years? In response to an argument then often heard, that Ukrainian and Russian soldiers had eaten from the same pot at the front, Pylkevych pointed out the pot had been filled with Ukrainian wealth that Russia had arbitrarily extracted in the form of colonialist exploitation – an arbitrary extraction continued by the Bolsheviks.

The author included an extended condemnation of Bolshevik Russia. Real socialists were opposed to conquest, war, and exploitation, whereas the Bolsheviks, like true imperialists and the tsars, wanted to forcibly annex Ukraine to Russia and steal all its wealth: "We now look to Europe but they are pulling us back to Asia." Pylkevych went on to condemn all Russian socialists as imperialists of the worst kind. The Bolsheviks were simply thieves who had to be destroyed if Ukraine hoped to live in peace and prosperity. Ukrainians were better off than the Russians because they had better land and worked harder. If they had wealth it was because they had worked for it. The national government, meanwhile, would help the poor. Nikifor Hryhoriiv, in another pamphlet, explained that even Russians who called themselves socialists and liberals were denying Ukrainians independence. Those who claimed that independence was "bourgeois" did so because they exploited Ukraine and feared that independence would deny them their ill-gotten wealth. The Bolshevik idea that Ukrainian separatism was "bourgeois" was nonsense, because the real bourgeoisie opposed Ukrainian independence. Hryhoriiv nowhere claimed that all of Ukraine's bourgeoisie were Russian, or that that there was no Ukrainian bourgeoisie.

Pamphlets also dealt with practical issues. Some were especially detailed, which suggests they were intended to serve as texts for novice officials.[112] They included explanations of administration, observing that not every Tom, Dick, and Harry could be a government administrator because the task required education. Pamphlets explained what states were, how they functioned, and why states should exist. One author explained that almost everything metal in a peasant's household, even something like a needle, had been produced by others, often far away and from materials not locally available. Such items included salt and gas. This meant that workers, along with transportation, machinery, communications, and security for thousands of cities, towns, and villages, had to be organized and controlled by a central political authority: "without which we farmers would all die even on the best land." Just as in a village, many tasks required cooperation and a leader. A government, then, was necessary and had to be obeyed so that it could cooperate with other governments and trade for goods and services. Like a village, a state had to levy taxes in order to buy commodities and provide welfare services, public safety, and defence. This text included a discussion of money and inflation, explaining that a state's financial losses were its *people*'s losses and that if states were defeated in war their populations would suffer. If people refused to provide their state with conscripts and taxes, the conqueror would end up taking more in war booty than the taxes would have been. The author included an account of why the Russian empire collapsed, making his argument in terms of national rights. He pointed out that non-democratic nations suffered national and social oppression. Nations that were ruled by oppressors (e.g., the Poles, the Irish, and the Serbs) inevitably took up arms in the name of liberty. This was followed by an account of the Russian oppression that justified the Ukrainian struggle for independence. The author explained that Russia was an autocracy, contrasted that regime with various forms of democracy, and concluded that a republic was the most desirable form of government. Faced with the Bolsheviks, the Whites, and the Poles, the UNR needed taxes and cooperation if it was to provide a good life for its citizens and defeat its rapacious enemies.

Another author explained that political independence was necessary to ensure that wealth remained in the country and that education and administration would be in the native language. Because intellectuals and learning were necessary for the government to function, and educated Ukrainian professionals were few, they should not be persecuted or killed, but instead respected. The purpose of the struggle was to establish a decentralized Ukrainian national republic free of any foreign yoke. The immediate task was to equip the army so that it could defeat the Bolsheviks and end their looting and pillaging, which was impoverishing the population. The elected government had plans to deal with the economic collapse caused by the Bolsheviks. It realized that it needed not only military might but also schools and education, all of which the UNR, unlike the Bolsheviks and Hetman, would provide.

A number of pamphlets focused on historical themes.[113] One outlined the importance of national co-ops to the national revival as sponsors of schools, publishing, and libraries. The central theme in the historical materials was that Ukraine was endowed with natural wealth that was coveted by the Poles and Russians. Hryhoriiv explained that the tsar, Kerensky, and Lenin were all the same: they were interested only in appropriating Ukrainian wealth for the betterment of Russia, and in return "they gave us what dropped from their nose." It was no business of Ukraine that Russians were fighting among themselves, yet that war had produced anarchy and common suffering. As a result, in Ukraine, "people elected at various meetings" had decided to separate and to rule themselves. Poland, for its part, wanted to control western

Ukrainian oil, to reimpose its yoke, and was just as bad as Russia. After 250 years of tsarist oppression, Ukrainians needed political independence so that they could decide their own fate. Ukraine had separated in 1917 because Russia had ignored its autonomy, repressed and exploited the Ukrainian people, and distributed Ukrainian land to Russian and Polish landowners. It consistently took more in taxes from Ukraine than it returned in services, all the while imposing policies that hindered economic development and made Ukrainian advancement contingent on cultural Russification. Despite claims to the contrary, Russia did not need Ukrainian grain, and Ukraine did not need Russian manufactured goods. Bolshevik policies were just as inimical to Ukrainian interests as were tsarist ones, and only political independence would allow the Ukrainian nation to decide for itself what to do with its wealth. "We listened to the Russians for 250 years and no good came of it. Now let the Russians listen to our nation." Only a strong army could secure independence, and this required high taxation so that the government could support the collective national interest.

A group of pamphlets addressed perceived differences between western and eastern Ukrainians. These explained that both peoples were Ukrainians and had a common interest in political independence and that they had to cooperate with and fight alongside each other. Some explained that soldiers with Austrian-style uniforms were Ukrainian soldiers and that western Ukrainians had been "slaves" much like eastern Ukrainians. Some authors offered creative explanations as to why the Whites hated western Ukrainians: "Western Ukrainians are better educated than us [easterners]. That is why they cannot be so easily fooled as us ... They trust neither Bolsheviks [n]or Mensheviks. The westerner only trusts those he knows well and takes all street-talkers [agitators] either to his superior officer or the police." Western Ukrainian troops were warned that all Bolshevik claims – including that they would free western Ukraine from Poland – were lies. The truth was that they were exploiting and Russifying Ukraine just like the tsars. The Ukrainian Soviet Republic was a fiction, and western Ukraine could be freed from the Poles only after eastern Ukraine was secure.

The sample texts rarely address foreign policy. One item that did broach the subject described Ukraine's position at the Versailles Conference. The victorious powers were hostile towards Ukraine because it had been a German ally, and accordingly, they supported the Poles and the Whites. The pamphlet included a copy of the pro-Ukrainian resolution of the Second International Socialist Conference at Lucerne in 1919, which called on the Allied powers to recognize Ukrainian independence and its borders.

Two pamphlets in the sample presented the Ukrainian case in the form of fables.[114] The first of these labelled Ukrainians (*Ukrainsti*) "okradentsi," meaning "stolen from," and Russians "Rozsiiane," meaning "spread out." These terms were meant to reflect the two sides' respective historical realities. Thus, Ukraine's neighbours were always trying to take its wealth and to "spread out" their conquered neighbours to Siberia. In the tale, Russians one day all contracted a strange disease that made them want to steal everything in sight and infect all their neighbours. Criminals were especially prone to this disease, and nothing, not even assistance from abroad, could stop it from spreading. Only Ukrainians themselves could eradicate that disease, once they finally heeded their own honourable and intelligent leaders. The second fable recounted a conversation between a pro-Bolshevik "Little Russian" worker and a Ukrainian soldier. A Ukrainian officer intervened while the other two were discussing the Ukrainian and Bolshevik versions of current events. After the worker fled, the officer explained to the soldier that the worker was not a real worker but a Bolshevik anti-Ukrainian provocateur. He then refuted each of his claims regarding Ukrainian independence and explained the bitter realities of Bolshevik rule.

In a final group of pamphlets published in 1919, some of which had bilingual Hebrew/Ukrainian texts, focused on Jewish issues. *Ievrei ta Ukrainska Respublika* summarized the minutes of a meeting in July 1919 between Petliura and Jewish representatives, during which each side presented its point of view. The Jews declared their loyalty, requested protection from pogroms and punishment for pogromists, and noted the gap between the government's declarations of Jewish rights and the reality of pogroms. The Bund representative pointed out that while there were as many Ukrainians as Jews in the Red Army (if not more), the latter were being shot when captured, while the former were released. Petliura said he would do what he could to combat "hooliganism" and to publicize how Jewish citizens supported the army.

Borys Martos, a government minister, addressed a pamphlet to Jewish citizens and workers. It explained that the Bolsheviks were exploiting the darker instincts of the masses, and as could be expected, one result was pogroms, which the socialist UNR government opposed. Martos noted that the government had already established commissions to deal with pogroms. It was also providing compensation for victims and executing perpetrators. The government was aware of the importance of the Jewish contribution to Ukrainian independence, and Jewish parties had places in ministries. He pointed out that the only protection against Bolsheviks and Whites was an independent Ukrainian state. Another pamphlet warned readers not to believe anything they heard about all Jews being Bolsheviks or benefiting from the war. It stated that pogroms typically erupted during times of upheaval and only helped those who opposed the revolutionary struggle. Ukraine's enemies – landlords, capitalists, Russians, and Poles – had failed to repress Ukrainians by force alone and were now resorting to anti-Semitism to provoke strife between workers and peasants of different nationalities. They were doing this because they knew that Christians would rather attack Jews than other Christians. Some pogromists were paid provocateurs; others were naive people who had been conned by anti-Semites. The former had to be arrested, the latter enlightened.

A more sophisticated attempt to explain why "so many Jewish workers were Bolsheviks" began by explaining that the difference between socialists and Bolsheviks was that the latter imposed socialism at bayonet point immediately and were nationalizing everything in a country where the vast majority were still peasants. As a result, the poorest suffered. This especially affected Jewish workers, because almost all of them worked in small workshops. Poor owners meant low wages and bad working conditions. Jewish workers, consequently, were more susceptible than gentile workers to Bolshevik promises of immediate improvement. The author blamed pogroms on Whites who had entered the UNR army with the collapse of the Hetman's government, as well as various "demoralized" elements who remained in that army after the vast majority of peasant-volunteers left in January 1919. The Jewish response to the pogroms had been to join the invading Bolshevik army. In other words, the nominally Bolshevik Jewish workers were not motivated by ideology. The author concluded that, because as of July 1919 it was UNR policy to punish pogromists and forbid requisitioning, Jews on the Ukrainian side of the front were supporting the UNR, as would Jews on the Bolshevik side once they learned that Jews in the UNR were safe.[115]

In 1921, UNR propaganda included a series titled "Letters of the Peasant Hory" to the Ukrainian peasantry. Three of these publications are included in the sample (Doc. 234–6). The series was perhaps intended to accompany the UNR's Second Winter Campaign of October 1921. In the wake of its failure, these texts declared that the dead had not died in vain and explained why their deaths had to be avenged. "Sharing his thoughts" with his "fathers, brothers and sisters," Hory explained that the whole world supported Simon Petliura and Ukraine's struggle for liberation, which would succeed if only Ukrainians would unite. Throughout Ukraine's thousand-year history, its worst enemy had been "the Muscovite-Jewish Bolshevik party," which in three years had managed to inflict more suffering than other rulers had done in centuries.

The party's title, in Cyrillic "RKP," the leaflet explained, could only stand for Russian Company of Torturers, in light of their massacre of 360 UNR soldiers from the campaign who had surrendered.

An example of what today would be called "black propaganda" is a leaflet supposedly issued by Trotsky in late 1919 or early 1920. It is most likely phoney because there is no known original of this document, nor is there a copy of it in Trotsky's published works. Its orthography is tsarist rather than the modernized version used by the Bolsheviks, and it refers in uncharacteristically positive, non-Marxist terms to Ukrainians, their government, and Petliura. This phoney text was likely the work of a UNR political officer, Vasyl Sovenko, and a local UNR partisan commander, Iuryi Hulai-Hulenko. Their likely intent was to compromise the Bolsheviks and indirectly enhance the Ukrainian cause by claiming its enemy was awed by its power and resilience.

Vasyl Sovenko first appears in documents in August 1917 as a representative from the Minsk front at his native village in Katerynoslav province.[116] In the UNR he was the political commissar in his native district. In December 1919 he was appointed a propaganda/intelligence officer with troops assigned to the Winter Campaign in Bolshevik Ukraine. In light of the continuing armed mass resistance, UNR leaders had hoped the appearance of a 2,000-strong Ukrainian force on Bolshevik territory would tip the fortunes of war in their favour and re-establish their authority.[117] Having survived the campaign, Sovenko submitted his report in June 1920. That report is especially relevant to this book because it is by an Ukrainian official in charge of propaganda. Significantly, he noted that while the army had only reached Cherkassy, UNR leaflets were circulating as far east as Kharkiv and Katerynoslav.

A Soviet manifesto dated 17 December 1919 told Ukrainians that the Soviet regime had been reborn and that they could now decide their own future and the nature of their relations with Russia. Ukraine's Bolshevik government had no army of its own. However, the manifesto claimed that this imaginary force would be brought together to form a single "Russian-Ukrainian Red Army" that would be the army of both worker/peasant republics. There were Ukrainian Bolshevik and pro-Bolshevik Ukrainian SR irregulars who did have support, especially in their fight against the Whites, but already in May 1919, Trotsky had issued secret orders to systematically and ruthlessly disarm and disband such units. Partisans deemed loyal would be allowed to serve only in rear units.[118] Against this background, Sovenko related that in early January 1920, just north of the town of Balta, he had obtained from Bolshevik prisoners copies of one of Trotsky's public orders stating that the Red Army, after liberating Ukraine from the Whites, would return home. The order explained that Ukraine was independent and that troops were to behave themselves.[119] This was an actual document issued by Trotsky, and it suited UNR interests. Sovenko reproduced and circulated the order to surrounding villages still held by Red troops to remind the people of the Bolsheviks' declared intentions.

Some days later, he claimed that a group of partisans "in a village whose name I forgot" had handed him a second captured Bolshevik document. This was a secret instruction issued by Trotsky, in line with the earlier secret policy, ordering all irregular detachments be disbanded and disarmed. This contradicted the publicly proclaimed Soviet line about independence and "uniting" a "Ukrainian army" with the Russian one. Because the local populace disliked Bolshevik troops remaining in their towns and villages after the Whites had fled, Sovenko decided to reproduce and circulate this secret order as well, in order to discredit the Bolsheviks and win support for the UNR. Simultaneously with this document, Sovenko and Hurenko circulated a leaflet of their own. It addressed Russian soldiers, asking them what they were doing in Ukraine now that the Whites had been defeated. Sovenko claimed that this leaflet had sparked mass desertions from the Red Army.[120]

Towards the end of March 1920, Sovenko claimed that local partisans near the southwestern town of Balta had delivered to him a third Bolshevik document. This was a copy of another, supposedly secret instruction, whose contents, like those of the second document noted above, supposedly contradicted publicly proclaimed policy. He claimed that Trotsky had written these instructions, which detailed how agitators in Ukraine were to carry out their work. Sovenko explained why he decided to reproduce this document, attached a rebuttal, and distributed it as proof of Bolshevik perfidity. "The captured instructions were valuable counter-propaganda material for me; it sufficed to read them at a meeting to [immediately] hear curses rain down on the communists."

In "Instruction for Agitator-Communists in Ukraine," which Sovenko had most likely compiled, Trotsky allegedly stated that each Bolshevik offensive in Ukraine was more difficult than the previous one. Attributing a key role to "good agitators" in the spring 1919 occupation of Ukraine, Trotsky then (supposedly) praised the "free spirit of the zaporizhian cossacks and haidamaks." That "terrible force," aroused by "Communes, the cheka, requisition squads and Jewish commissars," had led Ukrainians to miraculous feats of bravery, which was how they had been able to defeat their historical enemies, who included the Russians. "Only unimaginable credulity and pliancy," and their failure to maintain unity after the battles were fought, led to them quickly lose their independence. If Bolshevik agitators remembered this, they would succeed. There followed ten points to guide agitators. These included established propaganda themes found in leaflets and pamphlets, as well as other recommendations, such as these: it should be claimed that Petliura was allied with the Bolsheviks; Bolshevik pillaging should be blamed on Ukrainian soldiers who had joined the Red Army, and that pretext should be used to shoot them; and non-Bolsheviks should be barred from the *soviets*. "Do not forget for a moment Ukraine must be ours, and it will be ours only when it is soviet and Petliura is forever erased from the national memory."[121]

The Message: The Ukrainian Radical Socialists

The two Ukrainian radical socialist parties, the left-SRs (Borotbists) and left-SDs (Independendists – later the UCP), broke with their respective centrist factions, the ruling parties in the UNR, in January 1919.[122] The left-SRs envisaged an autonomous Ukrainian socialist state and party federated with Russia. The left-SDs stood for a Ukrainian socialist state and communist party independent of Bolshevik Russia and its party. The leaders of both parties claimed there could be no Ukrainian revolution without a Ukrainian communist party. The sample includes only one SD and two SR leaflets with catching graphic design (Doc. 186–7, 201).[123] Most of these leaflets were simple typed text and tended to be long on detailed explanations and short on sloganeering. Both these parties placed as much importance on national liberation as they did on social justice, and this was reflected linguistically in their published materials, in which they used Ukrainian as an adjective much more frequently than as a genitive. Such usage underscored that Ukraine and its people were distinct national entities – thus, "Ukrainian revolution," "Ukrainian workers" "Ukrainian peasants." This was unlike the Bolsheviks. Choosing to avoid national issues, as will be shown, they used in their materials the genitive form almost exclusively, as in, for example "workers of Ukraine" or "revolution in Ukraine." Their usage presented Ukraine as a region no different from Tula or Riazan. It located Ukraine as part of a larger whole and obfuscated the fact that Ukraine was inhabited overwhelmingly by ethnic Ukrainians.

Left-wing Ukrainian parties differed little from the Bolsheviks with regard to their land policies. They differed markedly in matters of national independence. The "[u]nited national-proletarian organizations of Ukraine's left-socialists" in January 1918 called on "principled" Bolsheviks to end their invasion of Ukraine. The war their party had launched against independent Ukraine was contrary to basic socialist principles, which the leaflet duly cited. That war also prevented "Ukraine's revolutionary forces from deepening the struggle in Ukraine" and would benefit only the common enemy and third party – the exploiter bourgeoisie. In the summer of 1919, centrist SRs pointed out that the Bolsheviks were as imperialist as the tsarist bourgeoisie and were not interested in *soviets* or freedom but only in Ukraine's wealth. They called on the population to support the government, the army, and the party: Russian Bolsheviks "are the same kind of Russian rapacious imperialists as the Russian bourgeoisie, landowners and capitalists. They brought you neither freedom nor soviets" (Doc. 180, 183).[124]

After splitting from the UNR, left-SRs (Borotbists) denounced it, declaring that its leaders had betrayed the Ukrainian revolution by turning it to the right. The UNR had destroyed peasant and worker organizations and fomented pogroms; it avoided fighting the Whites and now based itself on part of the army and "a small group of nationalist intellectuals." A leaflet from the left-SRs' Poltava branch called for opposition to the UNR and the warlord Hryhoriev, who had just switched sides to fight the Bolsheviks, with whom the Borotbists were by then allied. Leaflets that summer called on men to join the Red Cossacks, noting that "Ukraine's true revolutionary power united under the Ukrainian Communist Party [the Borotbists] had defeated the Whites" and that revolution would soon sweep all Europe. Leaflets now omitted reference to Bolshevik depredations. They included calls for an "independent" Ukrainian Soviet Republic, world revolution, and a "Ukrainian Red Army" (Doc. 181, 184–5).[125]

The Ukrainian left-SDs directed one of their first leaflets in February 1919 to the UNR's most important military unit, the western Ukrainian Sich Riflemen. It told them they were being forced to shoot Ukrainian workers and peasants in the name of independence by a government that had denied those same workers and peasants the opportunity to build a socialist state. It accused the UNR of preparing to sell the country to the Entente, whose only interest was in rebuilding the Russian empire with the Whites, and it urged the soldiers to understand that there could be no national liberation without social liberation. "Ukrainian workers and peasants must have help from their comrades so they do not have to wait for help from Moscow." This leaflet urged the soldiers to join the nation, fight under the red flag, and become the core of a national Red Army that would create "our own independent socialist republic" (Doc. 188).[126] That spring, the left-SDs elaborated their position, explaining that they opposed the UNR because it privileged national over social issues. They warned that Ukraine would be smothered in any alliance with the Anglo-French bourgeois capitalist powers, whose primary interest was in supporting the Whites and re-establishing the tsarist empire. The Bolsheviks represented a foreign country that had conquered Ukraine. They had caused civil war and imposed an occupation regime through their puppet Communist Party of Ukraine, and they had created a phoney pro-Kremlin left-faction within the Ukrainian left-SD to weaken the revolutionary struggle. The Bolsheviks had so alienated the people that, despite their fundamentally radical socialist ambitions, they supported the "bourgeois" UNR.[127] The solution lay in a Ukrainian Red Army, all-party *soviets*, and an independent socialist Ukraine (Doc. 189–91).[128] Party leaders explained that after failing to convince the Bolsheviks of their errors in Ukraine, they had attempted to take control of the massive anti-Bolshevik uprisings that spring through an All Ukrainian Revolutionary Committee. They condemned every aspect of Bolshevik policy in Ukraine, pointing out that the Bolsheviks had become counter-revolutionary and had turned Ukraine into a "Russian colony." Their program specifically included rule by *soviets* without any party dictatorship.

Especially noteworthy are "Order no. 48" and the Independentist Ukrainian Revolutionary Committee's "Ultimatum to Rakovskii's So-Called 'Ukrainian Worker-Peasant Government'" (Doc. 196, 197).[129] In the Order, the Revkom referred to itself as the representative of the soviet power of the "Ukrainian working nation" and declared the government of the "Muscovite conqueror in Ukraine" dissolved. It directed people to depose and arrest all agents of both the UNR and the Russian Bolshevik government if they resisted. In the ultimatum, Iury Mazurenko, the Independentist military commander, explained: "The workers and peasants of Ukraine rose against you [the CPU] as the arm of Russian conquerors, who, under the guise of slogans that are holy to us ... not only ruin [them] and destroy the true authority of the workers and poor peasants of a neighboring state, but exploit them for purposes far distant from any kind of socialist order." He called for power to the *soviets*, self-determination of nations up to and including separation, and struggle against imperialist conquerors. Russian Bolsheviks in Ukraine called themselves a worker's government, the ultimatum continued, yet they had taken raw materials and even machinery out of Ukraine and had created unemployment. Instead of ruling through *soviets*, they rigged elections in their favour and ruled through commissars and secret police, who were no different from tsarist governors and gendarmes. "Instead of an independent Ukrainian Republic, wherein power had to lie with the Ukrainian working nation, you have made it [Ukraine] into a Russian colony and Ukrainian workers and peasants into slaves working for Russia who send the product of their labour in return for packages of [worthless] Kerensky roubles, leaflets, and your hired agitators." This was not internationalism "but merely the subordination to Moscow of all states where worker and peasant power exists, which, as a result, opens the door for the Whites." Instead of uniting nationalities, the Bolsheviks were intensifying the antagonism between Jews and the rest of Ukraine's population and thereby inciting pogroms. Mazurenko concluded: "Let the blood and curses of the Jewish nation fall on your head."

The left-SDs differentiated neutral/indifferent and loyal Russians and Jews from those who supported the Bolsheviks in their propaganda. They usually specified that they were targeting the "Jewish commissar Bolshevik," or "Jewish communist," or "Russian communists" (Doc 193, 194, 195, 197).[130] One leaflet specifically warned people to ignore Black Hundred attempts at provoking pogroms and to reject national-based enmity in general (Doc. 192).[131] The left SDs opposed the Bolshevik Committees of Poor Peasants, "all chauvinists, be they Ukrainian, Russian or Jewish," and swore they would hunt down "all Petliuras be they Russian or Jewish. These new Petliuras are just as counter-revolutionary, if not worse, than ours." Another leaflet declared: "Down with Russian and Jewish Petliura-commissars." Another: "Down with communes ... Save your houses and goods from the communist gangs, long live Soviet independent Ukraine." These leaflets told Red Army troops that their commissars were lying to them and that they were not fighting for soviet power in Ukraine, but to *conquer* Ukraine; and that they were not fighting wealthy peasants, but poor Ukrainian peasants and workers (Doc. 198).[132] Furthermore, the Bolsheviks were dispersing all *soviets* that did not elect Russian communists. Ukrainian workers and peasants could not be allowed to suffer the Russian invasion, which would steal from them and, like the tsars, oppress their culture and language. Nor did they need their Russian, Chinese, and Latvian brothers to introduce soviet power in Ukraine – that was something they could do themselves. Red Army men should surrender their arms and go home.

The most important left-SD commander, Danylo Zeleny, did not condemn all Jews in his leaflets; he did, though, issue an ambivalent ordinance upon taking the town of Rzhytsiv. Here Jews were addressed as a group. They were told they did not have to flee; however, those who had supported the Bolsheviks had to surrender their arms. At the same time, the text referred to all Jews behaving in an anti-Ukrainian manner because they had attempted to flee (Doc. 200–1).[133] In other leaflets Zeleny gave details of repression as examples of Bolshevik perfidy. His leaflets noted how the Bolsheviks shot simple peasants on the pretext that they must be counter-revolutionaries because they had protested Russian communist thievery. When the "Bolshevik-communist brothers" came, instead of asking anybody whether they wanted commissars and Cheka agents, they imposed communes, shot innocent people, "the best people who devoted their entire lives to the people," and burned villages. "What kind of peasant power is this?" (Doc. 199).[134]

Having failed in its attempt to lead the mass anti-Bolshevik uprising, and faced with the White invasion of the summer of 1919, the left-SDs stopped fighting the Bolsheviks. In a public declaration they blamed their failure on their lack of organization, which had allowed Petliura sympathizers who had infiltrated its ranks and White-funded subterfuge to undermine the uprising. They now maintained that the reactionary counter-revolutionary Bolshevik policies they had condemned were only a temporary consequence of unfavourable circumstances. In 1920 they opposed the Polish-Ukrainian offensive alongside the Bolsheviks (Doc. 202, 203).[135]

Three Borotbist pamphlets from 1919 outlined their relationship to the national and Bolshevik governments. The first was a collection of articles and declarations from earlier that year that described the Bolsheviks as a Russian party of Russian workers ignorant of Ukraine; the Bolsheviks implemented unsuitable policies and had no business in Ukraine. Their presence only provoked resistance and lent credence to counter-revolutionary claims that revolution in Ukraine was a foreign imposition. Only Ukrainian parties could realize the socialist revolution in Ukraine. In the interests of the revolution, the Borotbists called on Ukraine's Bolsheviks to join them in one Ukrainian Revkom.[136]

In the second pamphlet, Vasyl Blakytny provided readers with a short history of recent events. It explained that because the tsarist ruling class had oppressed the Ukrainian bourgeoisie, the Borotbists supported national independence. "Socialist appeasers [*uhodovtsi*]" in the Rada refused to oppose the national bourgeoisie and worker representatives were too few. As a result, the Rada had not kept its promises to the people and had instead made anti-revolutionary agreements with foreign bourgeoisie. When workers and peasants realized that the Rada was not socialist, they took up arms against it, and then against its bourgeois ally, Germany. The Hetman's alliance with the Russian bourgeoisie alienated the Ukrainian bourgeoisie, which then turned to the "petite bourgeoisie" and "appeasers" to establish the Directory. It, in turn, repressed "worker-peasant power" and made agreements with the exploiting imperialist European bourgeoisie. To prove his claim that the Ukrainian bourgeoisie had sold the country as a colony to the international capitalist cabal, Blakytny included transcribed documents from the Ukrainian–French negotiations in Odessa that spring that contained the harsh terms the French had set the UNR. For Ukrainian communists to send goods to Russian communists, he continued, was a qualitatively different act of exchange than the kind the Directory was considering with regard to the Entente. The former did not involve buying and selling, but rather mutual "fraternal aid" between workers. That "aid" was a necessary aspect of world revolution that would finally bring an end to hardships, exploitation, and war.[137]

The third pamphlet summarized Borotbist party history, as well as its policies and differences with the Bolsheviks.[138] In Ukraine,

> fortuitous circumstances resulted in a part of its population always having been under the cultural influence of Russia – both now and under the tsars. The communist-Bolshevik party that leads the construction of soviet power in Ukraine belongs to that part of the population. The majority in this party are Ukrainian [territorially] but these Ukrainians, under the influence of Russian culture and, particularly, under the influence of the Russian revolution, absolutely refuse to recognize that in Ukraine the communist revolution has to follow a different path than it did in Russia. In response to all the efforts of the borotbists to point out that this or that cannot be done because in the context of Ukrainian life it will hinder the revolution, they reply "well in Russia this is has already been done." And the communists-borotbists say that it is not enough for Ukraine to be an independent republic and have its government. There must also be people in this government who will guide it not bothering about whether this or that has been done in Russia or in other soviet states, but who will first and foremost look at what the Ukrainian proletariat wants and then carry out policies accordingly.

Disagreements were over tactics rather than programs, and the party would handle disputes with the Bolsheviks "only verbally, on paper."

The Borotbists' approach to national issues differed from the Bolshevik one, and in their publications they promised to transform Bolshevik policy. A pamphlet issued in 1920 briefly summarized the issue.[139] National oppression had opened the gates for the petite bourgeoisie to use nationalism to mask its class interests and to derail the socialist revolution. This was not to be confused with the natural desire of the working masses for "cultural development in the national form of the population of a given region." The issue of nationalism had to be raised carefully (unlike what the Bolsheviks had done) so that it would not be exploited for counter-revolutionary purposes. Policy could not be left in the hands of the Russian or Russified proletariat, for that would nullify assertions about cultural equality in Bolshevik party declarations. To attain that equality and overcome the legacy of tsarist Russian oppression, political support for the Ukrainian language, culture, and education was necessary.

According to Independentist pamphlets published during the summer of 1919, "the working people of Ukraine" had supported the UNR until it allied itself with the Entente to establish a bourgeois republic. The poor peasants and workers then extended a brotherly hand to Russian peasants, asking for help. That assistance was not forthcoming. Instead, Russian communists along with Chinese and Latvians appeared, destroyed the economic and cultural life of the "Ukrainian working people," and turned workers and peasants again into Muscovite serfs. "Russian communists" established a dictatorship of their own party and, backed by Chinese and Latvian mercenary bayonets, set out to return Ukraine to its status as a "Muscovite colony." "Our working people realized the plundering occupation nature of Russian communist policies and, rising in the name of liberty, instructed us, the All Ukrainian revolutionary Committee, to lead its revolutionary act." The pamphlet called for struggle against the conquerors and for power to worker/peasant *soviets* in an independent Ukrainian Soviet Republic.[140]

Included in the sample are two UCP pamphlets published in Ukraine. One is a preliminary draft of the party program, the other a reprint of articles by the Party's co-founder, Anatole Richytsky. Together they outlined the party's basic positions and its differences with the Ukrainian left-SRs and the Russian-dominated CPU.[141] They pointed out that socialist revolution in Ukraine had failed largely thanks to the "bourgeois imperialist" desires of Bolshevik leaders and their CPU subordinates in Ukraine. As the party of Russian communism in Ukraine, the CPU had its roots in a tiny Russian proletarian minority backed by the foreign power of Russia, and as such, it was ignorant of and isolated from "the national Ukrainian revolution." Richytsky compared the platforms of those parties with that of his own, noting they were basically the same except that one represented the interests of the proletariat in a ruling nation that still carried the legacy of imperialism with it, and the other, those of the proletariat of a ruled nation – a colony. Accordingly, the UCP program inevitably detailed issues that were of only passing interest in the RCP program. In particular, these concerned the relationship between national and economic oppression. Given its complete isolation from the Ukrainian revolutionary process, "the dictatorship of the northern worker" – that is, Russians represented by the CPU – had to be replaced by the "dictatorship of the southern worker" – that is, all the workers in Ukraine as represented by the UCP. The latter was the only group that could realize the tasks of the Ukrainian national revolution, thereby attracting the majority of the working population away from the UNR, and then introduce communism. Richytsky pointed out that the CPU, as a provincial affiliate of the RCP, had less authority than did the Rada under the provisional government. The Rada was at least the product of the Ukrainian revolution and not the "Russo-Ukrainian" revolution. If Bolshevik Ukraine was truly independent and had a real Ministry of Foreign Affairs, he asked, why was there no Ukrainian communist party in the International? Why was all party and government business conducted in Russian, and why did Ukrainian peasants in Bolshevik posters wear Russian straw shoes (*lapti*)? As Russia had shown, the proletariat becomes the carrier of national interests, and that is normal. But to use Russian national ideas to justify the Polish campaign of 1920 was absurd. In another article, Richytsky explained that all talk of cultural and national rights was meaningless in the context of Moscow's economic centralization.

The Message: The Warlords

The UNR government-in-exile maintained contact with as many anti-Bolshevik partisan leaders as it could.[142] For at least three years, through them, it tried to channel discontent with Bolshevik rule into a coordinated mass uprising. After 1920, when retreating some UNR commanders were ordered to remain in Bolshevik territory to organize opposition, UNR leaders continued issuing leaflets telling people to support the Ukrainian government and its army and that a planned uprising was imminent. People were urged to be patriotic, to distrust the Bolsheviks and the bourgeoisie, and to do whatever they could to sabotage their initiatives (Doc. 204).[143] Actual and nominally pro-UNR irregular military commanders did not always indicate their affiliation in their propaganda. The sample suggests that partisans distributed leaflets only. They likely had no access to presses in Ukraine, and it was easier to smuggle leaflets than pamphlets published in Polish-controlled territory across the border. Some leaflets were handwritten. Some have survived only as Bolshevik Russian-translated transcriptions, some of these made in multiple copies for the many officials ignorant of Ukrainian (Doc. 222–4).[144]

In an undated "testament," the prominent UNR commander Iurko Tiutiunnyk issued standing orders for what the UNR leaders-in-exile believed would be Ukraine's "National War" against the Bolsheviks. They insisted the only outcome of that war would be victory because no treaties could be signed with criminal occupiers. The entire population was to be armed, disciplined, and prepared to obey a central command and was to use every means possible to seek out and destroy the enemy (Doc. 205).[145]

Another prominent commander, Iuliian Mordalevych, developed two themes in his leaflets. One of these, from July 1920, directed to Bolsheviks, focused on the differences between theory and reality. He explained that their ideals existed only on paper. In reality, people experienced only the deeds of Red Army plunderers and thieves, who were imposing oppressive imperialist policies that had nothing in common with socialism or with the right of self-determination. Such actions demonstrated that the Bolsheviks were not friends of working people but "bloody imposter gendarme-terrorist oppressors and imperialist exploiters." Put simply, they were counter-revolutionaries. He told his Bolshevik audience that Ukrainians, as democrats and proletarians, opposed both the bourgeoisie and "extremist leftism," which was unsuited to Ukraine. Mordalevych's second leaflet was an appeal to the populace based on romantic nationalism. Faced with so much struggle and suffering, the weak had surrendered and made peace with "the foreign oppressor in Ukraine." But there was salvation from disaster for those who knew they were Ukrainian, not Russians or "Little Russians." Their only hope lay in the Ukrainian soldier and his democratic government, which was opposed both to the "absurd utopian politics" of Muscovite Bolshevik communists and to a bourgeoisie that still could not accept the need for democratic reforms. This second leaflet ended with a call for all possible support.[146]

Mordalevych's leaflets focused on the gap between fine-sounding theories and the bitter realities evident to those living in Bolshevik-controlled territory. The Bolsheviks were in reality counter-revolutionaries. Ukrainian democrats and proletarians were equally opposed to "bourgeois tendencies and your ultra-leftism." He declared that Ukrainians did not fear terror and would fight as long as necessary to convince Bolsheviks to become real socialists, to show them they were unwanted, and to get them to leave Ukraine. "The Jews as a nation are not our enemy ... We will not allow pogroms and plundering," he wrote elsewhere. Ukrainians would protect them, but they should not support Bolsheviks or engage in hostile acts against the Ukrainian state, for such activities could provoke "a desire for revenge among insurgents." Pro-Ukrainian behaviour was in the Jewish interest because Ukrainian independence would come sooner or later (Doc. 206–7).[147]

Partisan commander Orlyk (Fedir Artemenko) in 1920–1 issued texts more radical than those of 1917 or early 1919. These implicitly condemned all Jews as enemies. He explained that a Bolshevik yoke had replaced the old landowner yoke, and in October 1921 he was still calling for people to stand ready to join an imminent centrally planned uprising: "Who gave these Muscovite torturers and Jewish mercenaries the right to occupy Ukraine? By what right? On what grounds? They bring freedom to peoples on Chinese and Latvian bayonets." Those who "sold themselves to the Jews and betrayed our fighters ... will have their property destroyed." Those who worked in Bolshevik institutions would, when captured, have their property destroyed. Those apprehended a second time would be shot. "We will repay in kind the Red Terror." Those bourgeois who had not fled, "together with the Jews and lost ignorant people [who] all joined the 'COMMUNIST' [*sic*] party to re-establish the tsarist regime via terror ... Whoever threatens our freedom from left or right is our enemy" (Doc. 208–9).[148] Andryi Levchenko, a formally pro-UNR commander, used less violent language and did not label all Jews enemies (Doc. 210–11).[149]

Between 1919 and 1921, UNR and partisan leaflets, which may or may not have been issued by a central propaganda official, highlighted the rapacity of Bolshevik requisitions. They focused on the reality of misery and death on their territories, and on the Bolsheviks' broken promises, and promised an imminent mass uprising that would expel them:

> We have no life but all want to live. They mobilize you into the Red Army so that it will be easier to rob your families and to send you all to Siberia to fight the Japanese. Think and act. Will you go and serve our enemies and [blank space] your brothers, or follow us for the great holy deed of liberating your brothers and dear Ukraine from its eternal enemy Russia, and now, in particular, from the Bolshevik communist red occupiers.[150]

One leaflet related that the Ukrainian nation in 1917 had thrown off the chains of the Muscovite tsars but after that, the "entire Muscovite nation," desiring Ukraine's wealth, had descended on the country. Russian workers and peasants, workers and peasants like Ukrainians, chanting slogans like "all power to the working people," had set out to conquer Ukraine. The communists had promised everything but instead had taken everything to Russia or stored it in "Jewish basements." The Petliurites, fed up with this anarchy, had also fought against the Hetman and the Germans. Communists included Jews, Russians, native collaborators, and the "imprudent," who had sold their souls to foreigners and tortured and killed their brothers for money. All who could now had to do what they could to retake "our native land from these occupiers."[151]

Some leaflets specified that the planned uprising against Bolshevik rule would be nationwide and called on all Ukrainians, including women and children, to maintain discipline and fight back however they could. "The final judgment is upon these bloodsuckers who destroyed all economic life, tortured the innocent, caused price rises and shortages, disorder, theft, violence, and illegality." In the autumn of 1920, months after the Bolsheviks had reoccupied Ukraine, "regional insurrectional committees" declared their rule dissolved and called on local people to form new government bodies, which, among other tasks, would return seized assets to the poor. Leaflets almost certainly of UNR provenance identified Bolsheviks and Russians as the enemy and told people not to allow pogroms or disorder (Doc. 213–14).[152] Besides claiming that a mass anti-Bolshevik uprising was imminent, some leaflets falsely claimed that the Entente had recognized Ukrainian independence (Doc. 238).[153]

An anonymous group, the Main Military Council of the Insurrectionary Army, issued an undated leaflet titled "Why the Partisans Fight: We Fight to Establish True Worker Peasant Power" (Doc. 231).[154] It explained that Ukraine was ruled by Russian communist commissar-occupiers who had dispersed all elected *soviets* by force and turned Ukraine into a colony ruled from Moscow by "Leiba Trotsky, Moishe Nakhamsin, Rozenfeldy, Bronshteins who sat on Nicholas I bloody throne and continue his bloody work." While sending Ukrainian Cossacks to fight who knows who or where, they sent Latvian and Russian-Jewish communist regiments to loot Ukraine. "We are fighting against foreign occupiers, who came armed to our native land. And how not to oppose them? They came as vicious enemies. They burn our houses, steal our goods, rape our women and daughters, kill our fathers, our children. These are not our brothers, but Cains, whom God damned."

Some leaflets declared that all Russians regardless of political affiliation were enemies and opposed to Ukrainian independence (Doc. 215).[155] Most identified the Bolsheviks as the cause of all of Ukraine's problems. They had dispersed the Constituent Assembly, launched an invasion that compelled the Rada to ally itself with Germany, and divided the nation along class lines. The peasants worked tirelessly, but then the Bolsheviks exported what they produced, along with everything else in Ukraine, to Russia. In return they gave nothing except trains full of propaganda, hungry agitators, and punishment battalions. According to the communists, "justice would exist only when Ukrainians with their labour feed all the Muscovite, Jewish, Latvian and Chinese layabouts." Just like all the other "uninvited guests," the communists promised much and gave little. Warlords called on the population to organize and to take up arms for the UNR, which would call a constituent assembly, refuse to return land to landowners, and establish an eight-hour workday. "Try arrested Bolsheviks and communists on the spot in front of the community. According to conscience. No pity for those who belonged to the CHEKA." Ukrainians were urged to form district and regional executive committees subject to local insurgent committees, to take charge of affairs, and to prevent anarchy (Doc. 212, 214, 216).[156]

In the summer of 1920, local commanders issued mobilization orders that included warnings that shirkers would be punished according to martial law, as well as prohibitions against serving the Bolsheviks in any capacity. One leaflet from April 1921 warned the local "Jewish-criminal authority" that if it did not end its terror against peasants, the insurgent and Ukrainian authorities would impose "vicious terror on the families of all party-workers and Red Army men." Some leaflets set out penalties that reflected the brutality of the times: "Otherwise, those who ignore this [mobilization] order will be cut with holy knives, their goods will be confiscated and villages will be destroyed and burnt." One creative local commander declared the Zaporozhian Sich organized in Ukraine. Another urged "Ukrainian Cossacks" not to believe the anti-Ukrainian propaganda of the "the prison warders of Great Russia," to refuse to serve as foreign mercenaries, and to join Ukraine's army to fight for the republic. Another warned that if those mobilized by the Bolsheviks, for whatever reason, assisted in despoiling the population, they would be arrested, their property destroyed, and their villages burned. It called on those mobilized by the Bolsheviks to refuse to serve in any capacity (Doc. 216–19).[157]

Appeals to Russian Red Army men urged them to defect and not to follow "Godless Jews, Chinese, and Latvians" who were telling them to take up arms against their brother Ukrainians. They asked who had seen any Bolshevik promises realized, and what they were doing in Ukraine while at home their families were starving and their lands remained untilled. Conscripts were told that "Yid-Russkies" were calling them to service and that if they went, they would have to obey the Jews Trotsky, Kamenev, and Rakovskii. "Come over to our side and we will help you get rid of slavery in your tortured, blood-soaked country." Ukrainian Red Army men were asked why they were destroying their native villages and stealing from their own families. Other leaflets threatened to punish those who tore down notices, and offered amnesty to former soviet officials who helped the Ukrainian cause (Doc. 221–6).[158] In April, near Balta, the regional partisan unit warned local Bolshevik officials that if their "Jewish-criminal government" continued robbing the people and burning their homes, in the future "the Ukrainian government" would respond against the families of all Red soldiers and party members with "vicious terror" (Doc. 222–3).[159]

In March 1921, railway workers were told to strike when the promised uprising began. Leaflets instructed people to resist. They urged men to join partisan units and at least die in Ukraine, rather than submit to conscription and die in Siberia. They explained that reporting for call-up would not, as the Bolsheviks promised, protect parents' households from requisitions. People were reminded that *soviets* meant rule by commissars. Bolshevik Ukraine was not independent but a "Muscovite colony." It was controlled by Russian Jewish Bolsheviks who were sitting on the tsar's throne, stripping Ukraine of everything, and sending its men to fight in parts unknown, all the while "importing from Moscow their hungry Latvian, Ruski-Jewish communist regiments to steal from us." The solution was independence: "Long live a free independent worker-peasant soviet Ukraine" (Doc. 226, 229, 230).[160]

Alongside the irregular pro-UNR partisan commanders were independent warlords who were not common criminals and who claimed to represent particular regions or local parties. Presumably one of the latter formed an anonymous "Political Committee of National Ukraine," which explained in a leaflet that communists were imperialists who had conquered Ukraine and who were ignoring the "holy right of every nation to self-determination and political liberty." It told Russians that Ukrainians were not their enemies and that the two nations had fought their common enemies together. The communists and the monarchists, however, wanted power over all of the old empire and the world. The former wanted to make its peoples slaves of "the insane commune." The latter wanted to turn people into the slaves of the ruling eastern European dynasties. Accordingly, Russians and Ukrainians together had to rid their respective countries of the communists and then create a worker/peasant government without communists or communes in Russia, as well as a national democratic republic in Ukraine. An anonymous leaflet urged Russian soldiers not to be herded, as they had been under the tsars, to shoot those who fought for liberty. The Red Army should not be a tool for torturers and the "tyrants Lenin and Trotsky," who had turned the free citizens of 1917 into the lowest of slaves. "Comrades, they send you here to Ukraine against some kind of [alleged] bandits while they mobilize Ukrainians and send them to Russia to shoot and kill your fathers and brothers who want the same thing as the Ukrainian 'bandits.'" The leaflet called for both Russians in Ukraine and Ukrainians in Russia to go home. A second anonymous group, "Political Committee of National Ukraine," which opposed the UNR and stood for rule by *soviets* without communists, told Red Army soldiers in December 1921 that the Ukrainian nation wanted only independence from communist as well as monarchist dictatorship. Each of these was seeking its own version of world domination. It told them not to oppose the Ukrainian nation when it rose against the communists (Doc. 227, 228).[161]

Some anti-Bolshevik commanders published standing orders they had issued, presumably to demonstrate that their units were not the criminal gangs Bolshevik propaganda claimed they were. These ordered insurgents not to get drunk and not to consort with women. There were to cut all ties to friends and family and observe strict secrecy. They were to leave no wounded or dead on the battlefield, shoot the seriously wounded, and commit suicide rather than surrender. Anyone who witnessed an obvious act of treason among his fellows was to shoot the man on the spot. Rise, take up arms, urged another, because if you sit at home doing nothing while "the Jews and Russkies shoot our best people, then you will [never] see either land, freedom or your rights but only the sinewy yoke on your neck" (Doc. 232, 233).[162] Some of these units called for a "free Ukraine," others for "free worker and peasant soviets." Some reminded all of the need for strict secrecy and urged people to defend their goods against expropriation. Warlords repeated slogans about an independent Ukraine with non-party *soviets*, free of communists and Jews. None in sample proposed anything more detailed (Doc. 240–2).[163] An anonymous 1920 warlord leaflet from southern Ukraine read:[164]

> Wherever you look there are Jewish commissars, Jewish power is everywhere, on all doors in all halls stand guards, Russkie [*katsapy*] Jewish hirelings guarding their masters – the Khaims and Revkas. And the Ukrainian, the master of his own native land – stands ragged, barefoot, hungry – wandering in dark forests. They hound him everywhere, everywhere they beat him, everywhere they curse him and do not allow him to live in his own native house. And what is this brother. Why do they so beat all Ukrainians.

Ideological anti-Semitic texts like the *Protocols of the Elders of Zion* were circulated in Ukraine, in Russian, by the Black Hundreds before 1917, and later by the Whites, but there is no known pre-1922 Ukrainian translation of the *Protocols*.[165] Tsarist troops were regularly exposed to ideological anti-Semitism in the ranks, officially and unofficially. Against this background, and given the disproportionate number of Jews in Bolshevik party and government positions, warlord-printed materials identifying all Jews as enemies or communists had resonance (Doc. 229, 237–43).[166] Some explicitly told readers to kill or destroy them *and* Russians. They insisted that Bolsheviks had allowed Jews to rule over "our peasants and workers" and that "the Jews and Russkies drink your blood." "Why do our Yids wait so anxiously for and agitate in favour of Russian Bolsheviks? Because the Bolsheviks allow Jews to rule us peasants and workers." On becoming commissars, they had made vast profits by selling stolen Ukrainian goods in Russia. "BEGIN THE INSURRECTION and as one man DESTROY the Jewish-Russkie gangs."[167] One leaflet paraphrased a well-known poem by Shevchenko, replacing his words "enemies' evil blood" with "Jewish communist blood." Another warned that "Jews control everything. Look at the corpses in the Kamianets cemetery ... Did you see among them Jews, bourgeois landowners or speculators? No. You didn't." It continued: "Don't let the Jews put their yoke on you ... They say they are communists but they await Kolchak [the White general] who will protect their stores." A partisan unit near Uman issued a leaflet instructing all "Russian peasants" within the half hour to place icons in their windows because otherwise the Cossack unit "will slaughter all indifferently [*rizaty ne rozbyraias*]." "Peasants" urged another, "once more I tell you to wake up and help us as you can. Destroy these unbaptized Jews and Russkies, destroy village communist informers, destroy small Red Army units, take their weapons and horses, and give them to us."

The sample includes original handwritten appeals, presumably from 1921 or later, when Bolsheviks strictly controlled publishing materials even for their own agencies. These warned men not to answer the draft because they would be sent to Murmansk as part of plans to "dilute our Ukrainian combat potential." One item warned people they were fighting a partisan war in which all questions from officials must be answered, "I don't know and did not see." Leaflets warned informers they would be executed and their property razed. They told hungry Red Army men that their real enemies were their well-fed and well-clothed communist commissars, not those the commissars called "bandits." Peasants were told not to surrender their crops or their sons "to defend Yids and communes," but to send them to the partisans. One ends: "Death to the Jews and Communists" (Doc. 244–7).[168] Translated transcriptions of partisan leaflets by that time had presumably become routine, as shown by a collection of multiple messages typed consecutively on single sheets. These include appeals to women for help. They gave instructions on how to make bandages and sheets. They dealt with public health issues and advised people about traditional remedies. Included was advice to abstain from sexual intercourse to counter the spread of syphilis. If the urge became intolerable, then "at least choose one that is not infected" (Doc. 248–9).[169]

The last sample item, dated September 1923, is a manifesto signed by warlord Ignatius Ratytsia. It called on Ukrainians to take the rod "to our torturers" and chase them out of Ukraine like Christ had chased the moneylenders from the temple. It ordered mass mobilization on Good Friday throughout Ukraine. "Don't look to see which neighbour joins or not but take your example from Christ who fought alone against the world and its injustices" (Doc. 250).[170]

ТОВАРИШІ--ГРОМАДЯНЕ!

Въ м. Вінниці організовано Центральне Інформаційне Бюро при Директорії У. Н. Р. Запрохуються свідомі агітатори, особливо ті, що раніш працювали в Інформаційнім Бюро, які мають посвідчення від соціялістичних партій, негайно з'явитись по адресі: Вінниця, вул Богдана Хмельницького № 10 Центр. Інф. Бюро.

При роз'їздах агітаторам видаються добові гроші.

Голова Бюро **М. Гризодуб.**

Завідуючий Інф.-агітаційним відділом **М. Лебединець.**

28 Leaflet with an appeal to "Comrade-Citizens" for those with previous experience as agitators to report to the local Information Bureau. DNAB.

До вояк-учителів!

Довгий час, як ви відірвані від своєї так дуже відвічальної роботи серед селянства, в яке ви вносили головний перший світильник і свідомість нашого істнування.

Ви зараз стоїте з рушницею в руках на сторожі нашого знова поневоленого народу, нашої дорогої батьківщини, України.

Від часу нашого відродження, ви стали певними проводирями, невехітними вождями нашої ідеї серед селянства.

Ваша ініціятива, — що з революцією, на Україні знова відродились просвітні організації. Під вашим приводом повстав наш нарід проти гнобителів Москалів-комуністів і Москалів-денікінців. Завдяки учительству велась і ведеться сильна праця в тилу ворога-большевика, де учительство являється головним чинником повстання, яке і зараз розгоряється на нашій поневоленій землі. —

Отже вояки-учителі! Будьте великими й могутніми, як і ваші попередники. Будьте яркими світилами та головними проводирями нашої великої, святої ідеї і серед козацтва нашої армії. Як найбільше свідомі, — ви піддержуйте серед нашого козацтва настрій — в критичних хвилинах; з'ясовуйте їм, наше становище. Станьте ближче до козака, щоби своїм авторітетом вплинути на його культурно. Освідомлюйте його з нашим великим минулим, — із нашою історією. Неграмотних научайте рідньому слову. Закладайте співучі гуртки. В пісні козак найде відпочинок і розумну розвагу; душею торкнеться він далекої минувшини нашої батьківщини. Хай із змучених його грудей понесеться наша краса-пісня аж на стени нашої неньки-України! „Пісня не вмірає"! Її страждучий гомін понесеться до наших рідних хат, до наших батьків, матерів, братів, сестер. Вони почують, і на її голос спішитимуть помогти нам розбити страшного тирана нашої волі, нашої незалежности! —

Вояки-учителі! Візьміться щиро за працю. Сійте чисте зерно на нашій рідній ниві.

До праці! Завдання велике і важне!

Культурно-просвітний відділ

І. Запоріжської Стріл. Дивізії.

УВАГА. Всі бажаючи бути співробітниками Культ.-просвітн. відд.; І. Запор. Стр. Дивізії на місцях повинен зголоситись в відділі. —

Матеріял історичний, (сьогочасний) белетристичний, а також різні малюнки та нові пісні з життя козацтва, просимо надсилати до Культурно-просвітнього відділу (при штабі дивізії). —

29 Leaflet with an appeal "TO SOLDIER-TEACHERS!" in the army to devote time to educate their fellows.
TsNB.

НАКАЗ Ч 38

26 Вересня 1919 року.

Об'їжаючи по службовим справам повіт, я нігде не знаходив не тілько у Сільських, але і у Волостних Комісарів посилаемих в повіт Наказів, Распоряджень, Оголошень, Відозв і т. и. як мійсьцевої так і Центральної Влади Української Народньої Республіки.

Вважаю таке явище не допустимим, НАКАЗУЮ всім Волостним і Сільським Комісарам Могилів-Подільського Повіту, з одержанням від Мійсьцевої і Центральної Влади Української Народньої Республіки Наказів, Распоряджень, Об'яв, Відозв і т. и. обов'язково підшивати по одному примірнику до діла, по одному вивішувати в *помешканню Комісара* (волост. Народ. Управа, збірні хати, а також на людних місцях села) для відома населення, а решту—роздавати населенню.

Крім того НАКАЗУЮ: всі Накази, Распорядження, Відозви, Оголошення і т. и. негайно по одержанню їх прочитувати населенню на сходах і з'ясовувати прочитане, коли цього буде вимагати справа.

Про вражіння яке робить на населення то чи иакше распорядження Влади, а також про те, як населення відноситься до прочитанних йому Распорядження і Наказів кождий раз доносити мені, складаючи протокола.

Повітком'сар ХРИСТИЧ.

30 "Order no. 38." Leaflet with orders concerning the display of government publications, issued by an official who observed during a tour that no propaganda or notices were being displayed in government offices.
Arkhiv druku.

С украинского-.

БРАТЬЯ СЕЛЯНЕ.-

овольно спать пора встать,пора добывать свободу.Мы проспали хлеб
роспали скот.Коммунистическая неволя ложится тяжелым ярмом на на-
их отцов и матерей.Кровавые слезы заставляют нас итти на послед-
ий решительный бой с врагами трудового народа.Вперед братья.Не ду
айте а делайте.Вся Украины пылает восстаниями.Врага мы безусловно
азобьем.Но не думайте выезжать на чужих шеях,ибо это стыдно/позор/
дите к нам,помогайте.Берите оружие и патроны и идите с нами.За на
и сила за нами,свобода и правда святая.

Политический Отдел при Штабе Повстанческой Дивизии.
/Печатано на шапирографе/-.

Отрывок из неизвестной про
кламации.Писан карандашом
на регистрационной карточ
ке КПБУ.-

.......не будет сам хозяином в своей хате.Пусть же действительно
процветает независимость нации,свобода и братство-эти символы,на-
ертанные на нашем знамени.
ДА ЗДРАВСТВУЕТ СВОБОДА НАЦИИ.

олитический Отдел Штаба Повстанцев,-

Набросок некролога,повиди
мому с целью издания листо
вки.-

-o Ooo-

2 сего сентября в бою погиб от вражеской пули старший доктор пол
а И.З.Патерило.Происходит Ив.Сн.из бедной крестьянской семьи.Еще с
младенчества остался он круглым сиротой и только благодаря своему со
ственному труду и энергии смог он одолеть тяжелую медицинскую нау
у.На национально-общественной арене,еще совсем молодым человеком,
н выступает с начала революции когда он с особенной энергией боре
ся за национальный вопрос на фронте,в Эрзеруме,а потом в своем род
ом селе.Работая здесь еще в качестве ветеринарного помощника он поль
уется полным уважением и любовью своих односельчан.Когда же запыла
огонь восстания Ивановича как его звали крестьяне встал в первых
ядах повстанцев.Назначенный на должность доктора он не ограничил-
я исключительно медицинской работой и с винтовкой в руках бывал пе
вым в рядах бойцов.Во время последнего фатального боя,он с несколь
ими казаками прорвался к вражескому пулемету и захватил его..но в это
т момент пули положили конец его светлым стремлениям.
Казаки и селяне.
Ряды наши уменьшились на одного честного,храброго рыцаря,на одно
о верного сына своего народа.Но ряды наши от этого не дрогнут, а
е больше сплотятся и дружно станут на нерушимую борьбу за те идеи
оторые навеки похоронены в могиле нашего усопшего товарища.Спи же
спокойно верный сын Украины.За твою смерть мы жестоко отплатим ве-
ным врагам нашего народа.Вечная память тебе-честный рыцарь и друг

Подписей нет.Писано рукой Секретаря Политотдела Пов-
танческой гр.Оп ра.

Товарищество.Помни и не забывай своего постановления которое
осит.Постановляем:
Раздел 2-й.
I. Придерживаться в войске самой строгой революционной дисциплины
дисциплинированность считать за измену трудовому народу и карать

31 Page from Bolshevik collection of warlord leaflet transcriptions translated into Russian.
TsDAVO f. 3158 op 2 sprava 7.

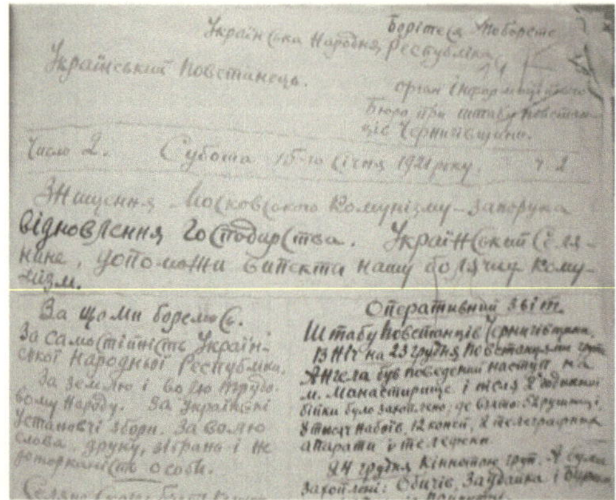

Українська Народня Республика

Боріться — поборете

Український Повстанець.

Орган Інформаційного Бюро при штабі повстанців Чернигівщини.

Число 2. Субота 15-го січня 1921 року.

Знищення московського комунізму — запорука відновлення господарства.

За що ми боремося.

За самостійність Української Народньої Республики. За землю і волю трудовому народу. За Українські Установчі Збори. За волю слова, друку, зібрання і недоторканість особи.

Оперативний звіт.

32 Handwritten copy of the newspaper, *Ukrainian Partisan*, the organ of the Information Bureau of the Chernihiv Provincial Insurrectionary Headquarters. Issue no. 2, Saturday, 15 January 1921.
Full version, TsDASBU f. 6 sprava 71538 no 15-16.

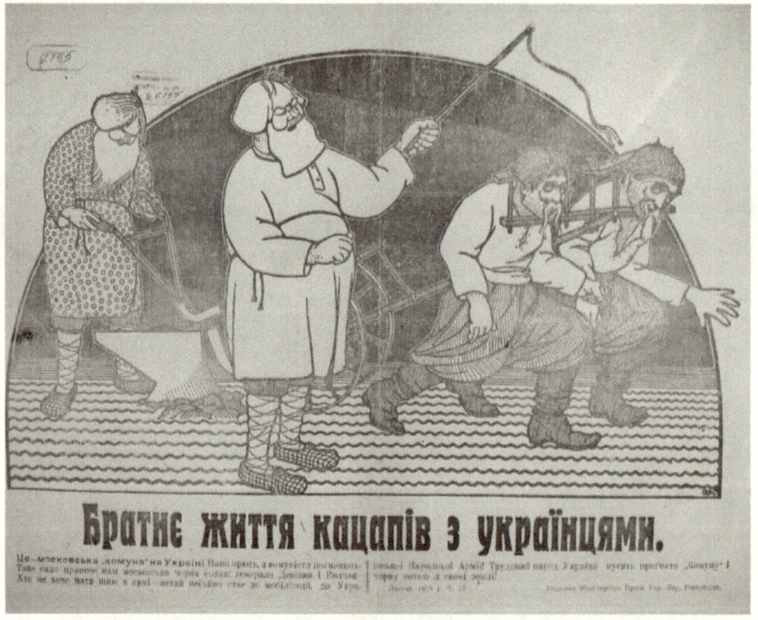

33 UNR Poster (1919): "The fraternal life of Russkies with Ukrainians." "This is Muscovite 'Commune-ism' in Ukraine. Our people plough and the communists sik them on. Russian Black Hundreds, Generals Denikin and Kolchak will bring the same. Whoever doesn't want their neck in a yoke – immediately volunteer in the Ukrainian National Army. The working people of Ukraine must chase 'commune-ism' and the Black Hundreds from their land."
TsNB (Vyddil plakat).

Chapter Four

The Bolsheviks

Representing between ninety and ninety-five of Ukraine's three hundred *soviets*, Ukraine's Bolsheviks seized power in Kharkiv on 12 (25) December 1917. They set up a government backed by approximately 4,500 troops and Red Guards, of whom half had arrived from Moscow the previous week. Of the twelve members of the newly formed People's Secretariat, four were Ukrainians and four were Ukrainian-born Germans. This People's Secretariat claimed to be the true government of the Ukrainian National Republic – that is, the five provinces that the Provisional Government had allotted to the Central Rada in June 1917. Bolsheviks in the remaining provinces remained formally under Petrograd. The Kharkiv People's Secretariat arrived in Kyiv on 30 January (12 February) 1918, from where the Germans evicted them in March. That month, with the signing of the Treaty of Brest-Litovsk, the Bolsheviks were required to recognize all of the provinces claimed by the Central Rada as an independent state. They then placed all *soviets* in Ukraine under the authority of their local party affiliate there. The order amalgamating these *soviets* under one local Bolshevik centre explicitly avoided legitimating Ukraine's Soviet republic in national terms. The entity was defined as a "soviet republic on Ukrainian territory," within which *soviets* in the previously excluded Ukrainian provinces had to unite, the better to face the German threat.

In November 1918 in Moscow, Lenin and Stalin decided to create a second Soviet government for Ukraine in Kursk. When Stalin arrived in Kursk on 19 November, he told the local leaders: "The Central Committee of the RCP has decided to create a Soviet government – headed by Piatakov."[1] Ukraine's Bolsheviks duly proclaimed the Ukrainian Socialist Soviet Republic in January 1919 and created a Council of Peoples Commissars for it. Its core territory, in northeast Ukraine, by August 1919 had shrunk to 300 square kilometres centred on Chernihiv. In the west and southeast, the borders shifted back and forth, reflecting the progress of the war with the Directory, the Whites, and Makhno's anarchists. Formally, by 1920, the Bolsheviks ruled all of what had been tsarist Ukraine. In reality, the guerrilla war led by Makhno and continued by the *otamans* raged through to 1923, and central control was tenuous outside the big cities. The Bolshevik government's bureaucracy, unlike that of the national governments, included large numbers of Russians and Jews born outside Ukraine.

The Medium

In 1917, Ukraine's Bolsheviks controlled the Agitation Section attached to the Executive Committee of Kyiv's Soviet, which they did not yet dominate. Once in power, as of January 1918, they began confiscating presses and paper stocks and centralizing control over the press, archives, and libraries. The records of the Agitation Section of Bolshevik Ukraine's first Central Executive Committee are presumed lost. During these first months of Bolshevik rule the local branch of the censorship and propaganda section of Russia's Military Revolutionary Soviet (*VoenRevSovet*) published materials for Ukraine. Its records are in Moscow archives. While retreating in the spring of 1918, the Bolsheviks stripped Ukraine of whatever they could, including presses and publishing materials. In Surazk in northeastern Ukraine, for instance, local Bolsheviks rebuilt a bridge damaged during the German offensive in order to transport the town's entire paper factory to Russia. They brought in 160 rail cars to do it. When local Ukrainian authorities moved to stop them, the Bolsheviks threatened to blow up the factory.[2]

Throughout the Hetman's rule, when they were illegal, Ukraine's Bolsheviks published using underground presses. They also distributed wagonloads of materials published in Moscow, which dozens of agitators brought in almost daily. Ukraine's police had neither the manpower nor the means to keep surveillance over those hundreds of agents. Operations were carried out by the Agitprop section of the army staff in Kursk, which had subsections in Kyiv and Kharkov. By July, Bolshevik papers were being sold openly in Kharkiv.[3] Agitators entered Ukraine either illegally, with forged papers, or on trains assigned to diplomatic personnel, which were not subject to inspection. Some of these trains included as many as three wagonloads of such "personnel."[4] A Ukrainian report from October 1918 records thirty-one people in a diplomatic delegation that was supposed to consist of one person. According to secret police reports, twenty well-financed agitators were arriving daily through the border station at Kursk, and they began their work while still riding the trains. In November another report explained: "Kharkiv is now overflowing with Bolsheviks among whom are entire organizations of agitators with literature and cash."[5]

On forming their second government in December 1918, the Bolsheviks recentralized publishing and propaganda, and just as in Russia, the local branch of the secret police (Cheka) was tasked with closing anti-Bolshevik publications. In 1919 the Bolsheviks folded all civilian presses and their distribution networks into the Kharkiv Provincial Agency of the Moscow-based *TsentroDruk* (Russian: *TsentIzdat*) – that summer renamed All Ukrainian Publishers (*VseVydav*). The following year, they subordinated this organization to the All Ukrainian Central Executive Committee. Distribution was assigned to a single central unit (*UkrTsenrah*). Centralization was carried out over several months. Co-op presses were not nationalized until mid-1920.[6]

The CPU re-formed its agitation section on 22 December 1918, while still based in Kursk, and six days before it publicly declared the formation of Ukraine's second Soviet government.[7] In February 1919 the section was renamed the People's Commissariat for Soviet Propaganda and assigned all publishing and distribution tasks; meanwhile, Russia's VoenRevSovet continued to function in Ukraine.[8] The final paragraph of the original decision establishing this department was marked secret. It stipulated that the commissariat would receive its directives directly from the CPU Central Committee and that all heads of local departments were to be members of local party committees. The version released for distribution that same day, accordingly, did not include this last paragraph. Concealing the reality of subordination to the party, the commissariat's published organizational statute claimed that all personnel were to be appointed by the Council of People's Commissars (*Sovnarkom*) – a supposedly elected *soviet* organ that few at the time realized was controlled by the party's Central Committee.[9]

The following month, printed propaganda was classified as military supplies; this gave couriers priority on trains. The commissariat was replaced that May by an Agitation and Propaganda Department within the CPU Central Committee. Mainly non-Ukrainians were in charge of Bolshevik Ukraine's propaganda sections.[10] In 1919 these were Fedor Artem, Georgii Piatakov, and David Erde. Among the principal authors of anti-Ukrainian propaganda who can be identified were the Ukrainian-born Russian Piatakov, the Russian Maksimilian Saveleev, the Ukrainian Jew Ivan Kulyk, and the Ukrainian Evhen Kasianenko (pen name Larik). As far as can be established, most of the ethnic Ukrainians in the various propaganda agencies were rank-and-file agitators.[11] That spring, the commissariat's leaders projected 215 personnel for each provincial commissariat unit. Of these, twenty-five were instructors who did the walking and talking and sixteen were watchmen and janitors. Twenty-five personnel (including five instructors) were allotted to each district and four (one instructor) to each county. Besides preaching, instructors were expected to mobilize all of the local literate people and instruct them to serve as ancillary instructors among the illiterate (Illus. 37).[12]

A few months after party leaders established this system, Oleksandr Shumsky, the Ukrainian left-SR Education Commissar, submitted a critique pointing out that, through its economic function as sole legal supplier of paper, the Propaganda Commission had *de facto* control over everything published, including literary and cultural texts that were not supposed to be within its purview. He recommended that all publishing be placed under his commissariat's control. Had that happened, all Bolshevik propaganda would have been *de facto* under Ukrainian left-SR rather than Russian Bolshevik control.[13]

Although some Bolshevik-published materials were in Ukrainian, the pro-Bolshevik Ukrainian left-SRs in 1919 nevertheless viewed that ostensibly "Ukrainian press," especially the newspapers, as part of a "huge Russification machine," because the materials in Ukrainian were almost all translated from Russian originals. Released days, if not weeks later, they were of little interest to anyone. This observation was made by Ukrainian left-SR Vasyl Blakytny in an undated latter to Agitprop in which he recommended the creation of a committee on Ukrainization. Perhaps in response to this, in January 1920, Ukraine's leaders ordered the creation of a Section for Work among the Peasants, with its own bureaucracy and agitators. Formed just after the appearance of Lenin's conciliatory "Letter to the Workers and Peasants of Ukraine," the section resembled its Russian counterpart. It was to have branches attached to the party provincial committees responsible for generating propaganda and all governmental work in villages. Its mandate specified that its staff would have to know and work in Ukrainian and that all of its literature would have to be in Ukrainian and marked "for the village" when published. Because of the Polish offensive, the section did not begin work in the central and western provinces until July of that year, when Blakytny became its head. By then it had 358 personnel. It was incorporated as a subsection of Agitprop in 1922.[14]

Besides the Peasant Section, Agitprop, and the army's propaganda department, all of which were centralized bodies, agitators were attached to various commissariats and agencies, such as the "Section for Town Agitation and Propaganda," and propagandized their respective activities to various audiences. One these, as an example, was Ukraine's Food Procurement Commissariat. In the spring of 1920, one of its instructions for agitators specified what was likely true for all similar agencies – that all *soviet* work was by definition political: "Every assembly, speech and meeting must be turned into a political meeting [where the focus will move] from issues of food procurement to class struggle and from questions of politics to procurement practice."[15]

An unsigned and undated memorandum from Kharkiv province, likely written in early 1920, was probably an attachment to the Peasant Section's founding mandate. Written in Russian, apparently by Russians, the document included remarks reflecting the position of the CPU as an organization foreign to Ukraine that no native organization would have had to tell its personnel. "A Guide for Organizers Sent to Do Party Work among the Peasants of Ukraine" began by noting: "It is necessary to approach the Ukrainian peasant carefully, taking into consideration his psychology, economic circumstances, historical background, cultural level and attitude to religion and the social revolution." Agitators/instructors were to be intimately familiar with Ukraine's particularities and to realize that "Ukrainians are often implacable advocates of independentist opinion." For that reason, agitators would have to disseminate their communist ideas very carefully, as middle-stratum peasants in particular distrusted communism. There followed instructions on how to present policies. In particular, agitators were to emphasize that communes would be totally voluntary and that middle-stratum peasants would be well treated.[16] A similar instructional guide, written in Russian, was issued at the end of the year, when the Ukrainian left-SRs still had places in the government and when the still legal UCP was demanding a separate party and army for Ukraine. Titled "Instructions to all Provincial and District Revkoms," it specified that differences in attitudes regarding the political relationship between the Ukrainian and Russian republics were to be treated as secondary to the main topic of the time, which was how to combat the "international counter-revolution." It recommended that all soviet workers "under the threat of strict responsibility" adopt a "very cautious [*berezhnoe*] attitude to Ukrainian language and culture and support all Ukrainian national issues, otherwise they would be immediately replaced."[17]

Bolshevik leaders gave much thought to propaganda. Initially, they distributed their materials however they could. This included randomly giving any and all demobilized soldiers as many materials as they could carry. To forestall their using the leaflets and pamphlets for cigarette paper, Lenin ordered they also be issued with old calendars for that purpose – good for as many as 365 smokes.[18] Centralization eventually resulted in leaders issuing detailed instructions concerning propaganda to ensure that delegated agents delivered a standard message everywhere (Illus. 34–5). That control applied to oral and text messages, and to matters related to health, lice, cigarettes, and liquor, as well as to politics and economics. The top leaders identified issues at Politburo meetings. They also often formulated the underlying ideas, which were then passed down to specialists in given areas, who elaborated on them. The detailed expositions were passed down in turn to lower-level officials, who used them to phrase their articles and leaflets.[19] Instructions included lists of slogans. For example, a short guide outlining how to explain the Bolshevik seizure of power (which Bolsheviks called "the October Revolution") explained that that event had involved "the workers and peasants of Russia under the leadership of their party, the RCP, taking power." The terms "Russian [*Russkii*]" workers and "workers of Russia [*Rossiia*]," were used interchangeably. This implied that all workers in the Russian empire were Russians. The Bolshevik state was to be presented as a victim that, from its first day in power, had had to defend itself against the entire "world bourgeoisie" while coping with blockades, shortages, and breakdowns. Because of war and disastrous conditions, "soviet power" had been unable to meet all workers' needs.

Also printed were short pamphlets explaining terms from the Bolshevik perspective – for instance, that socialism was an order without rich or poor, under which all the means of production worked for the common good. For the time being, however, there had to exist a "dictatorship of the working poor." These booklets described Republican Russia as a voluntary federal union of regions with the right to speak their own languages and practise their own traditions. A soviet republic, unlike a bourgeois republic, did not allow the rich to vote in the *soviets*. Descriptions of how elected deputies in *soviets* controlled administration and public functions made no mention of the party. The pamphlets avoided mentioning the party.[20]

An example from June 1919 illustrates how a propaganda campaign was launched. Ukraine's Bolshevik leaders that month considered how to explain away the abolition of the Ukrainian SSR, after having insisted for two years that they supported the "right of nations to self-determination." Ukraine's leaders had a bureaucratic interest in territorial autonomy and that May had argued against centralization. But by the end of that month, once central leaders had decided to centralize, they were no longer discussing whether their republic should be dissolved but only how best to do it.[21] Denikin's offensive from the southeast and the Ukrainian offensive from the west, which had expelled the Bolsheviks from most of Ukraine in August, cut short these plans. Even so, the minutes of the meeting of late June, during which top leaders discussed how to publicly justify the abrupt turn, provide an example of how a propaganda campaign was planned.

The ethnic Ukrainian Hryhoriy Petrovsky, in his status as representative of the central government, opened the meeting by declaring that the "joining" would have be to carried out with maximum care and careful tactics so that "we not place ourselves in sharp conflict with nationalist parties in soviets and the nationalist inclined mass." He added that the propaganda campaign should focus on economic and military issues and that force would have to be used against those Borotbists who would not go along. "We must be as flexible as possible so we can change our tack [*peremenit front*] in 24 hours if upcoming [provincial] assemblies adopt different resolutions." One local official present said that the task was "an unexpected flying bomb"; another, however, pointed out that in Katerynoslav and Kharkiv the issue had long been thought about. Others present asked whether in upcoming provincial conferences the change was to be discussed or imposed and noted that, since the new policy represented a radical change, the relevant propaganda had better begin immediately so that enemies would be unable to exploit the issue. In reply to accusations that the dissolution of the Ukrainian republic represented a sharp reversal of national policies, Petrovsky retorted: "There is no reversal. This is a continuation of CC CPU policy." Speakers suggested that it would be best to start in the southeastern provinces. In Poltava and Kyiv provinces the campaign would have to be slower and more systematic, and even more so west of the Dnipro, where there would undoubtedly be a struggle. The campaign would have to avoid "irritating chauvinist attitudes" and leaving the impression that "the Muscovites came and annulled Ukraine." Insofar as those present imagined that "chauvinist sympathies among peasants had disappeared," and that the idea of a tie with Moscow was now strong, they felt they could start their campaign by first convening conferences with pro-Bolshevik villagers, who would then convince the "non-party peasantry." One participant thought: "The objective conditions for the inevitable joining here in Ukraine are fully ripe." The propaganda argument would be that it was impossible to create the Soviet order without union with Russia. Notwithstanding Petrovsky's opinion, some viewed the Borotbist threat as minimal.[22] A leaflet announcing the decision thus explained that it was necessary to "fuse into one single indestructible union" all Russian-ruled republics in order to counter the plans of "the imperialists" to divide workers from peasants and turn them into "the slaves of western European capital." In light of the spreading revolutions in Hungary and Bavaria, the moment was at hand (Doc. 260).[23]

Another example of how the Bolsheviks organized propaganda is provided by their campaign against Nestor Makhno. Local Bolshevik officials had condemned him by the end of March 1919; central leaders decided to break their alliance with him in mid-May. Trotsky categorized him as an enemy at the end of the month and instructed Rakovskii to launch a press campaign against him, "otherwise [our] liquidation of the Makhno regime will not be understood." Trotsky then penned an unequivocal condemnation of Makhno in June 1919 that characterized him as an anti-Bolshevik anarchist.[24] In May 1920 a two-page analysis titled "Thesis on the Makhno Regime [*Makhnovshchina*] and Its Elimination," by Viacheslav Molotov and Maksimilian Saveleev, elaborated the main ideas of the anti-Makhno campaign at that time. As a movement initially comprised mainly of wealthy peasants, it was a tool of international imperialism whose goal was to disrupt soviet power from within and to smooth the way for the restoration of capitalism. By 1920, because rich peasants were neutral towards the Bolsheviks and no longer supported him, Makhno had had to rely more on terror, anti-Semitism, and criminal gangs to control territory. There followed a two-page "Thesis on Agitation in the Struggle against the Makhno Regime," which included a short history and socio-economic analysis, followed by two pages of suggested anti-Makhno slogans and lecture themes, divided by subject, for agitators to use. These included accusations that Makhno promoted drunkenness, demoralized the young, built a Great Wall between town and village, starved workers, disrupted communications, and interfered with the importation of fuel and manufactured goods.[25]

Once leaders had made decisions and elaborated arguments, secretaries summarized these now party positions in one-page "Agitator Notes" (*pamiatka ahitatora*) for local activists. One of these sheets, from Poltava province in late 1920, made the expected points: Soviet power protected the "entire working people," Revkoms were only temporary, and there would be no requisitions from poor or middle-stratum peasants. In addition, the notes stressed that what had been taken from the rich was for "Ukrainian cities" and the "Ukrainian Red army," although no such entity existed. Agitators that year were instructed to emphasize, contrary to fact and earlier leaflets, that "under no circumstances will grain be exported beyond Ukraine's borders." Earlier hostility to Bolshevik rule was to be explained to people not as a reaction to erroneous policies since revised, but as an unexplained change in attitudes: "The earlier middle peasant hostility towards Soviet authority was undoubtedly an aberration [*nesomnenno zabluzhdenie*] that should no longer exist, because the middle peasants now recognize that soviet authority defends their interests."[26] In Akhtyrsk district, Kharkiv province, instructions from 1919 specified that agitators should emphasize the following themes: that the Red Army opposed capitalism, that national quarrels were not in the peasants' interest, that Bolsheviks were to be the only leading force in the local soviets, that party membership was voluntary, and that world revolution was imminent.[27] When possible, courses were organized for agitators and instructions were issued on all subjects ranging from foreign policy to dealing with unions behind enemy lines and the mechanics of spring sowing.[28] Since for its members the party was always right, agitators who realized that peasants who supported Soviet power simultaneously hated Jewish commissars, the Cheka, and communes, had to make circumlocutions in their reports: "The peasants' and some of the urban proletariats' understanding of these issues is very mixed up."

Bolshevik leaders devoted much energy to creating a professional central cadre of propagandists. One such initiative involved special courses established in 1918 by the Red Army in Moscow. Another involved courses established by the Ukrainian section of Petrograd's Party. Both centres recruited already leftist-inclined individuals from all parts of Ukraine and trained them to expound on the virtues and logical nature of Marxism and the Marxist ideal. The training included decorum and etiquette. Russians in Ukraine, for instance, were notorious for their profuse use of expletives, whereas Ukrainians rarely used profanities in everyday speech. An eyewitness who met such a group of Ukrainian Bolshevik agitators near Poltava was surprised when he realized that they never used profanities – something that would have ingratiated them with Ukrainians, especially the literate and educated.[29]

By 1920, party officials were issuing very detailed instructions to agitators, local offices, and activists that aimed at controlling the messenger as much as the message. Bolshevik agitators and lecturers were to visit settlements with literature, whether they had been asked or not. The instructions detailed distribution and financing practices at local levels and told agitators to

> discover ways to prevent workers and peasants from using journals and newspapers as paper and [to instead] read and keep them. For this it is necessary to have an appropriate complement of lecturers from the local party committee that would from time to time visit villages factories and enterprises and read newspapers aloud to comrade workers and peasants, explaining the contents to them, thus, creating among the audience interest to do individual reading.

A pamphlet written for couriers included twenty-one specific transit and delivery instructions. These detailed when they were to appear at railway stations and where they were to collect their materials. Couriers were to witness the packaging of those materials, sign for them, and follow detailed travel instructions (Illus. 34). Each instructor was to keep a log to record loads, destinations, and departure times. They were told where to post their materials, how to prove that they had indeed posted them, and how to ascertain whether earlier posted materials were still posted. They were to post two copies of a newspaper and two copies of a poster on each side of the wagons they were riding at an appropriate height for reading. They were to post materials in all the stations they passed through and get confirmation from the local stationmaster that they had done so. They were to report their itineraries, provide proof of arrival at all stops and destinations, declare what they had disseminated at those destinations, and bring back copies of local publications. On return, those whose tallies of returned materials did not correspond to their original receipt invoices were subject to court martial. In April 1921, the Central Committee was still instructing agitators in newspaper articles to ensure that they used good glue and that hung posters were shielded from the elements, away from direct sunlight but not in shaded corners. If there were too few copies of a newspaper, agitators were to make handwritten summaries of contents for posting and to forward those summaries to editors, who were then to publish them and distribute copies, so that others could make more handwritten copies.[30] Instructors had the authority to mobilize all local party members to travel to villages as agitators. Instructors who failed to organize would be treated as saboteurs.[31] Agents, besides having to attend all courses available, and being obliged to return regular reports often, had to fill out detailed questionnaires about their work and to make recommendations for future work.[32] A small printed form about the size of a hand issued by the Agitation Sections of provincial executive committees in late 1920 indicates that the propaganda process was about as automated as it could be. The form contained spaces for a number, agitator name, topic, and destination, as well as a note at the bottom specifying that the agitator had to report within two days of return about his mission. It also stated that he was fully responsible for executing the order.[33]

An undated policy brief intended for Shumsky, possibly written in early 1920, listed agitation tactics intended to facilitate requisitioning and to expand influence generally. Agitators were to focus on practical matters and were not to directly express any political positions or make decisions, but only to provide information to existing local agencies. This included giving rewards to loyalists, being tactful when dealing with illegal trading and home brewing, and interacting directly only with local sympathizers when dealing with the "consequences of the diseases of the Soviet system." These chosen sympathizers would then convey official explanations to the rest of the population. This would give the illusion that the ideas did not emanate from the party, thereby making them more credible. Agitators were to carefully study the sympathies of the majority and not openly condemn speculators or Whites if they supported Bolshevik rule. They were to appeal to local Bolshevik troops for help only as a last resort.[34]

Rakovskii wrote the first reference guide for village requisition agents, which included twenty-two points specifying their duties. These points included setting a personal example, viewing themselves as propagandists rather than grain expropriators, and explaining that peasants had to give grain in return for the land the government gave them, otherwise workers would go hungry and not produce the manufactured goods that peasants wanted. Agitators had to stipulate that delivery totals were not negotiable. They were to avoid discussions about communes or God and to emphasize that Ukrainian grain was not destined for Russia. There followed ten pages of text summarizing Bolshevik positions on key subjects such as *soviets* and poor peasants' committees and providing details of requisition regulations. There was no mention of the RCP.[35]

The well-preserved provincial records of the Peasant Section contain detailed instructions written in Russian. These were labelled "circular letters" and covered not only specific subjects but also rhetorical techniques. The first such letter of one series was issued in Katerynoslav in the spring of 1920. It claimed that armed opposition to Bolshevik rule stemmed primarily from an "incorrect presentation" of Bolshevik aims and that where party work was done well, the peasants, even in difficult moments, remained "revolutionary." The instructions list divided the population by class, referred to fighting partisans as bandits, and called for the formation of poor peasants' committees. They also outlined organizational and administrative tasks. The second letter specified that, even in their spare time, agitators were to talk to and meet with inhabitants, share their work, and try to turn local reading rooms previously established by prewar Ukrainian Enlightenment Societies (*prosvita*) into party agitation centres. Agitators were not to talk condescendingly about abstract theoretical matters; rather, they were to discuss practical daily problems in simple terms. Letter no. 6 amounted to a short course on advertising techniques. It specified that all agitators had to be intimately familiar with peasant life and learn as much about the locale as possible before arriving. Before giving speeches, agitators were to determine how their audience was divided by age, status, and gender and structure the presentation accordingly, making it short, simple, practical, and entertaining. Letter no. 11 specified that besides the church, agitators should target and endeavour to destroy the *prosvita* organizations. The head of the Poltava province department that year, Iuriy Kotsiubynsky, specified that all local agitators, party members, and poor peasants were to join the *prosvita*, thereby taking over the organization from within.[36] Letter no. 12 addressed how to explain the Polish invasion of 1920. Letter no. 62, from January 1921, specified that the best way to deal with partisans was to ensure that the poor peasant committees carried out requisitions against wealthy peasants (*kulaks*). A note specified: "The agitator should do this work with tact and skillfully, not personally, but through the resolutions of the Poor Peasant Committee."[37]

Until 1921, as much as 95 per cent of all published materials in Bolshevik Ukraine were devoted to political agitation and propaganda. Thereafter, the figure dropped to 10 per cent. As of 1921, 70 per cent of all production was in Ukrainian and intended for villages, 17 per cent was in Russian for towns, and 13 per cent was bilingual. That year, publishers in Moscow were obliged to send 7 per cent of their periodical production and 10 per cent of all other publications to Ukraine, while Ukraine was expected to send 10 per cent of its total output to Russia – to persons or audience unspecified.[38]

The bulk of government-published materials during the first months of 1919 were produced by the publishing unit of the Political Directorate of Soviet Ukraine's War Commissariat. Not all presses were nationalized yet, but by July 1919 the party had established a formal monopoly over all publishing and had militarized the entire industry. Nothing could be printed, and no materials could be purchased or obtained, without the permission of the Publishing Bureau of the Commissariat of Education and the Paper Division (*Bumagotdel*) of Ukraine's Council of People's Commissars – a subsection of its Russian parent body. This included governmental decrees and instructions. Within days of occupying a settlement, the Bolsheviks would issue leaflets instructing the inhabitants to register, among other items, all writing materials. No publishers were to accept orders without permission, and those who did not comply were threatened with court martial and confiscation (Illus. 39). Even notebooks had to be registered on pain of confiscation and were not to be sold on the open market.[39] By 1920, as a result of fuel and paper shortages, as well as anti-Bolshevik sentiment, so many people were tearing down posters, along with the boards and fences they were attached to, that local and central officials issued leaflets warning that those caught would be considered enemies of the revolution and tried by court martial (Illus. 40–2). In May 1920 at least one Bolshevik provincial secretary instructed his subordinates not to distribute printed materials directly, but to deposit them in libraries and reading rooms so that after they were read, if they were read at all, they would not end up as cigarette smoke.[40] Bolshevik publishing statistics are neither accurate nor complete and do not necessarily include distribution totals by destination. Nonetheless, they can give some idea of the degree of media saturation in Bolshevik-controlled territories (see Appendix).

By one estimate, as of December 1920 there were 1,029 presses of all kinds in Ukraine (excluding Volyn and Podillia provinces); of these, 727 were in Kyiv, Kharkiv, and Odessa provinces. But of 24 rotary presses (13 in Kyiv, 6 in Odessa, 4 in Kharkiv, 1 in Katerynoslav), no more than 5 or 6 were functioning because they lacked the necessary huge rolls of paper. In addition, only 25, at most, of Ukraine's 43 typesetting machines were operational because their matrices were broken and could not be repaired or replaced. Worn parts, poor-quality paper, and diluted ink sometimes resulted in illegible publications.[41] Another set of figures, from October 1921, reports 872 presses of all kinds in all of Ukraine, with the greatest number in Kharkiv and Kyiv provinces (136 and 126 respectively).[42] Apparently, the most productive printing establishments, until they were taken over by the Bolsheviks in April 1920, were Ukraine's two dozen or so co-op presses, which published millions of copies of literature of all kinds.[43]

By 1921 almost all print shops were under the jurisdiction of a poligraphy department attached to the Council of Ministers (*poligraficheskii otdel*). That year the department was formally in charge of 12,825 personnel, all but 700 of whom were directly involved in printing. The most personnel were in Kyiv (2,528), Kharkiv (2,336), and Odessa (2,044); the least, in Oleksandrivsk (343 – today Zaporizhzhia), Podilsk (387), and Kremenchuh (431). Of 4,819 typesetters, 85 worked typesetting machines.[44] By 1922, all presses and the entire distribution system were under the control of the secret police (GPU), and all publications from the years 1918 to 1922, except for Bolshevik and academic works, had been declared illegal and not to be bought or sold without permission. That same year, apparently, all of these nominally illegal publications were still being bought and sold *en masse* at bazaars and markets – something the GPU was ordered to stop.[45]

All paper mills were nationalized in February 1919, but neither Ukraine's Publishing Bureau nor central publishers controlled the supply of paper, which was in the hands of the Moscow-based Supreme National Economic Council (*Sovnarhoz*) through its GlavBumaga.[46] Private stocks were subject to seizure, no paper could be purchased legally in stores, and Ukrainian paper orders had to be sent to the Promburo of Ukraine's Sovnarhoz. However, the archives contain order forms from Ukraine's Central Committee to private shops and co-ops for office supplies that listed paper.[47] The Bolsheviks had centralized in order to control and rationalize available resources, but this system created other problems. Theft was one, overlap in jurisdictions was another. Also, local officials often had to wait as long as six months for permission from the centre to acquire supplies or withdraw them from local stocks. They were forbidden to buy on local markets, although, as noted, they did.[48]

Total production fell. The first reference to smaller press runs is from February 1919, when all Kyiv papers cut back production. In October 1919 the paper allotment to provincial presses was cut by 30 per cent and allotments to ministries by 50 per cent. By August 1920, officials were being instructed not to publish separate posters or leaflets announcing meetings or performances and to run such advertisements only in newspapers. In March 1921 a special decree instructed the ministry in charge of paper collection and distribution (*Glavbumag*), to reserve 25 per cent of its paper for the army.[49] In June 1919, officials in Kharkiv reported that they had 1,083 tons of paper but needed 353,000. In June 1919, Ukraine's Paper Department (*Bumazhnyi Otdel*), the agency responsible for paper, apparently had no contact with the central Moscow office and was proposing to re-establish links with Ukraine's prewar suppliers, Finland and Estonia, as local production was insufficient to cover needs.[50] According to the department, that summer five working mills were producing 296 tons monthly (of which 108 was cigarette paper), and another five mills then under repair were expected to produce another 502 tons by the winter (32.5 tons being cigarette paper). The following month, it seems that Kyiv had restored rail links with Moscow, and it received a shipment of 632 tons.[51] As of spring 1919, half of Ukraine's twenty-one mills were working, but none of them at more than 60 per cent capacity.[52] In 1920, the 14 of Ukraine's 23 paper mills still functioning produced 6,374 tons. Ukraine's state publishers had no more than 90 tons in stock, however, and needed 1,083 tons.[53] By March 1921 the number of functioning mills had fallen to ten.[54]

In August 1919 in the town of Malyn, the last functioning paper mill in the Kyiv region burned down; it would remain out of commission for over a year. Besides producing a small amount of writing paper, this mill had been the only supplier of cigarette paper, not only for Ukraine but for all of Russia. Furthermore, it had already been shut down for ten months in 1918 due to lack of fuel. That same month, the only paper mill in Podillia province reported that it no longer had any paper.[55] The consequences were serious – millions of men were using leaflets and newspapers to roll their cigarettes, wrap their rations, and wipe their bottoms, and all of this severely limited the dissemination of information. By 1920, all governments were using cigarette paper for correspondence and publishing some newspapers and posters on thin, soft cardboard. An incomplete Bolshevik report from April 1920 covering eight paper mills estimated their combined total monthly production at 740 tons and their total production capacity at 813 tons – half of what officials deemed necessary. That December, two months after the Bolsheviks reoccupied Podillia province with its six printing shops, officials in Vinnytsia reported that they had just under three tons of paper in stock and were using 181 pounds daily to publish the town's two newspapers. With the army regularly requisitioning stocks, there was no paper to publish anything except newspapers.[56] In the Crimea, the price of 36 pounds (1 pood) of newsprint had risen to 80,000 roubles in 1921, from 3 roubles in 1917. Printing shops in Katerynoslav met that year's orders by pulping 375 tons of archival documents considered unimportant.[57]

Paper allocation was a complicated process that in practice routinely involved bypassing official channels. Ukraine's leaders would order supplies or send personnel to Moscow to buy them. Central authorities often intervened directly to supply scarce paper to provincial offices. Thus, on 17 May 1921, provincial officials in Katerynoslav informed Kharkiv that their paper allotment for 10,500 daily copies of the city's party paper, and a further 5,000 daily for the countryside, would run out in eight days. On 19 May, the Central Committee ordered immediate resupply; it is not recorded, however, whether the shipment arrived.[58] Paper shortages led to squabbling among bureaucrats over allocation. In early 1921, for instance, the editor of Kharkiv's *Kommunist,* informed the Central Committee that he had enough paper for either a run of 30,000 copies for eight days or of 10,000 copies for one month – which was as long as it would take for more paper to arrive through official channels. Since this was unacceptable, the Central Committee instructed the army's typographic office to surrender some of its stocks – which it refused to do. In 1921, when officials wanted 1,080 tons of paper monthly, they received between 470 and 500 tons, of which 75 per cent went to newspaper production.[59] When necessary, leaders allocated arbitrarily – for example, in April 1921 they ordered seven tons of paper for Volyn province in addition to the normal allocation, in order to increase the volume of anti-UNR propaganda there.[60]

The Bolsheviks pulped archival holdings to make paper. This included private commercial as well as tsarist government collections. In June 1920, just after they had reoccupied Ukraine, the head of Buzhotdel reported that country's three working pulp mills could supply no more than 328 tons for that month and that the main source of paper was pulped archival documents. He noted that 46 tons of documents allowed one mill to produce enough paper for one week of printing. He requested from his superiors fifteen to twenty wagons to cart seized documents to the mill. That August, in a more detailed report, he indicated that the paper factories still functioning could produce only 10 per cent of needs. To compensate, he had ordered that half of all archival holdings that officials had classified as "insignificant" be pulped, with the reverse blank side of the other half to be used directly for writing or printing. He estimated that his subordinates, working as quickly as they could, could provide 3,112 tons of paper from Ukraine's archives, with totals for each archive allocated by province. This would supposedly cover three months of publishing. A special department was established for the task in 1920, the *Otdel po utilizatsii arkhivov.* In 1920 it delivered 1,350 tons, and in the first six months of 1921, 594 tons.[61] Detailed figures from Poltava province for a five-month period in 1920 indicate that local workers received 17 tons of writing paper, 16 tons of cardboard, and 200 tons of waste from 273 tons of documents.[62] The Kharkiv government requested paper from Russia but did not always receive it. By October 1920, Moscow had agreed to send Kharkiv 8,720 reams (*stop*) per month, but nothing seems to have arrived.[63]

In response to an order to print a poster in July 1920, the central publishing office wrote to the Central Committee that it could not produce the poster for three weeks due to a back-up and a lack of paper. Bolshevik statisticians that year calculated that forty-five presses turning out six thousand printed sheets daily required forty pounds of paper each day. Planners that year estimated that in total, Bolshevik newspapers required eighty-two tons of paper per month.[64] A publishing department official in August 1920 reported that, as of that year, Ukraine had three working paper mills producing 271 tons of paper, of which 145 tons could be used for printing. He estimated that if no supplies were forthcoming from Moscow, after three months Ukraine's government would be unable to publish anything except one or two central newspapers. The army had paper, he pointed out, because it could confiscate stocks in the territories it occupied.[65] As of August 1920, all supplies of paper were supposed to be at the sole disposition of VseIzdat, but army officials surrendered their stocks reluctantly and only when pressured hard to do so.[66]

A 1919 report from Katerynoslav provides some insight into the circumstances surrounding printing outside Kyiv and Kharkiv. On occupying the provincial capital, the Bolsheviks learned that there were thirty-five printing shops in the city and thirteen in the rest of the province; also, ten typesetting machines and one rotary press. But only half of the pre-1917 stock of type was still usable, and to make up for a lack of ink, printers had concocted a substitute made from oil and soot.

To supplement the insufficient stocks of paper, local officials between April and January 1920 had pulped 376 tons of archival documents to produce 306 tons of newsprint.[67]

Materials shortages affected output. Early in November 1920, Rakovskii complained to the Kremlin that Ukraine's Bolshevik newspapers were unreadable because the paper and ink were of terrible quality and publishing officials were indifferent towards their work. His patron Trotsky was listening, and at the end of the month he delegated two special envoys to correct the matter.[68] By April 1921 not much had changed, which suggests that Russians in Moscow sent little or none of their recent 7,000-ton paper purchase from Estonia to their comrades in Kharkiv.[69] The head of VseIzdat reported that output was minimal owing to lack of materials, including electricity, ink, and paper, and that Moscow had not sent any paper. Workers were few because of low rations and low pay (or no pay at all). Ukraine needed 5,420 tons of paper per month, but that April it had only 321 tons in stock. Summarizing Ukrainian needs, he estimated that to provide one hundred readers per newspaper, the country had to print 306,000 copies daily, which required 144 tons of paper monthly, plus another 150 for special and extra editions. And this figure did not include paper for leaflets, books, stationery, and posters.[70] Only at the end of 1922 did Ukraine's Agitprop report that it had received most of the paper it needed to provide more or less sufficient amounts of materials to all assigned destinations. The same report drew attention to the removal by that year of printed "anti-soviet" materials from stock rooms and libraries.[71]

In Bolshevik Ukraine by 1921, the estimated total of print workers ranged between 6,868 and 7,708 (excluding Volyn province). However, as many as 75 per cent that year did not come to work regularly because of low pay and food shortages. By the end of 1921 the count of printers and print shop workers had risen back to the 1897 total of approximately 10,000, with more than half located in Kyiv, Kharkiv, Odessa, and Katerynoslav provinces. As of September 1922, 976 worked in Kyiv city.[72]

For Kharkiv province, incomplete figures of union membership from 1920 indicate that there were 2,137 workers in nine towns, with more than half working in Kharkiv. More than half were between the ages of eighteen and twenty-three, around half were either typesetters or printers, and 32 per cent of typesetters were women. A survey of printers in Poltava province shows that Jews and Ukrainians comprised 379 of the 410 personnel in 1921, with the total number of Ukrainians rising from 20 per cent in 1920 to 50 per cent in that year. Almost 60 per cent had completed primary school and 36 per cent were typesetters. During those years, working conditions were apparently so horrific that the

Bolsheviks shut down some establishments in Kharkiv, despite their need for printed materials. Premises tended to be filthy and covered in fine dust from the machines. Not the least of the issues in one factory was no indoor toilets. This meant that in winter, workers running from hot rooms through sub-zero temperatures and back would catch colds, which would lead to complications since people were emaciated and weak. In Kharkiv, no one bothered to reply to the question of whether the buildings had sinks and soap. Death rates among printers, who as noted earlier were mostly young men, were so high that party reports claimed the entire profession was slowly dying away – primarily from tuberculosis and lead poisoning.[73]

During the first months of Bolshevik rule, the Publishing Bureau had little control over anything outside the city of Kharkiv. According to Ukraine's Military Commissar, Mykola (Nikolai) Podvoisky, during the first half of 1919 little printed or oral propaganda reached Ukrainian peasants and the responsible commissariat and Central Committee section did almost nothing.[74] The various agencies did not produce or disseminate as much as they might have in part because of overlapping jurisdictions and bureaucratic rivalries. The War Commissariat publishing unit complained that spring that, although it was doing all the work, the Publishing Bureau was not supplying it with enough paper or funding. Kharkiv was the capital, yet until 1921 it had no lithographic press, so posters could only be printed in Kyiv – when it was under Bolshevik control. To supplement their own travelling agitators and materials, they received imported Russian papers and at least 150 agitators sent from Russia, each of whom carried as much printed material as he could.[75] Ukraine's Bolsheviks complained that imported Russian materials were too few. In May 1919, at least one agency gave a representative cash to go and buy paper in Moscow.[76]

Distribution depended on communications and transportation. These were especially significant, given that the publishing infrastructure was centred in Moscow and Petrograd. Russia's infrastructure declined after 1917 but was still much stronger than Ukraine's. For the Polish campaign alone, Moscow published an estimated 10 million leaflets, pamphlets, and announcements directed at Polish soldiers. Leaflets and pamphlets saw runs of up to 300,000 copies per title, and posters averaged 100,000 copies each. The huge volume of political publications contrasted sharply with the miserly press runs of a few thousand copies allotted to the Commissariat of Public Health, which was having to deal with unprecedented death and infection rates. In the autumn of 1920, health officials submitted plans for leaflets in runs up to 100,000 and for pamphlets and medical texts in runs of 20,000 to 30,000, but they were never sure whether they would be allotted the necessary paper.[77] In 1920 the highest press run of a published health information leaflet was no more than 17,000 copies. Professional medical journals circulated between 50 and 100 copies per province. Ukraine's rail system in October 1920 was allotted 12 pamphlets on health matters in 15 to 20 copies each for its 61 stations and post offices.[78] By 1921, in the town of Radomysl and enivrons, near Zhytomir, a UNR agent reported there was no paper whatsoever. Whenever the odd leaflet was posted men tore it down to roll their tobacco. The local Bolsheviks could only disseminate their message orally, but that was unnecessary the agent noted, because they were in any case imposing "their communism" by force. In villages people would still shout-down Bolshevik speakers with catcalls until they left the podium.[79]

Moscow and Petrograd used trains and couriers to supply Kyiv and Kharkiv with Russian-language publications. Every day the *Ukrainskoe ekpeditsennoe biuro,* a subsection of the Central Publishers in Moscow (Tsentrpechat), sent 49,500 copies of Russian papers for distribution in Bolshevik Ukraine to Kyiv and Kharkiv; in addition, those two cities published 300,000 copies of their own papers. Kyiv was the best-covered province, with 41,000 copies going to sixteen towns, while Poltava was the least covered, with 8,000 copies going to twelve towns.[80] Overall, during the first half of 1921, fifty-five of Ukraine's eighty-three papers (fifteen of them in Ukrainian) were published in the country, and twenty-eight in Russia. While 95 per cent of the 538,873 leaflets distributed in Ukraine were published there, only 61 per cent of the 159,911 copies of posters were.[81] Bolshevik airplanes in July and August of 1919 alone[82] spread 100,000 leaflets behind enemy lines.

As of January 1919, Bolshevik-controlled Ukraine east of the Dnipro (left-bank Ukraine), had 333 locomotives (186 functioning) and 9,506 wagons (8,645 functioning). Ukraine west of the Dnipro (right-bank Ukraine), had 177 locomotives (90 functioning) and 701 wagons (359 functioning). One set of figures noted that as of May 1919 the totals in left-bank Ukraine had declined to 135 locomotives (90 functioning) and 2,902 wagons (2,591 functioning).[83] Just before Denikin's June offensive, Ukraine's total rolling stock was estimated at 39,302 functioning wagons and 1,475 locomotives; of these, 2,547 wagons and 49 locomotives were on the left-bank system.[84] After the Bolsheviks lost territory to Denikin that June, they were left with 77 locomotives (51 functioning) and 52 wagons (34 functioning).[85] Shortages of fuel and parts significantly reduced the speed and frequency of functioning trains. Trips that before 1914 took hours by 1919 were taking days. It took two or three days to travel from Kyiv to Moscow, which allowed literature published in the centre to reach Ukraine within a reasonable time. But *within* Ukraine, the journey from Kyiv west to Kamianets-Podilsky took eighteen days.[86] From Kharkiv by rail, it took an average of six or seven days to get to Odesa, seventy hours to Chernihiv, Kyiv, or Cherkas, thirty hours to Poltava, and fifty hours to Katerynoslav or Moscow.

A report from August 1919 indicates that Kyiv by then had functioning telegraph links with twenty-two of forty-six towns.[87] That same month, because lines were still being cut as troops moved back and forth, the Post and Telegraph Commissariat was obliged to report every twelve hours on the condition of Ukrainian lines as well as the line to Moscow. Apparently, by the first half of 1920, all districts except those controlled by partisans had been reconnected to the telegraph network. In the summer of 1919 there were fifty-five couriers in the Publishing Bureau's Collection and Distribution Unit and sixty-three distribution offices on Bolshevik-controlled territory. The most were in Kharkiv province (fifteen) and the Donbass region (eleven), the fewest in Katerynoslav (one), Tavrida (one), Volyn (one), Podillia (two), and Kherson (three) provinces.[88] By the following year the Bolsheviks had increased the number of couriers to more than 1,000. Couriers had priority, but as trains were usually overcrowded, they often rode outside the cars. In cold weather, couriers would refuse to travel unless they were issued winter clothing.[89]

Destruction, paper shortages, and technical restrictions led to clogged telephone and telegraph lines. In July 1919 the Post and Telegraph Commissar wrote to Rakovskii that because of overloaded lines, messages from Kyiv to Odessa were arriving as much as six days after submission. He explained that telephones used lines to Odessa for twelve hours daily, while telegraphs used five hours daily. The remaining time, lines were either down or being repaired or rerouted. Leaders had resorted to giving special precedence to various agencies and the military, but so many permissions were being issued that lines remained clogged and wait times long – while tempers ignited. In Odessa in May 1919, the commissar in charge of establishing the Bolshevik government in the newly occupied city issued an edict stating that launching invective at post and telegraph employees was not permitted and that employees of *soviets* found guilty of doing so would be severely punished.[90] These problems persisted into 1921. That August a circular of Ukraine's Sovnarhoz to the Polygraphy Department stated that there was no point in sending constant, expletive-laced complaints to the rail ministry regarding failed deliveries. In light of the acute fuel shortage, the allocation of trains was in the hands of a Sovnarhoz bureau, not the rail ministry, and complaining about delivery only clogged the telegraph system.[91]

The Message

The Bolsheviks in Ukraine focused their propaganda on social issues, with additional emphasis on public health and sanitation in 1920–1. Through 1917 and early 1918 their major themes were most clearly manifest in the Decrees on Land and Peace, summarized by the slogan "Bread. Peace. Land." Agitators claiming to represent the Petrograd Soviet showed Lenin's Land Decree to peasants, who took it as justification to continue doing what they were doing – expropriating land from big landowners (Illus. 42). In early 1917, when the postal system was still functioning, some sympathizers in Petrograd sent thousands of copies of the Bolshevik leaflet "To Brother Peasants" to relations in Ukraine. Most of the major landowners west of Kyiv were Polish, and it was they who suffered the most. Anti-Polish attitudes were further enflamed by publications issued by local Russian monarchists.[92] However, leaflets calling for "death to the enemies of the working people" or for "mercilessly spilling the blood of traitors and the enemies of the much-suffering fatherland" (Doc. 303, 322)[93] were rare in the sample.[94]

Mass propaganda ignored national liberation issues and was rarely in Ukrainian in 1917–18. This is reflected in the seventy-three leaflets (including multiple copies) reproducing Lenin's speeches, articles, and decrees released in Ukraine between 1917 to 1921. The first of twenty-two (including bilingual versions) Ukrainian-language translations of one of them appeared in February 1918: "Appeal of the Council of Peoples Commissars to the Workers and Peasants of Russia [*Rossiia*] to Defend the Socialist Homeland." Lenin's first specific public reference to national problems was in his "Letter to the Workers and Peasants of Ukraine," released in January 1920. He noted necessary "concessions to the survivors of national distrust" and discussed why Russians had to suppress with "the utmost severity the slightest manifestation in our midst of Great-Russian nationalism."[95]

Leaders' belated exploitation of national issues in their propaganda can be explained in part by their Marxism, which attached little significance to national matters. Also, almost the entire Ukrainian branch of the party was not politically or ethnically Ukrainian and thus was ignorant of, or indifferent if not hostile to, Ukrainian national issues. Indicative of all this is a speech made in Kyiv by a man named Khaifets, the chairman of the city's executive committee (*ispolkom*), on Red Army Day in March 1919, about how "the Russian [*Russkaia*] army was reborn" and served the proletariat.[96]

The overwhelming majority of party members in Ukraine were Russians or Russified Jews, few of whom could understand let alone speak

Ukrainian. They identified with Russia culturally, socially, politically and intellectually.[97] Because few members had any understanding of, let alone knowledge of or sympathy for, Ukrainian national issues, Ukraine's Bolshevik party was "Ukrainian" only in a territorial sense. Local leaders united the separate provincial RSDLP branches into one "Ukrainian" branch in 1918, while in exile in Russia. Ukraine's status in the Bolshevik order as a Russian province was described in two often overlooked articles in the 30 June 1918 edition of *Pravda*. The anonymous articles essentially set the agenda for the CPU's first congress and as well as the basic principles of its propaganda. One article began: "In some sections of our party in Ukraine." It continued that economic development under the empire had supposedly made political separation from Russia impossible. The authors saw the Hetman's Ukrainian state as a temporary result of German occupation that only served the interests of a "Ukrainian bourgeoisie." In reality, the Treaty of Brest-Litovsk had simply replaced "the southern part of Russia" with "the southern part of the provinces occupied by the Germans in the east." Afterwards there was to be a "voluntary unification for revolutionary unity." The resolutions of the First CPU Congress that July made no mention of federalism, let alone independence, and categorized relations between Russia and Ukraine as "reunion" and "centralism."[98] The overwhelming majority of Ukraine's Bolshevik party members, accordingly, can be compared to Dutch settler-colonists in Indonesia or the French in Algeria who formed the first socialist parties in their respective colonies. Those French and Dutch claimed to represent the local population even though they identified with the metropolitan ruling nationality. They based their policies on an imperial metrocentric understanding of their local situation, and they did not envision political secession from the imperial metropole.[99] In much the same way that settler French and Dutch radicals shared imperial prejudices and a metropolitan perspective with regard to Arabs and Indonesians respectively, Ukraine's Russian/Russified Bolsheviks shared tsarist imperial prejudices against non-Russian, non-ruling "small" nationalities in the tsarist empire, notwithstanding their leader's theoretical pronouncement on "the national question."[100] Their attitude resembled that of English socialists, who believed that English oppression in Ireland would be ended by English socialists, not an independent Irish Socialist Republican Party.

Lenin's version of Marxism legitimized the imperial Russian centralist perspective. Lenin claimed, for instance, that the Bolshevik party was the only radical socialist party that could legitimately exist within former imperial space (i.e., the tsarist empire). He did not consider that, contrary to his belief, ruled nations might not want to "voluntarily" reunite with former empires after they been "federalized" and "democratized," or that "the proletariat" of the imperial metropole might be as chauvinist as its ruling class. He did realize that Russian settlers in former tsarist Central Asia constituted a "creole" minority and included workers "strongly infected with a colonialist psychology." But he never elaborated theoretically on the role of settler-colonizers in empires, on colonialist imperial loyalism, or on creole-led independence movements, which did not necessarily call for decolonization for native populations. Lenin condemned Russian "great power chauvinism." Yet he did not categorize or criticize Russians in Ukraine as settlers, nor did he propose exiling all Russian officials there to Russian concentration camps as he did for those for Central Asia.[101] When Nestor Makhno met Iakov Sverdlov and Lenin in Moscow in June 1918, he was annoyed that the two men shared that Russocentric bias and talked of "south Russia" instead of Ukraine. In one reply he called them "you Communist-Bolsheviks who try [to] avoid the word 'Ukraine.'"[102]

Lenin himself contended that "robbers deprived her [Russia] of Ukraine and other territories." There is no evidence that he used analogous terminology to describe the separation of other dependent countries from other empires – for example, he did not speak of Japan or Britain or France being "deprived" of Korea or Ireland or Algeria.[103] In 1918, his close associate Lev Kamenev stated: "We won't allow the tools of imperialism, the nationalist bourgeoisie, to break apart the Russian empire [*Rossiia*]." No Bolshevik leader is known to have made analogous statements about the French or Spanish or British or Portuguese or Dutch empires.[104] It was Ukrainian and Muslim communists who first drew attention to this myopia. As Vasyl Shakhrai observed in 1918: "The socialization of the means of production will not automatically end the domination of one nation over another."[105]

The sample includes Russian-language leaflets referring to Soviet or Worker-Peasant "Ukrainian" government or authority. An early recruiting poster in Ukrainian mentioned a "Ukrainian worker's government." Another stated: "the Ukrainian nation, after the Russian, throws-off the bourgeois yoke" (Doc. 253, 300–1).[106] But using this adjectival form was exceptional during the first months of Bolshevik rule. Russian Bolsheviks in Ukraine explicitly condemned the idea of Ukrainian independence and opposed exploiting it in the interests of revolution. An anonymous author in a Krivyi Rih newspaper in March 1918 wrote: "We must extirpate [*vytriavliat*] the idea of an 'independent Ukraine' by all possible means from the people's consciousness, which through inertia, might still smoulder among certain inconsequential groups as events have shown." The July 1918 resolutions of the First

CPU Congress specified that propaganda must oppose any attempt to assign the party's planned uprising that year a national rather than a social character.[107] How little attention Bolsheviks initially paid to language or nationality issues is illustrated in a Ukrainian military intelligence report from Poltava province dated February 1919. In the wake of the advancing Red Army came numerous, primarily Jewish and most probably Russian-speaking, agitators extolling the virtues of the new world. Instead of swaying their peasant audience, they infuriated them. Villagers complained: "What kind of commune [*kommuna*] is this where the Jews have all the power." Their sympathies, the report continued, lay with "their Bolsheviks," that is, the Ukrainian left-SRs, who spoke Ukrainian, and decidedly not with the Russian Bolsheviks.[108] The Bolsheviks adapted when faced with this kind of reaction and the massive anti-Bolshevik uprisings that underlay the territorial expansion of the UNR that summer.

As noted, leaders made concessions in 1919. These included an agreement with the Ukrainian SRs. Then, after dissolving that party, they allowed some of its members into the Bolshevik party. In the realm of propaganda, concessions the following year took organizational form with the founding of the Ukrainian Peasant Section. In May 1920, four days before the Bolshevik counteroffensive against the Poles, Ukraine's Rakovskii instructed all Army newspaper staff to "take into consideration the fact of the existence of a Ukr SRR and to carry out newspaper work accordingly." Propaganda now began referring at length to Ukrainian culture and language and using the adjective Ukrainian positively. By 1920, after Ukrainian Bolsheviks in Moscow organized around Pavlo Popov had impressed upon their Russian superiors the significance of nation-related concessions, the Russians further modified their propaganda agenda. One result was that Trotsky ordered that the destruction of Ukrainian partisan units be carried out in such a way that "the working masses" did not perceive it as the destruction of Ukrainian independence. Another was the idea that Ukrainian was not a "bourgeois" language – that it had equal status with Russian and was to be learned and used in government.[109]

Select concessions did not mean unbridled exploitation of national matters. Presumably to forestall messengers getting carried away with national messages, the following month the RCP's *orgburo* under Stalin ordered the head of the secret police (Cheka), Feliks Dzerzhinskii, "to begin systematic exchange of Ukrainian railway agitators [*politrobitniki*] with Russian agitators."[110] Also, leaflets continued to be issued in Ukraine that could just as well have been issued in any Russian province. One from Bakhmut in 1919 read: "The Russian [*Russki*] people wanted to end the war, the Entente opposed, so they ignored, isolated and invaded the SNK [Council of Peoples' Commissars]." They supported the Whites and "obedient governments warring with us at their command." The leaflet mentioned small states – Estonia, Finland, Poland, Latvia – but not the UNR. "But having taken power the Russian nation suffered through and overcame all." In Donetsk, the provincial party in one of its leaflets referred to the "Russian [*Russki*] nation" as a victim, and referred only to a "Russian working class."[111]

The semantics, syntax, word choices, and lexical categories of Bolshevik propaganda reflected authors' Russocentric preconceptions and Russian Marxist socio-economic terminology. That terminology did not always reflect Ukrainian socio-economic realities – which raises the as yet unstudied matter of how those Russian ideas influenced Ukrainian behaviour during the revolutionary years. For example, as noted in chapter 1, *kurkul–kulak* was not used at all or had a different meaning in pre-1917 rural Ukraine than in post-1917 Bolshevik propaganda.

The Bolsheviks' select use, when not complete avoidance, of the adjective "Ukrainian" also reflected Russocentric preconceptions. In the sample texts, writers typically used the genitive "of Ukraine" rather than the adjective "Ukrainian," except in the territorial sense, as in the "Ukrainian Soviet Socialist Republic." Ukrainian sometimes preceded "landlord," "capitalist," "proletariat," or "working people," but rarely "nation." In the sample, the adjectival form appeared most often in materials directed at Ukrainian soldiers or partisans. The terms "Ukrainian National Republic," and "Ukrainian banditry" are rare in the sample. "Ukrainian Revolution" appears once, as does the term "Russian Ukrainian revolution." The usual term for the events of 1917–19 was "workers' and peasants' revolution in Ukraine." Where mentioned, the collective historical actor was normally "working people of Ukraine." By contrast, "Russian revolution" and "Russian workers" appear frequently. In 1920, propaganda aimed at Poland addressed "Polish Workers and Peasants." The term "Brother Ukrainians" appeared once in a leaflet appealing for unity in face of the 1920 Polish-Ukrainian offensive. Materials directed at western Ukrainians in eastern Galicia used "Halychna" rather than western Ukraine, in reference to the territory and the people, alongside "workers and peasants of Galicia."[112] Bolshevik leaders did not associate the two parts of Ukraine with each other because they had decided to give the western lands to a planned Bolshevik-Polish client state.

In April 1917, Kyiv's Bolsheviks condemned the Central Rada's anti-Russian Ukrainian socialists as "separatists" whose actions had weakened "the revolutionary Russian [*Rossiskyi*] proletariat."[113] That

June, in the wake of the Central Rada's First Universal, which declared Ukrainian autonomy, Lenin wrote a much-cited article titled "Ukraine." In it he recognized the right proclaimed by the Rada of "the Ukrainian nation [*narod*]" to secede, explaining that this was a precondition for it to voluntarily unite with Russia in an imagined future centralized socialist state. He did not discuss the possibility that "the Ukrainian nation" might not want to rejoin a Russian state after secession. But he did implicitly recognize the Rada as the representative of "the Ukrainian nation" inasmuch as the Rada was the body that claimed the right.

Even so, the next day, the Kyivan Bolsheviks declared explicitly that they did not consider the Rada the representative of "the Ukrainian nation." They clarified their position that August in a declaration stating that "Ukraine's population [not the Ukrainian nation] must decide its own fate."[114] Then, in a series of articles published on 9, 11, and 14 November 1917 in their Kyivan newspaper *Proletarska mysl*, they explained that the Rada ignored "the organizations of the working class" and that it could not be trusted with "the defense of the interests of the broad masses." They claimed that the Rada was concerned only about Ukrainians and was threatening to place other nationalities under Ukrainian domination. They did not mention that non-Ukrainians were 10 per cent of the total population or that 202 representatives of those non-Ukrainians were present in the Rada as of that August.

Local Bolsheviks considered themselves somewhat distinct from their central Russian colleagues only in that they faced the task of reinforcing the class-consciousness of "the Ukrainian proletariat" and of instilling the notion that it had a common interest in fighting "nationalism" alongside the workers of other nationalities. From their perspective, people in Ukraine were part of an empire-wide class struggle that included a struggle against the Rada. Ukrainians were not involved in a national struggle against empire. The imperial preconceptions and Russocentrism that Bolsheviks shared with their monarchist and liberal rivals were summarized in a March 1918 declaration: "We never regarded the Ukrainian Soviet Republic as a *national republic* but exclusively as a Soviet republic on the territory of Ukraine. We were never of the opinion that the Ukrainian National Republic is totally independent [*nezavisima*], and regarded it only as a more or less autonomous [*samostoiatelnoe*] whole tied federally with the all-Russian worker peasant republic."[115]

During Hetman Skoropadsky's rule, in August 1918, a seven-page leaflet/pamphlet titled "Prepare Yourselves, Workers and Peasants of Ukraine" (*Gotuites rabochie i krestiany Ukrainy*) was released for illegal distribution in Ukraine. It addressed its intended readers as "workers and peasants of Ukraine," not as Ukrainian workers and peasants, and told them there was no such thing as a national struggle. The leaflet did use the adjectival forms German, Austrian, and Hungarian when referring to workers in those countries. The text included only once the term "Ukrainian people [*narod*]." It did not classify "workers and peasants" as Ukrainian, applying the adjectival form only to bankers, the wealthy, capitalists, landlords, and oppressors. The text implicitly identified "Ukrainian" with "reactionary" and with everything the Bolsheviks claimed people should oppose.

A prominent Bolshevik propaganda theme through to 1920 was that the workers and peasants of Russia and Ukraine had made one revolution together. CPU leader Volodymyr Zatonsky summarized the approach that January: "We will try that the idea [*sic*] enters the proletariat's consciousness that Great Russia is totally uninterested in oppressing Ukraine in any way, and that only with the powerful assistance of the Russian proletariat will we be able to protect the soviet country from the attacks of international predators and internal counter-revolution."[116] A version of this theme also appeared in a leaflet from 1920 produced for the Red Army's Polish offensive: "The workers of Russia freed Ukraine not only from national but also from social oppression." This accompanied another claim that the Red Army marched to liberate "Polish workers and peasants."[117] Bolshevik propagandists used the term "national war" instead of "imperialist war" when talking about the First World War to their Ukrainian audience. They then juxtaposed that with "class war," making no mention of "national liberation wars."[118]

Russian Bolshevik leaders did not conceive of such a thing as a "Ukrainian" revolution, nor did they publicly refer to their taking power in Ukraine as a "conquest." On 22 November in Petrograd, Lenin phrased relations between his new republic and Ukraine as follows: "As Ukrainians you can organize your lives as you wish. But we will extend a brotherly hand to Ukrainian workers and tell them: we will fight together with you against your and our bourgeoisie."[119] Mikhail Muraviov, commander of Bolshevik forces that took Kyiv in January 1918, did not obfuscate in a declaration subsequently reprinted in Kyiv newspapers: "We brought this [Bolshevik] power from the north on the points of our bayonets." He wrote to Lenin "I handed the government [I] installed with bayonets to Ukraine's soviet." In his speech to the city council he said: "We come from the north with fire and sword," not against the Ukrainian nation but "the bourgeoisie."[120] The message in a leaflet circulated just after he had occupied Kyiv, nonethless, reiterated Lenin's obfuscation without mention of "Ukrainian workers": "The revolutionary workers soldiers and sailors of Ukraine with the help of their brothers from all parts of the Russian worker-peasant republic ... gave power to the Soviets of workers peasants and soldiers deputies" (Doc. 252).[121] Among themselves, Bolshevik leaders – including Lenin – realized that Muraviov had, as he had claimed, militarily conquered Ukraine. In March 1919 Georgii Piatakov summarized the view of Ukraine's party members: "Without the armed intervention of armed Russian soviet power there cannot be a successful independent revolution and establishment of soviet power in Ukraine." In July 1919, Dzerzhinskii complained to Ukraine's Cheka head that the Bolshevik administrations in all the non-Russian republics "were taking themselves seriously as if they were state governments" and not subject to the RCP Central Committee. In May 1920 during a trip there he wrote: "Ukraine can and must be conquered only by the stubborn daily work of workers [i.e., Cheka operatives] from the center coming here for an extended time ... In general our Cheka [people] work here as if in a foreign country."[122]

Although the occasional leaflet or article rebutted the Ukrainian claim that Russian Bolsheviks had invaded and conquered their country, as a rule, propagandists used circumlocutions to explain how the party had come to power in Ukraine.[123] Thus: "To all citizens of Kiev. On the 26th of this month [January 1918] revolutionary troops entered Kyiv coming here in the name of establishing in Ukraine, as in all Russia, the authority of the Soviet of workers, soldiers, and peasant deputies." From another leaflet: "The friendly onslaught [*druzhnym natiskom*] of Ukrainian and Russian workers, soldiers, and peasants chased from Kyiv the government of the bourgeois Rada that betrayed the interests of the people." The worker/peasant Ukrainian government elected in Kharkiv in December had "spread its authority over Ukraine" and "entered" Kyiv. Throughout "all Russia [*Rossii*]," it noted, workers and peasants had one and the same interest (Doc. 251, 253).[124] Ukrainian-language leaflets explained that the Rada had tricked some Ukrainians with ideas about national liberation in order to turn them against Russians. The aim of this had been to "drown the revolution in rivers of fraternal blood" and thereby restore the rule of generals, landowners, and capitalists. This was followed by an account demonstrating that Rada policies were counter-revolutionary (Doc. 299).[125] A Bolshevik-controlled Rail Union leaflet portrayed the Bolshevik invasion and occupation as a popular uprising, making no mention of Russia's Red Army. A government declaration read: "The tight historic, economic, and cultural ties of worker peasant Ukraine with Soviet Russia make it our duty to make a single revolutionary class front with the Russian proletariat." This declaration ended with reference to a "Ukrainian Red Army" – although no such entity existed. Nor was it clear how "tight" historical "ties" could be with an entity that only came into existence in November 1917. The Rada claimed that it represented all of Ukraine's workers and peasants, but it had then "declared war on [*obiavila*] all the soviets." Thus began a struggle in Ukraine from which "our soviet of workers and peasants emerged totally victorious." This leaflet made no mention of any alliance or help from Russians. It stated that the bourgeoisie had allied with the Germans and that they were guilty of treason.[126]

The basic message was that the "workers and peasants of Ukraine" had established Soviet power. This was associated with the idea that they had done so with the help of their worker and peasant comrades in Russia. "Ukraine liberated itself from the yoke of foreign invaders and its own landowners and capitalists only with the help of the workers and peasants of Russia." Texts noted that all workers had be united regardless of national differences (Doc. 260).[127] The rest of the message was that after taking control of the land and factories in a struggle against landowners, the bourgeoisie, and their foreign allies (with "foreign" never associated with Russia or Russians), the people had to fight to hold on to them. Direct denial was rare: "We did not conquer Ukraine as foreigners but took the lead of an uprising, organized the worker-peasant Red Army, the broad masses of the Ukrainian proletariat and workers and overthrew the officer-landlord Directory." The sample materials contain no mention of borders, unlike with regard to Poland in July 1920, when texts explained to Red Army troops: "You cross the border not as imperial conquerors but as defenders of workers' rights."[128]

In one leaflet, Bolshevik propagandists explained away Ukrainian political separatism by linking it to "the bourgeoisie," who, according to them, did not play the same role during Ukraine's revolution as they did in other imperial dependencies. The "bourgeoisie" in Ukraine had wanted to impede the comradely unification of the workers and poor peasants of Russia and Ukraine, so they had declared the Ukrainian bourgeoisie independent from the Russian and Ukrainian workers and peasants. To the degree that Bolsheviks recognized that an entity called the Ukrainian nation could be revolutionary, they associated that sentiment not with political secession from empire but with the restoration of imperial unity. Thus: "the Ukrainian working nation" had caught on to the bourgeois ruse, and the "Ukrainian nation" had overthrown the Rada (Doc. 253, 299).[129] Another leaflet explained that in 1917 "the Ukrainian working people" had understood that independent Ukraine was only a "bourgeois yoke," so they overthrew it.[130] No Bolshevik publication in the sample explained who exactly the "Ukrainian bourgeoisie" were, or how they could be so powerful in a country where urban dwellers with capital who owned the means of production were overwhelmingly non-Ukrainians – as explained by CPU leader Khristian Rakovskii himself in January 1919.[131]

A leaflet, likely printed shortly after Lenin's "Letter" of late 1919, titled "Katsap i Khokhol" (the derogatory terms Ukrainians and Russians use to refer to each other), explained the Bolshevik Russian presence in Ukraine in terms of duty and biological-ethnic ties (Doc. 254).[132] It pointed out that Russian peasants and workers, whose rulers had once used them to oppress non-Russians, were now coming as brothers fulfilling a duty to right the wrongs that their grandfathers, in their role as generals, princes, and landowners, had inflicted on Ukrainians in the past. The sons of the former oppressors had come to rid Ukraine's workers and peasants of the "leeches on their necks." Those Russians who had been forced to fight by former landowners allied with the Entente now proclaimed the right of self-determination in Russia and the world. Because Russian princes and nobles dispossessed in the name of liberty and socialism had fled to Ukraine, Russian workers and peasants had to pursue them there. "Not as conquerors or oppressors, but as brothers, comrades and friends have the "*katsaps*" now come to the "*khakhly*." Only after they were liberated from the old ruling class by Russians could Ukrainian workers and peasants decide whether they wanted to secede or federate. "The workers and peasants came from the north as brothers to finish-off together [with Ukrainians] the landlords and other enemies."

This presentation of Russians as agents of Ukrainian liberation was reinforced by the claim that the Bolsheviks were *not* a Russian party despite their formal name. The left wing of the Russian Social Democratic Labour Party was presented as comprising all nationalities and as having merely taken the lead in the uprising in one part of one country. In 1918 the Bolsheviks formally adopted the name Russian Communist Party (RCP). Leaflets explained that despite the change, it remained the same party with the same aim (Doc. 256).[133] But no leaflet in the sample includes the term RCP – only "Communist Party" appears as the new name. Some leaflets, assuming it was self-evident that *soviets* ruled, declared that it was impossible to be simultaneously pro-Soviet and anticommunist. These did not mention that the *soviets* were subordinate to the party (Doc. 255, 257, 302–3, 306).[134]

An anonymous pamphlet – which saw three editions by 1919 – explained that, contrary to what Ukrainian leaders claimed, it was not "the workers and peasants of Russia" who were invading and despoiling Ukraine. It argued that the conflict in Ukraine was a class war, not a national war, the assumption being that class trumped national ties. "The workers and peasants" of Russia *and* Ukraine had suffered under the tsars and had now united to overthrow him. After they together established soviet power in Petrograd, in Ukraine "Ukrainian rich peasants and landlords" "stabbed the workers and peasants of Russia" in the back, and the Rada declared war on "the soviets of Ukraine" and "the soviets of Russia." That the Bolshevik government in Petrograd had declared war first was not mentioned. In the resulting war, "our soviets" had emerged triumphant. "Under the cover of war against the 'Russkies' [*katsapy*] Ukrainian rich peasants called the Germans, who returned the landowners and bourgeoisie to power as soon as they came and then surrounded Worker-Peasant Russia with a steel bayonet wall." The ensuing conflict was one of "our [Ukrainian] rich peasants against Russkie peasants and Russkie workers. Rich-peasant Russkies and Russkie landowners helped." Meanwhile, the Germans exported Ukrainian coal and grain to reinforce the Kaiser's power over German workers and peasants.[135]

A constant theme was that the leaders of the national Ukrainian governments were traitors because, in league with landlords and "the bourgeoisie," they had allied with foreign capitalists for purposes of exploitation and profit. "Petliura makes agreements with all who want to drink Ukrainian peasants' and workers' blood."[136] Propaganda occasionally used the term Central Rada. It otherwise usually avoided referring to other Ukrainian governments by their official names, the Ukrainian State and the UNR. Texts instead referred to them and to anti-Bolshevik organizations by their leaders' names.[137] This implied that Ukrainian opposition to Bolshevik rule did not involve a government representing a people leading a national war against a Russian invasion. Opposition to Bolshevik Russia was thus presented as individuals pursuing class or private interests backed by various "imperialists" who wanted to divide Russia (*Rossiia*). From such a perspective, the Bolsheviks in Ukraine were fighting a civil war against rebels and criminals.[138]

Nikolai Podvoiskii, Ukraine's War Commissar in 1919, wrote a number of articles explaining that Ukrainian independence was an Anglo-French and White Russian plot to starve Russia. Since the "workers and peasants" of Russia and Ukraine shared a common will and interests, the former had naturally helped the latter hold on to power. "The workers and peasants of Ukraine must not forget that without the support of Soviet Russia they could not hold on to power." At the time, holding on to power meant that "Ukrainian workers and peasants" had to dissolve their partisan units, which had just overthrown the Hetman, and fight in the Red Army. Podvoiskii argued that no rival forces could defeat the Bolsheviks because they represented the majority of the working poor. But the party's task was not easy. It faced the "general and political ignorance of the Ukrainian population" – a product of the illiteracy resulting from Russification and tsarist rule. National independence, he explained, was being promoted by nationalist intellectuals attempting to gain village support against the "foreign city" and steer the revolution in a "petite bourgeois nationalist" direction. This appealed to wealthy peasants, who were terrified at the prospect of heavy requisitions by hungry Russia.[139] The Rada, whose sole interest was in establishing an independent state, had advocated both left- and right-wing policies. It failed because it was backed only by rich peasants. But the "anarchic partisan movement" it had fostered persisted, as evidenced by Makhno, whose banditry betrayed that movement's anti-commissar, anti-Jewish, anti-Russia, anti-communist aims. Makhno attracted support, Podvoisky admitted, by exploiting the slogan "Power to the soviets – without commissars."

Podvoiskii explained that the *soviets* were weak because the Bolsheviks had failed to support middle-stratum peasants, had imposed a much-reviled state land fund, and had only a "vague requisition policy." He noted that they had also failed in their propaganda work. As of that August, he stated, the responsible agencies existed only on paper. He concluded that re-establishing control would require a close association with Russia. This was especially necessary because Ukraine's historical and socio-economic characteristics had fostered "an unfavourable base for the flowering of Ukrainian soviet power." A single Red Army had to be formed that excluded all partisan formations, even those that were pro-Bolshevik.

The idea that landowners, officers, and wealthy peasants, backed by the "world bourgeoisie," were waging war on the worker/peasant soviet republic and refusing to let its population work in peace, was developed in two anonymous pamphlets that appeared the following year. They explained that the Bolsheviks were defending the common people and were giving peasants land, while Petliura and his foreign sponsors looted and pillaged. People believed Petliura's lies about Ukrainian national liberation and building a national republic, yet the reality was that only "soviet power" gave the people what really mattered – control over capital, land, and factories. Petliura's national liberation was a facade concealing the ongoing bourgeois rule of wealthy peasants and landlords.[140] In the wake of the failed Ukrainian-Polish offensive, propaganda explained why Ukraine was a Bolshevik republic and Poland an independent state. The difference was that in early 1920 the Bolsheviks were "willing to agree with the Polish [independent bourgeois] government, for as long as the Polish nation tolerated it, so as to prevent further bloodshed of Russian and Polish workers and peasants."[141]

A surviving collection of lectures to activists, given in Russian in Kharkiv in July 1920, instructed them to explain that Ukraine before 1917 had been like a vassal state and that only a "gendarme tie" linked it to Russia. Once soviet power "appeared" (with no explanation of how it appeared), both countries met the common enemy of international capital. Victory was possible only through united struggle. That is why both countries had been united since 1918. The text claimed that the two countries had common interests because they had been side by side for years, their populations were mingled and their economies tied. Economic dependency had been established over the centuries. That meant Ukrainians did not need manufacturing, which existed in Russia, and Russia did not need heavy industry, which existed in eastern Ukraine. Because history had produced a single economic organism, there was no need for separate Russian and Ukrainian commissariats. Culture, justice, and internal affairs could be kept separate to reflect the circumstances in Ukraine. Railways, defence, finance, and economics could have Ukrainian subagencies that would look out for Ukrainian interests while adopting centrally determined policies as appropriate. Problems could be resolved after the enemy was defeated.[142]

An important propaganda theme in the sample concerned grain exports to Russia. Rakovskii had explicitly ordered such exports in February 1919, as confirmed the following month at the Third CPU Congress: "The biggest possible amount of [food] is to be sent first of all to the hungry brothers of Soviet Russia."[143] Between January and April 1919, exporting was proclaimed to be a magnanimous duty to Lenin and the revolutionary capitals. Lenin that March told Russian workers in Petrograd that "it is the primary socialist duty of every citizen of Ukraine to help the north." After that, however, faced with mass uprisings provoked by forced requisitioning, Rakovskii explicitly instructed requisitioning agents to deny that grain would be shipped to Russia and to tell people that Russia had enough grain of its own.[144]

Miron Vladimirov, in charge of food procurement in 1919, explained to Ukrainian peasants that Russian peasants had learned through experience that it was in their interest to meet government demands.[145] If the state had grain, it could feed the army, which would then not arbitrarily requisition, and cities, which could then produce manufactured goods for villages. Once they had schools and the opportunity for self-government through *soviets,* peasants would stop listening to enemy anti-Bolshevik rumours and lies. Precisely *when* poor and middle-stratum peasants in Ukraine would have their own schools and *soviets* would depend on how soon they freed themselves from the control of rich peasants. The "Ukrainian peasant" had to understand that soviet power could not function properly without grain and that it would do whatever was necessary to obtain it. "The Soviet government of Ukraine," Vladimirov carefully noted, would demand only 25 per cent of any remaining surplus and put part of that in a reserve fund. He did not mention Russia in his brief discussion of distribution.

After March 1919, agitators and leaflets denied outright that Russians were exporting Ukrainian grain, although forty-six of Ukraine's seventy-one requisition squads, involving as many as 80,000 men, were shipping their plunder to Russia that spring.[146] Vladimirov now claimed that bread was going only to the Red Army in Ukraine, which was defending "our Soviet Socialist Independent Ukrainian Republic." "Ukrainian bread is only for Ukrainian workers, peasants, and the Red Army." Elsewhere: "None of us ... is about to export bread or sugar from Ukraine to other countries. Although, truth be told, our brother workers of Russia should be helped."[147] Leaflets now only urged peasants to help the starving Russian proletariat, or referred only obliquely to sending bread to Ukrainians' brothers on "other fronts of the Red proletarian land." Or: "The bread you hesitate giving to your hungry brother workers in Russia will end up in the rapacious mouth of the French bourgeoisie to whom Petliura sold himself and his robber gangs." Another argument was that not giving bread to Russia was against Ukraine's interest because Russia was defending it against wealthy generals and landlords.[148] In the autumn of 1920, Hryhory Petrovsky, to a local conference of poor peasants, offered an oblique justification of what was not supposed to be happening. He explained that those present should not complain about grain requisitions because it was "our holy brotherly obligation to our fraternal Russian republic," and in any case, while the Germans had exported seven million tons, "we Bolsheviks" had exported no more than 500,000.[149]

The sample includes one leaflet claiming that Russia had received only a few tons of surplus food stocks, while its massive "brotherly help," in the form of money, manufactured goods, and arms, had liberated Ukraine and saved it from "the yoke of the hetman and petliura." Here was included the argument that Ukrainians and Russians were brothers who had lived together for centuries, that there existed temporary difficulties imposed by landlords and speculators, and that both peoples would again help each other once they had liberated each other. "And, while we get almost nothing from you, fraternal Russia gives you almost everything." Some leaflets claimed that while "Judas traitor Petliura" was accusing Russia of exploitation, he was shipping foodstuffs west to Galicia, and that only the Red Army had stopped him from shipping "everything." In Odesa, local party leaders blamed shortages on the hoarding and speculation of the "urban bourgeoisie." They addressed a leaflet to peasants calling for their support because they were confiscating those scarce goods in their interest. Any food sent to Russia was insignificant, had been taken from stores collected by the Hetman, and had been paid for with manufactured goods. Otherwise food went only to the "army of peasants and workers" (Doc. 264, 304, 319, 340).[150]

The sample includes a number of other explanations for urban food shortages. Some blamed the "petliurites," who had destroyed rail lines. Others, the war, which meant the army had to have priority. War was invoked to justify army requisitioning. People were told to register complaints and that because soviet power was *their* power, it made no sense to oppose it. The Bolshevik order was a perfect direct participatory democracy based on *soviets* with elected commissars. Leaflets claimed that the massive anti-Bolshevik uprisings of 1919 had in fact been part of the world revolution, which in Ukraine was directed against the landlords and Petliura.[151]

A third propaganda theme in the sample appears in materials related to the 1920 Polish-Ukrainian offensive and subsequent invasion of Poland. Ukrainian national ideas figured here. On the one hand, materials reflected the Bolshevik decision to use Russian nationalism. A twelve-point program from May 1920, penned by Trotsky, specified that the Ukrainian-Polish offensive was to be presented in terms of a war for the "independence of socialist Russia" – although he certainly must have known that Poland never intended to invade Russia. Some leaders warned Lenin against exploiting Russian nationalism during the war, something he had not been averse to earlier. In November 1918 he had called on the previously vilified Russian "petite bourgeoisie" to defend Russia as patriotic Russians and for party members to accept them because soviet power guaranteed Russian independence. This coincided with an influx of Russian Menshevik, SRs, and monarchists joining his party for nationalist rather than for Marxist reasons. Stalin, like most of the top leaders, conflated ethnic Russia with its empire in February 1919 when he defended Bolsheviks as restorers of "Russian unity [*edinstvo Rossii*]" – by which he meant Russian imperial unity.[152] But by the time of the Polish offensive, Lenin had modified his earlier opinion, adding that editors should distinguish between the Polish people and their rulers. Not all officials bothered. Faced with the Polish offensive, leaders openly exploited Russian nationalism and imperialism in their propaganda. Authors wrote about the national unity of the Russian nation, ignoring the fact that at least half of those under Bolshevik rule were not Russian and that Polish forces were far from Russian territory. Moscow's *Pravda* ran an article about how the Polish gentry in the seventeenth and eighteenth centuries had ravaged Ukrainian lands inhabited by "Russian workers and peasants" and "Russian lands inhabited by more than five million Russian inhabitants." The Jewish-born former Austrian citizen Karl Radek characterized the war as a Russian national struggle of liberation against foreign invasion in which "Russians" were defending Mother Russia. Their goal was to "reunite all the Russian lands and defend Russia from colonial exploitation." Trotsky agreed with Lenin about not exploiting Russian nationalism. Nonetheless, he wrote articles about a "single united Red Rus" and the Red Army as defender of the "independence of the Russian nation," as if Ukraine was not involved. He made speeches praising Russian officers for saving the "freedom and independence of the Russian people."[153]

Propagandists often used the term "Soviet Rus."[154] In Odesa a Ukrainian translation of a decree issued in May 1920 by Lenin, Trotsky, and Mikhail Kalinin still used the term Ukraine only in the territorial sense. The principal historical actors mentioned were "the Polish working nation," "Polish workers and peasants," the "Russian nation," and "Russian workers and peasants." "Ukrainian nation" appeared once in a sentence noting that the Bolsheviks did not recognize the right of Polish landlords to expropriate the lands of "Russian [*Ruskii*] peasants." The sentence ended with the note that they did not recognize the right of the Polish military to strangle and belittle the "Russian [*Ruskyi*] and Ukrainian nation."[155]

But Ukrainian national issues *were* broached alongside the Russocentric neo-imperialist anti-Polish propaganda. Leaflets explained that claims that Polish landlords would leave Ukrainians alone to rule themselves as a "Petliura republic" were untrue. In reality, Poles would be in control and landlords would be taking back their land. "Petliura promised your land to the lords, they promised him power." This message was reinforced in Ukrainian-language leaflets with phrases such as "independent Soviet Ukraine," "glory to free Ukraine," and "native Soviet Ukraine." These were absent or less prominent in the Russian-language sample, where only one leaflet included the slogan "Long live an independent [*nezavisimaia*] worker-peasant Soviet Ukraine." The latter group included items announcing that it was not enough for the Bolshevik counteroffensive to liberate Kyiv "and chase the Poles from Russia [*Rossiia*]." The red flag had to be planted in Warsaw. A leaflet to "the population of right-bank Ukraine" referred to defending "our native land soaked with our sweat and blood." It did not specify who were the natives of the land in question (Doc. 268–71, 322, 324).[156]

In the wake of their counteroffensive, the party's Kyiv province committee issued a leaflet in Russian: "The Communists are liberating Ukraine." It explained that three years earlier, the common effort of workers and peasants of Ukraine and Russia had destroyed the Muscovite autocracy. But then, the native Ukrainian bourgeoisie and gentry, who wanted to liberate Ukraine only to exploit it, took power and established a new bourgeois slavery. They persisted until "the working people of Ukraine" "cleansed itself [of] the nationalist waste [*ugar*]" and rose up to achieve true freedom alongside fraternal soviet Russia. "The party of working and poor peasants all the time standing steadfast in stubborn struggle against the bourgeoisie advanced and liberated Ukraine." "Ukraine is Soviet. Ukraine is free!" (Doc. 272).[157]

Leaflets with titles like "Glory to a Free Ukraine" told UNR soldiers: "We are Ukrainians like you and, like you, love our dear Ukraine," and reminded Ukrainians about historical injustices their ancestors had suffered under Polish rule (Doc. 323–5).[158] In 1921, in a singular example of its kind, someone in the eastern Ukrainian town of Bakhmut issued a leaflet citing a Shevchenko poem in large letters in bold type: "I love my poor Ukraine so, that I would curse God and lose my soul for it" (Doc. 356).[159] It was printed in one hundred copies at a time when leaflet press runs were in the tens of thousands.

Two documents from June 1920 addressed to teachers and "educational workers" explained that the Polish army was the agent of international capital and Ukraine's historical enemy, the Polish gentry.[160] One told teachers to remind their pupils that the invasion threatened Ukraine's future well-being. The Russian Revolution, the vanguard of world revolution, ran the argument, had freed "Ukrainian workers and peasants," but European imperialism had then turned the country into a battleground between world revolution and counter-revolution. In a rare use of the term UNR, it described the 1918–20 Russian-Ukrainian war as a civil war between the Ukrainian Soviet Republic and the UNR. UNR leaders, the text continued, had exploited the deep desire of the working masses of Ukraine for national liberation, fanned national enmity, and betrayed the country to the Germans, the French, the Poles, and the Whites. This item then noted that only Soviet Ukraine had fought all of Ukraine's enemies, among whom Russia was not included, and given land to the peasants. In the struggle against the

Poles, no one could be neutral, and teachers in particular had to understand these political and cultural aspects of the struggle.

A second text, issued the same day, was titled "The National and Cultural Tasks of Soviet Ukraine's Struggle against the Polish–Petliura invasion." It admitted that at the beginning of the revolution the "Ukrainian bourgeoisie" had exploited the issue of national liberation from Russian imperialism; now, however, all had to realize that soviet power was the sole true representative of the interests of "workers and peasants of Ukraine." Making no mention of Russia, the text related Bolshevik rule in Ukraine only to "the heroic efforts of the leading Kharkov and Donetsk workers, who took over [*ovladela*] the whole proletariat – poor peasants and all workers – from Kharkiv to Podillia, from Chernihiv to the Black Sea, and organized them into a proletarian state." This message, directed at teachers, accused the UNR of betraying national interests, because all it did in the realm of education was translate into Ukrainian the old bourgeois educational system. According to the Bolsheviks, the UNR's aim was to spiritually imprison workers and peasants and separate then from workers and peasants in other countries – first and foremost, from "the heroic proletariat of Russia." The UNR was to blame for the dearth of Ukrainian schools and "Ukrainian proletarian literature," because its allies, the Whites and the Poles, had destroyed both. Propagandists sometimes claimed that national-ethnic and class ties converged. After "the Poles" won their independence, they had begun to plunder and conquer their neighbours, unlike "our Russian brothers." The latter not only overthrew the tsar but also "established popular soviet power for themselves and extended the hand of love and assistance to Ukraine."[161]

N.I. Faleev used Ukrainian patriotic ideas in a pamphlet that began with a description of how, through the centuries, Ukraine had been invaded because it was such a rich and beautiful land. But now, thanks to soviet power, which was worker and peasant power, the land belonged to the peasants. Faleev explained that by joining the "Russo-Ukrainian worker-peasant Red Army" and providing food for it and the cities, the peasants were defending their land and securing manufactured goods and schools for themselves.[162]

In the materials issued that year, Grigorii Zinoviev used a disease metaphor in one item to explain the Ukrainian drive for independence – perhaps to remind all that Bolshevik Ukraine was not to be confused with an independent Ukraine. Like many Bolsheviks, he reduced the Ukrainian struggle to the term "Petliura regime or movement" (*Petliurovshchina*). He classified it as "a bacillus" made up of rich peasants, petite-bourgeois nationalists, anti-Semites, and independentists that resulted in villages hoarding grain while urban workers went hungry. The disease had even infected the party inasmuch as it had allowed the petite bourgeois to join and become corrupt commissars, who, he admitted, were widely despised. The solution was to take the rich-peasant and Petliura movements "by the throat" and "mercilessly destroy all gangs." Such initiatives would simultaneously defeat the "White Guardist" invasion that the Poles had sponsored. This was to be accomplished through "iron organization, strong centralization and real proletarian dictatorship." Corrupt commissars had to be crushed "like lice."[163]

A thirty-page pamphlet published in Moscow explained that because every major capitalist country in the world except the United States needed Ukrainian resources, they supported wealthy anti-Bolshevik Ukrainian peasants and their leader, Petliura. The Polish offensive was only the most recent example of this resource-driven imperialism by a historical enemy, which again was threatening Ukrainians with cultural Polonization. Only through union with the "working masses of Soviet Russia" could "Ukrainian workers" defend their language and culture. "How much blood have Russian workers and peasants shed on Ukraine's fields in fighting for its freedom and fortune! And compared to those flows of blood and heroic self-sacrifice of Russian workers and peasants, what are those paltry 145 tons exported to Russia during the most recent period of soviet rule in Ukraine."[164] The author then declared that association with Soviet Russia – which would soon transform itself into a world socialist federation – was preferable to association with Britain, France, and the big European countries. While *they* were exploiting colonial populations, Russia was offering ex-colonial peoples their freedom and the prospect of cultural flowering. He then listed leading Ukrainian politicians like Hrushevksy, who in 1920 had publicly conceded that Bolshevik rule would, in the end, free Ukraine from oppression.

Propagandists exploited Ukrainian patriotism in their treatment of UNR treaties with Western European countries. As of mid-1919 those treaties included a nominal truce with the Whites. Such treaties were condemned as treason committed by the "Judas Petliura," who was selling the country to foreign exploiters, French, German, and Polish, for his own personal gain. One leaflet called on the "Ukrainian poor" to defend Ukraine from those who had sold "their native nation to a foreign bourgeoisie." An appeal to Ukrainian troops told them: "We are Ukrainian like you and love our dear Ukraine as much. We have soviet power, the power of workers and peasants to which you belong" (Doc. 270, 321, 323–5).[165] Mobilization efforts included patriotic slogans such as "long live worker-peasant Ukraine," as well as calls to support the Red Army, which had evicted the landlords. "Who does not give bread to the Red Army betrays the revolution and aids the Polish gentry." The entire Soviet republic, not just individual villages, had to be freed and defended by a single army, not by partisans, because the main enemy was "western capital" (Doc. 320, 327, 341).[166]

In their propaganda Russian Bolsheviks never explicitly targeted Ukrainians as the enemy. The enemy were "bourgeoisie," "counter-revolutionary gangs," "kulaks," "bandits," or "Petliurites." Printed materials in the sample delivered the message that the "Ukrainian bourgeoisie" and Petliura were traitors because they had signed, or tried to sign, treaties with European powers, which themselves were sitting atop revolutionary volcanoes because their "slaves" were waking up. Entente troops in Odesa, one leaflet related, would not fight because they were reading soviet papers about socialism in their own languages (Doc. 261).[167] This idea appears in published letters sometimes written back and forth between opposing front units. In one reply to UNR Ukrainians, pro-Bolshevik Ukrainians, in Russian, explained that their enemy's leaders were "little judases" and liars who gave nothing despite their promises and who only killed innocent, ignorant common people. The true brothers of "judases" like Skoropadsky and Petliura were the foreign powers and the rich, to whom they had sold Ukraine. The Bolshevik Ukrainians declared that their only true brothers were Russian workers and peasants and all those who fought to liberate the workers (Doc. 262, 312).[168] Appeals to pilots called on them not to defend the interests of capital and to defect with their planes, and assured them they would not be shot when they landed. They were told: "Our Ukraine is federated [with] and decidedly not a part of Russia" (Doc. 266). [169]

In leaflets issued during the summer of 1920, Bolsheviks addressed western Ukrainians as "Galicians." They avoided referring to national liberation, or to eastern and western Ukraine as a single national entity. They explained that the "workers and peasants" of the soviet republics would help western Ukrainians and that they should demand from their commanders and authorities "an immediate tie with the workers and peasants army of Soviet Ukraine," without which they would be unable to overthrow their Polish landlord enemies and win land and liberty. Western Ukrainian soldiers were told to defect and not fight "Ukrainian workers and peasants," for doing so would only help Polish landlords and again enslave "our free Soviet Ukraine." Petliura had betrayed Ukraine to European imperialists: "The Workers and peasants of Ukraine, fraternally linked with the workers of Galicia, want to help you free yourselves from the chains with which Petliura has tied you [by allying with France and Poland] ... Only the fraternal unity of

Ukrainian and Galician workers and peasants can bring the true liberation of labour from the yoke of capital." A separate leaflet assured western Ukrainians that "Petliura's" accusations about Bolshevik repression of Ukrainian culture and language were lies. It pointed out that primary schools were in Ukrainian and that the government was publishing Ukrainian books (Docs. 328–31).[170]

In their western Ukrainian propaganda, the Bolsheviks avoided the issue of national liberation in the sense of political secession from empire, while claiming to defend Ukrainian cultural and linguistic concerns as eastern Ukraine's rulers. In 1921, Bolshevik Ukraine's Foreign Affairs Commissariat published *Zashchitu Sovetskoi Ukrainy. Sbornik Diplomaticheskikh dokumentov i istoricheskikh materialov,* a collection of forty-one documents purporting to show what "the worker-peasant government did 'in defense of Soviet Ukraine' as a separate independent state, during the second period of its existence." In the introduction the authors imputed a Ukrainian national character to the Red Army in Ukraine by labelling it "Ukrainian soviet units" and "Soviet Ukrainian." They referred to that army's occupation of Kyiv as a "liberation." They stated that the "Red Ukrainian army" was calling on the "working masses of Galicia" to follow the example of "their Ukrainian brothers." As noted below (p. 178), claiming that a draft unsigned agreement between France and the UNR was an actual treaty, they accused the leaders of the national governments of turning Ukraine into a French colony, praised the Bolshevik government for protesting against the France–UNR negotiations, and defended soviet Ukraine as "an independent state."

A fourth group of sample texts are directed specifically against Makhno, the UNR, and all Ukrainian irregular units that Bolshevik leaders classified as "bandits." This term included "nationalists" and "anti-Semites" but not actual criminal gangs. In the Bolshevik lexicon, "bandits" were wealthy peasants who fought against "workers' power," economic justice, and socialist revolution. "Rich peasants" included deserters and criminals. Bolshevik leaders knew that all of these groups represented different phenomena and used different slogans, but this was not reflected in their propaganda.[171]

Once Trotsky had laid down the basic ideas of the anti-Makhno campaign, pamphlets about him were released. Moisei Ravich-Cherkasky, the one-time anarchist, then party member, and later first official historian of the CPU, added details to Trotsky's "Thesis" in a pamphlet that traced Makhno's movement back to anti-German uprisings. These had their roots among wealthy peasants who "self-determined themselves as a class" and who supported landlord and bourgeois power. After Germany withdrew, by guile and force they compelled the poor and the middle classes to join their criminal gangs. Although in reality only wealthy peasants waged war against Ukrainian cities, he continued, the uprisings had a national aspect in that the cities were Russian. This allowed "gang leaders" to drape their movement in national colours while calling for an independent Ukraine. All of these leaders were linked in one way or another to Petliura, who had sold Ukraine to the Germans, then the Entente, then the Poles, and finally the Whites. Makhno, however, as an anarchist, stood apart from these others, Cherkasky explained. He then summarized anarchist ideas, noting that although Makhno would ultimately be defeated, the Makhno movement, "Makhnovshchina," was a disease that "had infected all Ukraine. All its party civilian and military institutions. Every Ukrainian revolutionary, Bolshevik, communist, and left-SR, to a greater or lesser degree, is infected by this disease."

A second pamphlet, by G. Rakitov, provided Red Army troops with a twenty-three-page description and rebuttal, from the Bolshevik perspective, of Makhno's key ideas and slogans. "According to Makhno, bandits, rich peasants, speculators and ex-officials should all have freedom. Judge for yourselves and tell me. What kind of life will workers and peasants have if their enemies have freedom?" Rakitov concluded by telling all soldiers to carry not only bullets but also party resolutions so that they could explain to peasants why Makhno was being destroyed, and that they should use every possible opportunity to destroy him.

Two simpler accounts characterized Makhno as a bandit surrounded by criminals and deserters who wanted an easy life. They were described as foreign hirelings whose destructive activities made peasant shortages and struggles even worse. The authors claimed that Makhno had established a dictatorship of bandits and anarchists and that anarchism was impossible to implement because no society could function when all did as they willed whenever they pleased. Social justice required order, and only the Red Army and the communist *soviets* comprised of elected workers could provide it.[172]

Leaflets discredited Makhno, claiming that he was fighting only for himself, that he could not stand against disciplined White troops, and he would have had no victories if the Red Army had not been fighting the White Army. He was accused of "shooting us in the back" and of opposing the inventorying of confiscated goods and property before redistribution, because that was not in the interests of his wealthy peasant supporters. He was accused of murdering peaceful villagers, pillaging their homes and slaughtering unarmed or surrendering Red troops. By definition, Makhno and his supporters could only be bandits, because it was impossible for workers and peasants to oppose a worker-peasant power established by themselves. One leaflet, responding to calls for

Red Army soldiers to defect, included explicit death-threats: "It is pointless for you to think your subversive call from June 1920 to us Red Army men will convince us to join you ... Know you little shits [*merzavtsy*] ... we won't play games with you, you evil parasites ... We will openly destroy your criminal gang. We will sweep you from the face of the earth forever" (Doc. 274–6, 335).[173]

In 1921 a ten-page instructional pamphlet for agitators declared "Makhnovism" a manifestation of "Ukrainian banditism" – a subset of a broader phenomenon supposedly based on the 10 to 20 per cent of the rural populace opposed to the "proletarian revolution" because they were a "rural bourgeoisie." Ukraine's particularity stemmed from frequent changes of government there as well as the presence of foreign imperialist interventionists – among whom the authors did not include Russians. All of this produced "independentist tendencies among the populace and an inclination for people to individually defend their private interests," which was possible, because the men had military training and access to massive amounts of arms. Thanks to the Red Army, by 1921 only criminal elements were maintaining an armed opposition. Makhnovism was one of "banditism's" ideological expressions. Petliurism, its second ideological expression, was distinguished by its call for a national constituent assembly. A short organizational/territorial description of each movement was followed by detailed instructions for combating both, which combined military and organizational initiatives with propaganda directed at the misinformed and uninformed.[174]

A fifth group in the sample are texts addressed to peasants in general or specifically to Ukrainian soldiers and partisans. These include appeals by defectors urging their former associates to join them. Some of these texts appealed to reason rather than to fears or emotions. Because these used logical argument to explain positions, they could be classified as information materials as much as propaganda. Two pamphlets from 1919 offered reasoned arguments, written in response to anti-Bolshevik propaganda, explaining aspects of Bolshevik policy and why it merited support.[175] As noted, none of these pamphlets stated the full version of the Bosheviks' new name, the Russian Communist Party. Leaflets included short definitions of terms such as Mensheviks, socialists, and communism, explained what "middle stratum" peasants were, and discussed why it was in their interest to support the Bolsheviks and the poor rather than the rich. Another set explained what "middle-stratum peasants" were and appealed to them for support, providing assurances that the party would not dispossess them: "Comrade middle-peasant, understand once and forever that the rich peasant is as much your enemy as he is of the poor peasant. To help the poor take bread from the rich is tantamount to helping yourself." Another message was that only liars and "Judas-imposters" claimed that *soviets* would be good without Jews and Russians because, in reality, *soviets* beat the rich and defended the poor regardless of their nationality. The enemy, a Ukrainian-language leaflet explained, was not the Polish lord, the Ukrainian *kulak*, the Russian merchant, or the Jewish bourgeois, but "the rapacious beasts and thieves of all nationalities." Those who opposed communists were bloodsuckers and parasites "for whom work means death" (Doc. 303, 337).[176] Shortages resulted from circumstances, not policy. All wealthy peasants were bloodsuckers who supported bandits and the Whites. They were the cause of all problems and were to be flattened (*prizhimat*) through taxation. It was totally justifiable to seize not only their land but also their tools and livestock (Doc. 278, 305).[177] That, in turn, was why it was important for peasants join the Poor Peasants Committees (*KomBid*). Otherwise, rich peasants would become landowners and again force the poor to work for them. Furthermore, *soviets* did not persecute the faithful. The party criticized the clergy but did not close churches or forbid services, leaflets explained (Doc. 308).[178] "We swear before God," one finished, "that we do not shut down churches."[179] Leaflets explained that, contrary to rumours spread by enemies, communes were not military prisons where all ate from one big pot and shared women, but purely voluntary organizations of honest hard workers (Doc. 258, 277, 280, 338).[180] Anyone who claimed the contrary was to be ignored and immediately arrested. It was not mentioned that forcibly imposing communes had been policy during the first months of the year.[181]

A leaflet specifically addressed to "those dissatisfied with Soviet power" explained that anything bad anyone had heard about soviet power was lies and that opposition to *soviets* amounted to people opposing themselves, since soviet power was *their* power. If errors occurred, they were not be dealt with individually in a way that disrupted the ongoing struggle, but by complaining to the *soviets*, which would address them in an orderly manner. On the third anniversary of the Bolshevik seizure of power, Ukrainians were reminded that of all the regimes that had come and gone, only the Bolsheviks remained, because "it is the power of the workers, because it only defends their interests." In the Ukrainian army, common soldiers were treated like animals, whereas in the Red Army, they were on equal terms with their commanders and controlled them via *soviets* (Doc. 263, 265, 281, 309, 310).[182] Pamphlets elaborated on why peasants who did not want to be slaves of landlords and factory owners had to join Poor Peasant Committees and win middle-stratum peasants over to their side. Only *their* organization could counter the wealth and power of the rich, ensure that the poor could defend their material interests, and deliver grain to the army and cities.[183] Peasants were told in 1921 that to overcome hunger and disorder they had only to destroy the partisans and fulfil their delivery quotas (Doc. 311).[184]

Leaflets in the sample directed against Ukrainian anti-Bolshevik partisan units did not mention those units' stated political aims. They categorized all such irregular units as a single group with one centre, allied to the Whites, with a shared desire to destroy. Their activities benefited only enemies of workers' power by weakening what should have been a common front. Partisan leaders were robbers interested only in "freedom to rob the nation." They obeyed the orders of Polish landlords and tsarist generals for money. If they triumphed, only they, the wealthy, foreign capitalists, and bankers would benefit. In return for all their foreign loans, the "petliurites" and "bandits" would allow the Whites to reinstitute serfdom – something the rich peasants did not fear. "Whoever does not want serfdom must fight Zeleny [a partisan commander] as they would Denikin." By disrupting grain deliveries, fighting the Red Army while it was fighting the Whites, and putting Ukraine at odds with Russia, the partisans would starve Russia. The Red Army would be weakened, soviet power would collapse, and the foreigners would easily "devour" Ukraine. "Woe [peasants] for you and your children if the gangsters and the warlords succeed and Ukraine falls to the Whites. They will make gallows from the trees and force your children and wives to make your nooses. And the warlords will become administrators, gendarmes and policemen serving tsarist generals and Polack [*liakhski*] landlords." These leaflets refuted accusations about forced collectivization, church closures, and Russian exploitation. They explained that excluding Russians and Jews from *soviets* as supposed enemies would only weaken those bodies, for such exclusion would remove only poor Jews and poor Russians. Some leaflets countered the charge that soviet power was Russian-Jewish power by pointing out that the criteria for party and soviet membership were political, not ethnic. One leaflet refuted various Ukrainian claims regarding the Bolsheviks' policies, including the charge that they would restore tsarism and persecute the religious and had enlisted White officers. The activities of the Cheka and the party executive committees were fully justified because these were directed against enemies. Shortages had resulted not from soviet power but from the partisans' disruptions. "Take grain from the rich peasants so they don't turn it into moonshine. Take it to rail-stations to feed our Red warriors who defend peasants and workers from the White landlord-bourgeois horde, serfdom and slavery" (Doc. 267, 298, 313–17).[185] Partisans were told that their leaders only wanted to be rulers like the old pre-revolutionary ones: "You have been given a sword to beat the enemy not your brothers" (Doc. 273, 279, 307).[186] An appeal from December 1921 by a local Revkom head in Podillia province, who may have been a former Borotbist, explained that Bolshevik rule was not rule by Russians and Jews. He noted that in his district only 5 or 6 per cent of *soviet* members were Jews. There were more Russians than Jews in general, he continued, but who was preferable? The landlords and Poles behind their partisan commanders, or the "workers and peasants of Russia," who were helping Ukrainians rid themselves of the tsar, landlords, and bourgeoisie? "If you are honourable, if you love Ukraine ... join us ..."[187]

Anti-partisan materials during the years 1920–2 indiscriminately labelled all partisans as "bandits," adding that the Ukrainian irregular units combined within them "village garbage, wild butchers, dumbed by moonshine, poisoned by the smell of wine, blood and 'the green monster' [opium]" (Doc. 332–6, 341).[188] The campaign included appeals by former partisan commanders, of whom perhaps the most important was Mordalevych, who had defected in June 1921. His pamphlet, *To Insurgents: My Path from Democratism to Socialist Revolution,* explained that he was a democratic socialist disillusioned with consecutive Ukrainian governments that had pursued capitalist politics under the guise of democratic fictions, and with the opposition and indifference he had encountered among the peasants whose interests he had sought to defend. Ukrainian reactionaries and the European bourgeoisie were using democratic and nationalist slogans to build a bourgeois bureaucratic republic at a time when a socialist revolution was necessary. Such a revolution would be impossible if it was modified to placate peasants' desires. The Ukrainian nation's future, he wrote, could only be built on soviet lines. If some Bolshevik officials did not understand that only social liberation brought national liberation, then peacetime evolution would eventually show them the error of their ways.[189] In a second leaflet, Mordalevych insisted that no revolutionary could pretend to base himself on the "petty bourgeois" village and that anti-Bolshevik activities would only benefit "class enemies." The villages had to be supported and should not be changed using force. Communism was ethically correct and represented the future, he wrote, but at some point it would have to use force to overcome resistance. These remarks, directed towards the committed and their leaders, were reinforced in a leaflet that quoted former Ukrainian SR officials, recently convicted in a show trial, explaining why they had decided to support the Bolshevik order (Doc. 342–5).[190]

Leaflets that appealed to the partisan rank and file asked them how they could have committed atrocities against innocent victims like Red Army soldiers and party and non-party government officials, whom they had lumped together with poor Jews. Others, written in the wake of the NEP, asked why they were not at home with their families doing honest work. Why were they fighting a regime that was not imposing communes, that had cancelled requisitioning, that guaranteed landownership for nine years, and that was promoting Ukrainian language, education, and culture? This message included the idea that malfeasance, problems, and injustice should be dealt with through established procedures and due process, not by force of arms. Amnesty offers continued to link partisans with international capitalism, wealthy peasants, and the restoration of the tsar and contended that the partisans were wreaking havoc and destruction in order to invoke nostalgia for the supposed strong hand of the old regime, which they wanted to restore. People were told that partisan "White terror" would be met with Red terror and that "bandits" could only be destroyed if poor peasants helped the Red Army by fighting the rich peasants (Doc. 345–7).[191]

The journalist Stepan Vasylchenko, who decided to live in Soviet Ukraine in 1920, wrote two pamphlets endorsing Bolshevik rule.[192] Whatever his motivations, he, like Mordalevych, quite possibly influenced others like themselves – educated and literate Ukrainians who had concluded that, in light of the collapse of the UNR, the scale of repressions, and Lenin's promises in his December 1919 "Letter," it made more sense to accept Bolshevik rule than to continue fighting. In one of these pamphlets (30,000 copies), Vasylchenko elaborated on Lenin's December 1919 concessions. In the other, which was based on his impressions of Ukraine from a 1920 tour he had taken with a choir, he contended that "all the workers and all the working peasants have applied themselves to realizing the tasks of the revolution and are building the foundations of the successful life [that had been] bought for such a high price." He explained that the Red Army would deal with any opposition, and he listed as the main Bolshevik accomplishments land distribution to poor peasants and Lenin's concessions on linguistic and cultural matters. Thus the soviet regime was not Russian, and "the Red Army of Russian workers and peasants" had not come to oppress the Ukrainian poor but to free them from torturers and landowners. "And, first and foremost, Russian soviet power announced that the Ukrainian poor had to organize its own authority in Ukraine by themselves – the authority of the Ukrainian proletariat and poorest peasants." They would now be deciding what exactly their relationship would be to Russia. Since the capitalists, landlords, and bourgeois counter-revolutionaries realized that they could not rule Ukraine as long as the Ukrainian and Russian proletariats were united, they had sponsored independence. In reality, as demonstrated by the Hetman and Petliura, that meant rule and exploitation by foreign capitalist countries. That threat made soviet federal unity necessary.

Propaganda related to Jewish issues was published in Hebrew, Ukrainian, and Russian. The basic message in the Ukrainian and Russian materials was that landlords and wealthy peasants were provoking pogroms as they had under the tsar, in order to divide the working population and weaken soviet power. Leaflets explained that people should hate their oppressors, not nations. In a pamphlet written as a dialogue between a Ukrainian peasant and a Jewish plumber, the plumber explains that under the tsars, poor Jews were even more oppressed than poor non-Russians, while rich Jews had privileges. Analogously, it was not just Jews who were capitalists and speculators. The Jews may have killed Christ, but to persecute today's Jews for that made as much sense as punishing a grandson for the crimes of his grandfather. In reply to accusations heard even from Red Army troops that many commissars were Jews, the plumber replied: "So why cannot Jews be commissars? Any good revolutionary can be a commissar. Only the ignorant can think otherwise." The peasant concluded that the only fight that mattered was the one against social and economic inequality.[193]

One leaflet described pogroms as the sword with which the enemies of the soviet order hoped, with one blow, to destroy all the gains that poor peasants and workers had made and kill the revolution. Various anti-Bolshevik Black Hundred gangs were preparing another 1905-style pogrom as agents of their landlord and capitalist masters, whose goal was to regain their wealth and power. This leaflet warned people to reject all provocations to commit pogroms, because they would lead to counter-revolution (Doc. 259).[194] "The Petliurites" defeated in battle, explained one leaflet, wanted to instigate strife among nationalities and to reanimate pogroms in order to destroy *soviets* and weaken the Red Army. This same pamphlet claimed that while the Bolsheviks had the slogan "Workers of the world unite," the "petliurite" slogan was "Beat the Jews, beat the Russkies, beat the Polacks." This particular leaflet ended with Lincoln's adage about not being able to fool all of the people all of the time (Doc. 318). [195]

Leaflets relating to public health normally gave matter-of-fact descriptions of symptoms and urged people to practise daily hygiene and to seek medical help when necessary. Information provided on subjects like smoking and drinking contain much that is still read now in health brochures. An army leaflet dealing with syphilis explained that the best way to avoid infection was "to summon all your willpower" and not indulge. It reminded soldiers that doctors said abstinence did no harm. Soldiers were warned to avoid prostitutes because they were all infected, not to believe them if they claimed otherwise, to wash, and to see a doctor as soon as they felt pains. Some other recommendations seem odd today. One advised not indulging more than once a night, and, to be safe, to smear the organ concerned with tallow or fat just before insertion. Afterwards, soldiers were advised to wrap their organ for ten to fifteen minutes in a cloth, or medical gauze if available. Those with condoms were told to give them two or three good pulls beforehand to check there were no holes. Like most Bolshevik leaflets, this one included the slogan "workers of all countries unite." Given the subject matter, the slogan undoubtedly stimulated creative barracks commentary.[196]

All governments issued regulations and ordinances, but the Bolsheviks surpassed them in total published because they aimed to place almost all activities under government and party control. Those in the sample suggest that officials made these decrees more graphically appealing than their political leaflets. These ordinances and decrees were not propaganda as such. Nonetheless, they deserve attention because the policies they announced brought home the reality of Bolshevik rule in a way that probably disabused most urban dwellers of any illusions or sympathies that propaganda may have created.[197] Townspeople faced endless registration, mobilization, confiscation, restrictions, and arbitrary arrest; fear of informers and anonymous denunciations was widespread (Doc. 348–51).[198] In the newspapers they regularly saw lists of those who had been shot; they learned the grizzly details from old women, who were allowed to look at the bodies.[199] After the Bolsheviks claimed power in a specific region, however, not all orders explicitly threatened the death penalty for opposition (Doc. 335, 282).[200]

The sample includes an undated call for "proletarian forces" to "go to the village for bread and meat" to "strengthen the muscles of your arms with normal eating." A leaflet issued during the 1921 famine insisted that hunger was a relic of the old regime "that should not exist in a soviet republic." It was now "an all national [*vsenarodny*]" rather than a "proletarian" task to save the country (Doc. 294).[201] One leaflet attributed famine not to requisitioning but to excessive logging and called for forest conservation (Doc. 352).[202] A notice from Novozybkivsk in 1918 declared Rada decisions invalid and that all institutions not working in contact with *soviets* would be re-elected. One year later, another in Chernihiv ordered all individuals and organizations to register on pain of arrest. In Tokmak in central Ukraine, foreigners as well as officers in the tsarist and Ukrainian armies were required to register. Martial law was declared, and a four o'clock curfew was imposed. Here, it was specified that those who did not register their weapons would be shot on the spot if discovered. Searches were to be conducted only between the hours of nine in the morning and seven in the evening. Anyone conducting a search who was not a Bolshevik official was to be reported and would be subject to the death penalty. In April the town's two commissars issued Easter greetings to the population, expressed best wishes to the parents of serving soldiers, and urged men to volunteer rather than wait to be drafted to fulfil their "holy duty of victory over bourgeois reaction" (Doc. 283–90).[203] In Pryluky in 1919, a leaflet urged people to conserve and protect works of art, churches, old buildings, and books. If such items were not saved, "all of us and our children will be sad and maybe even ashamed" (Doc. 351).[204]

The first decrees in Konotop in December 1918 forbade free trade and ordered merchants, tradesmen, and craftsmen within three or four days to provide lists of all their commodities, tools, and materials, or face military tribunal and confiscation. Order no. 5 ordered all who had information about any enemies to immediately report it, ensuring them anonymity and secrecy. Order no. 6 ordered all telephones registered, and Order no. 9 declared that all of those who refused to accept soviet roubles would be sent to a concentration camp. Order no. 19 ordered all able-bodied men, except for officials and communications and press personnel, to report for municipal labour duty on pain of death; also, all clocks were to be reset 2 hours and 38 minutes ahead.[205]

In Pervomaisk, where the mobilized repeatedly failed to show up for their assigned tasks, the recalcitrant were warned they would face detention in a concentration camp. In Kremenchuh, those who did not appear at the appointed time to clear the city's garbage faced arrest and a concentration camp. In Kherson in December 1920, each housing committee had to supply two light bulbs from each household to the authorities within two days or be disconnected from the electrical system. In Pyriatyn, inhabitants saw one day a leaflet requiring all within the week to report all building materials in their possession. As of that moment, such materials could no longer be bought or sold, and anyone not reporting would have their items confiscated (Doc. 291, 348).[206] A committee established to oversee a public sanitation week in Zaporizhzhia province in June 1920 declared the entire population, including soldiers, liable for cleaning duty. Shirkers would be sent to concentration camps (Doc. 349).[207]

Leaflets called on communists who discredited the party to be expelled. An undated appeal to women was unlikely to have been very appealing to any woman who cared to think about it. The only concrete achievement it listed was equal pay. It claimed that insofar as soviet power cared about poor peasants, work would be easier for wives. The leaflet stated that the government offered day care and education. It went on to tell women that if they were displeased, it was their duty to improve the situation. How women were supposed to undertake improvements while at work was not explained. Women were told that if they wanted what soviet rule promised, they would have to support soviet power and be organizationally active alongside their men (Doc. 350).[208]

In cultural matters, a leaflet for the newly established Kharkiv Officer Academy called upon "Ukrainian Red Youth" to enrol. The list of qualifications did not specify knowledge of Ukrainian. The government had by then begun to sponsor free six-week courses in Ukrainian for officials. Local offices in 1920 began receiving instructions from their superiors reminding them to know and use Ukrainian and that they would be "severely punished" for refusing to deal with citizens in Ukrainian. Such behaviour, it noted, gave a pretext for the Bolsheviks' enemies to accuse them of Great Russian chauvinism (Doc. 353–5).[209] The official literacy campaign included instructions telling people what to do physically with a book when reading. Leaflets had titles like "The Hygiene of Reading" and "The Ten Commandments of the Red Army Reader." These told people not to read for too long a time, not to lick their fingers before turning pages, and not to read while eating, at night, when lying down, or after meals "when the muscles are relaxed." Read all subjects purposefully, read with others so that discussion is possible, and keep a dictionary and pencil at hand for notes. "Don't tear out pages and don't be tempted [to do so] by the pictures: don't be a barbarian" (Doc. 295–6).[210]

The Bolsheviks used what today would be called "black ops" to undermine their enemies and spread their message. Lenin, for example, wrote a radio-telegram on 21 January 1918, broadcast the next day, in which he claimed that the Rada had collapsed and that his Kharkiv government "holds undivided sway over Ukraine." Two days later, *Izvestiia* reported that Bolshevik troops had entered Kyiv on 16 January under the Ukrainian Bolshevik Iury Kotsiubinsky and that the government had arrived five days later. This was a blatant lie. In reality, Muraviov's Bolshevik troops took the city on 27 January, followed by the government on the 30th. The dates were not coincidental. This incident exemplifies the masterful exploitation of medium and message in aid of a political objective. The ploy was intended to undermine the Ukrainian delegation's claim that it represented Ukraine at the Brest-Litovsk talks and to depict a conquering Russian-led army as a revolutionary Ukrainian army. The 16th of January was one day before Trotsky was scheduled to return to negotiations at Brest-Litovsk, two days before the dispersal of the Constituent Assembly in Petrograd, and seven days before the Rada declared Ukrainian independence at its Fourth Universal. Lenin released the phoney telegram the day the Rada declared independence. The newspaper version, with added dates, appeared the day after the convocation of the stacked Third Congress of Soviets, which called for the legitimizing of his party's claim to rule former imperial territories – including those it did not control.[211] This ploy had no effect on the Germans, but it did influence some of those Ukrainians who believed that Bolshevik troops were actually a Ukrainian Red Army under Ukrainian command.

A second example involved the circulation in Kyiv of a forged treaty purportedly signed between France and the UNR on the eve of the All Ukrainian Labour Congress (*trudovyi kongres*) in January 1919. The phoney document was meant to discredit the UNR government by claiming it had agreed to federate Ukraine within a "single indivisible Russia." Another instance involved a later draft agreement that did include broad economic concessions to the French, but was never signed. This was broadly circulated that winter and spring as a concluded treaty to prove that the "bourgeois" Directory had sold Ukraine to French capitalists.[212]

Bolsheviks also distributed brochures and leaflets with phony sponsors and places of publication. In the spring of 1919, Ukrainian Galician Army intelligence officers discovered anti-Ukrainian brochures supposedly published by the Ukrainian Social Democratic Party. Tests on the paper and print revealed that the Bolsheviks had published the materials when they still controlled Odesa, then sent them for distribution to one of their agents in Ukraine, who posed as a Ukrainian SD activist. On raiding the office they discovered tens of thousands of copies of such phony publications, which they summarily burned.[213] In another instance, UNR intelligence arrested a group of Bolsheviks in February 1919 who carried with them detailed plans to organize uprisings in seven towns at midnight on 14 February. The plot failed. Nonetheless, on 15 February, Bolshevik radio falsely reported fighting in the towns backed by non-existent peasant supporters. In a third instance, they produced a phoney leaflet written in ungrammatical Ukrainian calling on peasants and Cossacks to form *soviets* and signed it "General Staff of the UNR Army."[214] A leaflet from June 1920 had the boldface title "Glory to Petliura." The text then explained how the Bolsheviks with the help of the peasants had saved Ukraine from capitalists and foreign bourgeoisie.[215]

Инструкция

Центрального Отдела распространения печати Всеукраинского Издательства

ДЛЯ КУРЬЕРОВ-ПРОВОДНИКОВ,

отправляющихся с литературой по Украине.

1. Курьеры, находящиеся в Харькове, обязаны ежедневно являться в Команду Связи не позже 10 ч. и расписываться в книге.

2. Курьеры получают назначение накануне своего отправления по наряду Иногороднего под'отдела.

3. Мандаты и контрольные книжки курьеры получают в Команде Связи, а дубликаты накладных в Жел.-дор. Экспедиции.

4. Курьеры обязаны присутствовать при подсчете и упаковке, предназначаемой для его маршрута, литературы.

5. Курьеры расписываются на копиях накладных в Центральной Экспедиции, откуда они обязаны сопровождать литературу на вокзал.

6. Перед от'ездом курьеры получают подробные инструкции в Жел.-дор. Контрольной Секции, куда они являются по получении мандатов.

34 First page of an instructional pamphlet for agitators (Russ.). Instructions for couriers – leaders going to Ukraine with literature issued by the Bolshevik Central Section for the distribution of printed matter of the All Ukrainian Publishers (1920).
Arkhiv Druku.

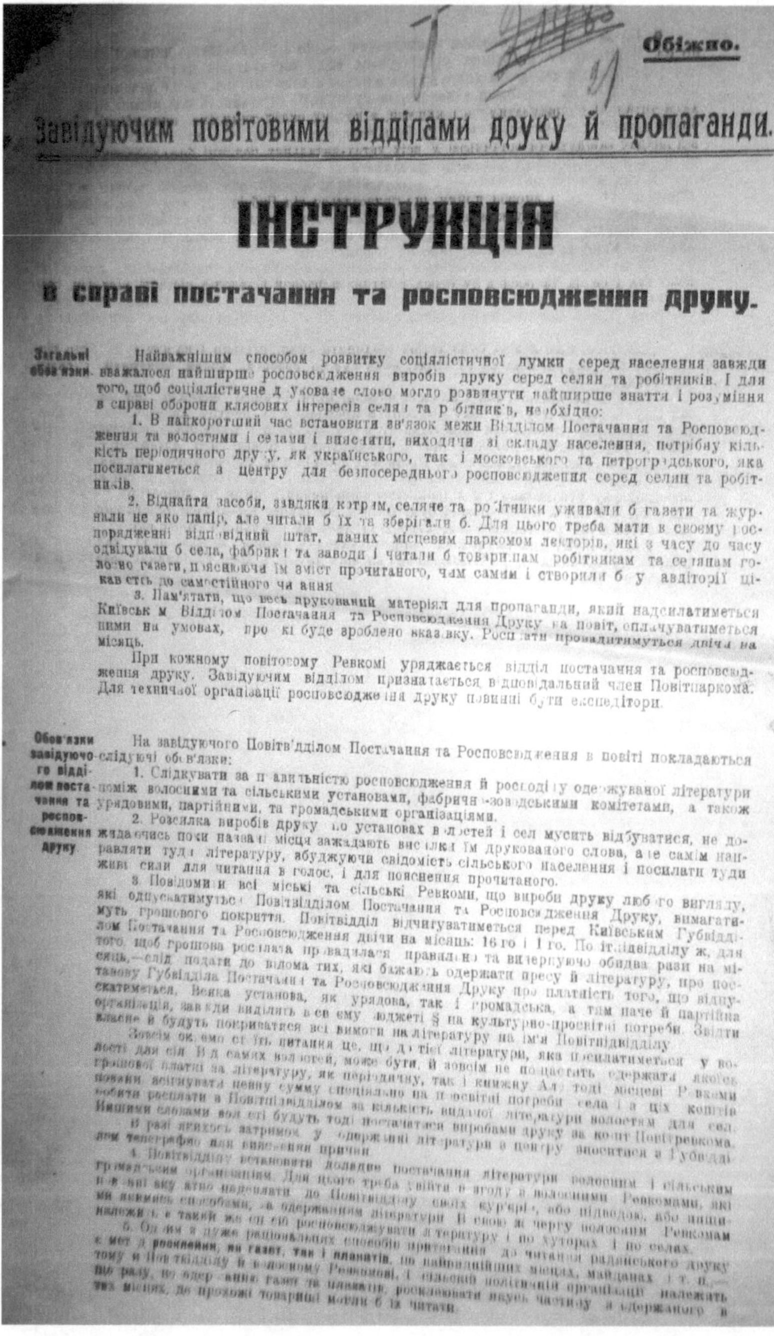

Обіжно.

Завідуючим повітовими відділами друку й пропаганди.

ІНСТРУКЦІЯ

в справі постачання та росповсюдження друку.

Загальні обов'язки.

Найважнішим способом розвитку соціялістичної думки серед населення завжди вважалося найширше росповсюдження виробів друку серед селян та робітників. І для того, щоб соціялістичне друковане слово могло розвинути найширше знаття і розуміння в справі оборони клясових інтересів селян та робітників, необхідно:

1. В найкоротший час встановити зв'язок межи Відділом Постачання та Росповсюдження та волостями і селами і вияснити, виходячи зі складу населення, потрібну кількість періодичного друку, як українського, так і московського та петроградського, яка посилатиметься з центру для безпосереднього росповсюдження серед селян та робітників.

2. Віднайти засоби, завдяки котрим, селяне та робітники уживали б газети та журнали не яко папір, але читали б їх та зберігали б. Для цього треба мати в своєму росporядженні відповідний штат, даних місцевим паркомом лекторів, які з часу до часу одвідували б села, фабрики та заводи і читали б товаришам робітникам та селянам голосно газети, пояснюючи їм зміст прочитаного, чим самим і створили б у авдиторії цікавість до самостійного читання.

3. Пам'ятати, що весь друкований матеріял для пропаганди, який надсилатиметься Київським Відділом Постачання та Росповсюдження Друку на повіт, оплачуватиметься ними на умовах, про які буде зроблено вказівку. Росплати провадитимуться двічі на місяць.

При кожному повітовому Ревкомі уряджається відділ постачання та росповсюдження друку. Завідуючим відділом призначається відповідальний член Повітпаркома. Для техничної організації росповсюдження друку повинні бути експедітори.

Обов'язки завідуючого відділом постачання та росповсюдження друку.

На завідуючого Повітвідділом Постачання та Росповсюдження в повіті покладаються слідуючі обов'язки:

1. Слідкувати за правильністю росповсюдження й росподілу одержуваної літератури поміж волостними та сільськими установами, фабрично-заводськими комітетами, а також урядовими, партійними, та громадськими організаціями.

2. Розсилка виробів друку по установах волостей і сел мусить відбуватися, не дожидаючись поки названі місця зажадають висилки їм друкованого слова, а не дожидаючись поки названі місця зажадають висилки їм друкованого слова, а треба самім направляти туди літературу, збуджуючи свідомість сільського населення і посилати туди живі сили для читання в голос, і для пояснення прочитаного.

3. Повідомити всі міські та сільські Ревкоми, що вироби друку любого вигляду, які одпускатимуться Повітвідділом Постачання та Росповсюдження Друку, вимагатимуть грошового покриття. Повітвідділ відчитуватиметься перед Київським Губвідділом Постачання та Росповсюдження двічи на місяць: 16 го і 1 го. Повітвідділу ж, для того, щоб грошова росплата провадилася правильно та вичерпуючо обидва рази на місяць,—слід подати до відома тих, які бажають одержати пресу й літературу, про постанову Губвідділа Постачання та Росповсюдження Друку про платність того, що відпускатиметься. Всяка установа, як урядова, так і громадська, а тим паче й партійна організація, завжди виділить в своєму бюджеті § на культурно-просвітні потреби. Звідти власне й будуть покриватися всі вимоги на літературу на ім'я Повітвідділу.

Зовсім окремо стоїть питання це, що до тієї літератури, яка посилатиметься у волості для сіл. Від самих волостей, може бути, й зовсім не пощастить одержати якоїсь грошової платні за літературу, як періодичну, так і книжну. Але тоді місцеві Ревкоми повинні асігнувати певну сумму спеціяльно на просвітні потреби села і з цих коштів робити росплати з Повітвідділом за кількість виданої літератури. Іншими словами волості будуть тоді постачатися виробами друку за кошт Повітревкома.

В разі якихось затримок у одержанні літератури з центру зноситися з Губвідділом телеграфно для вияснення причин.

4. Повітвідділу встановити доладне постачання літератури волосним і сільським громадським організаціям. Для цього треба увійти в згоду з волосними Ревкомами, які [illegible] до Повітвідділу своїх кур'єрів, або підводою, або іншими якимись способами, а одержанням літератури в свою ж чергу волосним Ревкомам належить в такий же спосіб росповсюджувати літературу і по хуторах і по селах.

5. Одним з дуже раціональних способів притягання до читання радянського друку є метод росклейки, як газет, так і плакатів, по найвиднійших місцях, майданах і т. п.,—тому и Повітвідділу й волосному Ревкомові, і сільській політичній організації належить по разу, по одержанні газет та плакатів, росклеювати якусь частину з одержаного в тих місцях, де прохожі товариші могли б їх читати.

35 Leaflet [Ukr.]: Instructions concerning the supply and distribution of printed matter (1920).
TsDAVO.

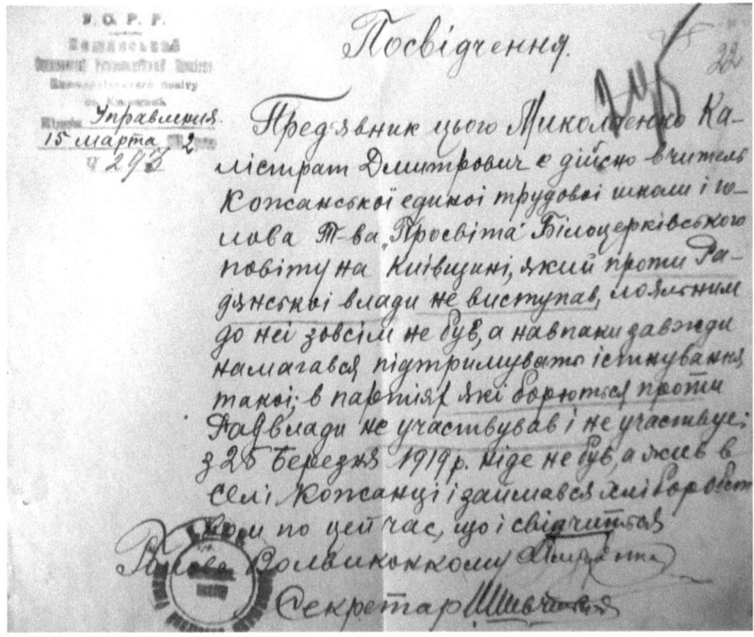

У.С.Р.Р. [illegible] Управління 15 марта 1922 ч 293

Посвідчення.

Предявник цього Миколаєнко Калістрат Дмитрович є дійсно вчитель Копсанської єдиної трудової школи і голова Т-ва „Просвіта" Білоцерківського повіту на Київщині, який проти Радянської влади не виступав, ворожим до неї зовсім не був, а навпаки завжди намагався підтримувати існування такої; в партіях які борються проти Радвлади не участвував і не участвує; з 25 березня 1919 р. ніде не був, а жив в селі Копсанці і займався хліборобством по цей час, що і свідчиться

Голова Волвиконкому [illegible]

Секретар Шевченко

36 Document confirming that the bearer is a teacher and head of the Enlightenment Circle in Bila Tserkva county and has never been involved in anti-Bolshevik activity.
TsDASBU.

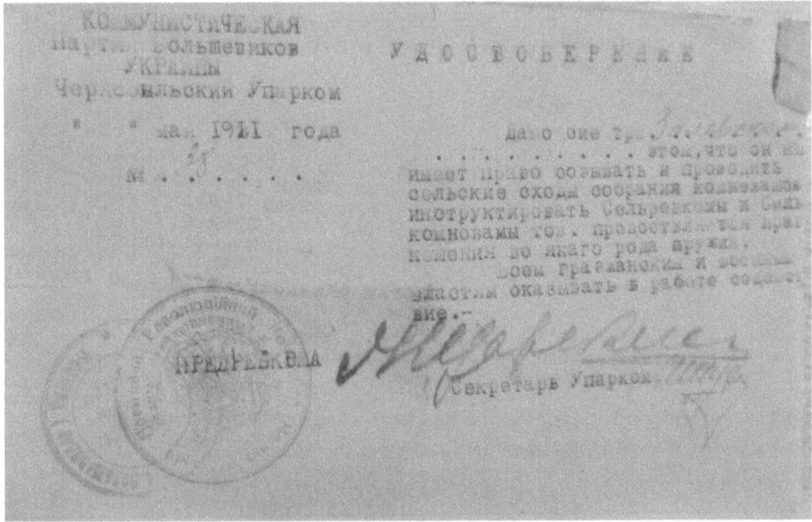

Коммунистическая партия большевиков Украины [illegible] Упарком

« » мая 1921 года

№ . . . . . .

УДОСТОВЕРЕНИЕ

Дано сие тов. [illegible] в том, что он имеет право созывать и проводить сельские сходы собрания комнезамов [illegible] инструктировать Сельревкомы и [illegible] комнезамы тов. предоставляется право ношения всякого рода оружия.

Всем гражданским и военным властям оказывать в работе содействие.—

ПРЕДРЕВКОМА [illegible]

Секретарь Упарком [illegible]

37 Document confirming that the bearer is a party agitator with the right to organize meetings and carry a weapon.
TsDASBU.

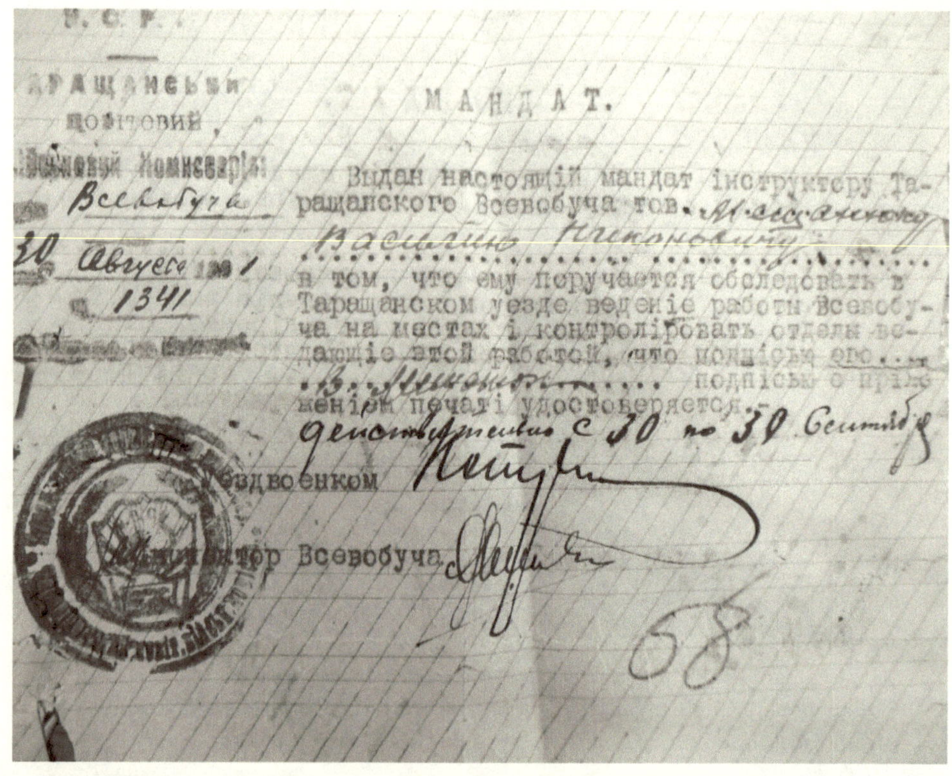

У. С. Р.

Таращанський
повітовий
Військовий Комісаріят
Всевобуча

30 Августа 1921
№ 1341

МАНДАТ.

Выдан настоящій мандат інструктору Таращанского Всевобуча тов. ...
Василию ...
....
в том, что ему поручается обследовать в Таращанском уезде веденіе работы Всевобуча на местах і контролировать отделы ведающіе этой работой, что подписью его ...
.В. .... подписью с приложеніем печаті удостоверяется.
действительно с 30 по 30 Сентября

...здвоенком

...тор Всевобуча

68

38 Document confirming that the bearer is a supervisor responsible for overseeing instructor-agitators in Tarashcha district.
TsDASBU.

ПРИКАЗ № 1/26

Волынского Губернского Революционного Комитета

по Полиграфо-Бумажной Секции Химотдела Волгубсовнархоза.

Житомир, 24 Июня 1920 г.

§ 1.

Приказывается всем учреждениям и владельцам писче-бумажных магазинов и складов, также и торговцам, имеющим в наличии разную бумагу, канцелярские принадлежности, сдать на учет Полиграфо-Бумажного Под'отдела Химотдела в течение 3-х дней со дня опубликования сего в помещение Совнархоза, Бердичевская, № 16, комната № 25.

§ 2.

Все гражданские и военные учреждения, также и частные лица, имеющие в своем распоряжении пишущие машины, обязаны в течение 3-х дней сообщить Полиграфо-Бумажному Под'отделу.

§ 3.

Всем типо-литографиям и переплетным предприятиям запрещается принимать заказы на типографо-переплетные работы без наряда Полиграфо-Бумажного Под'отдела. Военным и гражданским учреждениям предлагается направлять все заказы на типографо-переплетные работы для распределения таковых по типографиям в Полиграфо-Бумажный Под'отдел Совнархоза.

§ 4.

Все счета на выполненные типографо-переплетные работы должны учреждениями предварительно направляться в Полиграфо-Бумажный Под'отдел для утверждения таковых.

§ 5.

Невыполнение настоящего приказа повлечет за собой привлечение к ответственности по законам военного времени. Не сданные на учет указанные в сем приказе предметы, при обнаружении таковых будут конфискованы.

Зам. Председателя Волгубревкома **Г. Шепелев.**

За Заведывающего Отделом
Управления Ревкома **Кийко-Шелест.**

Председатель Волгубсовнархоза **В. Зиновьев.**

39 Leaflet: Order to register all printing materials and forbidding publishing without permission (1920).
TsDAVO F. 573 op 1 sprava 816.

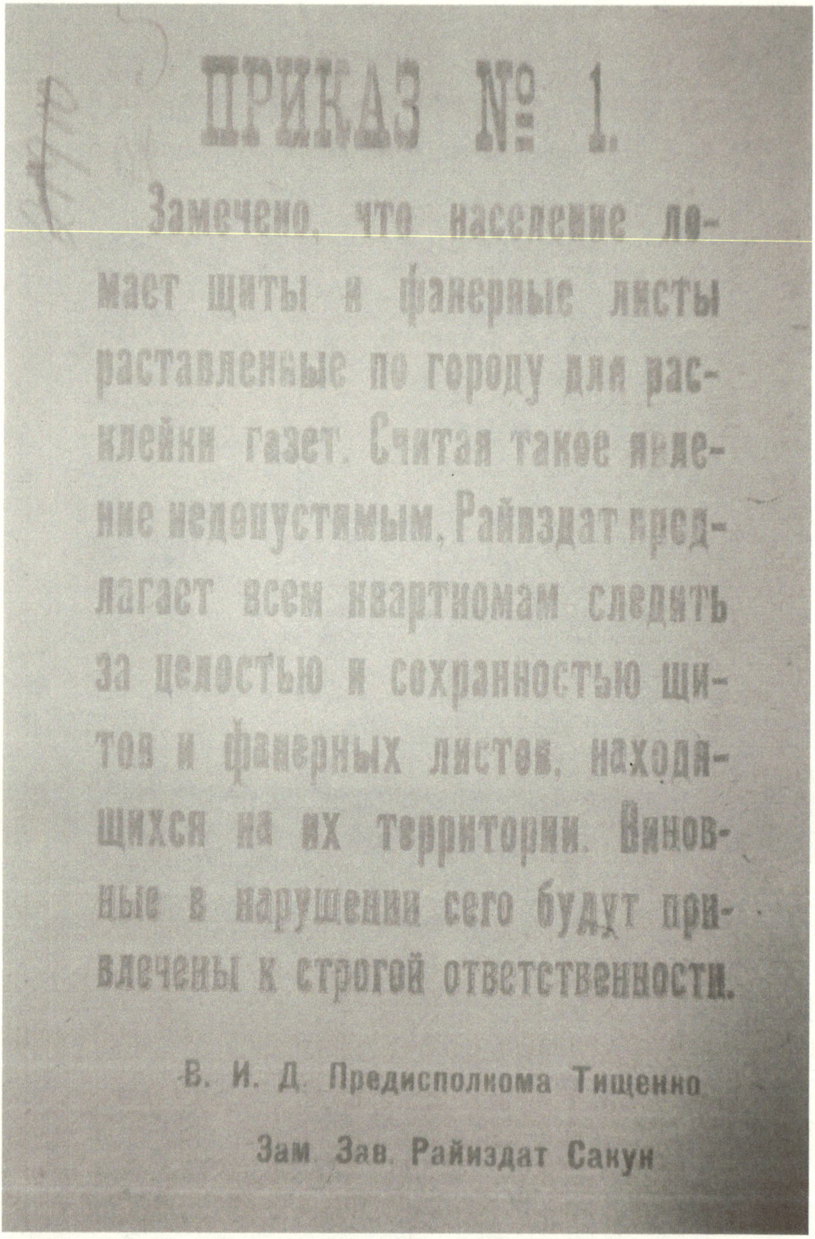

ПРИКАЗ № 1.

Замечено, что население ломает щиты и фанерные листы раставленные по городу для расклейки газет. Считая такое явление недопустимым, Райиздат предлагает всем квартномам следить за целостью и сохранностью щитов и фанерных листов, находящихся на их территории. Виновные в нарушении сего будут привлечены к строгой ответственности.

В. И. Д. Предисполкома Тищенко

Зам. Зав. Райиздат Сакун

40 Leaflet: "ORDER No. 1" warning of severe punishment for anyone caught tearing down fences or boards used to post newspapers (1921?). Arkhiv druku.

ПРИКАЗ № 14

Злонамеренными лицами и хулиганами систематически срываются плакаты и листовки, расклеиваемые Губагентством.

Приказываю Чека и Милиции, срывающих плакаты, немедленно арестовывать и привлекать к ответственности, как ВРАГОВ РЕВОЛЮЦИИ.

Предлагаю всем гражданам, видевшим срывающего плакаты, немедленно сообщать об этом ближайшему постовому милиционеру или агенту Чека

Председатель ревкома Д. ПЕТРОВСКИЙ

41 Leaflet: "ORDER No. 14" warning that those tearing down leaflets and posters will be considered enemies of the revolution. (1920?).
H. Ivanushchenko, *Zalizom i kroviu.*

21 586

Приказ № 7

Роменского Уездного Отдела Управления по Уиздату

В виду того, что до сих пор замечается злоумышленное срывание афиш, объявлений, приказов, расклеиваемых на витринах, Отдел Управления приказывает всем гражданам, до сих пор занимающимся подобными действиями прекратить.

Лица замеченные в этом, будут преданы суду Ревтрибунала.

Заведующий Отд. Управления ОГИП

Зав. Уиздатом БОБОВИЧ.

42 Leaflet: "ORDER No. 7" - The Romni district administrative printing office threatens court martial for those caught tearing down notices. Arkhiv druku.

Conclusion

This book has reviewed and summarized messages that rival elites wanted to transmit to audiences. It is based on an illustrative sample of printed texts intended for mass distribution. These included instructions, ordinances, commands, informative materials, and exhortatives phrased to encourage sympathizers or dishearten opponents. Texts explained what the issuing body represented, who its allies were, and why it should be supported. They explained who were enemies and why they should be opposed, as well as who were minorities and how they should be regarded. Rivals appealed to the uncommitted and called for each other's supporters to desert or surrender, or to rebel. Each magnified its opponents' internal divisions and refuted its rivals' claims. Texts resorted to manipulation and black propaganda, appealing to emotion and fear. Some included lies, stereotypes, derogatory allusions, and exaggerations. Other texts used explanation and logic to instruct, to explain terms and concepts, or to recount events that had actually happened. Rivals used moral appeals to obtain goods, food, and recruits. The sample indicates that the Bolsheviks demanded a much greater range of items from their civilian populations than their Ukrainian rivals. More often than their Ukrainian rivals, they threatened severe penalties in order to obtain those items – including summary execution or deportation to a concentration camp. Bolshevik materials circulated in all of former tsarist Ukraine, whereas UNR texts rarely if ever reached the extreme southeastern territories.[1] People obviously were also swayed one way or another by information from "the grapevine" and rumour mills, but it is unlikely anyone will ever be able to study how and what messages circulated by word of mouth.[2]

Cynics might claim that Ukrainian intellectuals no more represented a Ukrainian nation than Bolshevik intellectuals represented workers and peasants. The pronouncements of the latter, like those of the former, from such a perspective, amounted to empty rhetoric and lies by self-appointed leaders who had usurped power and represented only themselves. But such a sweeping generalization is no more true for the Ukrainians than it is for the Bolsheviks. The messages of both contained lies, but not everything printed was lies. A lie found in the propaganda of both sides was that more land for peasants would improve their lot. This idea was widely promulgated by socialists of all nationalities before the war, and it did appeal to peasants, despite the fact that reformers realized the key to rural prosperity lay in improved techniques, not redistribution. On average, prewar Ukrainians peasants had more land than did their western European counterparts, who nonetheless produced at least twice as much more per acre. We shall perhaps never know whether those who promulgated this particular idea believed it or simply exploited it for their own ends, realizing, as Napoleon had observed, "The truth is not half so important as what people think to be true."

The main message in the sample Bolshevik materials was that "the workers and peasants of Russia" had "helped" the "workers and peasants of Ukraine" establish "soviet power." Workers and peasants of different nationalities had a common socio-economic interest in controlling land and factories that overrode national differences. Texts never referred to Russia or Russians as "foreign" or explicity targeted Ukrainians as the enemy, although, in practice, in Ukraine, local agents did target Ukrainians as Ukrainians when they used the euphemism "petliurite" to describe them.[3] Texts rarely refuted the Ukrainian claim that Bolshevik rule was tantamount to a military conquest by foreigners. They did not mention the true role of the party in *soviets*, and they rarely, if ever, used its full name, the Russian Communist Party. The names of top leaders, with the exception of Lenin, appeared infrequently before 1920. The enemy was identified as landlords, capitalists, tsarist generals, and wealthy peasants, who threatened to overturn "soviet power" and turn the poor and middle-stratum peasants into serfs again. Texts equated "Soviet power" with popular rule and land distribution for poor and middle-stratum peasants and emphasized that communes were voluntary. Materials dealing with religious issues stressed that the Bolsheviks allowed freedom of worship and did not desecrate churches. Ukrainian national leaders were "bourgeois" liars who exploited national issues in order to retain their class privileges. They were traitors because they had signed treaties with the Entente powers and then duped peasants and criminals to fight the Red Army and disrupt "soviet power." Their alliances with western European countries were presented as a capitulation to imperialism. Some texts were didactic, providing explanations of concepts like socialism.

Bolshevik propagandists' use of Ukrainian national issues changed during the revolutionary years. By late 1919 they had replaced isolated abstract assertions about "national self-determination" made in 1917–18 with an emphasis on issues such as sponsorship of mass education and opposition to Ukraine's centuries-old enemy, Polish landlords. One document treated the Bolshevik presence in Ukraine as an altruistic self-sacrifice by Russians in the name of the socialist ideal. Another, as Russians' atonement for past wrongs. The sample texts show that after 1920, due to the influence of former Ukrainian left-SRs and the Ukrainian Bolshevik faction in Moscow, propaganda sometimes equated national independence with "soviet power," explaining that it was possible only thanks to Russia and the Red Army. Propagandists used some national motifs in both Ukrainian and Russian texts, but whether these motifs appeared more frequently in Ukrainian- than in Russian-language materials cannot be determined on the basis of the sample.

While the Bolsheviks did disseminate lies, not everything they published was lies. The biggest lie they told was that they represented "soviet power" (*sovietskia vlast*). Originally, in practice and theory, *soviets* were elected councils of peasants, workers, and soldiers' deputies, who were either independents or members of any left-wing party. In reality, the Bolsheviks began systematically usurping and taking over the *soviets* after they took over a region. At the top of the *soviet* hierarchy, in theory, the Council of People's Commissars (Sovnarkom) made decisions. In reality, it only implemented the decisions of the Bolshevik party's Politburo. This at the time was a secret entity, one whose existence, decisions, and resolutions were also secret. And so on down the hierarchy, with local party committees ensuring, by force if necessary, that only Bolshevik members were "elected" to all *soviet* executive offices. In August 1918, Dzerzhinskii specified that *soviets* had no authority over the Cheka. In August 1919, Ukraine's Politburo explained the relationship as follows in a secret circular: "It is forbidden to raise arguments regarding central party decisions at soviet meetings, and to reveal the *party's predetermined decisions* [sic *predreshenie voprosov*] concerning soviet institutions: a recess must be declared when necessary."[4] Three other mendacious assertions appeared in the sample. One was the claim that the Bolsheviks were not exporting large amounts of Ukrainian grain to Russia. Another was that the UNR had dissolved itself and agreed to federate with a White Russia and had given Ukrainian assets to France in return for troops to fight its imperialist war. Third was Lenin's claim that Bolshevik forces had occupied Kyiv before they actually did.

Ukrainian leaders, governmental and non-governmental, stressed the idea of national independence attained after centuries of tsarist

Russian oppression. The sample suggests they rarely used Russian to promulgate the national message. One key theme was that the honest and hard-working would have social justice and equitable land reform only in an autonomous and (later) sovereign state organized as a parliamentary republic. If Ukraine did not establish its own national government, rapacious imperialist neighbours, Russia in particular, drawn by Ukraine's resources, would reimpose their rule and oppress the people. Government materials described Ukraine's Bolshevik government as a foreign Russian regime imposed by military conquest and dominated by commissars, layabouts, lowlifes, drunkards, and disloyal or foreign (i.e., Russian) Jews. Texts highlighted Bolshevik depredations and injustices, stressing that they promised everything and gave nothing. Radical Ukrainian socialists called for an independent country with its own Communist Party based on non-Bolshevik *soviets*. Governmental and party materials labelled Bolsheviks as foreign imperialists whose vicious exploitation menaced everyone, including the poor. Didactic texts explained matters such as what Ukraine was, who Ukrainians were, or what a republic was. By the end of 1917, faced with the Russian invasion, leaflets were paying more attention to identifying enemies and explaining why they had to be fought than they had at the beginning of the year. In 1919, when western Ukrainian troops wearing Austrian-style uniforms and helmets appeared in eastern Ukraine, UNR leaflets and pamphlets explained that they were not foreigners, but the same nationality as eastern Ukrainians. That year, propaganda identified Russian Bolsheviks and Whites as one and same – Ukraine's historic Russian enemy. Materials from 1917 explained that tsarist Russia had economically exploited the country. In 1919–20, texts described how the Bolsheviks were stripping Ukraine of everything they could grab, shipping it to Russia, and leaving all Ukrainians, including the poor, with nothing. Government propaganda did not explicitly condemn as enemies all Russians or Poles living in Ukraine.[5] Some texts distinguished between pro- and anti-Ukrainian Poles, and between Polish landlords and the Polish people.

The Hetman's government identified itself as a national Ukrainian state to peasants not thanks to a propaganda campaign, but due to its decrees rescinding land reforms. That link was reinforced by illegally circulating Bolshevik texts that explained that peasant economic interests were incompatible with Ukrainian independence. During the last weeks of its existence, the by then decidedly pro-White ministers issued a spate of leaflets intended to organize resistance to the Bolsheviks as well as Ukrainian national forces. They called on the population to fight for a Ukraine within a restored imperial Russian state. This association of independence under the Hetman with old-regime restoration was neutralized to a degree in southern Ukraine in 1918 by the western Ukrainian Sich Riflemen Legion.

The sample materials indicate that the presentation of enemies in general, and Jews in particular, changed over time in Ukrainian texts. They do not allow us to pinpoint the exact dates of those changes. Rada materials in 1917 initially identified only White or Bolshevik Russians, and Bolshevik Jews, as "the enemy," and condemned pogroms. The reviewed sample contains a non-governmental poster from late 1917, and anonymous army leaflets from 1919, that did refer to all Jews as enemies. From late 1919, Ukrainian materials, as a rule, classified Bolsheviks, communists, and Russian Russians, not Ukrainian Russians, as "the enemy." The sample contains one warlord leaflet that condemned all Russians as enemies. Some warlords also began to group all Jews into the enemy category in verbal statements as well as in their leaflets, much as English propagandists assumed that all Germans in Britain, and their German counterparts assumed all Belgians in Belgium, were potential traitors (Illus. 43). One leaflet in the sample explicitly urged Ukrainians to kill Jews.[6] By 1920 almost all the warlord leaflets in the sample condemned all Jews as enemies. An analysis from Odesa written in July 1921 noted, however, that while ideological anti-Semitism figured as a reason for pogroms, more significant were situational issues – specifically, hatred of communists and the desire for loot.[7] Some detailed witness accounts specified that local military commanders allowed or ordered soldiers to initiate violence against Jews and pillage their property, or they tolerated such activities, in which civilians then joined.[8]

UNR propaganda, like its Bolshevik opposite, contained lies. One was the claim that it was supported by the European powers. A second, encountered mainly in warlords' materials, was that all Jews were Bolsheviks. A third example was the claim that, on Petliura's signal, Ukrainians would rise as one and overthrow the Bolsheviks. By the end of 1921, Petliura's conservative critics had dismissed this as naive speculation: "No uprising was prepared. The peasants did not trust S. Petliura."[9] Nonetheless, at the time, significant armed opposition did predispose many, including the pragmatic Chykalenko, to view the claim as possibly true.[10] The Ukrainian troops in Polish POW camps who were supposed to spearhead an invasion planned for 1921 that would spark the mass uprising believed it would happen.[11] The authors of Bolshevik secret situation reports in Ukraine thought so as well. However, by the end of 1921, the doubters had been proven correct, and the Bolsheviks knew that nothing could shake their rule in Ukraine. Their million-strong army stationed in Ukraine far outnumbered any available trained Ukrainian troops. They also knew in 1920 that the British had lifted their Baltic blockade. By August of that year, in the wake of their retreat from Poland, the Bolsheviks had begun receiving vast supplies of munitions, paper, medicine, arms, uniforms, and rolling stock from Germany, Estonia, Sweden, Denmark, and Switzerland.

A fourth dubious assertion was that the 1920 alliance with Poland and subsequent independence would not involve the return of Polish landlords – the strongest Polish group supporting the alliance. As noted in chapter 2, peasants in Volyn and Podillia provinces were reluctant to support the UNR, or even opposed it, because of its alliance with Poland, which they associated with the return of the hated Polish landowners.

Leaflets reveal that parties used fictional, now forgotten, popular characters to promulgate their messages, analogous to the Père Duchesne of the French Revolution – a straight-talking working commoner who explained things simply and convincingly – although it cannot be acscertained today how popular such figures actually were. Leaflets also offer insight into aspects of life at the time that have since been forgotten: the salutation "mister comrade," a call for workers to form a "proletarian free Cossack" militia, Ukrainian SD appeals to "proletarian cossacks," " Christ Has Risen" titles on appeals to Red Army soldiers, and Bolshevik commissars issuing Easter greetings to citizens.

It is not easy to assess the impact of "paper bullets." The volume and ubiquity of printed texts varied with time and place. While in cities there could be many copies of items for each individual, in villages it was often the opposite; many individuals per single copy. Historians of the war in western Europe, where there were functioning distribution networks behind the front lines, have concluded that propaganda successes were closely related to circumstances. Propaganda could not be totally divorced from daily realities if it was to have an impact. British recruiting posters, for instance, initially alienated many of the men they were supposed to attract because they sold war as a commodity and focused on monarchism, imperialism, and militarism. None of that motivated the workers they were intended to attract, as much as they did the gentry and the upper middle class, whose members had created the posters. Once the exuberant first year of the war had passed, German domestic propaganda, focused on national issues, also stopped influencing soldiers, of whom 30 to 50 per cent were peasants. Their experiences at the front did not make them receptive to nationalist perspectives or interpretive models.[12] Conversely, German propaganda in 1917 was successful in maintaining popular support for the war domestically and in disintegrating the Russian Army on the Eastern Front.[13]

Where and when "paper bullets" reached their targets, they were most effective – at least in the short term – when events reinforced their message. If too many expectations aroused by mobilization remained unfulfilled, loyalties among most soon evaporated. Successful propaganda, in the words of one historian, required propagandists who knew how and when to exploit an opportunity – precisely when to throw a left hook at an opponent who was about to fall as a result of a right hook.[14] British propaganda, for instance, stimulated anti-German sentiment in the United States by exploiting the sinking of passenger liners, the execution of nurse Edith Cavell, and publicizing the Zimmerman telegraph. This propaganda helped ensure that the United States would enter the war and that the Central Powers would collapse sooner rather than later. In the last six months of 1918, when defeats and losses at the front and hunger at home were seriously crippling Germany, Entente propaganda describing the futility of resistance against overwhelming odds decisively complemented its military offensive and the civilian dissatisfaction that finally toppled the Kaiser. It spread knowledge of the massive retreat and intensified the psychological impact of the harsh reality. That year, the Entente dropped more than 15 million leaflets on German troops between August and October alone, which the wounded and those on leave then passed to civilians. That same year, propaganda was singularly successful on the southern front, where it undermined the fighting capacity of the Austrian army through massive coordinated appeals for surrender directed at Slavic soldiers.[15] Party and Cheka reports from the Urals in 1919–22 also reported that it was living conditions more than propaganda that shaped attitudes towards the Bolsheviks – attitudes that ranged from indifference to hostility.[16]

Generalizations derived from study of the western European countries seem applicable to the Ukrainian case, with three caveats. First, the production and distribution of printed texts in Ukrainian lands was seriously hampered by shifting fronts, shortages and destruction. Second, there were more than two sides in Ukraine and the dissemination and impact of Russian SR, Menshevik, White, and Bundist propaganda has not yet been studied. Third, not all readers necessarily understood texts exactly the way authors intended.

It is undeniable that on the territories of the former Russian empire in 1917, the Bolshevik slogan "Land. Peace. Bread" was singularly successful in demoralizing the army and turning the population against the tsar and the Provisional Government. Supported by German anti-Russian propaganda directed at the army, the slogan worked because it coincided with, and exploited, widespread war-weariness, food shortages, and the desire for land reform.[17] Because most of the major landowners in Volyn and Podillia provinces were Polish, Bolshevik propaganda there also successfully inflamed traditional national hatreds in 1917. The demoralized soldiers who engaged in looting and land seizures, like the peasants who joined them, knew little of Bolshevik theory, but they knew that Bolshevik slogans justified their violent behaviour. Also successful were the Bolshevik agitators who persuaded General Kornilov's soldiers that their officers were using them to restore the tsar; thus these soldiers stopped their march on Petrograd in July 1917. German soldiers told their Bolshevik captors in October 1918 that their massive barrage of German-language leaflets had been decisive in persuading them not to fight.[18] Ukrainian leaders claimed that Bolshevik propaganda had a decisive impact on Ukrainians in late 1917. It persuaded already demoralized soldiers not to fight while the naive peasants "hoodwinked [*zadurene*] by agitators from Russia followed the communists against the Central Rada" (Doc. 97).[19] UNR officials in January 1919 reported that of two thousand recently captured Red Army POWs, seven hundred avowed that they had fought on the Red side because the Bolsheviks had explained to them that Petliura was defending the bourgeoisie and that the Bolsheviks opposed the bourgeoisie.[20]

Leaders at the time perceived the propaganda of their rivals as omnipresent and influential, although that was not necessarily the case.[21] American historians have claimed that during 1919–20, Bolshevik publications were not as decisive in swaying opinion as were Entente materials in western Europe. As noted even at the time, this was due to technical problems of production and delivery, as well as the failure of newspapers to attract attention with creative layout, typefaces, and headlines and to publish photographs. No less a problem was ambiguous and grammatically incoherent language.[22] Reports on the impact of propaganda by those who disseminated it, and of Bolshevik and Ukrainian national government sympathizers or agents behind front lines, show that "paper bullets" in Ukraine between 1917 and 1920, when and if they reached their targets, had much the same impact as anywhere else. Success or failure in swaying opinion depended on local circumstances. In some cases, reports from different people covering the same area at the same time contained similar conclusions.

Ukrainian troops in Kyiv in the winter of 1917 were addressed by Bolshevik agitators, but meanwhile, Bolshevik troops were addressed by Ukrainian agitators – that was standard procedure during those months. One Ukrainian soldier wrote in a letter that Bolshevik agitators alone did not always turn opinion. There were instances where they exploited Ukrainian soldiers' utter disbelief to disarm them – albeit under threat of shooting. "For long years we all together fought the hated autocracy ... And now the Bolsheviks declare war on us Ukrainians," wrote an incredulous eyewitness Ukrainian soldier. "Brother comrades, workers, soldiers and peasants! Must you strangle freedom in Ukraine? Do you see in us [Bolsheviks, and our] democratic Ukraine, worse enemies than Hindenburg's landlords? No, we can't believe that!" The Ukrainian soldiers concluded they did not, and did not fight.[23] In a report from the town of Trypillia, just after it had been freed from Bolshevik control in January 1919, a UNR agent reported that the garrison's morale was good but that it was leftist-inclined because of earlier Bolshevik influence. However, "there is strong propaganda from the left-wing Ukrainian socialists that is neutralizing what remains of communist propaganda."[24] During the 1920 summer Polish offensive, Ukrainian peasants were little moved by pro-Polish UNR leaflets or by calls for support in the name of independence. Most associated independence with the re-establishment of Polish landownership and with the vicious depredations of the irregular and regular Polish armed units that enforced that re-establishment. No more than three thousand men from those provinces volunteered for the Ukrainian army that summer.[25] In western Volyn province in May 1920, peasants in the Zhytomir area did greet the troops warmly in the wake of the offensive, but only because they saw them as harbingers of stability and order. Politically, they wanted a tsar, or for Petliura to become tsar or president: "it is best if one man rules us."[26] In August 1920, Bolshevik officials in the Kryvyi Rih area reporting to their superiors did attribute strong partisan resistance, including among poor peasants, in part to UNR propaganda. The UNR's defeat and the general internal collapse and mayhem by the end of that year left people with little alternative but to believe the Bolshevik message about a Ukrainian Bolshevik Ukraine populated by landowning peasants.

Printed materials must be produced and distributed. The available data on the distribution and production of Ukrainian and Bolshevik propaganda indicate that more texts than images were disseminated and that more of each went to towns than to villages, although some villages were well covered. Total volume published declined as paper became scarce. In villages far from major roads or rail lines, and thus distant from agitators, inhabitants might, or might not, get information on the events surrounding them. Someone may or may not have arrived to explain terms like "Ukraine" or "the Russian Soviet Republic" or "imperialism." Kazatyn, south of Zhytomir, was the terminus of the local rail network and within Bolshevik territory in the summer of 1919. A Bolshevik agent reported it had one kiosk with fifty or sixty copies of various assorted newspapers and that beyond there was no contact of any sort with the "political centre." Agitators and activists refused to travel in the region because local anti-Bolshevik units were shooting Ukrainian and Russian Bolsheviks on the spot as "Jewish hirelings."[27]

Nor would people necessarily read materials that did arrive. A report from Volyn province is typical: "They [residents of Dubno region] used unread journals and 'literature' as scrap paper [*bumazhki*] because paper [*papertsi*] was hard to find."[28] In 1920 in central Ukraine, an eyewitness wrote: "There was no paper. Soviet newspapers are published so poorly that 'even with a priest you can't make it out.' The peasants smoked [used for cigarette paper–SV] all the books they had, including psalters and books of hours. That is why they grab what Bolshevik literature they can."[29] On UNR territory agitators reported that it was unwise to give published materials to passersby and expect them to distribute it. What often happened was that the lucky man took his bundle home, hid it, and used it thereafter for wrapping food.[30]

Uncertainty made many cautious. When the village of Napadiivka in Kyiv province came under UNR control in September 1919, its notables heard that government inspectors were coming to their village, the county seat. So they decided to decorate the county office with portraits of Shevchenko, Alexander III, and Lenin. Asked by the shocked inspectors why they had done so, they replied: "If Ukraine wins, then we have Shevchenko; if Denikin, then we have His Imperial Majesty; and if the Bolsheviks win, then we have Lenin. Don't you see we are surrounded by three foes and we don't know which of them to serve and obey. If we had newspapers or information that told us what to do, then we would know whom to support and whom to serve."[31] This incident suggests how audiences reacted to messages at a time when no one government or party could control communications and isolate an audience from rival messages for an extended period of time.

Individuals were important. The right person in the right place at the right time could sway moods with the spoken word. One town or village might have teachers who subscribed to Ukrainian papers; the next might have Black Hundred or Bolshevik activists who subscribed to *their* newspapers. Political positions evolved accordingly. One member of the Central Rada, Mykola Kovalevsky, a Ukrainian SR co-op activist, saw a Bolshevik agitator in front of Kyiv City Hall (today the Maidan), in June 1917 urging a crowd of a few hundred, mainly soldiers, to reject the Rada's recently proclaimed First Universal. He was using a theme common in Bolshevik propaganda at the time, claiming that the Rada was comprised of generals, as proven by the name of its executive organ, the General Secretariat. The crowd began to turn ugly, and some wanted to march on the Rada, located nearby in the Pedagogical Museum, to depose it. Kovalevsky took the podium, introduced himself, told the crowd he was a member of the Rada but not a general, and declared that the Bolsheviks were taking money from German capitalists. The crowd turned, and some wanted to lynch the Bolshevik agitator, who by then had slinked away. The threat of lynching faced by this particular fellow was an occupational hazard for agitators whose messages departed too radically from what their audiences wanted to hear. According to Rada agitators, popular opinion became decisively pro-Rada only after July 1917 and the failure of the Kornilov's coup.[32]

Language influenced reception. One Ukrainian SR claimed that had Ukrainian SD leaders published more in Russian, they would have attracted more workers.[33] Yet Ukrainian agitator reports from 1917 often mention how, after hours of stubborn argument, a persistent Rada activist could swing meetings from hostility or suspicion expressed in Russian, to support expressed in Ukrainian. Reports from Kharkiv and Kherson provinces indicate that activists in those places, too, could swing opinion. In August 1917 in some areas, for instance, peasant but not worker-soldier *soviets* were pro-Rada, and local Russian officials allowed the transit of large amounts of Russian but not Ukrainian literature.[34] In Kherson province in the summer of 1917, well-developed Russian networks and the lack of Ukrainian literature and personnel were key factors not only in peasant support there for Russian parties, but also in identification with Russian-imperial rather than Ukrainian national values. One agitator noted that "the Russians are swamping us here with their literature, their money, their agitation and organization." Another report noted the result: "The people have been propagandized [*propagandazuvani*] that they are not Ukrainian, but the opposite [i.e., Russian] and they do not recognize any Ukraine or Central Rada."[35]

A student in a group of travelling instructors related how at their first meeting he spoke in Russian. He asked the assembled crowd whether he should continue in Russian or Ukrainian – a word that at the time few peasants applied to themselves. They replied "in Russian" (*po Rusku*). The instructors learned their lesson. In the next villages, the Ukrainians asked whether they should speak "in the landlord's language" (*po pansku*) or "in our language" (*po nashomu*). The crowd replied "in our language," and the meetings continued in Ukrainian. Some reports from the south note that peasants spoke Ukrainian without realizing it was Ukrainian they were speaking.[36] During the summer of 1917, one agitator related how he had begun a meeting, in Ukrainian, about establishing a town reading club. The peasants all spoke Russian and explained that they would have to speak Russian in the club because they had all forgotten Ukrainian. As the meeting went on, more and more began speaking Ukrainian. By the time it ended, the entire proceedings were being conducted in Ukrainian and, according to the agitator, in a much more relaxed atmosphere. When the people assembled again the next day, they asked one another: "When did you learn Ukrainian if yesterday you said you did not know it?" In Kharkiv province on 8 October of that year, a Vovchansk county meeting considered a proposal from the *zemstvo* to hire a teacher who would teach in Ukrainian. The meeting decided against because "it was unnecessary to teach in Ukrainian." A Rada agitator heard about this, travelled there, and explained to the people why they should have a Ukrainian teacher. On 15 October the council annulled its previous decision. It voted to hire the teacher, saying it had been a misunderstanding "and that we did not know that it [Ukrainian] is our native language which we ourselves speak."[37]

Early Bolshevik reports on their rule in Kharkiv and Poltava provinces during the first months of 1919 show how circumstances determined the impact of spoken and printed propaganda where it appeared. They repeat an observation found in almost all agitator and instructor reports from all sides. Namely, agitators who could communicate well and distribute plenty of literature were decisive in swaying opinion. Another observed that too few agitators, little or no literature, and poor communications meant that printed messages reached few if any people outside the big cities. Reports contain many complaints about weak distribution and an almost complete lack of printed materials outside city limits: "There are no newspapers and peasants have nothing except a chance dirty old leaflet." Just as skilled agitators could win sympathy, bad ones alienated their audiences. Among those who did reach villages were the ignorant, the incompetent, and "commissar autocrats." A report from April 1919 noted that "incompetent agitators did more harm than good." Reports the following year noted that such persons discredited Bolshevik rule by doing things such as harassing priests, closing churches, and establishing departments within district party committees with odd names like "for the struggle against the feelings and moral failures of the people," or "for the struggle against family unpleasantries – too many children." None of which did much to win support. One strange project noted by an inspector was titled "How to work like a dimwit [*neumenye*]."[38]

Wise agitators sometimes realized that peasant dissimulation, "the weapon of the weak," could leave outsiders with a false impression of their reception. A Bolshevik report from Volyn province in June 1919 noted that despite the population's favourable reaction to the Bolsheviks, and the resulting easy passage of all resolutions and measures by local *soviets*, the situation was bad. This agitator realized that the people had passed all resolutions because, even if they did understand what they were about, they knew from experience that nothing would be implemented any time soon. Other agents flatly reported that people had no conception of what soviet power was about and often did not interpret messages as they were intended. From Kyiv province in the summer of 1919, one agent reported that peasants told him: "We could come to terms with the communists but it is just too bad they don't believe in God."[39] In territories recently taken back from the Bolsheviks in August 1919 south of Kamianets-Podilsky, a report cited peasants in Kytaigorod county: "We heard that somebody thought-up some kind of Ukraine. We don't know who, to what end, whether there is an authority [*vlast*] in that Ukraine, and what it is." Regarding other agitators who had come their way, the peasants "did not know who they were or why they came." In another village in the same area, a woman in the autumn of 1919 replied as follows when asked what was new: "There was a Petlia [sic] here, and now there are some Tabachniki [troops belonging to Tiutiunnyk, one of Petliura's commanders] but we don't know what they want."[40] Was this dissimulation born of caution, or from ignorance resulting from isolation?

In January 1918 some Ukrainian leaders claimed that their troops were refusing to fight thanks to Bolshevik propaganda. The usually reliable Evhen Chykalenko explained that was not the case with three regiments in Kyiv. These units had fought Bolshevik troops to get to Kyiv but then found, upon arrival, that their leaders had not prepared quarters, rations, or medical services for them. They decided not to fight in defence of a government that was unable to provide basic essentials. In November and December 1918, the Hetman and Chykalenko made no mention of UNR promises of land allotments for service, or its national ideals, as ideas that motivated men to volunteer for its army. They wrote that men were motivated to join its forces by hope of plunder and rumours of a promised three-day pillaging of the capital for all volunteers.[41] Just as not all in the UNR's army fought for an independent Ukraine that December, not all on the Bolshevik side were interested in soviet power. It was rumoured at the time that once the Germans retreated, the English and French would return, together with their tsarist allies, and shoot whoever had deserted in 1917. This predisposed men to support the Bolsheviks.[42]

Bolshevik complaints about failures to convince audiences in 1919 rarely if ever admitted that people rejected their policies because they were oppressive. In northeastern Ukraine after the first few weeks of occupation in 1919, there was hunger. Inhabitants had little interest in listening to speeches extolling the policies they regarded as the cause of that hunger. On the assumption that central policy could not provoke hostility because, by definition, it was correct policy, agents explained that hostility to their superiors in other ways: "The hostile attitude of the peasants is the result of incompetent agitators dealing with the issue of communism incorrectly." In Volyn, one admitted that the population called all agitators "liars."[43] Through May, June, and July of 1919, local party reports were unanimous about the anti-Bolshevik nature of the uprisings, which included Red troops and the poor. Troops shouted down agitators: "Don't feed the barefoot with words."[44] In Chernihiv in the spring of 1919, Ukrainian conscripts who had been mobilized by the Bolsheviks were apparently unmoved by their propaganda and refused to fight in Russia: "We will not fight for Russia. But we will fight for Ukraine." During those same months in southeastern Ukraine, Bolshevik agitators reported that despite intense propaganda within the army, Russian troops were not interested in fighting Makhno and Denikin: "Why should I fight for the *khokhly* [i.e., Ukrainians]. Why do I need Ukraine?"[45] Bolshevik propaganda had mobilized support during the first weeks of 1919, but its effects had vanished by the spring. Confronted with the realities of Bolshevik rule with its forced requisitions, and by the overwhelmingly Russian and Russified Jewish personnel who carried out those requisitions, tens of thousands of workers and peasants, including the poor, joined anti-Bolshevik partisan units.[46] Bolshevik reports from 1920 admitted that their propaganda was having little effect.[47]

Because circumstances mediate propaganda's impact, it is difficult to generalize about the role of printed text in instigating pogroms. There is evidence that verbal incitement to violence against Jews in 1919 did motivate perpetrators. Verbal pleas to refrain also had an effect. Did printed text decrying pogroms and calling on people to refrain from such behaviour have the desired effect?

When considering the Ukrainian side it must be remembered that the government, unlike the Bolsheviks, did not have a well-controlled propaganda organization. Nor did the governmental and anonymous army leaflets in the reviewed sample that did label all Jews as enemies incorporate ideological anti-Semitic ideas such as Masonic conspiracy or the blood libel. In this regard, the records of Ukraine's Politburo from May 1919, when it reviewed the subject of pogroms, are noteworthy. Those present decided that the best solution to what they saw as the anti-Semitism that sparked pogroms would be to replace Jews in government and party posts with Ukrainians and Russians. In briefs opposing that decision, Georgi Piatakov, then head of Ukraine's Agitprop, and later the head of the Ukrainian Bureau of the RCP's Jewish Section, did not link pogroms to ideological anti-Semitism. Semen Dimanshtien and Moishe Rafes, also members of the Jewish Section, stressed that pogroms were not the result of anti-Semitism because Ukrainian peasants had earlier readily followed Jewish Bolshevik leaders. Violence erupted only after "Soviet power presented itself to the peasants as communist [which people did not identify with "Bolshevik"] and began forcing communes upon villages." Analogously, they continued, in offices, the problem was not the presence of Jews per se; rather, it was the presence of too many "demoralized petit bourgeois" specialists. Piatakov attributed pogroms to hatred of the "pompadourism [*pompadorstvo*] of our young communists, or those who call themselves 'communists,'" and their arrogant and dismissive attitude towards peasants. Hatred was then channelled against Jews because of their preponderance in town populations and party organs. Jews with such attitudes had to be "ruthlessly suppressed" and replaced with "solid revolutionary Jews" who, by working with the villagers, would demonstrate to them that not all Jews were speculators, usurers, or idiots. Ukrainian anti-Semitism, Rafes and Dimanshtien maintained, if an issue at all, was the result of two things: a manifestly bad agricultural policy that alienated peasants, and local leaders' refusal to accept revolutionary Jews – among whom were locals who knew their regions – into the Bolshevik party and local administrative positions.[48] For Piatakov, Dimanshtein, and Rafes, the solution for pogroms was to hire more "good" Jews and rid offices of "bad" bourgeois Gentiles and Jews, who demoralized the government from within. In this context, what deserves study is whether Dzerzhinsky or his local subordinates, who knew there were almost no Ukrainians in Ukraine's Cheka, deliberately sought to exploit national hatreds by appointing Jewish Cheka personnel to Ukraine.[49]

This analysis of anti-Jewish violence as situational rather than ideological in nature is mentioned by two important Jewish chroniclers. They differed over whether or not peasants distinguished between "their" Jews, whom they had known for a long time as honest traders and craftsmen, and foreign or outsider Jews who in 1919 brought the much hated commune.[50] The comments of a western Ukrainian officer who traversed right-bank Ukraine in April 1919, just after the Bolsheviks had fled, on the situational nature of violence confirm that people did make the distinction. In Zhytomir and in Volyn province, he wrote, administrative offices had been filled with nineteen- or twenty-year-old Jewish students, "who by their inexplicable behaviour" had provoked the violent hostility of Ukrainians and Poles towards all the local Jews. The young, educated, atheistic Jews fled with the army and left their religious elders and family members to face the wrath of local Christians, who refused to accept that the conservative "older and wiser Jews" condemned and disagreed with their apostate deracinated radical youth. Working local religious Jews, whose livelihoods had been shattered by Bolshevik policies, had no love for their former coreligionists who sat in Bolshevik offices. When Directory forces reoccupied the territory in 1920, religious Jews were not displeased, and there were instances of Ukrainian peasants and soldiers protecting captured former Jewish commissars and office workers from the wrath of local religious Jewish militias.[51] The same situation was reported by a Bolshevik officer in 1921 who had conversed with local Jews in the wake of pogroms in northern Ukraine.[52]

In none of the examined reports did agents explicitly attribute pogroms to publications – though future research might show otherwise. Perhaps local UNR commissars implicitly stigmatized all Jews when they levied collective fines on an entire community. But was levying a collective fine tantamount to official sanctioning of violence? In such cases, the most that might be inferred is that imposing fines *could* have pandered to the anti-Jewish sentiments of local troops, over whom civilian officials had little control. For instance, when in March 1918 Ukrainian soldiers, having just retaken Kyiv from the Bolsheviks, met a delegation of Ukrainian politicians, the politicians implored them not to engage in pogroms. They were shouted down with anti-Semitic remarks.[53] The newspaper of the conservative Socialist Federalist Party, *Nova Rada,* edited by Andryi Nikovsky, did publish decidedly anti-Jewish articles in early 1918, but these did not reflect government policy.

A December 1920 UNR report noted that Bolshevik verbal exhortations were more effective than printed texts, which "in today's circumstances" no longer had any effect on the population. A French observer with the White Army confirmed this when he attributed pogroms to word-of-mouth transmission of anti-Semitic ideas and rumours, rather than to UNR policies.[54] Other witness accounts also attributed pogroms to verbal exhortations, not printed propaganda.[55] While anti-Jewish messages, text or oral, likely motivated some Ukrainians to carry out indiscriminate violence against Jews, these did not motivate *all* Ukrainians, some of whom helped victims.[56] Analogously, while some army officers did identify all Jews as enemies in anonymous published texts, others are on record as making distinctions and preventing pogroms.[57]

In the 1927 trial of Sholom Schwartzbard for the murder of Symon Petliura, Morris Goldstein, a Russian-Jewish lawyer from Petersburg, was a witness.[58] During the first six months of 1919 he was supposedly the head of a Jewish Committee in Kyiv documenting pogroms. In his testimony he claimed that Ukrainian government publications accused Jews as a group of being hostile to Ukraine and called for massacres.[59] While there are government leaflets in the reviewed sample that do label all Jews as enemies, none called for massacres.[60]

Given that situation reports by refugees and UNR agents, like those of Bolshevik agents, could reflect personal and/or institutional interests, it is significant that they often assessed the situation in Ukraine similarly. Reports from both sides by late 1919 explain that war-weariness and frequent regime change channelled dissatisfaction among the general populace into resignation, lack of interest, and willingness to support whoever could maintain order by force.[61] Desperation was making people indifferent to propaganda. One report, from Katerynoslav province in the summer of 1919, noted that peasants would support anyone who could provide "vodka, sugar, calico, nails, salt and kerosene."[62]

In the spring of 1919 in Kyiv, no one believed anything circulated by the Bolshevik press agency BUP (*Buro Ukrainskoi Pechati*) – popularly known as "Lies of the Ukrainian Press" (*Brekhnia Ukrainskoi Pechati*). A very realistic appraisal by two Bolshevik agitators from Kyiv province in early 1919 noted that propaganda alone had only a temporary impact. "The harsh reality totally and often [*riadom*] extinguishes the spirit of the peasants [that had been] aroused by agitators." They argued that to turn loyalties decisively, propaganda had to be followed up as soon as possible with concrete measures implemented by locally known men. Agents from both sides usually reported that they did sway opinion once they had physically got to a place with sufficient personnel and quantities of literature. Without that kind of prior preparation, noted a Ukrainian report from June 1919, things like draft notices struck villagers like "thunder from heaven." Without propaganda, villagers held meetings, talked much nonsense, and then decided they were neutral. They knew nothing about Ukraine or Russia or UNR policies, this report continued, except what they remembered from Bolshevik propaganda.[63]

By 1923 the Bolsheviks had won the war of weapons. Their attractive propaganda slogans undoubtedly swayed opinion and then, in light of the reality of their policies, at least kept the populace passive if they could establish a printing monopoly. In 1920, for instance, while thousands of partisans were resisting Bolshevik rule, newspapers reported nothing about them. People were forced to attend various meetings and conferences under threat of arrest or death. These issued various resolutions supporting one or another policy, which the local press then published to show that all was well. In areas where no other printed sources of information were available, people could learn about what was happening in the neighbouring village or town only by sending someone there to inquire. Such monopolies obviously facilitated Bolshevik counter-insurgency operations as well. In their ignorance, people either hesitated, or were reluctant to assist, armed men who appeared and might just as well have been bandits as actual partisans.[64]

In Russia, as in Ukraine, reality and circumstances trumped propaganda successes in the long term. By November 1918, workers in Petrograd were sending anonymous letters to Lenin and Trotsky telling them they were parting ways. "We all unanimously supported soviet power until we experienced it. When we saw what soviet power entailed, then we damn [*sic*] soviet power and those in command."[65] Ukrainian situation reports submitted to the government-in-exile by recently returned sympathizers observed that workers by 1921 were concerned only with their stomachs because of hunger. "No amount of agitation will change the passive-reactive mood of the workers."[66] Lumpenproletariat Red soldiers were telling one another, "We will smash the bourgeoisie and then slaughter [*rezat*] the communists." After one year of Bolshevik rule, claimed one report, peasants considered it their duty to help anyone who claimed he stood for Ukrainian independence.[67] UNR reports noted that Red Army soldiers, ill-fed, ill-equipped, and ill-clothed, still regarded the Bolshevik regime as transitory and thought a mass uprising was imminent. Reports from 1921 noted that the general destruction and lack of paper meant there were not enough newspapers for government offices and none for villages. Bolshevik propaganda was limited to posted press-summary broadsheets, which no one believed.[68] In 1921, Evgenii Kulisher, a member of Kyiv's Jewish Committee, wrote that Bolshevik foreign propaganda would be a colossal waste of money and resources if it told foreigners about what life with commissars, Revkoms, and secret police was really like. The anarchist Emma Goldman, who was in Kyiv in 1922, observed that Bolshevik reality trumped and nullified any impact that Bolshevik propaganda might have had: "Here the very atmosphere was charged with distrust and hatred of everything Muscovite ... In Kiev there was no attempt to mask the opposition to Moscow. One was made to feel it everywhere."[69]

By 1920, urban conditions had made even the thought of armed resistance in cities impossible. Those who had not fled resigned themselves to their fate.[70] During the 1921 famine, Cheka reports noted that the popular mood in cities became especially anti-Bolshevik when wages and rations were not forthcoming and prices rose. That year, protest took the form of strikes, work to rule, or walking away from jobs. Reports classified urban opposition as non-political but noted that people did blame "Soviet power" and the Bolsheviks for all problems. One report cited the public speech of an unidentified worker:

> What kind of freedom is this and who [really] has it; only the Hershes and the Shmuils [a reference to the disproportionate number of Jews in the Bolshevik regime] and the commissars [can] live; they have beer and wine, and we don't even have a slice of bread. They lied to us and continue to lie; they are destroying us and we are silent; our children swell from hunger.

The Cheka characterized the mood in the countryside that winter as passive and indifferent to politics. Yet wherever "Petliurist agitation" was strong it was able to rouse peasants to fight "at any moment."[71] A former UNR employee, after fleeing Bolshevik Ukraine, observed that although peasants seemed indifferent to propaganda, they still wanted to know whether what they read in announcements was true. He noted that after the Bolsheviks had reoccupied Ukraine in 1920, they disseminated posters and leaflets in villages that depicted destroyed churches in Kyiv and blamed the Poles and Ukrainian troops for their destruction. Some villages sent a representative to confirm the claim. When they returned and reported that the churches were intact, it destroyed any credibility the Bolsheviks might have had.[72]

Although Ukrainian national leaders had lost the war of weapons by 1922, the year the government-in-exile disbanded its army, their victories in the war of words should not be ignored. As they noted, bolshevized Ukrainian soldiers did refuse to fight invading Latvian guards, Russian sailors, and Red Guards under the influence of Bolshevik propaganda from December 1917 to January 1918. But during those months other Ukrainian soldiers were uninfluenced and refused to join the invading force. Ukrainian propaganda likely played a role here, and as a consequence, the Bolsheviks disbanded all Ukrainian military organizations in Russia.[73] One successful initiative by Ukrainian political leaders was to call their newly established representative body the "Rada." This Ukrainian word for council had very positive connotations of representative democracy and freedom that won mass support in 1917. Ukrainians carried out successful propaganda campaigns that year that brought huge wins for Ukrainian parties in elections for the Imperial Constituent Assembly. Hundreds of agitators with thousands of leaflets and pamphlets carried a propaganda message that linked peasant socio-economic demands with political autonomy. SR rural activists in particular told peasants to vote for Ukrainian parties that demanded autonomy. Only an autonomous Ukraine would ensure land reform without redemption payments, they explained, and that Russians would not flock into the country to take Ukrainian land.[74]

A Ukrainian fugitive characterized the situation in 1920 as follows: "Thanks to the Bolsheviks the Ukrainian national idea has strengthened. Among the peasants the idea has spread that Ukraine should be separate from Russia and be its enemy."[75] Bolshevik attempts to dismiss the notion of Ukrainian national independence in their mass propaganda by associating it exclusively with the name of an individual, Petliura, backfired. After experiencing the reality of Bolshevik rule, Ukrainians in 1920 still identified him as the authoritative leader representing an alternative: "I state this as a fact, and not as a patriot," wrote an observer.[76] A similar unintended consequence apparently happened with the word "bandit-gang" [*bandity*]. The Bolsheviks used it to vilify all partisan units. Peasants in the Bila-Tserkva region in 1920 associated it with their champions: "If not for them the Bolsheviks and Denikenites would have slowly eaten us [*uzhe z potrukhamy*] long ago. Only they, my pigeons [referring to interlocutor], defend us from all attacks."[77]

Both Bolshevik and White reports recognized the impact of ideas about Ukrainian nationality, independence, and self-awareness. In the eastern city of Krivyi Rih in March 1918, for example, the former expressed concern about the strength of Ukrainian national ideas among the population: "We must extirpate [*vytriavliat*] the idea of an 'independent Ukraine' by all possible means from the people's consciousness, which through inertia, might still smoulder among certain inconsequential groups as events have shown."[78] In the summer of 1919, White intelligence labelled Ukrainian peasants unreliable soldiers because they were influenced by "Petliurite propaganda" and supported independence. That is probably why White officers demanded Russian draftees and wanted Ukrainian draftees sent to Russia. In early 1920, when no more than 10 per cent of the Red Army in Ukraine was Ukrainian, Red commanders also wanted their Ukrainian recruits sent to Russia, and demanded Russians, whom they considered to be more loyal.[79] In 1921, an anonymous, presumably Ukrainian Bolshevik party member observed: "*Ukraine's population, including the very lowest, including a considerable portion of workers and urban dwellers who are linguistically russified have come to see themselves* [*sic*] as Ukrainians and distinctly contrast themselves both as a nation and a state to Russians and Russia."[80]

Two reports to the UNR government-in-exile describing the situation in Ukraine in late 1920 echoed the Russian reports. In one we read: "In the peasant's view, whoever speaks Russian [*po moskovskomu*] is a Bolshevik." In the second, the former head of the Odessa *prosvita* observed that in Kherson province, White and then Bolshevik regimes had made the population pro-Ukrainian. Whereas in 1917 no one in regional villages knew about the Ukrainian national movement, by 1920 even grandfathers understood that the "Russkies [*moskali*]" were thieves and foreigners, and were talking about a workers' or peasants' or communist Ukraine – but on the condition that it was an *independent* Ukraine.[81] Individual commanders, who, as noted, preferred to have Russian troops under their command because they doubted the loyalty of Ukrainians, indirectly confirmed such reports. The commander of Bolshevik forces in Ukraine, Mikhail Frunze, asked Trotsky and Rakovskii in August 1921 to immediately dispatch six thousand Russians (*chelovek velikorossov*) to Ukraine to guard rail lines and borders. He offered to send the same number of Ukrainians to Russia for military duties there.[82]

During a congress of provincial Agitprop heads in February 1922, delegates summarized the year's work and planned for the future. In his report on political parties, the Ukrainian Bolshevik Pavel Popov said that Bolshevik propaganda had had limited impact. He warned of massive sympathy for the national government-in-exile even though its parties were weak and disorganized. He noted a strong cult of partisan leaders, alongside a cult of Petliura among the people, built on their still strong memory of eighteenth-century popular uprisings. Every village, he continued, had a copy of Hrushevsky's one-volume history of Ukraine, and future propaganda campaigns would have to vigorously counter those "dangerous realities." He urged that any such campaign use Ukrainians and Ukrainian to a much greater degree than previously, and exploit the materials of the recent show trial of the Ukrainian right-SRs that had supposedly proven that all Ukrainian governments were agents of foreign powers. Most of the existing Ukrainian Agitprop agitators, he noted, had eventually to be replaced because they were usually ex-Ukrainian SR party members or sympathizers and did not always deliver strictly Bolshevik messages. That July and August, Agitprop officials adopted a series of measures incorporating these observations. One included a secret circular instructing local officials and the secret police to devote greater effort to intercepting Ukrainian national published materials still in circulation. Officials called for more publications in Ukrainian, a commission to study and then publish an anthology for all party members on "bourgeois ideology" with recommendations on how to oppose it, funding for works aimed specifically at countering foreign publications, and sizeable amounts of Ukrainian-language publications for Ukrainians in the Red Army.[83]

While each claimant to power had a circle of supporters, the attitude of the majority of the urban population from as early as 1918 was characterized by a progressive increase in apathy and indifference.

This was caused by the seeming endless regime change, by the killings, food shortages, and criminality, and by the collapse of services and infrastructure. The number of those swayed by the initial enthusiasm created by the slogans of each side decreased; no incoming power could maintain itself long enough to improve the harsh daily reality. In general, the internal administrative collapse in March–April 1918 discredited the Rada for the majority. The Hetman's attempt to restore landowners discredited the Ukrainian State, which as an entity was too Russian for Ukrainians and too Ukrainian for Russians. The reality of outsiders ruling via local Ispolkoms, Revkoms, and Cheka units, and the prohibition of private economic activity, discredited the Bolshevik version of Soviet rule. Bolshevik reports on the situation in late 1919 noted that peasants supported Soviet power "but feared soviet armies from Russia like the plague. They dream of 'their own' Bolsheviks." Opinion of Petliura ranged from favourable in the west to lesser evil in the east.[84] By 1920, few, be they rural or urban, were greeting incoming forces as liberators. By 1922, if not earlier, people's primary concern was survival and keeping what they had. By then, wealthier peasants had made their peace with the Bolsheviks, believing that once they had taken their booty, they would be left alone and able to sleep at night. People wanted order, and Bolshevik terror did bring order of a kind.[85]

From late 1919, Bolshevik propaganda included Ukrainian national ideas. Authors more often referred to the "Ukrainian nation" instead of "workers and peasants of Ukraine" and described the country's Bolshevik government as "Ukrainian." This was primarily the work of Ukrainian left-SRs, left-SDs, and the UCP. These materials influenced the fight against Denikin's Whites. They were not as effective against the UNR, which remained a symbol of Ukrainian national independence at least until 1923. By March of that year the last major pro-UNR partisan commanders had either surrendered, believing amnesty declarations, or been captured, and their forces had been dispersed or destroyed. The party's XII Congress ratified a wide-ranging program of de-Russification titled "Indigenization" or "Ukrainization."[86] The 1921 famine underlay the final collapse of Makhno's army. As armed resistance faded, it seemed that the Bolshevik regime had established itself, and through 1922 many of those opposed made their peace with it. Former opponents rationalized the new regime as a lesser evil than the Whites, Makhno, and the UNR. People hoped there was perhaps some truth in its slogans. In the words of a former pro-UNR warlord: "Compared to previous years, the face of Ukraine in 1924 was unrecognizable ... For many, a Ukrainian state with a red instead of blue and yellow flag seemed to be a reality."[87] Significantly, while older people ignored agitators, the youth listened.

In the likely representative words of one of them: "[T]hey offered hope in a time of general distress and pessimism ... I was caught between the skepticism at home and my own thirst for faith."[88]

On the other hand, although Ukrainian-language publication and education expanded after 1923, "kulaks" and "the bourgeoisie" were excluded from higher institutions of learning and from membership in libraries and reading clubs. After a short hiatus, mass arrests resumed. While peasants had land, as promised, as many as 40 per cent had no animals or tools to work it; meanwhile, the NEP replaced forced requisitions with high taxes. Workers knew they were worse off in 1923 than in 1913. Overall living conditions in Ukraine relative to other parts of the USSR were worse because Moscow extracted excessive foodstuffs and provided fewer imported finished goods than other regions got.[89] In short, despite concessions and improvements, people knew that the Bolshevik victory had improved the standard of life only for the party *nomenklatura*, their extended families and clients, and those involved in criminal activities. That reality ensured a receptive audience among the Ukrainian rural and urban populace for supporters of the UNR government-in-exile, which continued to circulate its messages in texts and verbally after 1923. Secret police reports noted that groups still considered Ukrainian independence, or even Polish occupation, as realistic alternatives to Bolshevik Russian rule through the 1920s and that leaflets to that effect were circulating despite the NEP and indigenization. Particularly frequent were references to and condemnations of Bolshevik rule as Russian colonialism – a theme in Ukrainian left-SD and later UCP publications.[90] Mensheviks, Anarchists, Russian SRs, and Zionists still had sympathizers among Russians and Jews.

This book suggests that no one should either exaggerate Ukrainian failures or overestimate Bolshevik successes in the war of words. In the longer term, circumstances were crucial in determining how influential messages would be among audiences. Both sides had successes and failures during the period examined by this book. While the Russian Bolsheviks had obviously won the war of weapons by 1923, it was not so obvious that they had won the war of words. That victory came only in the 1930s, when leaders imposed the kind of ideal conditions all propagandists seek – a monopoly on all communications and isolation of the target audience from alternative messages. The destruction and seclusion in closed collections of rival propaganda texts, and the death of millions during the famines of 1929 to 1933 who remembered UNR and partisan slogans, assisted in that victory.

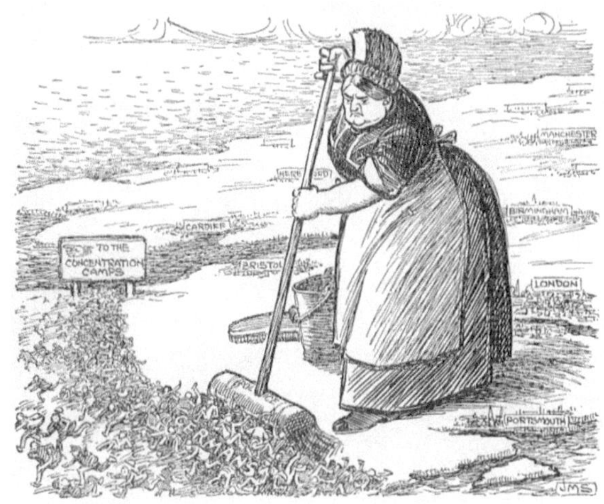

43 MRS BRITANNIA: "It has to be done: so I might just as well do it first as last – and so get rid of all the dangerous microbes."
Western Mail, 24 October 1914. cartoonww1.org.

Estimated Press Runs and Per Capita Distribution of Bolshevik Publications

This appendix compares 1919-21 publication data with the 1897 population totals. 1920 figures estimated the total population at 3 million less than in the 1897 census and the urban population at almost 2 million more than in 1897 and one million less than in 1917. The total rural population was approximately the same in 1920 as in 1897.[1] Accordingly, it is possible to estimate rural readers per copy in 1920 using 1897 figures. When considering average urban ratios, it must also be remembered that more printed materials were available to urban populations on main roads or rail lines with established printing shops and supplies than in towns distant from transit routes. The number of readers per copy would be lower also, if press runs are divided only between the total urban literate. In general, the available total figures for Ukraine confirm that as of 1921 published propaganda normally reached more people in cities and towns than in villages. There are no comparable figures from 1919. Bolshevik publications, it should be added, were free until 1921. There are no known figures for the Ukrainian side that are as detailed and that would allow comparable generalizations regarding dissemination of Ukrainian printed materials – which normally had to be bought, if only for a nominal sum.

It is possible to make only approximations of media saturation and readers per copy published, because the available figures for population, published materials, and dissemination in 1920–1 are incomplete and sometimes imprecise. The Bolshevik census of 1920 is incomplete. It did not cover Volyn and Podillia provinces and roughly 15 per cent of Ukraine's population. Insufficient paper for forms and locals killing enumerators also reduced the number of the recorded population. The destruction in Ukraine was immense. A review of what had been the prewar Iakovlev printing company in Kyiv revealed that as of January 1921, only five of its twenty-one presses were functional, and that it was working at 25 per cent of its prewar capacity.[2] Ukraine's Bolsheviks, however, could rely on imported Russian publications and paper – albeit sometimes irregular.

The pre-revolutionary differences in infrastructure, number of titles, and press runs between Russian and Ukrainian provinces remained after 1917, as shown by two surveys taken in Moscow and Kyiv in the summer of 1921. In Moscow, six of the city's largest print shops, with approximately 2,400 workers, had the following number of functioning presses: 113 all types, 30 rotary, and 52 lithographic, as well as 66 typesetting machines. Their maximum monthly capacity was 40 million printed pages. In Kyiv, comparable but incomplete figures from 13 of the city's shops with approximately 1,500 workers were, respectively, 92, 1, and 14, as well as 8 typesetting machines. Their maximum monthly capacity was 11 million pages, including 500,000 lithographed pages. In both cities, shortages and breakdowns ensured that presses did not print at maximum capacity. Actual monthly production is available only for the six Moscow shops, which apparently averaged 21 million printed pages, including 3 million lithographed pages, during the first six months of 1921.[3] After seven months of relative calm under the Hetman, 125 newspapers in all languages (25 in Ukrainian) were being published in Kyiv. By comparison, one year after war's end, 51 papers were being published in Belgium. With a population almost four times smaller than Ukraine's, Belgium averaged one newspaper per 150,000 population compared to Ukraine's one per 240,000.[4]

Available figures show that despite shortages of parts, paper, and printers, overall production in Moscow and Petrograd apparently remained considerable. In 1919–20, *Pravda* and *Izvestiia* together averaged 600,000 to 650,000 copies daily.[5] Between June and November 1919, the Red Army's Propaganda Department (*Politicheskaia upravlennia*) reported that it had published 241,000 pamphlets, 3.8 million leaflets, and 1.1 million posters, and that it had another 487,000 leaflets and 628,000 posters in press. Also, between June and December, it had distributed 3.4 million leaflets and 1.7 million posters. During the second half of 1919, Red Army presses alone averaged 300,000 to 400,000 newspapers a day. By 1920, Red Army troops were receiving, from all sources, an average of 2 million newspapers per day. Overseeing distribution in the army were 5,200 commissars, who in October alone were supplemented by 5,428 agitators sent directly from Moscow, along with an unknown number who came from local party organizations in the war zones. In June 1920, Moscow alone sent 113,000 pamphlets, 3,000 leaflets, and hundreds of thousands of newspapers daily to its western front.[6]

In the year following the tsar's abdication, Bolshevik newspapers represented no more than 1 per cent of all newspapers that appeared in Ukraine. By April 1918, during their first short three-month rule, Ukraine's Bolsheviks had published roughly sixty Russian-language newspapers with a combined daily run of about 200,000. That was fewer than the eighty-four Ukrainian-language papers that had appeared under the Rada, of which *Nova Rada* had the biggest run (200,000 copies).[7] This had changed significantly by July 1920, when Ukraine's Bolsheviks published 203 newspapers (46 in Ukrainian). Local leaders claimed that these covered only 10 per cent of their need and that month sent an urgent request to Moscow for thirteen tons of paper to publish propaganda specifically directed against Polish and Ukrainian forces. It is quite possible that Moscow did not meet this request, for the previous month, Ukraine's Bolshevik leaders had concluded that they could not count on Moscow for supplies. They were expecting ninety tons per month that year, but by June they were receiving only one ton per month. This meant that each province received no more than four tons during the first five months of 1920, and even that was from Ukrainian mills. An investigative committee recommended that coal supplies for Ukrainian mills be increased, otherwise there would soon be no more paper available. Also, that all possible resources under the state publishing committee be mobilized and that all paper held by the army be requisitioned unless the army had formal permission to hold it.[8] Overall, the amount of published materials had increased markedly over 1919. Yet until 1921, Bolshevik still thought they could not produce sufficient amounts of printed propaganda to counter an apparently huge distribution effort launched that summer by Makhno's army.[9]

In early 1920, by which time the UNR had collapsed, the number of Bolshevik newspapers in Ukraine had risen to ninety-two (ten in Ukrainian), with press runs ranging from 1,000 to 12,500 copies daily per title.[10] For the first half of 1920, the total press run of all newspapers ranged between 168,000 (August) and 250,000 (January). Monthly totals for February of 422,000 rose to 2,420,000 in July.[11] During the first half of 1921, total daily press runs of all newspapers was 260,500 copies, of which 83,000 were rural.[12]

In Kyiv province (1897 total population 3,560,000), between July 1920 and February 1921, the Bolsheviks published 4,364,615 copies of newspapers, including 828,447 imported from Moscow and Petrograd. This means that by the end of that seven-month period the Bolsheviks had produced more than one copy of a newspaper for every man, woman, and child in the province. By November 1921, total published copies had fallen to one for every four inhabitants of the province. That September in Poltava province, the ratio was one to nine. Urban residents got more copies than did rural residents. The figures for November show that on average, 33 per cent of all copies of Kyiv province newspapers were distributed in Kyiv city.[13] Figures from two counties in northern Kharkiv province from April–May 1920 indicate that in one, 7,000 copies of the local paper were printed, of which 3,400 were allotted to the countryside. This averaged one copy per twenty-one persons. In the other county, 800 copies of the local paper were supplemented with approximately 200 copies of three newspapers from Kharkiv – a distribution ratio of one to one hundred.[14]

For the first six months of 1921, different sets of figures give different pictures of overall newspaper distribution. The first set, from an undated survey probably compiled at the beginning of the year, was submitted to Agitprop with a report noting that because the paper situation was "catastrophic," press runs would have to be reduced to one copy per 160 persons. The survey indicated 139 published newspapers in all languages with a total daily run of 236,000.[15] This averaged one copy for every 120 people for the entire country, with the highest ratio in Kharkiv province (1:37) and the lowest in Podillia (1:441). The average for Ukraine, excluding Kharkiv province, which had the most newspapers and highest press runs, was 1:190.[16] This is confirmed by other reports that February from ten districts in central Ukraine: five reported no distribution, or very little.[17] Two later reports covering the first six months of 1921 give totally different figures. In one, almost 18,000,000 copies of eighty-three newspapers (fifteen in Ukrainian) were distributed among Bolshevik Ukraine's 26,752,000 people – roughly two copies for every three inhabitants. Of that total, twenty-eight newspapers, and approximately 30 per cent of all printed copies, were imported from Russia.[18] Another set of figures records 23,000,000 copies of 104 newspapers (sixteen in Ukrainian). Of this total, 6,400,000 copies (38 per cent) were imported from Russia. The highest per capita distribution was in Kyiv and Kharkiv provinces – approximately four and three copies per person respectively. As noted in this survey, the per capita published total of newspapers in Ukraine during the first six months of 1921 was almost one copy of a newspaper per person by July. This was impressive but far from western European norms. By comparison, the prewar French average was one newspaper for every four persons *daily*.[19]

Brochures, pamphlets, and leaflets had press runs between 10,000 and 30,000 copies. Documents and notices deemed especially important were released in as many as 100,000 copies. Between 1919 and 1921, reflecting their importance as an information medium, almost

70 per cent of all Bolshevik military publications comprised leaflets, handbills, posters, and cards. In June, July, and August 1920, the Red Army released a total of 7.5 million copies of various titles. In 1921, 70 per cent of the titles were published in Ukraine and 50 per cent of the total press run were devoted to propaganda.[20] Ukraine's Bolsheviks released at least 5,000 known leaflets between 1917 and 1921 in at least 4 million copies, published mainly in Russian. In Kharkiv between December 1919 and March 1920, they published nine pamphlets (320,000 copies), six leaflets (390,000) and eight posters (325,000). All of these texts were in Russian, although most of them were distributed beyond the city. The Agitation Section was allotted almost 1.5 million roubles from the provincial party's 7.7 million rouble budget, the highest by far of all its allocations.[21]

One set of figures from 1919 shows that of the roughly 4,000,000 leaflets and pamphlets released by the War Commissariat between March and June 1919, twice as many copies were in Russian than in Ukrainian (4,780 to 2,390). Of eighty-five leaflets and ninety-two pamphlets, twenty-seven and nineteen respectively were in Ukrainian. Figures for 1920 show 90,000 copies of eleven Ukrainian posters and 152,000 copies of nineteen in Russian – an average of one poster per 1,160 persons. One set of figures for that year shows 2.2 million copies of 210 leaflets, handbills, and official announcements released (1: 110). Of these, 78 (1.1 million copies) were in Ukrainian and 132 (1.7 million) in Russian. A second set shows 2.1 million copies of 190 leaflets, handbills, and official announcements, of which 72 (832,000 copies) were in Ukrainian and 118 (1,000,000 copies) in Russian. Among the leaflets were seventy-three (seven in Ukrainian, fourteen in Ukrainian and Russian) reproducing Lenin's speeches and letters, released in anywhere between 3,000 and 50,000 copies each. Four million copies of 334 political pamphlets (148 Ukrainian in 1.8 million copies, 186 Russian in 2.2 million copies) added to that would raise the percentage press run share of political literature for that year to almost 85 per cent of everything published.[22]

Figures on leaflet distribution, excluding Volyn and Podillia provinces, from February 1921 differ, but like the above set, they suggest dramatic increases in totals from the preceding two years. One set of figures gives 63,712 copies (1: 342), of which 43 per cent were released in Kharkiv province (1: 87). Another set gives 57,307 copies, with the highest percentage in Kharkiv (48 per cent). During the first six months of that year, 538,873 leaflets (1: 50) and 159,911 posters were disseminated.[23] By comparison, in Odessa province in August 1920, 13,500 copies of posters and 13,600 copies of leaflets were distributed. Also in Odessa, 14,057 of 20,376 copies of posters were distributed. For all of 1921, almost 500,000 copies of sixty-four leaflets and 71,000 copies of thirty-seven posters were distributed in Odessa province. Poltava province during the first six months of 1921 got 6,942 leaflets and 3,420 posters.[24] During the first four months of 1921, 1,000,000 copies of 116 leaflets and 200,000 copies of 20 posters were distributed throughout Ukraine.[25] These local totals were supplemented by Russian-language literature from Russia, where the Central Publishers allotted 10 per cent of all annual production for shipment to Ukraine via Kharkov. This amounted to 8.5 million copies of thousands of titles in 1919 and 1920.

Alongside stationary presses and imported materials, Ukraine's Bolsheviks ran twenty trains and four riverboats with presses. Through 1919–20, these disseminated propaganda, including more than 1 million copies of one hundred leaflets. In 1919 the presses of the First Ukrainian Soviet Division, carried in six rail carriages, could print 10,000 copies of a four-page newspaper three or four times a week, as well as various leaflets and pamphlets.[26] In June 1920, one such train, in the Oleksandrivsk region, released 75,000 leaflets and newspapers. It also distributed roughly three tons of paper to various local party organizations on its routes, as there was none to be bought in the region. In 1920 the 14th Army had five big presses transported in thirteen rail carriages. The War Commissariat between March and June 1919 turned out around 4 million leaflets and pamphlets alone. Even so, its officials complained about a paper shortage and demanded that the Central Committee do something.[27] Between April and June 1919, Ukraine's War Commissariat printing section (*redizdat*) published 2,672,000 pamphlets and 6,215,000 leaflets as well as 2,000,000 copies of *Krasnaia armiia*.[28]

Disparate local sources indicate that in reality, despite the seemingly huge press runs and number of titles, at least until 1922, for the reasons noted above, media saturation was uneven. Especially detailed reports on all aspects of publishing from Odessa province, for instance, illustrate how the mechanics of local publishing and distribution influenced production. Upon taking the city, the Bolsheviks folded its sixty-seven printing shops into ten publishing enterprises. Besides using confiscated paper and stocks, they requisitioned the output of Odessa's sole paper mill. In early 1920 it could produce four tons of paper in six days. By July, after the machinery was cleaned and repaired and the production process was rationalized, the factory was producing thirty-three tons a month. The main raw materials for paper-making were rags and archival documents. The recipe required thirty-six pounds of rags and thirty pounds of archival paper to produce thirty-six pounds of newsprint. During the nine months between February and October of that year, Odesa city (population 1.8 million), with its ten printing shops, 772 printshop workers, seven rotary presses, and seventy-seven presses of all other kinds produced a total of 22.3 million printed pages. This included 6.6 million pages of 10 newspapers, 288 million copies of leaflets, 741,000 copies of pamphlets, and 182,000 posters. Total printed pages fell each successive month during this period for each of these categories, except for posters, which reached a high of 62,000 copies in October before falling to 137 for November. Detailed figures for November, listing the difference between monthly maximum capacity and actual production in light of shortages or breakdowns, show an average monthly difference between the two of almost 6 million copies – 10 million versus 4.2 million.[29]

Incompetence, broken presses, ruined telegraph lines, railway breakdowns, a shortage of roving agitators, partisan activity, shortages of paper and ink, and distance from the main Bolshevik publishing centre of Kharkiv all combined to limit dissemination and make deliveries irregular. In August 1919, after six months of Bolshevik control, an agitator returned from a tour of duty in Ukraine reported a profound hunger for printed information everywhere he went. He wrote that no Bolshevik material was available in villages or in railway stations. In the latter, kiosks had only cockroaches, flies, and the odd left-over copy of one or another UNR pamphlet.[30]

Large press runs and centralized distribution – which by 1921 had established a centralized percentage allotment by city and region – did not guarantee that materials would reach local agents or readers. For example, in July 1918 the entire run of a pamphlet from the previous year was found in a printing shop in Vinnytsia, whose owner was using it for packaging. In the spring of 1919, Bolshevik military inspectors noted that incompetent propaganda personnel in Vasylkiv district had not distributed 722 pounds of leaflets and newspapers, which they had found stacked in the local Revkom office. In Volyn province a report covering the first half of November, just after the territory had been taken back from the Poles, observed that there was no gas, no paper, no office materials, and no money with which to buy office materials on the open market, and thus, no publications. The local Bolsheviks could publish only five hundred copies of one newspaper for the entire province.[31]

Statistics from Kyiv province indicate that most printed propaganda ended up in cities and towns. Between July 1920 and February 1921, the government distributed 58,542 copies of leaflets throughout Kyiv province (1: 86). Of these, 52 per cent (30,440) were distributed in Kyiv city (population 248,000), which gave a ratio of leaflets to inhabitants of

1:8. That February, of 19,574 copies distributed, 13,104 were distributed in the capital.[32] During first six months of 1921 in Kyiv province, of 277,000 leaflets, 165,000 went to the city and 21,000 to local army units. Of 81,000 posters, 41,000 went to the city and 15,000 to the army.[33] In January 1921, of 19,574 leaflets and 7,660 posters, 13,104 and 2,740 respectively went to the city.

The earliest available figures for rural areas are from the Peasant Section and date from 1920. These give a rough idea of how many newspapers, leaflets, and pamphlets were available per head of rural population in a given territory at a given time, if the agent in charge distributed his allotment. These figures indicate low and erratic distribution beyond city limits.

Volyn province (1897 rural pop. 2,756,000) in July and August 1920 had, on average one newspaper (62 per cent in Ukrainian) for every 1,060 rural inhabitants; one leaflet (7 per cent Ukrainian) for every 919 rural inhabitants; and one pamphlet (49 per cent Ukrainian) for every 725 inhabitants. The figures for Ovruch district (sixteen counties, rural population 198,000) for August–September were: leaflets 1:1,200 (400 Ukrainian); newspapers 1:3,000 (500 Ukrainian). This averaged ten copies daily for each county.[34] By November of that year there was no gas, no paper, no office materials, and no money to buy office materials on the open market, and thus there were no local publications. The local Bolsheviks published 500 copies of the provincial newspaper for the entire province of almost 3 million people, 100 of which were allocated to the villages.[35] Two districts in the province during the last months of that year received no literature whatsoever.[36]

In Kyiv province in September 1920, in the seventeen counties of Berdychiv district (1897 rural population 226,344), the 960 copies of local and central newspapers published daily averaged 1 per 236 persons and 56 per county. More detailed figures from July for Zvenyhora district (seventeen counties, rural population 257,781), show 15,026 copies of newspapers either published there or in circulation (12,622 Ukrainian), 277 pamphlets (231 Ukrainian), and 53 leaflets (28 Ukrainian). A local daily newspaper press run of 500 provided, on average, one copy daily for every 576 rural inhabitants – a ratio that would fall by the end of the month to 1:17. Detailed figures from eight counties show 1,413 copies of 102 pamphlets – an average of 176 copies and 13 titles per county. Distribution was uneven, and some counties apparently received no literature whatsoever.[37] Sometimes even cities received very little. A refugee university professor from Kyiv reported that just after the Bolsheviks reoccupied the city in the summer of 1920, there was no paper to be found. Newspapers had only two pages, and their entire runs were slated for street posting.[38]

Figures from Poltava province (1897 rural population 2,500,000) include a rare set of relatively complete statistics from Pereiaslav district (seventeen counties, 1897 rural population 171,000) covering five months from August to December 1920. The average numbers of rural inhabitants per copy of pamphlets, newspapers, and leaflets, in Ukrainian and Russian, distributed there in August, were, respectively 521, 800, and 609. For November the figures were 200, 9, and 52.[39] In Lokhvyts district (rural population 142,000), the corresponding distribution figures for pamphlets and leaflets were 1:35,500 persons, and for newspapers 1:10. For January 1921 the ratios were pamphlets 1:71,000, leaflets, 1:2,780, and newspapers, 1:14. Konstantynivka district (rural population 223,900), averaged one copy of one newspaper for every thirty-nine persons, and one pamphlet (Russian only) for each 178 persons for August 1920. For July, Mirhorod (rural population 148,000), persons per copy averaged as follows: newspapers – 1:14, pamphlets – 1:37, and leaflets – 1:170. While all the standard report forms contained a column for number of newspaper copies distributed daily, few such columns were filled in. Those that were indicate the following daily ratios: Lokhvyts district in December, 3,160 (1:45), Kobyliansk district (rural population 207,388) in August, 25 (1:8,296). In Kharkiv province, for Volchansk district (rural population 155,767), the August figures were 660 pamphlets (1:236), 4,867 newspapers (1:32), 3,310 leaflets (1:47), and 162 posters.[40] These higher ratios are perhaps explained by the location of the district capitals on rail lines. By contrast, figures for number of inhabitants per copy in Chernihiv province (November?), were 3,060 (1:682); for Sosnovyts county in August 1920, 250 (1:652), and for Horodynsk (undated – one month?) 550 (1:139).[41]

No one has yet determined whether Bolshevik printed materials reached more peasants in Ukraine than in Russia, or whether, as in Russia after a few months of Bolshevik rule, the literate simply stopped reading newspapers because they were so monotonously boring.[42] A study of Voronezh province in 1922 noted that villages there either had no newspapers at all, or at best had individual copies two weeks old that the peasants did not understand and in which they had no interest. The author wrote that official claims about one subscriber per 25 households (100–125 persons) were pure fiction. A more realistic distribution was 1 copy per 440 persons – with considerably fewer copies in villages than in towns. A county of 18,000 inhabitants, for instance, would get sixteen copies of one newspaper (1:1125). He estimated that fewer than 10,000 of the province's peasants read newspapers. A survey he took of forty-one peasants showed that whereas sixteen had regularly read newspapers before 1917, that year only four did. Apparently, peasants feared subscribing to newspapers because if local officials learned of it, they would consider the subscriber a rich bourgeois and raise his taxes. Before the war, he added, there averaged five or six subscribers per village and copies arrived within three days.[43]

Shortages of workers and materials, poor working conditions, and truncated press runs inevitably led to a decline in the total production of printed matter as compared to the prewar years.[44] For all of 1920, Moscow printed almost 400 million copies of the six major Bolshevik newspapers and 10 million copies of various posters. By comparison, in Britain between October 1914 and September 1915, thirty-six companies produced 12.5 million copies of 164 posters.[45] By May 1916, Britain's Parliamentary Recruiting Committee alone had released 34 million leaflets and 5.5 million pamphlets for the country's 42 million people. In September 1914, one English weekly, the *London Opinion*, printed more than one million copies.[46] As of 1914, Germany had 4,200 daily newspapers – around one title for every 16,200 persons. France in 1914 had 322 daily newspapers with a total press run of 9.5 million copies. That averaged one newspaper for every 124,000 people, and one copy for every four people. The biggest French paper, *Le Matin*, printed one million copies *daily*. The United Kingdom had 2,947 newspapers (1:14,000). Ireland in 1914 had 289 newspapers (1:13,800), of which more than 150 were politically nationalist.[47]

Notes

Introduction

1 TsDAVO f. 1114 op 1 sprava 44 no 83.

2 Recent overview: T.R. Paddock ed., *World War 1 and Propaganda* (Leiden, 2014). H. Lasswell, *Propaganda Technique in the World War* (London, 1927), provides a comparative analysis. On eastern Europe: M. Cornwall, *The Undermining of Austria Hungary: The Battle for Hearts and Minds* (New York, 2000); A. Watson, *Ring of Steel: Germany and Austria-Hungary in WW1* (London, 2014). Survey histories: P.M. Taylor, *Munitions of the Mind: A History of Propaganda from the Ancient World to the Present Day*, 3rd ed. (Manchester, 2003); G.S. Jowett and V. O'Donnell, *Propaganda and Persuasion*, 5th ed. (London, 2012); R. Marlin, *Propaganda and the Ethics of Persuasion*, 2nd ed. (Peterborough Ont., 2013); P.P. Pedrini, *Propaganda, Persuasion and the Great War* (London, 2018). L. Masterman, *C.F.G. Masterman: A Biography* (London, 1939). The lies disseminated by American publishers prior to and during the 1898 Spanish-American War were labelled "yellow journalism." Their false stories decisively swung opinion in favour of war. On Ponsonby: A. Gregory, *The Last Great War: British Society and the First World War* (Cambridge, 2008), 41–4.

3 A. Gleason et al., *Bolshevik Culture* (Bloomington, 1985), 131–74; P. Kenez, *The Birth of the Propaganda State: Soviet Methods of Mass Mobilization, 1917–1929* (Cambridge, 1986); S. White, *The Bolshevik Poster* (New Haven, 1988). Kenez, using the term "soviet people," but meaning actually Russians because his work focused on Russians, concludes that it will never be resolved whether Russians supported the Bolsheviks because they were successfully manipulated or because they agreed with their goals (251).

4 M. Stakhiv, *Ukraina v dobi Dyrektorii UNR*, 7 vols. (Toronto 1962–6) is the only survey history of the period that mentions press and propaganda issues throughout. The author was an army officer at the time. H. Basara,

"Politychnyi sotsium ukrainskykh provintsiinykh mist za zvitamy instruktoriv Tsentralnoi Rady," in *Ukrainska Tsentralna Rada: postup natsiotvorennia ta derzhavobudivnytstva*, ed. V. Serhiichuk (Kyiv, 2002), 158–68; V. Skalsky, "Obraz tsentralnoi rady u svidomosti selian na pochatkovomu etapi Ukrainskoi revoliutsii," *Ukrainskyi istorchnyi zhurnal* no. 1 (2008), 53. On foreign propaganda and organizational issues: D. Budkov and D. Viedienieev, *Slovo pravdy pro Ukrainu* (Kyiv, 2004). On Bolshevik propaganda among Ukraine's Red Army troops: O.V. Vilkhovyk, "Transformatsiia svitohliadu chervonoarmiitsiv na terytorii radianskoi Ukrainy ... (1917-1920)," Candidate Dissertation, Poltava National Pedagogical University (2018). On the failures of Ukrainian propaganda at Versailles, see Stakhiv, *Ukraina*, vol. 4, 255. The major figures on the Ukrainian and Bolshevik side who were involved in propaganda and are known to have written memoirs, gave little detail about their work as propagandists: D. Dontsov, *Rik 1918 Kyiv* (Toronto, 1954); O. Nazaruk, *Rik na Velyki Ukraini* (Vienna, 1920). The head of the Galician Army Press Office was Osyp Levytsky, *Halytska armiia na Velykii Ukraini: spomyn z chasu vid lypnia do hrudnia 1919 r.* (Vienna, 1921). See also idem, "Propaganda i presa," in *Ukrainska Halytska Armiia*, ed. M. Dolnytsky and O. Levytsky (Detroit, 1958), I: 325–34; V. Futuluichuk, *Ukrainska Halytska Armiia. Viiskovo-patriotychne vykhovannia ta vyshkil (1918–1920 rr.)* (Lviv, 2000), 50. Borys Antonenko-Davydovych served as a propaganda officer in a UNR regiment in 1919: B. Tymoshenko, ed., *Na shliakhakh i rozdorizhzhiakh: spohady, nevidomi tvory* (Kyiv, 1999).

5 The book does not discuss posters, objects (statuettes, ceramics), or songs. There is no Ukrainian equivalent of the detailed studies by A.J. Leinwald, *Czerwonym mlotem w orla bialego. Propaganda sowiecka w wojnie z Polska 1919–1920* (Warsaw, 2008); or B. Novick, *Conceiving Revolution: Irish Nationalist Propaganda during the First World War* (Dublin, 2001).

6 A collection of catalogued leaflets is in the Central State Historical Archive (TsDIA) in Lviv. A selection from the Lviv University Library is in: Iu. Lysy, M. Ilkiv-Svydnytsky eds, *Zakhidno Ukrainska Narodna Republika v kollektsiiakh LNU im. Ivana Franka* (Lviv, 2018). Fond 257 in the Lviv Oblast State Archive (DALO) contains leaflets.West Ukrainian local government materials, which included a few hundred leaflets and broadsheets, were collected by Polish officials when they occupied the territory in 1919 and then archived in Lviv (*Akta Ukrainskie*). The Bolsheviks took this collection to Kyiv in 1947, where it lies, unused, as of 2016. All these leaflets are in pristine condition. TsDAVO f. 3505 op 1 sprava 11–15, 31–5.

7 Historians in Soviet times collected and reproduced Bolshevik propaganda posters and leaflets. After 1991 Russian scholars began to locate, collate, catalogue, and reproduce surviving White propaganda materials. L.A. Molchanov, *Gazetnaia pressa Rossii v gody revoliutsii i grazhdanskoi*

voiny (Moscow, 2002); G. Mikheeva, *Beloe dvizhenie. Katalog kollektsii listivok (1917–1920 gg.)* (Saint Petersburg, 2000). On White propaganda: C. Lazarski, "White Propaganda Efforts in the South during the Russian Civil War 1918–1919," *Slavonic and East European Review* 4 (October 1992): 688–707; Ia.A. Butakov, "Russkie krainie pravye i beloe dvizhenie na Iuge Rossii v 1919 g.," in *Grazhdanskaia voina v Rossii: sobytiia, mneniia, otsenki*, ed. N.A. Ivnitskii (Moscow, 2002), 443–53; T. Mathew, "'Wish you were here': Anti-Bolshevik Postcards of the Russian Civil War 1918–1921," *Revolutionary Russia* 2 (December 2010): 183–216. M. Baker, *Peasants, Power, and Place: Revolution in the Villages of Kharkiv Province 1914–1921* (Cambridge, MA, 2016) 134–51.

8 Makhno's army had a Cultural-Educational Section and portable presses. His people also used the presses in cities they controlled. Makhno and his wife both gave speeches and wrote leaflets, but the bulk of his propaganda was coordinated and written by the Russian anarchists Piotr Arshinov, Isak Teper, and Vsevolod Volin (Eikhenbaum). A professional printer, Josef Gutman, ran his presses. Arshinov included thirteen leaflets from 1920 in his 1921 book, published later in English translation, *History of the Makhnovist Movement (1918–1921)* (Detroit, 1974), but no information about his propaganda activities. M. Protsyk, "Presa anarkhistiv i makhnovtsiv v Ukraini 1917–1920 rr." in *Ukrainska periodyka: Istoriia i suchasnist*, ed. M. Romaniuk (Lviv, 2008), 188–94; I. Kushnirenko, *Nestor Makhno: vid anarkhizmu do respubliky* (Zaporizhzhia, 2013), 107–40.

9 Between 1914 and 1917 Russian Orthodox clerics, Black Hundred party members (extremist empire loyalists), and monarchists, who later joined the Whites, issued mass explicitly anti-Ukrainian propaganda only in Russian occupied western Ukraine (eastern Galicia). In the tsarist Ukrainian provinces their mass propaganda was empire loyalist, anti-Catholic, anti-Polish and anti-Jewish. They published anti-Ukrainian materials in their newspapers. Ia. Tsetsyk, "Rol chornosotentsiv u zahostrenni mizhetnichnykh ta mizhkonfesiinykh vzaiemovidnosyn na Volyni u 1906-1916 rr.," *Naukovi zapysky Vinnytskoho Derzhavnoho Universyteta.* Seriia: Istoriia, vyp. 26 (2018) 69-72; R. Krutsyk, *Informatsiina polityka Rosiikoi imperskoi vlady v Ukrainskykh huberniiakh pivdennozakhidnoho kraiu (1914-1917).* Candidate Dissertation, Borys Hrynchenko University (Kyiv, 2018). M. Haukhman, "Formuvannia 'Malorosiiskoi pozytsii' hazetu Kievlianin u 1917 r.," *Kraeznavstvo* no. 3-4 (2017) 49-67.

10 O. Velikanova, *Popular Perceptions of Soviet Politics in the 1920s: Disenchantment of the Dreamers* (London, 2013).

11 It is estimated that in 1917 and 1918 at least 5,037 books and pamphlets in all languages were published on former tsarist Ukrainian territory. O. Vaskivska, "Drukovana knyzhkova produktsiia vydana na tereni

Ukrainy u 1917 rotsi," *Visnyk Knyzhkovoi palaty* no. 12 (2010), 25–8; idem, "Knyzhkova produktsiia u tretomu rotsi vidbuduvannia Ukrainskoi derzhavy," ibid., no. 10 (2011) 34–40.

12 Those with more than passing interest in this book's subject and doubts about the future cheap availability of electric power might consider copying and printing the posted reproductions at their earliest convenience. Websites shut down and Internet articles disappear. Intellectual barbarians and self-appointed thought police are also still with us and ready to intimidate authors, editors, and publishers to remove information-bytes they dislike, as with B. Gilley, "The Case for Colonialism," *Third World Quarterly* 28 (September, 2017): 1–17. See also https://www.tandfonline.com/doi/abs/10.1080/01436597.2017.1369037; https://www.mindingthecampus.org/2017/10/the-article-that-made-16000-profs-go-wild.

13 There is no biography of Hulak – possibly not the artist's real name. Around one hundred of his almost four hundred postcards are on the Internet. Most were published between 1905 and 1914. Some were either published for the first time or republished in early 1918. Some one hundred of his almost four hundred postcards on the Internet in 2016 have since been removed: http://kaktus-okamenel.livejournal.com/1105607.html; https://vk.com/album-63628701_203895375; http://his-v.livejournal.com/92651.html.

14 H.F. Jahn, *Patriotic Culture in Russia during World War 1* (Ithaca, 1995), 39; A. Rowley, *Russian Popular Culture and the Picture Postcard, 1880–1922* (Toronto, 2013); M. Zabochen et al., *Ukraina u starii lystivtsi* (Kyiv, 2000), reproduced seven thousand postcards but did not classify them chronologically. Most of those from the years 1917 to 1922 were apparently published in western Ukraine, Vienna, or Petrograd.

15 Ukrainian caricatures have not been studied, and little is known about them. S. Pankova and H. Kondaura, *Facie ad Faciem iliustrovanyi zhyttiepys Mykhaila Hrushevskoho* (Kyiv, 2017) contains a number of caricatures of, and related to, Hrushevsky, reproduced for the first time since they appeared almost one hundred years ago.

16 The best-known Russian-Soviet caricaturist was Boris Efimov (Fridliand). Born, raised, and educated in Ukraine, he moved to Moscow in 1922. He joined the Bolsheviks in 1919. His first cartoons supported no government. These are reproduced at http://rupo.ru/m/3393.

17 There were five radio transmitting and ten receiving stations on tsarist Ukrainian territory in 1919. O. Bohuslavsky, *Informatsiino-presova diialnist Tsentralnoi Rady ta Ukrainskykh uriadiv 1917–1920 rr.* (Zaporizhzhia, 2003), 120.

18 *Punch* (London), 3 December 1887; 13 October 1888. *Kommunist* (Kyiv), 7 May 1919. "Alongside the great creator of the new world – a drunken dwarf spitting in everyone's face. Must we tolerate this in these days?"

19 P. Opanashchuk, "Diialnist Ukrainskoi presy v umovakh tsenzurnoi polityky Rosiiskoho uriadu (1906–1914 rr.)," *Volynski istorychni zapysky* I (2008), 53. The war with Japan and the 1905 Revolution sparked the first mass demand for information throughout the empire's small towns and villages.

20 M.F. Dmytrienko, *Lystivky Bilshovytskykh orhanizatsii Ukrainy 1917–1920 iak istorychne dzherelo* (Kyiv, 1980), 13; A. Prykholko, "Knyzhkova produktsiia na Ukraini za chas revoliutsii," *Holos druku* no. 1 (1921), 30–1.

21 Pierre-Louis Robert in 1796 (*Essai analytique sur les divers moyens établis pour la communication des pensées entre les hommes en société)* was the first to draw attention to how mass publications create a national community among anonymous readers. J.L. Chappey, "Pierre-Louis Roederer et la presse sous le Directoire et le Consulat: l'opinion publique et les enjeux d'une politique éditoriale," *Annales historiques de la Révolution française*, no. 334 (2003): 1–21. Robert's ideas were developed by Benedict Anderson, *Imagined Communities: Reflections on the Origin and Spread of Nationalism* (London, 1983).

22 There is no Ukrainian equivalent of the digital collection of French Revolutionary pamphlets at http://libx.bsu.edu/cdm/landingpage/collection/FrnchRev. For an overview of the popular propaganda literature of the American English and French revolutions, see H. Chisick, "The Pamphlet Literature of the French Revolution: An Overview," *History of European Ideas* 20, nos. 2–3 (1993): 149–66. For a comparative perspective, see S. Sanyal, *Revolutionary Pamphlets: Propaganda and Political Culture in Colonial Bengal* (Cambridge, 2014).

23 Each archival leaflet has a card in a catalogue filed by title or first sentence and, where indicated, by year. Each reproduced leaflet in this book indicates the title. Not all are dated. The description gives the English translation of the title and an archive name.

24 "Dodatky do statti 'Bolshevytska agresiia proty Ukrainy,'" *Ukrainskyi Zbirnyk* (Munich) no.1 (1956), 22–9, reproduced leaflets from a collection in the Ukrainian Free University in Munich.

25 Dmytrienko, *Lystivky*. Includes reproductions.

26 A short description of a collection of three hundred leaflets in the Odesa Public Library is the first known article devoted to national government propaganda. O. Pohrebynsky, "Ukrainska lystivka – metelyk u 1917–1919 rokakh," *Zapysky Ukrainskoho bibliohrafichnoho tovarystva v Odesi* no. 2–3 (1929), 117–22. A random sample is reproduced in A. Shumilova, "Arkushevi vydannia periodu vyzvolnykh zmahan 1917–1919 rokiv u fondi knyzhkovoi palaty Ukrainy," *Visnyk knyzhkovoi palaty Ukrainy* no. 4 (2008), 37–43; "Tektstovi arkushevi vydannia 1917–1921 rr. iak unikalni pershodzherela istorii Ukrainy," idem (2015), no. 1: 32–5; no. 2: 33–8. C. Gilley, "The Ukrainian Anti-Bolshevik Risings of Spring and Summer 1919:

Intellectual History in a Space of Violence," *Revolutionary Russia* 2 (2014): 109–31, examines a small number of warlord leaflets.

27 S. Efremov, "Karna expedytsiia," *Knyhar* (January–March 1920), 72–80. Included is a list of 119 confiscated items from one bookstore.

28 Lenin ordered that White and Black Hundred materials be collected. These materials, however, were destroyed under Stalin. Mikheeva, *Beloe dvizhenie,* 15.

29 TsDAVO f. 178 op 8 sprava 39, no. 216; A. Kupelin, "Listovki 1917 goda v kollektsii gosudarstvennogo muzeia politicheskoi istorii Rossii," *Otechestvennye arkhivy* no. 2 (1993), 92; V. Ocheretianko, "Zahartovani knyhy. Vstanovlennia partiino-derzhavnoho kontroliu nad vydanniam rozpovsiudzhenniam ta vykorystanniam literatury u 20-30-i roky," *Z arkhiviv VUChK-GPU-NKVD-KGB* nos. 1–2 (1999), 129–41; V. Masnenko, "Tsenzura v pid radianski Ukraini 20-kh rokiv; systema, instytutsii represyvna polityka," *Suchasnist* no. 6 (1997), 81–90; K.I. Abramov, "Istoki sovetskoi tsenzury bibliotechnogo dela," *Sovetskoe bibliotekovedenie* no. 6 (1996), 66–77; O. Fedorova, *Politychna tsenzura drukovanykh vydan v USRR – URSR (1917–1990 rr.)* (Kyiv, 2009); V.A. Baviuk, *Politicheskaia tsenzura v sovetskoi Ukraine v 1920–1930-e gg.* (Kazan, 2012).

30 H. Kovalchuk, et al, "Kolektsiia istorychnykh lystivok NBUV i suchasni problemy vvedennia ii v elektronnyi prostir," *Naukovi pratsi Natsionalnoi biblioteky im. V. I. Vernaskoho* vyp. 31 (2011) 262–64.

31 Leaflets from 1917–1919 are reproduced in: V. Morenets, ed., *Sim spohadiv Vyzvolnoi viiny* (Kyiv, 2015); H. Ivanushchenko, *Zalizom i kroviu. Sumshchyna v natsionalno-vyzvolni borotbi pershoi polovyny XX st.* (Sumy, 2001); Ivanushchenko, *Ukrainska revoliutsiia 1917–1920 rr. v lystivkakh ta gazetakh* (Sumy, 2005); Ivanushchenko, *Ukrainske vidrodzhennia 1917–1920 rr. na Sumshchyni* (Sumy, 2010). Reproductions of rare warlord leaflets and transcribed leaflets from the years 1920 to 1922 in R. Koval, *Otamany haidamatskoho kraiu 33 biohafii* (Kyiv, 1998); idem, *Otaman Orlyk* (Kyiv, 2010); S. Zhovtyi, ed., *Iulian Mordalevych. Nashi zmahannia* (Kyiv, 2013). Transcribed copies are in: V. Verstiuk et al., *Ukrainskyi natsionalno-vyzvolnyi rukh. Berezen-lystopad 1917 roku* (Kyiv, 2003), passim; V. Verstiuk et al., *Dyrektoriia, Rada Narodnykh Ministriv Ukrainskoi Narodnoi Respubliki 1918-1920. Dokumenty i materialy* (Kyiv, 2006), passim.

32 On Hryhoriev's declaration in English, for example, A. Adams, *Bolsheviks in the Ukraine* (New Haven, 1963), 299–301, 320.

1 Message and Medium

1 On Benjamin Franklin's phony newspaper see: Carla Mulford, "Benjamin Franklin's Savage Eloquence: Hoaxes from the Press at Passy, 1782,"

Proceedings of the American Philosophical Society, no. 4 (December 2008) 490–530. In 1798 the Directory established a Bureau d'esprit Politique to forward favourable stories about itself to newspapers.

2 G. Creel, *How We Advertised America* (New York, 1920) 4. A. Axelrod, *Selling the Great War: The Making of American Propaganda* (New York, 2009) 81–3.

3 This perhaps explains the presence of many leaflets with closely typed long texts, sometimes two-sided. Presumably, their target was the literate/educated. Yet long messages may also have influenced the semi-literate/half-educated. Social psychologists note that short messages are effective if they are read. But people who only glance, or do not read but only look, are more likely to be persuaded by long messages, regardless of content.

4 S.B. Cunningham, *The Idea of Propaganda: A Reconstruction* (London, 2002), 15–23, 80.

5 C. Stuart, *Secrets of Crewe House: The Story of a Famous Campaign* (London, 1920). Stuart was deputy director of Crewe House.

6 Lasswell, *Propaganda Technique*, 207; L. Sanders and P.M. Taylor, *British Propaganda during the First World War, 1914–18* (London, 1982), 146–7.

7 One issue reproduced in K. Paduszek, *Działalność propagandowa służb informacyjno-wywiadowczych Wojska Polskiego w czasie wojny polsko-bolszewickiej 1919–1921* (Torun, 2004), 195–208.

8 N. Postman, *Amusing Ourselves to Death: Public Discourse in the Age of Show Business*, 2nd ed. (New York, 2006); Gustave Le Bon's *The Crowd: A Study of the Popular Mind* appeared in I895.

9 G.S. Messinger, *British Propaganda and the State in the First World War* (Manchester, 1992), provides biographies of fourteen non-governmental men who played key roles in developing communications media to influence populations in Britain.

10 On the 150,000-strong American Committee on Public Information, "the world's greatest adventure in advertising" according to its founder, G. Creel, see his *How We Advertised America* (New York, 1920). The committee had a subdivision that included every advertising agency in America (158) as well as a Ukrainian section headed by Mykola Tsehlinsky. S. West, *I Shop in Moscow: Advertising and the Creation of Consumer Culture in Late Tsarist Russia* (DeKalb, 2011).

11 F. Siffer and B. Schnitzler, eds., *L'autre Guerre: Satire et propaganda dans l'illustration allemande (1914–1918)* (Strassbourg, 2016). For a comparison of belligerent countries, see Messinger, *British Propaganda*, 14–23. See also M. Rickards, *The Rise and Fall of the Poster* (New York, 1971), 25.

12 For example, W. Dill-Scott, *The Theory of Advertising; A Simple Exposition of the Principles of Psychology in Their Relation to Successful Advertising* (Boston, 1903).

13 F. Wheen, *Karl Marx* (London, 2000), 385; J.D. Martinek, *Socialism and Print Culture in America, 1897–1920* (London, 2012), 3, 54.
14 Trotsky was much influenced by Freud; Lenin was not impressed. M.A. Miller, *Freud and the Bolsheviks: Psychoanalysis in Imperial Russia and the Soviet Union* (Yale, 1998). Wundt's student Isak Shpilrein worked in the Commissariat of Foreign Affairs as of 1919. He does not seem to have had anything to do with propaganda. LeBon's *The Crowd: A Study of the Popular Mind* appeared in I895 – Russian translation, 1896; English translation, 1908.
15 J. White, *Lenin: The Practice and Theory of Revolution* (London, 2001), 27, 38. Kremer's text, written in 1894, circulated widely as a typescript before and after it was published.
16 B. Bazhanov, *Vospominaniia byvshego sekretaria Stalina* (SPB, 1992), 112. A.G. Meyer, *Leninism* (New York, 1962), 54–5. B. Zaslavskii, ed., *Lenin o propagande i agitatsii* (Moscow, 1956), 244–5.
17 V.I. Lenin, *Collected Works* (Moscow, 1965), vol. 27: 265–6; F.M. Rudych, ed., *Vtoroi siezd Kommunisticheskoi partii (bolshevikov) Ukrainy 17–22 oktiabria 1918 goda. Protokoly* (Kyiv, 1991), 90–1.
18 TsDAHO f. 57 op 2 sprava 340 no. 71–2.
19 TsDAVO f. 2 op 1 sprava 281 no. 24; sprava 453 no. 24, 57. As of April only foreign commissariat personnel had access to radio-telegrams. Although the first public radio broadcast was in 1910, radio was still used primarily for station-to-station communication.
20 Regarding early legislation, see E.A. Dinershtein et al., *Izdatelskoe delo v pervye gody Sovetskoi vlasti* (Moscow, 1972).
21 *Statisticheskii spravnik po Kharkovskoi gubernii* (Kharkiv, 1911), 66–7; R.W. Pethybridge, *The Spread of the Russian Revolution: Essays on 1917* (London, 1972), 58. It is unclear whether these figures include 12,759 telephones run by Ukraine's *zemstvos* as of 1915. TsDAVO f. 2 op 1 sprava 453 no. 57.
22 Until 1917, *zemstvo* officials published annual listings of post office and telegraph station locations by province. For example, *Kalendar i zapisnaia knizhka zemskogo korrespondenta* (Kyiv, 1916), 154–7. These allow calculation of density. Iu. Rudenko, *Diialnist ustanov poshty i telehrafu na Pravoberezhnyi Ukraini (druha polovyna XIX – pochatok XX st.)*, Candidate Diss., Cherkassy National University (2018), 92, 94.
23 To prevent jamming, the Bolsheviks restricted access by dividing users into twenty-six categories with allotted daily word limits. The army, food production, and industrial commissariats were allotted 47 per cent of daily capacity, private citizens 1 per cent. There was no limit on party Central Committee messages. TsDAVO f. 342 op 1 sprava 55 no. 6, 123. In February 1919, and again in September, the UNR restricted access to phones and the telegraph to higher governmental and military personnel. Individual

citizens were prohibited from using either without the army's permission. TsDAVO f. 2537 op 1 sprava 40 no. 6.

24 O.O. Sukhov, *Ekonomichna heohrafiia Ukrainy* (Odesa, 1923), 103–4, 151, 167–73; *Bolshaia entsiklopediia*, XVI: 490–1. Maps of railway and telegraph lines are in P.P. Semenov, ed., *Polnoe geograficheskoe opisanie nashego otechestva*, 19 vols. (Saint Petersburg, 1899–1914). Ostapenko claims that Ukraine had almost 19,000 kilometres of track – about as much as Italy. *Ekonomichna heohrafiia Ukrainy* (Kyiv, 1920), 186–8.

25 *Ves Iugo-Zapadnyi krai* (Kyiv, 1913), 53–4. TsDAVO f. 2 op 1 sprava 463 no. 35–7. TsDAHO f. 1 op 20 sprava 18 no. 6–7. A Bolshevik report from 1921 notes 46,911 tons of production in 1914, of which 5,417 was printing-quality paper. TsDAVO f. 34 op 3 sprava 1311 no. 31.

26 *Kievskaia zemskaia gazeta* 1917 no. 38; H. Dmytrenko, "Tsiny na knyhy," *Knyhar* no. 5 (January 1918), 242–3; S. Panochini, "Ohliad Ukrainskoi knyzhkovoi produktsii v 1918 rotsi," *Knyhar* (April 1919), 1310–26. Surveys included only those Kyiv publishers that provided information.

27 TsDAVO f. 3487 op 1 sprava 5 no. 7, 73.

28 M. Shendrovich, "Poligraficheskaia promeshlennost i perspektivy na 1921 god," *Pechat i revoliutsiia* no. 1 (May–July 1921), 29, 33. TsDAVO f. 34 op 3 sprava 881 no. 48. Slightly different figures, perhaps more accurate, in Gleason, ed., *Bolshevik Culture*, 166–9.

29 Dmytrienko, *Lystivky*, 300; S. Petrov, *Knyzhkova sprava v Kyievi 1861–1917* (Kyiv, 2002), 59, 61, 63, 67. It is unclear if these totals include the small hectographs and poligraphs (*amerikanki*) that could print up to one hundred copies. These were widely used in offices and by illegal groups. L. Fit, *Knyzhkova sprava v Cherkassakh 1878–1920* (Cherkassy, 2015); S. Iesiunin, *Mista Podillia u druhii polovyni XIX-na pochatku XX st.* (Khmelnytsky, 2015), 124.

30 Kharkiv province as of July 1918, excluding the city itself, had thirty-two presses in its seventeen *povits*. TsDAVO f. 1325 op 1 sprava 378.

31 O. Fedotova et al., *Spetsfond knyzhkovoi palaty Ukrainy (1917–1921 rr.)* (Kyiv, 2002), 325–37; idem, *Dodtakovyi vypusk* (2003), 51–5. These figures are not classified by year and count an unknown number of enterprises twice: once as private firms and then again as nationalized Soviet enterprises. This publication also lists all publishing firms working during those years, but not does indicate if they had their own presses. See also *Bibliohrafichny pokazhchyk vidsutnykh v fondi Derzhavnoho arkhivu druku neperiodychnykh i periodychnykh vydan (1917–1918 rr.)* (Kyiv, 2010), 86–94, 148–57; *Bibliohrafichny pokazhchyk knyzhkovykh periodychnykh i prodovzhuvannykh vydan 1919–1920 vidsutnykh v fondi Derzhavnoho arkhivu druku* (Kyiv, 2011), 33–7, 58–62.

32 Katerynoslav province averaged five to ten shops per district capital; Kharkiv, two or three. TsDAVO f. 1184 op 1 sprava 11 no. 48–52; op 2 sprava 10 no. 9–16.

33 TsDAVO f. 573 op 1 sprava 857 no. 11. M.P. Kim et al., *Istoriia knigi v SSSR 1917–1921* (Moscow, 1983–6), III: 3: 97; N.N. Skatov, *Kniga v Rossii* (Saint Petersburg, 2008), 24; R. Mashtalir et al., *Rozvytok poligrafii na Ukraine* (Lviv, 1974), 44–59; D. Bagalii and D. Miller, *Istoriia goroda Kharkova za 250 let ego sushchestvovaniia* (Kharkov, 1912), II: 551; A.B. Molodchikov, "Knigoizdatelskoe delo v Ukrainskoi SSR (1917–1990)," *Kniga* 5 (1961), 63.

34 TsDAVO f. 34 op 3 sprava 1297 no. 8v.

35 TsDAVO f. 32 op 3 sprava 892 no. 33–6. Another inventory encompassing all of Ukraine that year, detailing personnel, press, and wages, contains column headings for only one province, thus making the survey hard to decipher. Idem, sprava 927.

36 Kim et al., *Istoriia knigi*, I: 66; III : 97. TsDAVO f. 34 op 2 sprava 138 no. 24.

37 *Vserossiiskaia vystavka v Kieve 1913 g. Katalog otdela pechatnago i pishche bumazhnago dela k 1913* (Kyiv, 1913), 33; M. Kogon and A. Sokolov, *Poligraficheskaia promyshlennost ukrpoligrafotdel* (Kharkiv, 1920), 12. There were 606 big presses and some 2,600 smaller presses. An incomplete inventory of typewriters counted 2,413 of which 1,896 were in Soviet offices. TsDAVO f. 34 op 2 sprava 138 no. 24.

38 N.S. Podoliaka, "Vydavnycha sprava Kharkova kintsia XIX–pochatku XX st. u dokumentakh," *Visnyk Kharkivskoi Derzhavnoi Akademii Kultury* no. 42 (2014), 45–6.

39 The fate of this distribution system in Ukraine is unstudied. E.G. Golomb and E.M. Fingerit, *Rasprostranie pechati v dorevoliutsionnoi Rossii i v Sovetskom Soiuze* (Moscow, 1967), 30, 75–80.

40 J.W. Markham, *Voices of the Red Giants: Communications in Russia and China* (Ames, 1967), 77. T. Leshchenko, ed., *Kataloh dorevoliutsiinykh gazet shcho vydavalysia na Ukraini 1822–1916* (Kyiv, 1971), 148–63, lists pre-revolutionary newspapers by town.

41 A.Z. Okorokov, *Oktiabr i krakh russkoi burzhaznoi pressy* (Moscow, 1970), 55.

42 Ia. Makhonina, *Russkaia dorevoliutsionnaia pechat (1905–1914)* (Moscow, 1991), 68–9, 116, 131, 152–7; I.V. Krupsky, *Natsionalno-patriotychna zhurnalistyka Ukrainy* (Lviv, 1995).

43 *Pratsia* (Lviv), August–September 1904.

44 D. Chorny, *Po livyi bik dnipra. Problemy modernizatsii mist Ukrainy (kinets XIX–pochatok XX st.)* (Kharkiv, 2007), 262–4, 278. Central publications arrived primarily in provincial capitals within three to five days.

45 B. Mironov, *Sotsialnaia istoriia Rossii perioda imperii (XVIII-nachalo XX v.)* (Saint Petersburg, 1999), II: 389–99. Mironov's figures are useless for detailed comparative purposes as they compare the Russian empire with national states, not other empires. Ukraine's press run and title figures should be compared with those of other colonized territories like Ireland, Korea, and Algeria.

46 V.E. Glandon, *Arthur Griffith and the Advanced-Nationalist Press: Ireland 1900–1922* (New York, 1985), 251–304.

47 Figures exclude Kherson and Katerynoslav provinces. [Anon.], ed., *Halychyna Bukovyna Uhorska Rus* (Moscow, 1915), 230; S. Balfour, *The End of the Spanish Empire 1898–1923* (Oxford, 1997), 85.

48 Iesiunin, *Mista Podillia*, 50, 123, 157. Including all available titles would raise the ratios. One title was a Ukrainian weekly that appeared after 1906 for the province's 1,222,000 Ukrainians, of whom 6,734 were literate.

49 V. Ihnatienko, *Ukrainska presa 1816–1923 rr.* (Kyiv, 1926), 70, lists only Ukrainian- and Russian-language items; his totals include publications that saw only one or two issues and exclude imported titles. It is unclear whether his totals include or exclude Bolshevik publications. V. Soldatenko, *Idti vperedi vsekh* (Kyiv, 1986), 65, 113–25. Through 1917 Bolshevik newspapers averaged one in ten of Ukraine's newspapers. Most appeared in Kyiv, Katerynoslav, and Kharkiv. Not all papers published regularly.

50 T. Karoieva, "Pidpryiemtsi v zabezbechenni ukrainomovnoho chytannia v Rosiiskii imperii 1881–1916," *Ukraina moderna* 22 (2015), 93–115. Once it became legal to publish specific subjects in Ukrainian, Russian publishers did so because they saw a market from which they could profit.

51 TsDAVO f. 34 op 2 sprava 132 no. 2; idem, sprava 138 no. 275, 494; sprava 140 no. 76. A disproportionately high percentage of printers died from scabies and malnutrition even before before the war. M. P. Kim et al, *Istoriia knigi v SSSR*, 2: 151–6.

52 Leshchenko, ed., *Kataloh*, 148–63; Ihnatienko, *Ukrainska presa, 70.* Russian-language newspaper titles fell from 751 to 151, Ukrainian-language titles from 106 to 79.

53 A.V. Vasilevna, *Kommerchiskaia reklama v Rossii; 1861- 1917 gg*. Kandytatska dissertatsii, St Petersburg University, 2002, contains a bibliography of histories of advertising in Russia. Verigin's booklet is online: http://www.nazaykin.ru/catalog/ru/tr-pr/russkaja_reklama.htm#.

54 *Ves Iugo-zapadnyi krai* (Kyiv, 1913), 382; West, *I Shop in Moscow.* On advertising in Ukraine, see V. Heorhiievska, N. Sydorenko, *Reklama- rushiy rozkvity: reklamno-dovidkova presa na terytorii Skhidnoi Ukrainy (XIX- pochatok XX st.)* (Kyiv, 2010).

55 J. Aulich and J. Hewitt, *Seduction or Instruction: First War Posters in Britain and France* (Manchester, 2007). Urban commercial culture in prewar Ukraine is unstudied. Little is known about two artists who did produce Ukrainian posters and postcards, Vasyl Hulak and Bohush Shippikh (Shipik?).

56 L. McReynolds, "Imperial Russia's Newspaper Reporters: Profile of a Society in Transition, 1865–1914," *Slavonic and East European Review*

2 (April 1990): 277–93; M. Sribliansky [pseud. Mykyta Shapoval], "Ukrainska pressa i publika," *Ukrainska khata* no. 6 (June, 1910), 396–405.

57 *Obshchii svod po Imperii rezultatov razrabotki dannykh perepisi 1897 g. po Imperii*. vols. 1 and 2. (Saint Petersburg, 1905), I: 1, 9, 11; II: charts 20, 20a, 23. *Pervaia vseobshchaia perepis naseleniia Rossiiskoi imperii 1897 goda* (Saint Petersburg, 1897–1905), vols. 8, 13, 16, 24, 32, 33, 37, 46, 47, 48 charts xxi, xxii. Petrov, *Knyzhkova sprava,* 36. The category "poligraphic manufacturing" (*poligrafischeskie proizvodstva*) included printers and printshop workers together with paper mill workers. At the imperial level the latter averaged 17 per cent of this census category. The category is not broken down into provincial totals. I have assumed the same percentage applied. Figures in parentheses indicate estimated total of printers and print workers (83%).

58 Hr. Hetmanets (pseud.), *Do Strashnykh dniv u kyivi* (1918), appeared in 10,000 copies. In an afterword he wrote that all trade union, Menshevik, Russian SR, and Bund party leaders were pro-Russian Jews. On the background to those events, see I. Cherikover, *Antisemitizm i pogromy na Ukraine 1917–1918 gg.* (Berlin, 1923), 135–9.

59 E. Goldenberg, "Kremenchugskie pechatniki ranshee i teper," *Drukar* no. 7 (November 1927), 12; ibid, [Anon.], "Iz Vospominanii," 8, for a Bolshevik account of Menshevik unionists in Kharkiv. There is no secondary literature on Ukrainian printers. For Russia, see D. Koenker, *Republic of Labor: Russian Printers and Soviet Socialism, 1918–1930* (Ithaca, 2005).

60 K. Kiriienko, "Viiskova presa chasiv hromadianskoi viiny," *Chervona presa* no. 8–9 (October–November, 1927), 14.

61 V.M. Shcherbak, *Bolshevistskaia agitatsiia i propaganda (oktiabr 1919-mart 1919 gg.* (Moscow, 1969), 19-22, 145; A.A. Iepishev ed., *Partiino-politicheskaia rabota v vooruzhennykh silakh SSSR 1918–1973* (Moscow, 1974) 80, 87. On the Four Minute Men: Axelrod, *Selling the Great War,* 113-34.

62 S.A. Tomilin, *Materiialy o sotsialno-gigienicheskom sostoianii Ukrainskoi derevni* (Kharkiv, 1924), 12; L.G. Protasov, "Klassovyi sostav soldat Russkoi armii pered Oktiabrem," *Istoriia SSSR* no. 1 (1977), 45–6; A.G. Rashin, *Naselenie Rossii za sto let. 1811-1913* (Moscow, 1956), 306.

63 A. Rublev, *Istoriia ...* (Zaporizhzhia, 2006), 103, 125. J. Brooks, *When Russia Learned to Read* (Princeton, 1985); M. Mykhailyk, "Ukrainske selo chasy natsion. revoliutsii," *Litopys chervonoi kalyny* no. 1 (1934), 10.

64 *Vilna Ukraina* (Kyiv) (1 January 1919). In Volyn the percentage fell to 40 per cent. In UNR territory the government forbade schools from enrolling non-Ukrainian citizens because they were allegedly filled to capacity. *Vilna Ukraina* (Kyiv), 19 and 20 April 1919.

65 TsDAHO f. 57 no. 2 sprava 260 no. 159–60. As of 1915, roughly 75 per cent of all students in all schools in the Ukrainian provinces were Ukrainians.

66 *Naselenie Ukrainy po dannymy perepisi 1920 goda*, Statistika Ukrainy, No. 28 Seriia 1, Demografiia tom 1, Vypusk 11 (Kharkiv, 1922), Table 3; *Pervaia vseobshchaia perepis naseleniia Rossiiskoi imperii*, chart no. 15, vols. 8, 13, 16, 32, 33, 41, 46, 47, and 48; TsDAVO f. 1115 op. 1 sprava 48 nos. 110–11. All figures rounded off. Jews, Poles, and Germans had high literacy rates, Ukrainians the lowest.

67 The major languages covered were Russian, Ukrainian, Hebrew, and Polish. Russian only – 242,752; Ukrainian only – 1,978; Russian and Ukrainian – 31,704; Russian and Hebrew – 54,845. Nine Jews and forty-five Russians indicated knowledge of Ukrainian; 24 per cent of the counted inhabitants (28,664) declared themselves Ukrainian, 43 per cent (232,148) Russian, 21 per cent (114,524) Jewish. *Perepis goroda Kieva* (Kyiv, 1919), Table XV.

68 S.N. Igumnov, "Naselenie Kharkovskoi gubernii po perepisiam 1897, 1917, i 1920 g.g.," *Profilakticheskaia meditsina* no. 1–2 (1923), 88–9; A. Marzeev, "Itogi vyborochnogo sanitarno-demograficheskogo obsledovaniia selskogo naseleniia Ukrainy," *Profilakticheskaia meditsina* no. 1 (1925), 99.

69 Pethybrige, *The Spread of the Russian Revolution*, 172. Ia. Shafir, *Gazeta i derevnia*, 2nd ed. (Moscow 1923), recorded that Russian peasants did not understand words in Bolshevik texts. On Russian surveys, see J. Brooks, "Studies of the Reader in the 1920s," *Russian History* 9, nos 2–3 (1982): 187–202. There is no known similar survey for Ukraine.

70 S. Anikin [pseudo.], "Sibirskoe," *Vestnik Evropy* (November 1915), 122–4.

71 Bolsheviks themselves did not know what the criteria were for categorization. Officials on the spot would make up their own and decide who was poor enough not to be rich. O. Nesterov, N, Zemziulina, and P. Zakharchenko, *U pokhodi za voliu* (Kyiv, 2000), 87.

72 L. Masenko, *Mova radianskoho totalitaryzmu* (Kyiv, 2017), 64–8; O. Mykhailiuk, *Selianstvo Ukrainy v pershi desiatylittia XX st.: Sotsiokulturni protsesy* (Dnipropetrovsk, 2007), 152–7, 318, 376–8.

73 *Nova Rada* (Kyiv), 15 December 1917. Popov, *Mizh vladoiu i bezvladoiu*, 320.

74 *Ukrainska stavka*, 3 January 1919.

75 B. Tymoshenko, ed., *Na shliakhakh i rozdorizhzhiakh: spohady, nevidomi tvory* (Kyiv, 1999), online: http://chtyvo.org.ua/authors/Antonenko-Davydovych/Nashliakhakh_i_rozdorizhzhiakh. TsDAVO f. 2 op 1 sprava 252 no. 41v.

76 *Kozak* (Kamianets-Podilskyi) 19 June 1919. The agitator related that he convinced the locals Ukraine was preferable to the Bolsheviks.

77 To keep his job, the postman paid boys a few kopeks to deliver his items. Once out of sight they would deliver them when it suited them or just throw them away. TsDAVO f. 2 op 1 sprava 252 no. 75v; ibid., f. 538 op. 1 sprava 116 no. 16.

2 The Central Rada and the Ukrainian State

1 V. Verstiuk et al., *Ukrainska tsentralna rada. Dokumenty materialy u dvokh tomakh* (Kyiv, 1997), I: 133, 158; II: 230. On organizational history, see O. Bohuslavsky, *Informatiino-presova diialnist Tsentralnoi Rady ta Ukrainskykh uriadiv 1917–1920 rr.* (Zaporizhzhia, 2003).

2 V. Verstiuk et al., *Serhyi Iefremov. Publitsystyka revoliutsiinoi doby (1917–1920)*, Tom 1 (Kyiv, 2014), 347–52, 493; M. Kovalevsky, *Pry dzherelakh borotby* (Innsbruck, 1969), 370–1.

3 Verstiuk et al., *Ukrainska tsentralna rada*, II: 71, 201.

4 TsDAVO f. 1115 op 1 sprava 44 no 59 v.

5 Basara, "Politychnyi sotsium ukrainskykh provintsiinykh mist za zvitamy instruktoriv Tsentralnoi Rady," in *Ukrainska Tsentralna Rada: postup natsiot-vorennia ta derzhavobudivnytstva*, ed. V. Serhiichuk, 158–68.

6 *Instruktsiia dlia viiskovykh ahitatoriv* (Kyiv, 1917).

7 Z. Kuzelia, *Z kulturnoho zhyttia Ukrainy* (Salzwedl, 1918), 73.

8 *Knyhar* no. 2 (October, 1917), 98; *Nova Rada*, 21 December 1917 (3 January 1918). Ukrainian Social Democrats in Winnipeg, Canada, in 1917 collected $12,000 for a press they purchased but then apparently never shipped. *Robitnycha hazeta*, 26 January 1918.

9 Petrov, *Knyzhkova sprava v Kyievi 1861-1917*, 289–90; Kuzelia, *Z kulturnoho zhyttia*, 79.

10 P. Fedoryshyn, *Presa i Ukrainska derzhvanist (1917–1920 rr.)* (Ternopil, 1996), 9; Petrov, *Knyzhkova sprava*, 279, 287–92, noted six hundred titles published in 1917, of which two hundred were in Ukrainian. T.R. Karoieva, "Dostupnist vydan, drukovanykh ridnoiu movoiu, Ukrainskym selianam Podilskoi hubernii pochatku XX st.," *Ukrainsky selianyn* no. 14 (2014), 69–71.

11 Kuzelia, *Z Kulturnoho zhyttia*, 29. Kuzelia lists publications according to publisher, without press runs.

12 TsDAVO f. 1184 op 2 sprava 11, no. 29–33; S. Panochini, "Knyzhkova produktsiia v 1917 rotsi," *Knyhar* no. 5 (January 1918), 243–50. T. Kivshar, *Ukrainskyi knyzhkovyi rukh iak istorychen iavyshche (1917–1923)* (Kyiv, 1996), 18.

13 Russian papers carried little on Ukrainian national issues. On wartime newspaper press runs in Germany, France, and Britain, see N. Ferguson, *The Pity of War* (London, 1998), 243–5.

14 N. Myronets et al., *Ievhen Chykalenko Andryi Nikovsky. Lystuvannia 1908–1921 rokiv* (Kyiv, 2010), 317, 324, 327, 334–5. Nikovsky claimed that Swedish manufacturers of rotary presses that summer sold their new machines only to the Bolsheviks. All others had been bought by the Germans.

15 Kuzelia, *Z Kulturnoho zhyttia*, 21, 70.

16 Fit, *Knyzhkova sprava v Cherkasakh 1878–1920 rr.*, 32, 38.

17 TsDAVO f. 2537 op sprava 53 no. 4.

18 TsDAVO f. 1035 op 1 sprava 82 no. 21.
19 [Anon.], "Lysty z Kyiva," *Volia* (Vienna), vol. 3, no. 8 (August 1920), 306–7; Ia. Pelensky, ed., *Pavlo Skoropadsky. Spohady kinets 1917–hruden 1918* (Kyiv, 1995), 50–1, 219–20. Dontsov does not mention the rotary press, financing issues, or passivity in his memoirs. *Rik 1918 Kyiv.*
20 A. Maliarevskii, *P. Skoropadskii Getman vseiia Ukrainy* (Kyiv, 1918); V. Smolyi et al., *Ukrainska Derzhava (kviten-hruden 1918 roku) Dokumenty i materialy u dvokh tomakh* (Kyiv, 2015), I: 28–9. The local unsupervised published texts are yet to be studied. I am grateful to Immo Rebitschek of Giessen University, who informed me of locally issued texts he had found in Moscow archives. He provided me with a copy of his unpublished paper "Pavlo Skoropads'kyj and the revolution in Ukraine," which includes a section on propaganda.
21 Pelensky ed., *Pavlo Skoropadsky*, 129.
22 The little that was done had little impact in western Europe. As reported in 1919 by a UNR diplomat: "Europe knew nothing about us and if it did, it was all only negative." Budkov and Viedienieev, *Slovo pravdy pro Ukrainu*, 50–7, 62.
23 The government did attempt to influence elite opinion via the press. Officials sponsored and allowed anti-Ukrainian articles in all of Kyiv's Russian newspapers while censoring all references to cultural and political Russification in Ukrainian papers. I. Davydko, ed., *Ievhen Chykalenko. Shchodennyk Tom 2 (1918–1919)* (Kyiv, 2004), 114, 117.
24 The last recorded allocation of 40 million marks was made in June 1918. Iu.F. Felshtinsky, ed., *Germaniia i revoliutsiia v Rossii* (Moscow, 2013), 220. In August, in an appendix to the Treaty of Brest-Litovsk, written after the collapse of the last German offensive on the Western Front, Germany agreed to cede to Russia Kharkiv, Katerynoslav, and Kherson provinces "on the conclusion of the general peace." Russia was required to pay 6 billion marks compensation for German war losses. Full text translated: http://images.library.wisc.edu/FRUS/EFacs/1918v1/reference/frus.frus1918v1.i0019.pdf.
25 TsDAVO f. 2537 op 1 sprava 53. no. 6.
26 TsDAVO f. 2537 op 1 sprava 53 no. 47–9.
27 TsDAVO f. 2537 op 1 sprava 53 no. 8–33. The PROTOFIS organization offered assistance, claiming that it was planning a big daily paper that would "defend the interests of Ukrainian industry and assist [*sodeistviet*] the growth of the young Ukrainian state."
28 In the Balta stationmaster's opinion, kiosks were needed – and he pointed out there were none in his station. "In Balta it would not hurt to have Ukrainian courses for passengers, and above all, Ukrainian kiosks so the yids [*zhydky*] not feed us with Russian newspapers." Ibid, no. 33.
29 TsDAVO f. 2357 op 1 sprava 54 no. 19.

30 TsDASBU – "To the Ukrainian Nation [*Do Ukrainskoho Narodu*]." DNAB – "Citizens [*Hromadiane*]," "Comrades and Citizens [*Tovaryshchi ta hromadiane*]," "The Common Council of Ukrainian Progressive Parties [*Spilna rada ukrainskykh postupovykh partii*]," "To Teachers in the Poltava Region [*Do vchyteliv na Poltavshchyni. Panove tovaryshi*]," "Respected Ukrainian citizen! [*Shanovnyi hromadianyne Ukrainets!*]," "To conscious Ukrainians in the Provinces [*Do svidomykh Ukrainstsiv na povitakh*]," "Ukrainian Central Council of the Southern Railway Lines [*Ukrainska tsentralna rada Pivdennykh zaliznyts*]." TsDAHO – "To the citizens in Poltava [*Do hromadian na Poltavshchyni*]." TsDASBU – "To Ukrainian Students [*Do Ukrainsoho studentsva*]," "To Ukrainian Professors [*Do Ukrainskykh profesoriv*]." Kharkivsky istorychnyi muzei – "Proclamation to peasants and soldiers [*Vidozva do selian i saldativ*]." Chernihivsky kraeznavchyi muzei – "Citizen Peasants, rural society and Intellectuals! [*Hrazhdane-seliane, ta selianske hromadianstvo i intellihentsiia*]." DNAB – "To Civilian government Officials [*Do sluzhashchim Grazhdanskikh Pravitelsvennykh uchrezhdenii*]."

31 Kharkivsky istorychnyi muzei – "Proclamation to peasants and soldiers [*Vidozva do selian i saldativ*]."

32 DNAB – "Respected Ukrainian citizen! [*Shanovnyi hromadiane Ukrainskyi*]."

33 Ivanushchenko, ed., *Ukrainska revoliutsiia 1917–1920 rr. v lystivkakh ta gazetakh*, 21.

34 DNAB –"Citizens [*Hromadiane*]," "COMRADES AND CITIZENS [*Tovaryshchi ta hromadiane*]."

35 TsDASBU – "To Ukrainian Professors [*Do Ukrainskykh profesoriv*]."

36 TsDASBU – "To Ukrainian Students [*Do Ukrainsoho studentsva*]."

37 TsDAHO – "To citizens in Poltava [province] [*Do hromadian na Poltavshchyni*]."

38 DNAB – "To Teachers in the Poltava Region [*Do vchyteliv na Poltavshchyni. Panove tovaryshi*]." Chernihivskyi kraeznavchyi muzei – "Citizen Peasants, rural society and Intellectuals [*Hrazhdane-seliane, ta selianske hromadianstvo i intellihentsiia*]!," "Respected Ukrainian citizen [*Shanovnyi hromadiane Ukrainskyi*]!," "To [nationally] conscious Ukrainians in the Provinces [*Do svidomykh Ukrainstsiv na povitakh*]."

39 DNAB – "Ukrainian Central Council of the Southern Railway Lines [*Ukrainska tsentralna rada Pivdennykh zaliznyts*]." TsNB (viddil starodrukiv) – "To Civilian government Officials. Comrades [*Do sluzhashchim Grazhdanskikh Pravitelsvennykh uchrezhdenii*]," "To Ukrainian Postal and Telegraph Officials [*Do poshtovo-teliehrafnykh sluzhachykh Ukrainstsiv*]."

40 DNAB – "Proclamation to our supporters [*Vidozva do nashykh odnodumtsiv*]," "UKRAINIAN NATION! [*Narode Ukrainskyi*]."

41 M. Hrushevsky, *Iliustrovana Istoriia Ukrainy*, 3rd ed. (Vienna, 1921), 558–9.

42 DNAB – "Proclamation to our supporters [*Vidozva do nashykh odnodumtsiv*]."

43 Ivanushchenko ed., *Ukrainska revoluitsiia 1917–1920*, 23. Kharkivskyi istorychnyi muzei – "Ukrainian Social Democratic Workers Party [*Ukrainska sotsial-demokratychna robitnycha partiia*]."
44 DNAB – "Citizens [*Hromadiane*]," "THE PEREIASLAV AGREEMENT [*pereiaslavskyi traktat*]," "The Kharkiv Literacy Society. What is a Republic [*Kharkovskoe obshchestvo Gramotnost. Chto takoe respublika*," "What is the Ukrainian Central Rada [*Chto takoe Ukrainskaia tsentralnaia rada*]," "Reports about Ukraine [*Zvistky po Ukraini*]."
45 DNAB – "What is the Central Rada [*Chto takoe Ukrainskaia tsentralnaia rada*]."
46 DNAB – "COMRADES [*Tovarishchi*]."
47 DNAB – "Reports about Ukraine [*Zvistky po Ukraini*]."
48 DNAB – "What do Orthodox Ukrainians want [*Choho khochut pravoslavni Ukrainsti*]."
49 DNAB – "From the National Council of Ministers [*Vid Rady Narodnykh Ministriv*]."
50 DNAB – "To Volost town and Village Executive committees of Balta District [*Volostnym ... komitetam Baltskogo uiezda*]."
51 DNAB – "From the General Secretariat [*Vid Heneralnoho Sekretariatu*]."
52 Ivanushchenko, ed., *Ukrainska revoluitsiia 1917-1920*, 8–16. Arkhiv Druku – "The Amateur Group presents Return from Siberia [*Liubitelskym hurtkom vlashtovuitsia Povernuvsia z sibiru*]," "(A Tragedy of Two Sisters). Victims of War [*Tragediia dvukh sester Zhertvy voiny*]."
53 DNAB – "Out with Russian disorder! [*Khet Rossiiske bezholovia*]." Chernihivsky Kraeznavchyi muzei – "From the Main Commission to the [Ukrainian] Constituent Assembly Elections of the Ukrainian National Republic [*Od holovnoi komisii po spravakh vyboriv do Ustanovchykh zboriv Ukrainskoi Narodnoi Republiky*]." DNAB – "From hand to hand from house to house! Good People! [*Z ruk do ruk, z khaty do khaty. Liudy dobri*]."
54 DNAB – "COMRADES, WORKERS, SOLDIERS, AND PEASANTS! [*Tovaryshi Robitnyky Saldaty Seliane*]," "The BLACK HUNDRED, List no. 3 yearns for the TSARIST WHIP on the Ukrainian back [*Chorna sotnia spysok no. 3 tuzhyt za tsarskoiu nahaikoiu na Ukrainsku spynu*]."
55 DNAB – "Mothers Wives Sisters! [*Materi, zhinky ta sestry*]."
56 Chernihivsky Kraeznavchy muzei – "Comrades and Citizens! Don't Vote For: [*Tovarishchi i Grazhdane. Ne golosuite*]." DNAB – "COMRADES, WORKERS, SOLDIERS, AND PEASANTS! [*Tovaryshi Robitnyky Saldaty Seliane*]," "All as one in Kyiv region vote for list no. 20 [*Vsi iakieden holosuite po Kyivshchyni za spysok No. 20*]," "All power in Ukraine to the entire working population: [*Vsia vlast na Ukraini vsomu trudiashchomu narodovi*]."
57 Chernihivsky Kraeznavchyi muzei – "Brother Ukrainians and Sister Ukrainians! [*Bratia ukraintsi Sestry Ukrainky*]."

58 DNAB – "Citizens! All Ukraine is going through hard times ... [*Hromadiane tuzhnyi chas perezhyvaie vsia Ukraina*]," "FROM THE UKRAINIAN CENTRAL RADA [*Vid Ukrainskoi Tsentralnoi Rady*]," "Citizens. The citizens of the Ukrainian National Republic must live through unprecedently difficult times [*Hromadiane. Tiazhki nadzvychaino tiazhni chasy pruishlosia perezhyty*]."
59 DNAB – "Warriors- Ukrainians! [*Voiaky-Ukraintsi*]."
60 DNAB – "To Ukrainians Patriots Brothers! [*Do Ukrainstsiv-patriotiv*]. "
61 DNAB – "To the population of Sloboda Ukraine [*Do naselennia Slobidskoi Ukrainy*]," "Citizens. The citizens of the Ukrainian National Republic had to live through unprecedently difficult times [*Hromadiane. Tiazhki nadzvychaino tiazhni chasy pryishlosia perezhyty*]," To all citizens of the town of Chernihiv and surroundings [*Do vsikh hromadia mista Chernihiva i ioho okolyts*].
62 DNAB – "Announcement. Citizens of Chernihiv Province!!! [*Vidozva. Hromadiane Chernyhivshchyny*]." www. hai-nyzhnyk.in.ua – "The Ten Commandments [*Desiat zapovidei*]."
63 TsDASBU – "ORDER 29/16 February 1918 [*Nakaz 29/16 February 1918*]," "Order #3 1/16 March 1918 [*Nakaz no.3 1/16 March 1918*]," "Comrade Peasants [deleted] To the Citizens of Budaiv County [*Tovaryshi seliane. Do hromadian Budaivskoi volosty*]."
64 Arkhiv Druku – "The Amateur Group presents Return from Siberia (A Tragedy of Two Sisters). Victims of War [*Liubitelskym hurtkom vlashtovuitsia Povernuvsia z sibiru (Tragediia dvukh sester Zhertvy voiny."*]
65 Ivanushchenko, ed., *Ukrainska revoluitsiia 1917–1920*. DNAB – "In the name of the Ukrainian National Republic we order [*Imenem Ukrainskoi Narodnoi Respubliky nakazuiemo*]."
66 TsDAHO f. 57 op. 2 sprava 266 no. 15. The man's father had been a wealthy industrialist.
67 Russian monarchists in Ukraine were ideologically anti-Semitic. Their publications explicitly called for violence against all Jews: "Now Jews are everywhere. Let us throw off this yoke ... Down with the Jews! ... Give us the tsar!" *Razsvet*, 6 September 1917. Russian Black Hundred texts were the main source of anti-Jewish ideas in before 1917.
68 The poster was signed in Latin letters by O. Valens, pseudomym of the radical nationalist Valerian Otamanovsky. Verstiuk et al., *Serhyi Iefremov*, I: 590–1. Russian Black Hundred texts were the main source of anti-Jewish ideas in before 1917. Their major Ukrainian publishing centre was in Volyn's Pochaiv monastery, whose prewar publications, regardless of hostile depiction of Jews in the present, did not incite violence and condemned pogroms.Taras Shevchenko depicted Jews as hostile exploiters in the past, not the present. K. Fedevych, *Za viru, tsaria i kobzaria. Malorosiiski monarkhisty i Ukrainskyi natsionalnyi rukh (1905–1917 roky)* (Kyiv, 2017), 211–15.

69 Verstiuk, ed., *Ukrainska Tsentralna Rada* 1: 354; E. Cherikover, *Istoriia pogromnago dvizheniia na Ukraine 1917–1921 Tom pervyi* (Berlin, 1923), I: 216–17.

70 P. Maltsiv, *Ukraina v derzhavnomu biudzheti Rossii;* S. Kulyk, "Iak Rossiia vyzyzkuie Ukrainu," *Pamiatkova knyzhka Soiuz Vyzvolennia Ukrainy i kalendar na 1917 rik;* I. Maievsky, *Chervonyi imperiialism. Po shliakhu kontr-revoliutsii,* reprinted in *Khronika 2000,* nos. 27–8 (1999), 286–96.

71 P. Syrotenko, *De povynna vyrishytysia zemelna sprava;* M. Iakymenko, *Zemelna sprava na Ukraini;* M. Baier, *Zemelna reforma i osnovy zemelnoi polityky na Ukraini, Sotsiializatsiia chy zemelna vlasnist?* In the second work, the *zemstvo* activist argued that the middle peasants opposed the Rada because it cancelled private landownership, a regressive move modelled on the archaic Russian commune, and not because of German policies.

72 Kh. Kolomeichenko, *Ekonomika i Ukraina;* A. Ternychenko, *Kryvdy Ukrainskoho Khliboroba.*

73 An anthology of some of these popular items is A.P. Demydenko, ed., *Velykyi Ukrainets* (Kyiv, 1992).

74 B. Zaklynsky, *Katekhizm Ukrainstia (Scho treba znaty kozhnomu Ukraintsevy),* 7th ed.; A. Pilkevich, *Kto takie Ukrainsty i chego oni dobyvaiutsia.*

75 Hryhoriev Nash, *Iakoi respubliky treba bidnym liudam?;* [Anon.], *Iakoho ladu nam treba;* V. Boiko, *Zemstvo i narodni upravy;* M. Zahirnia, *Pro derzhavnyi lad u vsiakykh narodiv;* V. Hryshchynsky, *Proletariat Panuiuchykh ta pryhnichennykh natsii.* A number of pamphlets were also devoted to immediate political issues such as A. Khomyk's *Vserosiiski Ustanovchi zbory chy Vsesvitnyi Mizhnarodnyi Konhres?* Khomyk condemned the Provisional Government, which refused to recognize Ukrainian autonomy while recognizing the re-establishment of a Polish state that included western and right-bank Ukrainian lands. It was not up to Russia but to the Versailles Conference to settle Ukrainian issues. In reply to arguments that Ukrainian claims were counter-revolutionary, he wrote: "Ukrainians have an older revolutionary tradition than the French so Muscovites should not lecture us about revolutionary thinking ... when every decade we raised the proud banner of insurgency against oppressors."

76 M. Cherkavsky, *Do intellihentsii na Ukraini.*

77 A. Boian, *Interesy robitnytstva ta natsionalne pytannia.*

78 Smolyi et al, *Ukrainska Derzhava* 1: 593; 2: 53.

79 Ivanushchenko, ed., *Ukrainska revoluitsiia 1917–1920,* 33–4. DNAB – "To the population of Poltava province" [*Do naselennia Poltavskoi hub*]," "To the Population of Podillia [*Do naselennia Podillia*]," "Citizens. With unimaginable thoughtlessness [*GRAZHDANE! S bezgranichnym legkomysliem*]."

80 Davydko ed., *Ievhen Chykalenko,* 114.

81 V. Petriv, *Spomyny z chasiv Ukrainskoi revoliutsii (1917–1921)* (Lviv, 1927–8) pt 2: 104–5, 136. Plans as of August 1918 to stop estate restoration to former lords were never implemented.

82 Cherikover, *Istoriia pogromnago dvizheniia na Ukraine*, 161. The paper was first sponsored by the War Ministry in 1917. Cherikover also noted that a popular print circulated approving of eighteenth-century pogroms committed by the Haidamaks.

83 When travelling by train the units draped the wagons in Ukrainian national colours and slogans. They sometimes marched into villages with band playing and flags flying. This impressed inhabitants, who had expected the worst from the troops in Austrian uniforms. Iu. Tereshchenko and T. Ostashko, *Ukrainskyi patriot z dynastii Habsburhiv* (Kyiv, 2008), 39–43; R. Koval, ed., *Hutsuly u Vyzvolnyi borotbi. Spohady sichovoho striltsia Mykhaila Horbovoho* (Kyiv, 2009), 154–64.

84 TsDAVO f. 2357 op 1 sprava 54 no. 16–19. Sales of *Neue Ziet* were low, presumably because few read German. The Railway's Cultural Education Union, together with local activists and *prosvita*, were willing to contribute to running the kiosks. In August the Zaporizhzhia region branch reported for the third time that the kiosk situation was bad and that it had no Ukrainian books and no directions from the ministry on their exact role. It requested full authority to run them. Ibid., sprava 53 no. 27.

85 None of these leaflets were signed by any government official or institution. Many were signed by various obscure organizations perhaps sponsored by General Keller's Defence Council. Keller, a man of decidedly Black Hundred convictions, was appointed as commander-in- chief reluctantly that November by Skoropadsky – who sacked him a week later. Keller filled his council with like-minded associates and during his short tenure tried to subvert the more moderate council of ministers.

86 Davydko ed., *Shchodennyk, Tom II*, 151–69. The Hetman issued his decree on reincorporating into a renewed Russian empire because he thought this would convince the Entente powers to recognize Ukraine. He later learned that the Entente had been prepared in any case to recognize his government and Ukrainian independence. Chykalenko claims he would not have issued the Decree had he known that earlier.

87 DNAB – "Peasants. Beauty and strength of Ukraine! [*Vidozva Seliane krasa i syla Vkrainy*]," "BROTHERS! [*Bratia*]," "Peasants! The day is nearing ... [*Krestiane Priblizhaietsia den*]," "Brother peasants! [*Bratia krestiane*]," "Peasants Ukrainians! [*Seliane-Ukraintsi*]," "Peasants. You are tired ... [*Krestiane Vy ustali*]," "To Government officials [*Do Uriadovtsiv*]," "Workers [*Rabochie*]," "Citizens At the Beginning of last November [*Grazhdane V nachale minuvshago noiabra*]," "Citizens. At the present deeply significant moment," "Citizens of the Ukrainian State [*Grazhdane Ukrainskoi Derzhavy Probil*

groznyi chas ispytaniia], "Citizens of Ukraine! [*Grazhdane Ukrainy*]," "Kievans [*Kievliane*]."

88 DNAB – "Women [*Zhenshschiny*]."

89 DNAB – Workers! [Russ.]

90 DNAB – "UKRAINIAN COSSACKDOM/ WARRIORS [*Kozatstvo Ukrainske. Voiny*]."

91 DNAB – "RESTORE RUSSIA!!! DEFEND UKRAINE!!! [*Vozstanovlaite Rossiiu Zashchishchaite Ukrainu*]."

3 The UNR, Radical Socialists, and Warlords

1 The relationship of warlords to the UNR is not straightforward, because individual ministers or parties were patrons to one or another of them. Consequently, is not easy to establish whether warlords represented the government or government policy, and if they did, which ones did so. Seven warlords were arrested during the spring and summer of 1919 and tried, when Petliura tried to curb their activities. However, when army intelligence or the justice ministry arrested one for what today would be called war crimes, ministers would intervene to release him. Faced with total collapse in October of that year, Petliura stopped the arrests. Iu. Mytrofanenko, *Ukrainska otamanshchyna*, 2nd ed. (Kirovohrad, 2016), 110, 186–7, 193–4.

2 *Ukrainska stavka*, 1, 2, January 1919.

3 On the army's Information Bureau, see S. Kost, *Narysy z istorii Zakhidnoukrainskoi presy pershoi polovyny XX st.* (Lviv, 2002) 107–14.

4 *Vistnyk UNR*, 12 February 1919.

5 *Zhyttia Podillia*, 23 March 1919; 5 April 1919; *Trudova hromada*, 22 October 1919.

6 Kost, *Narysy z istorii*, 23–30, 94–114.

7 TsDAVO f. 2357 op 1 sprava 54 no. 20; ibid. op 2 sprava 107 no 3.

8 TsDAVO f. 1 sprava 48 no. 122. The greatest number of copies for one leaflet was 61,000.

9 *Zhyttia Poddillia*, 5 April 1919.

10 *Novyny* (Kamianets-Podilskyi) 19, 21 October 1919.

11 Iu. Tiutiunnyk, *Zymovyi pokhid 1919-1920 rr.* (Kolomyia, 1923) 35.

12 *Zhyttia Podillia*, 4, 16 March 1919. The writer, who complained about spying, noted that the man in question did not know the difference between religion and nationality; because she was Catholic, he assumed she was Polish and therefore disloyal.

13 *Zhyttia Podillia*, 5 April 1919; *Trudova Hromada*, 22 October 1919; C. Lazarski, "White Propaganda Efforts in the South during the Russian Civil War 1918–1919," 691.

14 D. Doroshenko, *Istoriia Ukrainy 1917–1923 rr. Tom 1* (New York, 1954), 257.
15 M. Kukurudziak and M. Sobchynska, *Z istorii natsionalnoi shkoly i pedahohichnoi dumky v UNR* (Kamianets-Podilsky, 1997), 10.
16 O. Bohuslavsky, *Informatsiino-presova diialnist Tsentralnoi Rady ta Ukrainskykh uriadiv 1917–1920 rr.* (Zaporizhzhia, 2003), 119–45. No one has yet discovered as detailed a participant account of the Ukrainian propaganda effort as the one by George Creel about the American effort.
17 TsDAVO f. 1113 op 1 sprava 21 no. 5–6.
18 Verstiuk et al., *Dyrektoriia, Rada Narodnykh Ministriv Ukrainskoi Narodnoi Respubliki 1918–1920*, I: 382.
19 M. Obidnyi, "Iak ohoronialysia pamiatky," *Nova Ukraina* (Prague) no. 4–6 (1925) 97.
20 *Maiak* (Kremenchuh), 16 April 1919.
21 TsDAVO f. 1113 op. 1 sprava 12 no. 99; op 1 sprava 12 no. 86; op. 2 sprava 76 no. 72. I was unable to locate a second poster "To Arms. Red Imperialists Out!" (20,000 copies); idem, op. 2 sprava 76 no 83. Nor could I locate two others on typhus released that year: idem, f. 1109 op 1 sprava 11, no. 65, 266.
22 TsDAVO f. 1113 op. 1 sprava 6 no. 4–6, 28; idem, op. 2 sprava 1 no. 95; idem, sprava 2 no. 9–10; sprava 70 no. 19–20; idem, op. 1 sprava 76 no. 20.
23 M. Dolnytsky and O. Levytsky, *Ukrainska Halytska Armiia* (Detroit, 1958), I: 327.
24 TsDAVO f. 1113 op 4 sprava 3 no. 12–15. *Halytskyi holos*, 4 September 1919. The Directory apparently actually published only one poster. The order to print 25,000 copies: TsDAVO f. 1113 op 1 sprava 12 no. 86. Surviving order forms suggest more were planned. Ukraine had five broadcast radio stations (Kyiv, Odesa, Mykolaiiv, Zhmerynka, and Vinnytsia) and twelve radio receiving stations.
25 TsDAVO f. 2537 op 7 sprava 3 no. 140. Podillia railways that December had 125 locomotives (62 functioning) and 2,901 wagons. Idem, op 7 sprava 6 no. 2. Rail movement reports for January 1919 suggest that functioning stock was used primarily to carry German troops home. TsDAHO f. 57 op. 2 sprava 237 no. 8–14.
26 TsDAVO f. 2573 op 9 sprava 5 no. 32. Although the area had forests, wood was not available for locomotives because the government only gave promissory notes, not cash, to contractors. They consequently could not offer high enough pay to attract workers to cut and deliver to stations.
27 TsDAVO f. 1062 op. 1 sprava 7 no. 184, 246–9. These figures are from an inspection carried out in August and September 1919. Trains by then used only wood for fuel. The main cause of mechanical failures was the acute lack of grease. A November report estimated 5,246 functioning wagons of all kinds in Podillia province. TsDAVO f. 2537 op 4 sprava 2 no. 20. Slightly different figures: ibid. op 1 sprava 14 no. 15, 102–3, 129.

28 TsDAVO f. 2537 op 1 sprava 14 no. 6; ibid. op 2 sprava 107 no. 28–31.

29 TsDAVO f. 1113 op 1 sprava 16 no. 4; 2–4, 12–14; idem, f. 1078 op. 1 sprava 22 no. 376, 375, 380. Signature illegible. Minister at the time was Teofan Cherkasky.

30 TsDAVO f. 1113 op. 2 sprava 27 no. 58–63.

31 TsDAVO f. 1429 op 1 sprava 26 no. 24, 25, 29.

32 TsDAVO f. 1429 op 1 sprava 9 no. 1. A ten-page addendum to the report is missing. Stakhiv, *Ukraina v dobi Dyrektorii UNR*, 4: 198, notes that the Directory failed to exploit Bolshevik negotiations with the Entente to show that they were in conspiring with evil imperialists – although collaboration with imperialists was a main theme in Bolshevik anti-Ukrainian propaganda.

33 TsDAVO f. 1429 op 2 sprava 113 no. 65.

34 O. Zavaliuk and S. Oliinyk, *Ukrainska Halytska Armiia na Podilli (lypen 1919–traven 1920 rr.)* (Kamianets-Podilsky, 2013), 166–8.

35 TsDAVO f. 2188 op. 1 sprava 117 no. 97.

36 TsDAHO f. 1 op. 18 sprava 63 no. 1.

37 *Ukraina* (Kamianets-Podilsky), 16(3), October 1919; TsDAVO f. 1092 op. 2 sprava 354 no 4; V. Andriievsky, "Velyka ruiina," *Volia* (Vienna) 1, no. 3 (1920), 108–12.

38 TsDAVO f. 1092 op. 2 sprava 73 no. 4–5.

39 TsDAVO f. 1113 op. 1 sprava 16 no 3–4, 18–19.

40 Bohuslavsky, *Informatsiino-presova diialnist*, 136.

41 TsDAVO f. 1113 op 2 sprava 27 no. 59–60; P. Cherniavin, "1-ia konnaiia armiia," *Propagandist i agitator* no. 21 (November, 1939), 31–5; M. Kovalchuk, *Nevidoma viina 1919 roku: Ukrainsko-bilohvardiiske zbroine protystoiannia* (Kyiv, 2006), 99, 208.

42 TsDAVO f. 1092 op. 2 sprava 56 no. 25, 29, 35, 40; sprava 723 no 12. Claims about the total number of troops differ. Despite the efforts of the government-in-exile, not all irregular units had contact with one another, and their operations were uncoordinated. D. Krasnosilsky, *Antybilshovytskyi rukh selian v pravoberezhnyi chastyni USRR u 1920-1924 rr.* (Khmelnytsky, 2009), 267–70.

43 During May and June 1920, Stalin was in Ukraine and was impressed by the influence of co-ops and the *prosvita*. He characterized them as "authentic governmental institutions" that supported Petliura's government-in-exile. Local *soviets* paled in comparison with them, he wrote, as the superbly functioning co-ops provided commodities and the *prosvita* ideas. How powerful these institutions remained in 1921–2 and their relationship to local activists is unknown. V. Vasiliev, "Evoliutsiia pohliadiv kerivnytstva RKP(b) ta KP(b)U na svitovu revoliutsiiu v konteksti radiansko-polskoi viiny 1920 r," *Ukrainskyi istorychny zhurnal* no. 5 (2006), 162.

44 Krasnosilsky, *Antybilshovytskyi rukh*, 98.

45 V. Revehuk, *Otaman Poltavskoho kraiu – bortsi za voliu Ukrainy* (Poltava, 2011), 63, 78. The Bolsheviks shut down the press in 1922 and executed the printer together with other partisan leaders.

46 K. Lavrynovych, "Povstanchyi rukh," *Volia* (Vienna), no. 1 (April 1921), 14.

47 TsDAHO f. 1 op. 20 sprava 360 no. 44; idem, f. 57 op. 2 sprava 260 no. 38, 138–40. Editors questioned whether or not a mock-up poster they received of "The Jewish Deserter" should be published at all on the grounds that, as drawn, it was anti-Semitic. Idem, sprava 335 no. 23.

48 TsDAHO f. 8 op 1 sprava 41 no. 100; P. Bachynsky, ed., *Dokumenty trahichnoi istorii Ukrainy (1917–1927)* (Kyiv, 1999), 535–6, 544. English translation: C. Ford, "Memorandum of the Ukrainian Communist Party to the Second Congress of the III Communist International July–August 1920," *Debatte* 2 (August 2009): 248–62.

49 V. Gadzinskii, *Revoliutsionnoe dvizhenie v vostochnoi Galitsii* (Moscow, 1923), 49. The men are named and were most likely Ukrainian left-SRs. Gadzinskii does not elaborate on their activities.

50 TsDAVO f. 2188 op.1 sprava 117 no. 5–8. The report was written by a junior officer, Ivan Herasymovych.

51 Arkhiv Druku – "STOP ... Mykhailo Mukhin will read a lecture on the subject: [*Stii ... Mykhailo Mukhin prochytaie lektsiiu*]." TsNB – "LECTURE. SOLOMON GOLDELMAN [*Vidchyt Solomona Holdelmana*]." Arkhiv Druku – "Brother Galicians [*Do Brativ Halychan*]."

52 DNAB – "Stop Citizen! Ask yourself? [*Stii Hromadianyn. Zapytai sebe*]." Arkhiv Druku – "The Ukrainian national republic army ... will soon arrive [*Ukrainske Narodnie Respublikanske Viisko ... shvydko priyde*]," "Citizen! Ask yourself ... [*Hromadianyn Zapytai sebe*]," "Workers. Enough hesitation [*Robitnyky Hodi khytatys*]." DNAB – "Townsfolk! The national army of the Ukrainian Republic [*Horodiane Narodna armiia Ukrainskoi Respubliky*]." Arkhiv Druku – "Citizen! You have two pairs ... [*Hromadianyne Ty maiesh dvi pary*]," "MOBILIZATION. Orders of the Minister of the Army [*Po Mobilizatsii Nakaz viiskovoho ministra*]." DNAB – "Only with Iron and Blood will we liberate Ukraine [*Tilky zalizom i kroviu vyzvolymo my Ukrainu*]." Arkhiv Druku – "Brothers. Though the enemy is powerful [*Braty Khoch syly voroha velyki*]." "CITIZENS. General Tarnavsky ... [*Hromadiane Heneral Tarnavsky*]."

53 Arkhiv druku – "Dear sisters wives and girls [*Dorohi sestry zhinky i divchata*]." DNAB – "Attention Womanhood. A Cossack at the front awaits your work [*Pozir Zhinotstvo. Vashoi pratsi chekaie kozak*],"

54 Arkhiv druku – "Citizens. You have two pairs ... [*Hromadianyne Ty maiesh dvi pary*]."

55 DNAB – "Kozak reply to the order of the Revolutionary Military Council [*kozatska vidpovid na nakaz Revoliutsiinoi Viiskovoi rady*]."

56 Arkhiv druku – "Dear Ukrainian peasant [*Myli Ukrainski seliane*]."

57 Arkhiv druku – "To the population in regions of Ukraine occupied by Bolshevik-communists [*Vidozva do naselennia mistsevostei Ukrainy zaniatykh bolshevykamy-komunistamy*]."

58 TsDAHO f. 1 op. 20 sprava 1457 no. 33–6.

59 DNAD – "Only with Iron and Blood will we liberate Ukraine [*Tilky zalizom i kroviu vyzvolymo my Ukrainu*]." Arkhiv druku – "Brother Galicians [*Do Brativ Halychan*]."

60 DNAB – "Brave Cossacks [*Khorobri kozaky*]."

61 Arkhiv druku – "HEY TO ARMS [*Hei do zbroii*], Peasants Don't sleep. Rise up [*Hei do zbroi Seliane hodi spaty*]," "Proclamation of the Directory of the Ukrainian National Republic [*Opovishchennia dyrektorii*]," "RESOLUTION of the Directory [*Postanova Dyrektorii*]," "A Proclamation to all from the Directory [*Vidozva vsim vid dyrektorii*]," "ORDER To the Army [*Nakaz Viisku*]." DNAB – "Who Defends the Hetman and the Landlords? [*Khto oboroniaie hetmana ta pomishschykiv*]." TsNB – "CITIZENS OF KYIV! [*Hromadiane M. Kyiva*]," "To the population of the Town and District of Pryluky [*Do naselennia m. Pryluky i povitu*]," "Order no. 2 [*Prykaz no. 2*]," "Brother Peasants! The time has come ... [*Braty seliane Nastav rishuchyi chas*]."

62 Ivanushchenko, *Ukrainske vidrodzhennia 1917–1920 rr. na Sumshchyni*, 37–9.

63 TsDAHO f. 57 op. 2 sprava 266 no. 10.

64 TsNB – "To the inhabitants [*Do naselennia*]."

65 DNAB – "Ukrainian Democracy and the Bolsheviks [*Ukrainska demokratiia i bolshovyky*]."

66 DNAB – "To The Peasant Farmers of All Ukraine [*Do selian Khliborobiv vsiieii Ukrainy*]."

67 Arkhiv Druku – "Proclamation of the Directory of the Ukrainian National Republic [*Opovishchennia dyrektorii*]," "Comrade Peasants – Insurgents [*Tovaryshi Seliane- Povstantsi*]." DNAB – "Don't' Believe Provocations [*Ne virte provokatsii*]," "To the Ukrainian nation [*Do narodu Ukrainskoho*]." Arkhiv druku – "Against whom and why we fight [*Z kym i za shcho my boremosia*]."

68 Shumilova, "Arkushevi vydannia periodu vyzvolnykh zmahan 1917–1919 rokiv u fondi knyzhkovoi palaty Ukrainy," 3. DNAB – "Whom do Bolshevik 'soviets' care about?" [*Pro koho dbaiut bolshovytski 'saviety'*].

69 DNAB – "Who Defends the Hetman and the Landlords? [*Khto oboroniaie hetmana ta pomishschykiv*]."

70 DNAB – "Don't Believe Provocations [*Ne virte provokatsii*]," "What did the Bolsheviks DO? [*Shcho zrobyly Bolshovyky*]."
71 Arkhiv druku – "What to Do? [*Shcho robyty*]."
72 DNAB – "UKRAINE – LAND FOR THE PEASANTS [*Ukraina – zemlia dlia selian*]." TsNB – "Brother Peasants and Workers [*Tovaryshi seliane-povstantsi*]." DNAB – "Ukrainian working people [*Trudiachyi narode Ukrainskyi*]," "What every kozak must know [*Shcho treba znaty kozhnomu kozakovi*]."
73 TsNB – "PEASANTS! [*Seliane*]."
74 The word "khokhol" had the same implications of inferiority and naivety as "yokel" or "bumpkin" but was nationally specific because it referred only to non-Russified Ukrainians.
75 DNAB – "Protect the Ukrainian National Republic! Soldiers – Ukrainians [*Berezhit Ukrainsku Narodniu Republiku*]"; "What every kozak of the army must know [*Shcho treba znaty kozhnomu kozakovi*]."
76 TsNB – "Brother Peasants and Workers [*Braty seliane i robitnyky*]," "The Ukrainian National Army will not take revenge [*Ukrainska narodna armiia ne maie pomsty*]." Arkhiv druku – "Ministry of Labour order no. 5 [*Rosporiadzhennia Ministra Pratsi*]."
77 DNAB – "Who Defends the Hetman and the Landlords? [*Khto oboroniaie hetmana ta pomishschykiv*]," "Ukrainian working people [*Trudiachyi narode ukrainskyi*]." DNAB – "Protect the Ukrainian National Republic! [*Berezhit Ukrainsku Narodniu Respubliku*]." Arkhiv druku – "What does it signify? [*Shcho vono za znak*]."
78 Besides Latvians, the Bolsheviks recruited Chinese into national units that fought and requisitioned in Ukraine. The Chinese had been migrant workers before the revolution and were unable to return home. DNAB – "Comrade Peasants and Kozaks! [*Tovaryshi seliane kozaky*]."
79 DNAB – "Comrade Workers [*Tovaryshi robitnyky. Tovaryshchi rabochie*]," "Comrades! Don't fear the democratic armies of the Ukrainian National Republic [*Tovaryshchi ne boites demokraticheskikh voisk Ukrainskoi Narodnoi Respubliki*]," "PEASANTS AND COSSACKS [*Seliane i Kozaky*]."
80 Shumilova, "Arkushevi vydannia," 5; Ivanushchenko, ed., *Ukrainska revoluitsiia 1917–1920 rr.* 20, 43.
81 Arkhiv druku – "What are our strengths and what are our weaknesses? [*de nasha slabist i v chim nasha syla*]," Brothers. Though the enemy is powerful [*Braty Khoch syly voroha velyki*]."
82 TsNB – "Peasants! In the districts of Poltava ... [*Peasants. V povitakh Poltavshchyny*]," "PEASANTS! The Russkie Bolsheviks ... [*Seliane. Bolshevyky katsapy*]," "PEASANTS! In the districts of Kharkiv ... [*Seliane V povitakh Kharkivshchyny*]." DNAB – "Comrade Peasants and Kozaks! [*Tovaryshi seliane kozaky*]." Arkhiv druku – "To the peasants of

Poltava ... [*Do selian poltavshchyny* ...]," "Just what do they still need? [*Choho im shche treba*]." TsDAHO – "CITIZEN PEASANT [*Grazhdane krestiane*]." DNAB – "What did the Bolsheviks DO? [*Shcho zrobyly bolshovyky*]." Arkhiv druku – "Be Thoughtful [*Budte rozvazhni*]." DNAB – "PEASANTS AND COSSACKS [*Seliane i kozaky*]," "From the Socialist Ukrainian National Republic government [*Od sotsialistychnoho pravitelstva Ukrainskoi Narod. Respubliky*]."

83 DNAB – "Peasants and Workers! [*Seliane i robitnyky*]." TsNB – "To the population [*Do naselennia*]."

84 Arkhiv druku – "The difference between the Directory and the Bolsheviks [*Iaka rizhnytsia mizh Dyrektoriieiu ta bolshovykamy*]," "How they provoke [*Iak provokuiut*]."

85 TsNB – "THE PRETENDERS [*Samozvantsi*]," "To the population [*Do naselennia*]." DNAB – "Socialists-imperialists and Socialists-provocateurs [*Sotsialisty- imperiialisty ta sotsialisty-provokatory*]."

86 TsNB – "FROM ONE KETTLE [*Z odnoho kazana*]."

87 TsNB – "Muscovite Communists are already preparing sacks [*Moskovski komunisty vzhe hotuiut mishky*]." DNAB – "PEASANTS AND COSSACKS [*Seliane i kozaky*]."

88 DNAB – "What did the Bolsheviks DO? [*Shcho zrobyly bolshovyky*]," Arkhiv druku – "Against whom and why we fight [*Z kym i za shcho my boremosia*]," "Are the landlords returning? [*Chy vertaiut pomishchyky*]."

89 DNAB – "Brother Poles! [*Bracia Polacy/Bratia Poliaky*]," "To Citizens Russian Polish Jewish and other ... [*Ko grazhdanam Russkim Poliakam Evreiam i druhym*]."

90 TsNB – "TO ALL PEOPLES OF UKRAINE [*K narodam Ukrainy*]."

91 DNAB – "Whom do Bolshevik 'soviets [russ]' care about? [*Pro koho dbaiut bolshovytski 'saviety'*]," "Bolsheviks send you to Siberia ! [*Bolshovyky posylaiut vas na Sibir*]," "What might the Bolsheviks do? [*Do choho mozhut pryzvesty bolshovyky*]." Arkhiv druku – "The Bolsheviks want to rob the peasants again [*Bolshovyky znov khochut ohrabuvaty selian*]."

92 TsNB – "To all commandants and commissars [*Vsim komendantam i komisaram*]."

93 Arkhiv druku – "From the Socialist Ukrainian National Republic government [*Od sotsialistychnoho pravitelstva Ukrainskoi Narod. Respubliky*]."

94 Tsentralnyi derzhavnyi istorychnyi arkhiv (Lviv) – "About the Jews [*Pro Ievreiv*]."

95 Arkhiv druku – "The Jews and the Ukrainian Republic [*Zhydy i Ukrainska Respublika*]," "To Jewish citizens and workers in Ukraine [*Do Ievreiskoho hromadianstva i robitnytstva na Ukraini*]." DNAB – "To Citizens Russian Polish Jewish and others [*Ko grazhdanam Russkim Poliakam Evreiam i druhym*." TsNB – "TO ALL PEOPLES OF UKRAINE [*K narodam Ukrainy*]."

96 DNAB – "Comrades! Don't fear the democratic armies ... [*Tovaryshchi ne boites demokraticheskikh voisk*]."

97 TsDAHO f. 269 op 1 sprava 32 no. 21, 40–7. Bundist leader Moishe Rafes belonged the Central Rada in 1917 and in 1920 joined the Bolsheviks. That year he claimed that anti-Semitism was government policy. He referred to a rumour about a supposed conversation between two unidentified Rada members in January 1918 that circulated among Ukrainian leaders in late 1919. In reply to one who bemoaned how few resisted the Bolshevik advance that month, the other said not to worry because "we have not yet played our trump. *No bolshevism can stand against anti-Semitism* [*sic*]. This latter means [*sredstvo*] began to act then and is put into play now [*pushcheno bylo v obrot*]." *Dva goda revoliutsii na Ukraine. Evoliutsiia i raskol "Bunda"* (Moscow, 1920), 132.

98 TsNB – "WHO WANTS BOLSHEVISM [*Khto khoche bolshovysmu*]."

99 TsNB – "Peasants! In the districts of Poltava ... [*Seliane v povitakh Poltavshchyny*]."

100 TsDAHO f. 269 op 1 sprava 32 no. 21, 39–47. All are transcripts. One was anonymous. One in Russian, of unknown provenance, is signed "The Socialist party of Red Army Men." Three from Ukrainian army units were signed "soldiers" or "commander." The warlords who signed the last two were Anhelenko, Hreshchenko, Shevchenko, and Mukoid.

101 Arkhiv druku – "Circular to national councils ... [*Obizhno. Do narodnikh uprav* ...]."

102 DNAB –"How the Bolsheviks help the landlords [*Iak bolshovyky dopomahaiut pomishchykam*]."

103 Arkhiv druku – "Why do the black hundreds old-regime sorts ... [*Cherez shcho chornosotentsi i starorezhimnyky* ...]," "To arms To battle [*Do zbroi do boiu*]," "CITIZEN! General Tarnavsky [*Hromadiane. Heneral Tarnavsky*]."

104 DNAB – "To the Peasant Farmers of All Ukraine [*Do selian khliborobiv vsiiei Ukrainy*]."

105 DNAB – "??? We ask one another [*Pytaiemos odyn odnoho*]."

106 DNAB – "Ukrainian Red Army Kozaks! [*Ukrainski kozaky chervonoarmiitsi*]," "RED ARMY MEN RUSSIANS [*Krasnoarmeitsy Velikorossy*]."

107 DNAB – "Why the Poles have come to us [*Choho pryishly do nas Poliaky*]."

108 DNAB – "Read!! [*Chytaite*]," "The landlords are coming [*Idut pany*]," "??? We ask one another [*Pytaiemos odyn odnoho*]," "Why don't they order 'them'? [*Chomu 'im' ne nakazuiut*]," "Where is our Ukrainian army? [*De nashe Ukrainske viisko*]."

109 TsNB – "To all commandants and commissars [*Vsim komedantam I komisaram*]."

110 Arkhiv druku – "Obligatory resolution of the Podillia province commissar [*Oboviazkova postanova huberniialnoho komisara Podillia*]."

TsDASBU – "Order no. 1. Commandant of the town of Tetiiv ... [*Nakaz ch. 1. Komendant m. Tetiiva*]." DNAB – "5000 karbovantsi!!! To the population of Kyiv [*5000 karbovatsi do naselennia Kyiva*]."

111 [Anon.], *Do robitnykiv i selian*; [Anon.], *Federatsiia chy samostiinist?*; [Anon.], *Pora vzhe buty nam svidomymy i korysnymy hromadianamy Ukrainskoi Narodnoi Respubliky*; [Anon.], *Bezsovisnyi obman*; [Anon.], *Pravdyve slovo pro bolshovykiv-komunistiv*; [Anon.], *Svoia sorochka*; [Anon.], *Lytsari*; O. Pilch [Pylkevych], *Choho nas Ukrainstiv Katsapy prozvaly burzhuiamy*; H. Nash, *Vchimosia panuvaty*; [Anon.], *Choho my povynni borotys iz bolshovykamy; Do zbroii. Het Chervonykh imperialistiv.*

112 [Anon.], *Shcho robyt pravytelstvo Ukrainskoi Respubliki dlia narodu*; V. Poliashchuk, *De-shcho pro orhanizatsiiu vlady*; Io. Ivanovych, *Pro Derzhavu. Shcho take derzhava i derzhavne vlada, chy vony liudam potribni, ta iak povynni buty vlashtovani shchob trudovomu narodovi bulo dobre zhyty*; [Anon.], *Shanuite narodniu intelihentsiiu*; O. N[azaruk], *Za shcho my boremsia.*

113 [Anon.], *Cherez shcho Ukraina musila oddilytsia vid Rosii.* Although not indicated, this was a reprint of H. Nash, *Cherez shcho Ukraina musila vidriznytsia vid Rosii* (Kyiv, 1918), with some revisions. Most notably, the last paragraph, referring to a possible confederation with Russia, was deleted and replaced with sentences stressing the value of independence: "Better your own hut than a foreign palace." Also added was this phrase: "we listened to the Russians for 250 years and no good came of it. Now let the Russians listen to our nation for a while." I. Iurkivsky, *Chomy my musimo borotys za samostiinu Ukrainsku Narodniu Respubliku*; [Anon.], *Cherez shcho chornosotentsi starorezhimnyky a vsiaki ynshi tsarsko-hetmanski prysluzhnyky tak nenavydiat i obbrikhuit Halychan*; [Anon.], *Do Halytskykh zhovniriv*; [Anon.], *Natsionale vidrozhennia i kooperatsiia (zbirnyk stattei)*; [Anon.], *Shcho tse za liude v avstriiskii formi idyt do nas?*; [Anon.], *"Shcho to za Ukraina?"*; [Anon.], *Ukraina v mizhnarodnii politytsi.*

114 S. Palyi-Fastivsky, *Pro te shcho bulo i bude, abo zhyv sobi sashka syva-semeriashka*; [Anon.], *Iak vony duriat.*

115 M. Hlushkivsky, *Sterezhitsia provokatsii*; B. Martos, *Do Ievreiskoho hromadianstva i robitnytstva na Ukraini*; S. Zolotarenko, *Chomy sered Zhydivskykh robitnykiv ie bahato bolshevykiv*?

116 Verstiuk et al., *Ukrainskyi natsionalno-vyzvolnyi rukh*, 625.

117 In Kyiv province alone in December 1919, White intelligence estimated that partisan forces totalled 15,000 of whom no more than 3,000 were pro-Bolshevik. M. Kovalchuk, *Bez peremozhtsiv* (Kyiv, 2012), 306.

118 M. Rubach et al., *Radianske budivnytsvo na Ukraini v roky hromadianskoi viiny (1919–1920)* (Kyiv, 1957), 14–17. J. Meijer, ed., *The Trotsky Papers* (The Hague, 1964), I: 389, 431. Iu. Tiutiunyk, *Zymovyi pokhid 1919-20 rr.*, (Kolomyia, 1923), 84–6, reproduces a secret document dated 28 February 1920

not in the *Trotsky Papers* but whose contents are confirmed in other documents: Kovalchuk, *Bez peremozhtsiv*, 56–7; S.M. Korolivsky, ed., *Grazhdanskaia voina na Ukraine* (Kyiv, 1967), 2: 538–40. Trotsky condoned forming Ukrainian regiments from loyal Ukrainians as a core for a future Soviet Ukrainian army. Ibid., 675–6.

119 Also in *Kommunist* (Kyiv), 18 December 1918).

120 O. Dotsenko, *Zymovyi pokhid* (Warsaw, 1932; reprint Kyiv, 2001) 154–5. Trotsky's proclamation: Korolivsky, ed., *Grazhdanskaia voina na Ukraine*, 2: 518. L. Hrynevych et al., *Istoriia Ukrainskoho viiska 1917–1995* (Kyiv, 1996), 188–91.

121 Dotsenko, *Zymovyi pokhid*, 91–2, 283–7, http://chtyvo.org.ua/authors/Dotsenko_Oleksandr/Zymovyi_pokhid. See also https://zn.ua/SOCIETY/desyat_zapovedey__ot_lva_trotskogo.html. A French translation was published by the local UNR representative in *Gazette de Lausanne*, 15 July 1920.

122 Russian left-SRs in early 1919 supported the Bolsheviks. In Ukraine they called themselves the Ukrainian Party of Left Socialist Revolutionaries (*Borbists*). That February they appealed to rail workers, in Ukrainian, to support the Bolshevik regime as well as free *soviets* without appointed commissars, and to reorganize and operate the rail system. Neither Ukrainian independence nor the Bolsheviks were mentioned (Doc. 182).

123 DNAB – "Remember [*Pamiatai*]," "To the village and city worker [*Robitnyku sela i mista*]." TsDAHO – "ORDER NO 1 to the Rzhyshchev garrison [*NAKAZ NO 1 po harnizonu m. Rzhyshcheva*]."

124 DNAB – "AN OPEN LETTER [*Otkrytoe pismo*]." DNAB – "TO THE WORKERS AND PEASANTS OF UKRAINE [*Do selianstva i robitnytsva Ukrainy*]."

125 DNAB – "The Ukrainian Party of Socialist Revolutionaries [*Ukrainska partiia sotsialistiv-revoliutsiuneriv*]," "To the entire working population of Poltava province ... [*Do vsikh pratsiuiuchykh Poltavshchyy*]," "COMRADE WORKERS AND PEASANTS [*Tovaryshi robitnyky i seliane*]."

126 DNAB – "Comrade Sich Riflemen [*Tovaryshi sichovi striltsi*]."

127 It is unclear whether this leaflet appeared before or after their short-lived May 1919 coalition with centrist UNR parties. That agreement condemned Russian communist power in Ukraine as an occupation and called for an independent Ukrainian Republic based on *soviets*. The agreement established a ruling coalition of the three socialist party signatories that would organize the economy on the basis of a planned transition from capitalism to socialism. I. Mazepa, *Ukraina v ohni i buri revoliutsii*, 3rd ed. (Kyiv, 2003), 116. For the text of the proposed agreements with the UNR: P. Khrystiuk, *Zamitky i materialy do istorii Ukrainskoi revoliutsi*, reprint ed. (New York, 1969), IV: 111, 131–2; Bachynsky, ed., *Dokumenty*,

122–4, 156. Anonymous criticism of the UNR and opposition to cooperation is reproduced on pages 159–60 of Bachynsky. Bela Kun in Hungary also allied with SD "bourgeois nationalists."

128 TsNB – "A Concise Note [*Dokladna zapyska*]." DNAB – "Resolution of the Kyiv Committee of the USDLP [*Rezoliutsiia Kyivskoi orhanizatsii USDRP*]." TsDAHO – "To the comrade members [*Do tovaryshiv chleniv*]."

129 TsDASBU – "ORDER no. 48 [*Nakaz no. 48*]." DNAB – "ULTIMATUM [*Ultimatum*]."

130 DNAB – "To the peasants of Poltava province [*Do selian Poltavshchyny*]," "Workers and Peasants of Ukraine! [*Selian i robitnykiv Ukrainy*]," "To the Working Peasants and Workers of the Red Left-Bank [*Do trudovoho selianstva ta robitnykiv chervonoho livoberezhzhia*]," "ULTIMATUM."

131 DNAB – "Comrade Workers Peasants and Red Army Men! [*Tovaryshi robitnyky seliane ta charvonoarmeitsi*]."

132 DNAB – "Comrade Red Army Men [*Tovarishchi krasnoarmeitsy*]." E. Heifets, *The Slaughter of the Jews in the Ukraine in 1919* (New York, 1921), 75, 90, claims that the left-SDs were ideological anti-Semites and that one of their prominent leaders, Iury Mazurenko, published a "series of terrible Jew-baiting pamphlets." I have not seen any such publications.

133 TsDAHO – "BROTHER- PEASANTS! [*Braty seliane*]," "ORDER NO 1. Rzhyshchiv garrison [*Nakaz no 1 po harnizonu m. Rzhyshcheva*]."

134 TsDAHO – "TO LABOURING PEASANTS AND WORKERS [*Do trudovoho selianstva ta robitnykiv*]."

135 TsNB – "Comrades workers and Peasants! [*Tovaryshi robitnyky i seliane*]." DNAB – "Brother Peasants! For how many years ... [*Braty seliane Skilky rokiv* ...]."

136 A.P., *Ukrainska partiia Sotsialistiv-Revoliutsioneriv i tymchasove Robitnyche-Selianskyi uriad Ukrain.*

137 V. Blakytny, *Iak prodavaly Ukrainu.* The Bolsheviks also exploited this information to discredit the UNR. Like the Borotbists, they never revealed the UNR-rejected French conditions.

138 [Anon.], *Khto taki Kommunisty-Borotbysty.*

139 [Anon.], *Do rozrishennia natsionalnoho pytannia.*

140 TsDAHO f. 57 op. 2 sprava 266 no. 9.

141 A. Richytsky and M. Tkachenko, *Proekt programy Ukrainskoi Kommunistychnoi Partii*; A. Richytsky ed., *Nash Spir*. The latter work includes a polemical exchange between UCP and CPU leaders.

142 *Otaman* had two meanings. One referred to a military rank in the regular Ukrainian army. The other referred to irregular commanders among whom, already as of February 1919, were those who decided for themselves whether or not they would obey orders from UNR generals. Mytrofanenko, *Ukrainska otamanshchyna.*

143 DNAB – "To the population of Ukraine. Order no. 1 [*Do naseleniia Ukrainy. Nakaz ch. 1*]"

144 TsDASBU – "Ukrainian National Republic [*Ukrainskaia narodna respublika*]," "To Comrade Red Army Men [*Do tovaryshchyv chervonoarmiitsiv*]."

145 DNAB – "Commandments of the National Insurrectionary War [*Zapovidi naronoi povstancheskoi viiny*]."

146 TsDAHO f. 1 op. 18 no 63 no. 3–4.

147 DNAB – "Letter from a Ukrainian insurgent to Bolshevik Communists [*Lyst ukrainskoho povstantsia do bolshovykiv-komunistiv*]." www.hai-nyzhnyk.in.ua – "To the Jewish Population [*Do Zhydivskoho naselennia*]."

148 TsDASBU – "To You Brother Peasants and Workers of Ukraine [*Do vas bratia seliane ta robitnyky Ukrainy*]." DNAB – "ORDER No. 1 I propose that all peasants [*Nakaz no 1. Proponuiu vsim selianam*]."

149 TsDASBU – "Citizens of Ukraine [*Hromadiane ukrainy*]," "Workers Peasants and Red Army men [*Robochi seliane ta chervonoarmeitsi*]."

150 TsDAHO f. 1 op 18 sprava 63 no. 25v. An undated unsigned leaflet in a handwritten Russian scrawl, placed within a collection of documents from 1920, is addressed to urban workers. Titled "Notice," it begins: "Comrade workers, don't delay, they are sending you to collect bread for the Jews." It calls on workers not to join requisition squads, to resist also those "who sold you to the Jews," and to gather and await instructions at their factories on the 11th. TsDAHO f. 1 op. 18 sprava 63 no. 26.

151 TsDAHO f. 57 op. 2 sprava 266 no. 3, 7.

152 DNAB – "BE PREPARED [*Budte hotovi*]," "UKRAINIAN NATION! [*Narodie Ukrainskyi*]."

153 DNAB – "From the staff organizational section [*Vid orhanizatsiinoho viddilu shtabu*]."

154 DNAB – "Why the Partisans fight [*Zashcho boiutsia povstantsi*]."

155 Arkhiv Druku – "It is three years now ... [*Vzhe try roky iak*]."

156 TsDASBU – "Peasants! It is time to realize... [*Seliane Pora zrozumity*]." DNAB – "UKRAINIAN NATION! [*Narodie Ukrainskyi*]." TsDAVO – "ORDER. Chairman of the Horoshyn Volost Ispolkom [*Prikaz. Predsedateliu volostnoho ispolkoma Horoshynskoi volosti*]."

157 TsDAVO – "ORDER. Chairman of the Horoshyn Volost Ispolkom [*Prikaz. Predsedateliu volostnoho ispolkoma Horoshynskoi volosti*]," "Order to the mobilized [*Nakaz Mobylizovanym*]." TsDASBU –"Order no 2. In accord with the decision ... [*Nakaz no. 2. Zhidno rasporiadzhenniu ...*]." DNAB – "IMMEDIATE. Tarashchansk Military Administration [*NEHAINE. Tarashchanske Viiskove Upravlinnia*]."

158 TsDAVO – "Christ Has Risen! [*Khrystos Voskrese*]." TsDASBU – "Ukrainian National Republic [*Ukrainskaia narodna respublika*]," "To Comrade Red Army Men [*Do tovaryshchyv chervonoarmiitsiv*]."

TsDASBU – "PROCLAMATION ... We Address you ... [*Vidozva ... Zvertaiemosia do vas*]."

159 TsDASBU – "PROCLAMATION ... We Address you ... [*Vidozva ... Zvertaiemosia do vas*]."

160 TsDASBU –"PROCLAMATION ... We Address you ... [*Vidozva ... Zvertaiemosia do vas*]." DNAB – "Announcement. The fight for life and death ... [*Vidozva. Borotba na zhyttia i smert*]." TsDASBU – "ORDER No. 1 Kozaks who must appear for mobilization to the communists ... [*NAKAZ ch.1. Kozakam kotrii povynni ity po mobylyzatsiiu do komunistiv*]."

161 TsDASBU – "To Comrade Russian Red Army Men [*Tovarishcham krasnoarmeitsam Velikorossam*]." DNAB – "Red Army Men Red Cadets and Red Commanders [*Krasnoarmeitsy krasnye kursanty i krasnye komandiry*]."

162 TsDASBU – "PEASANTS You see for yourselves [*Seliane Vse zhe sami bachyte*]." TsDAVO – "REGULATIONS [*Ustav*]."

163 TsNB – "Brother Peasants and Workers [*Braty seliane i robitnyky*]." DNAB – "ANNOUNCEMENT [*Vidozova*]." TsDASBU – "PROCLAMATION [*Vidozva*]."

164 TsDAVO f. 2 op 1 sprava 732 no. 135.

165 L. Balatz, "Une Version Ukrainienne 'Protocols des Sages des Sion,'" *Revue Juive de Geneve* (May, 1935), 1–7. It is unclear if Balatz is referring in the article only to anti-Semitic publications that appeared in White-occupied Kyiv when he was there, or to the language of the item. He claims that the *Protocols* were unknown in Ukraine before 1917 outside a small circle around the court and secret police. He noted that the items he discussed were not the *Protocols*. They seem to have been leaflets by some Ukrainian group that linked anti-Ukrainian politics to the international Zionist conspiracy.

166 DNAB – "ANNOUNCEMENT. The fight for life and death [*VIDOZVA. Borotba na zhyttia i smert*]," "Why do our Yids in cities and towns so eagerly await the Bolsheviks ... [*Chomu tak chekaiut pryhodu bolshovykiv nashi zhydky*]," "From the staff organizational section ... [*Vid orhanyzatsiinoho viddilu shtabu*]." www.hai-nyzhnyk.in.ua – "NOTIFICATION [*OBIAVA*]," "Brother Peasants and Workers [*Braty seliane i robitnyky*]." DNAB – "ANNOUNCEMENT. Three months have passed ... [*VIDOZVA. Proshlo vzhe try mysiatsi*]." TsDASBU – "PROCLAMATION. Brother peasants [*VIDOZVA. Braty seliane*]," "Proclamation. Cossacks Wake-up ... [*Vidozva. Kozaky prokyntesia*]."

167 On 15 June the UNR formally forbade posting blatant anti-Semitic messages. A few days afterwards, a travelling Jewish citizen complained to the UNR's Jewish Ministry that this particular leaflet was displayed in a rail station. The ministry forwarded a complaint to the government to remove this material, which the irate citizen assumed was official, according to its own regulations. TsDAVO f. 2537 op 2 sprava 13 no. 5–8.

168 TsDAVO – "ANNOUNCEMENT. Comrade Workers [*VOZVANIE. Tovareshchi rabochie*]," "ANNOUNCEMENT Citizens [*OBIAVLENIE. Grazhdane*]," "Comrade Stop Read [*Tovarysh Ostanovys i prochytai*]." TsDAHO – "To the Peasants of Kyiv Province [*Do selian kyivshchyny*]."

169 TsDAVO – "Health information [*Ko i chto o zdorove*]," "UKRAINIAN WOMEN AND GIRLS [*Zhenshchiny Ukrainskoe i devushki*]."

170 DNAB – "MANIFESTO no. 3. Brother Ukrainians [*MANIFEST no. 3 Bratia Ukrainsty*]." Ratytsia was the pseudonym of Ivan Perlyk, a UNR officer turned partisan in eastern Ukraine who was shot in 1921. This manifesto was likely written in 1921 but apparently circulated widely in Poltava and Kharkiv provinces after his death. A few weeks after he wrote this appeal he decided further resistance was futile and to parley with the Bolsheviks – who promptly arrested him. http://tyzhden.ua/History/90742/PrintView.

4 The Bolsheviks

1 M. Rubach, "K istorii grazhdanskoi borbe na Ukraine," *Letopis revoliutsii* no. 4 (1924), 164; V. Zatonsky, "Iz spohadiv pro Ukrainsku revoliutsiiu," *Litopys revoliutsii* no. 5 (1930), 153–6. Zatonsky was present during all the meetings. In March 1919 he described the situation as follows: "the RCP CC without informing the CPU decided to form a provisional government of Ukraine." TsDAHO f. 1 op 20 sprava 22 no. 46. In the words of Moscow's emissary to Kursk (27 December), Leonid Serebriakov: "[Russia's] revolutionary war soviet [*revvoensoviet*] organized Soviet power in Ukraine on its own because the entire Ukrainian apparatus did not yet exist." TsDAVO f. 2360 op 1 sprava 3 no. 24.

2 TsDAVO f. 3766 op 3 sprava 7 no. 2.

3 Odesa's Bolsheviks published a short account of their underground activities in 1918. After paying outrageous rates to various private publishers, they bought and set up their own press in caves outside town, where they produced tens of thousands of copies of leaflets. NMIU l 1283. TsDAVO f. 1216 op 1 sprava 113 no. 4, 15.

4 The Hetman's secret police reports: TsDAVO f. 1216 op 1 sprava 93 no. 18; sprava 23 no. 46; f. 2469 op 1 sprava 7 no. 4–6.

5 TsDAVO f. 1216 op 1 sprava 110 no. 268; idem, sprava 113, no. 66, 174, 174, 201, 208. Samples of confiscated materials: idem, no. 37–41, 57, 91, 107, 127, 237.

6 N.S. Podoliakova, "Natsionalizatsiia polihrafichnykh pidpryiemstv Ukrainy v period 1917–22 rr.," *Sivershchyna v istorii Ukrainy* no. 8 (2015), 269–71.

7 The day before, 27 December, the CPU *revkom* had already requested paper, literature, and agitators from Moscow. On the 29th it created an Instructors Department to train 110 candidates already familiar with "the region" and its peasants. The word Ukraine was not in the resolution. TsDAVO f. 2360 op 1 sprava 3 no. 12a, 32.

8 On organizational history: I. Savchenko, "Ideolohichna skladova knyhovydavnytsva v USRR (1919–1920 rr.), *Istoriia Ukrainy. Malovidomi imena podii fakty* 35 (2008) 22–37; idem, 37 (2011) 96–111; Ie. Monastyrsky, "Formuvannia radianskoi systemy ahitatsii ta propahandy v Ukraini (1917–1928)," MA thesis, Ukrainian Catholic University (2016), 28–79.

9 TsDAVO f. 2 op 1 sprava 17 no. 108; idem, f. 1 op 1 sprava 15 no. 7, 193–7.

10 Judging by surnames only. Specifically: the central Agitprop kollegium, the Section for Party Education in Right Bank Ukraine, and the Agitation Commission for the Struggle Against Banditry and Petliurism on the Rail System.The protocols of all these agencies were in Russian. The protocols of the Ukrainian SR–dominated Peasant Section were often, but not always, in Ukrainian. TsDAHO f. 1 op 20 sprava 1457 no. 751, 752, 769; idem, sprava 333 no. 21, 74.

11 TsDAHO f. 1. op 6 sprava 7 no. 16. A 1919 list of personnel in the Informational Instructional Section of the Internal Affairs Commissariat indicates that the majority were Ukrainian-born Russians and Jews. TsDAVO f. 5 op 4 sprava 10 no. 90.

12 TsDAVO f. 1 op 1 sprava 15 no. 81, 200–6. Three versions of Kharkiv province factory worker Evdokyi Semenenko's 1919 party membership application survive, wherein he indicates he had "domestic education," could give speeches, and wanted to be an agitator. In the first form he wrote that he was Ukrainian and spoke Little Russian, in the second that he was Little-Russian and spoke Ukrainian, and in the third, that he was Ukrainian and spoke Ukrainian. TsDAHO f.1 op 20 sprava 81 no. 85–86.

13 TsDAVO f. 1 op 1 sprava 15 no. 116, 252–54. I found no response to this project.

14 TsDAHO f. 1 op 30 sprava 333 no. 65; TsDAHO f. 1 op 20 sprava 360 no. 1–3, 72; idem, sprava 355 no. 93. A short history of the department was written that summer: idem, sprava 355 no. 65–70.

15 TsDAHO f.1 op 20 sprava 368 no. 178.

16 TsDAHO f. 1 op 20 sprava 366 no. 24–5.

17 TsDAHO f.1 op 20 sprava 368 no. 43–4.

18 V.E. Mushtukov, ed., *Petrograd v dni velikogo oktiabra. Vospominaniia uchastnikov revoliutsionnykh sobytii v Petrograde v 1917 godu* (Leningrad, 1967), 438–40.

19 Example of Politburo decision to begin a propaganda campaign: TsDAHO f. 1 op 6 sprava 1 no. 64.

20 [Anon.], *Tezisy dlia sobesedovanii politrukov s krasnoarmeitsamy o znachenii Oktiabrskoi Revoliutsii* (np. 1920); M. Riesner, *Cbto takoe sovetskaia vlast* (Pyriatyn, n.d.).

21 In May, CPU leaders sent Rakovskii to Moscow to explain they wanted their republic to remain independent and discussion about centralization and unification to be open. TsDAHO f. 1 op 1 sprava 22 no. 4. The declaration on unification was issued 3 June. On 14 June, Ukraine's Central Committee rejected a Borotbist motion to establish a commission to work out the terms of the agreement that would have included representatives from all Soviet republics, including Hungary. TsDAHO f. 43 op 1 sprava 30 no. 17.

22 TsDAVO f. 2360 op 1 sprava 3 no. 204–11. Present were Petrovsky, Bubnov, Chubar, Bohuslavskii, Sapronov, Saveleev, Kin, Minin, Rafael, Rukhymovich, Angonov, and Sosnovskii.

23 DNAB – "To the entire population of Ukraine [*Ko vsemu naseleniiu Ukrainy*]."

24 Cited in V. Vasyliev, *Politychne kerivnytsvo URSR i SRSR: dynamika vidnosyn tsentr-subtsentr vlady (1917–1938)* (Kyiv, 2014), 78. Article translated in A. Skirda, *Nestor Makhno. Anarchy's Cossack* (London, 1975), 112.

25 TsDAHO f. 1 op 20 sprava 333 no. 13–18.

26 TsDAHO f. 1. op 20 sprava 363 no. 111; idem, 57 op 2 sprava 342 no. 4; sprava 340 no. 144; sprava 342 no. 142. On denial of grain exports in leaflets: TsDAHO f. 57 op 2 sprava 340 no. 137. In September of that year Ukraine's Bolsheviks specified they would deliver 542,000 tons of grain from Ukraine's estimated harvest of that year of 1,800,000 tons. TsDAHO f. 1 op 6 sprava 16 no. 53. Figures on grain export to Russia throughout 1919 are recorded in rail transport statistics. See also S. Velychenko, *Painting Imperialism and Nationalism Red: The Ukrainian Marxist Critique of Russian Communist Rule in Ukraine, 1918–1923* (Toronto, 2015), 139.

27 TsDAHO f.1 op 20 sprava 21 no. 6–10.

28 TsDAHO f. 1 op 20 sprava 368 no. 49, 96, 149, 134; idem, sprava 333 no. 13–48. In a seven-day course of fouteen lectures for agitators in Poltava, Ukrainian issues were mentioned once, in the last lecture, which was devoted to Ukrainian socialist parties. Idem, sprava 363 no. 193–4. In February 1919, a three-day course in Katerynoslav also had nothing on Ukraine. The national question figured as 1 of 24 subjects. TsDAHO f. 1 op 20 sprava 29 no. 17.

29 V. Shcherbakivsky, "Memuary," *Pamiatnyky Ukrainy* no. 4 (2007), 88. The author met and spoke with a group of these men in Poltava province in January 1919. L.D. Stepanova, "Ukrainska sektsiia petrohradskoho komitetu RKP(b) (Hruden 1918- Kviten 1919rr.)," *Ukrainsky istorychnyi zhurnal* no. 2 (1973), 34–6.

30 *Instruktsiia tsentralnogo Otdela rasprostraneniia pechati Vseukrainskogo Izdatelstva dlia kurerov-provodnikov otpravliaiushchikhsia s literaturoi po Ukraine* (Kharkiv, 1920); *Instruktsiia v spravi postachannia ta rospovsudzennia druku*, Arkhiv Druku, leaflet (1920). Dinershtein et al, *Izdatelskoe delo*, 99.
31 TsDAHO f.1 op 20 sprava 21 no. 27.
32 TsDAHO f. 1 op 20 sprava 368 no. 159
33 TsDAVO f. 342 op 1 sprava 96 no. 361.
34 TsDAHO f. 1 op 20 sprava 368 no. 185–6.
35 M. Vladimirov ed., *Spravochnik prodovostvennogo agenta Ukr. Sots. Sov. Respubliki.* Vypusk 1 and 2 (Kharkiv, 1920).
36 TsDAHO f. 1 op 20 sprava 363 no. 163, 169; idem, sprava 364 no. 82.
37 TsDAHO f. 1 op 20 sprava 359 no. 91, 93, 102, 107–9, 116–17, 139, 141.
38 TsDAVO f. 166 op 2 sprava 28 no. 22–8.
39 TsDAVO f. 1738 op 1 sprava 13 no. 150.
40 TsDAHO f. 1 op 20 sprava 364 no. 82v.
41 TsDAVO f. 34 op 2 sprava 138 no. 24; idem, sprava 872 no. 54–5. Of 4819 manual typesetters, 420 were women (15).
42 TsDAVO f. 34 op 3 sprava 975 no. 168. The fewest were in Zaporizhzhia province (25).
43 TsDAHO f. 1 op 20 sprava 372 no. 111–15. By the end of 1920 co-op publishing was taken over by the state agency *Vseizdat*.
44 TsDAVO f. 34 op 2 sprava 132 no. 113; idem, sprava 138 no. 15.
45 TsDAVO f. 166 op. 2 sprava 924 no. 4, 11, 12, 46–7.
46 Organizational structure as of April 1920: TsDAVO f. 573 op 1 sprava 833; also sprava 333 no. 69
47 TsDAHO f.1 op 20 sprava 173 no. 159, 261.
48 TsDAVO f. 573 op 1 sprava 831 no. 121,146.
49 TsDAVO f. 1738 op 1 sprava 31 no. 12. Dinershtein et al, *Izdatelskoe delo v pervye gody Sovetskoi vlasti*, 39, 49, 62, 85, 96, 165.
50 TsDAVO f. 166 op 1 sprava 723 no. 14, 28, 46–7. Kivshar, *Ukrainskyi knyzhkovyi rukh iak istorychne iavyshche*, 159, 172. The Publishing Bureau in February 1919 had 83 employees of which only 70 could come to work because there was no office space for the remainder. TsDAVO f. 2 op 1 sprava 463 no. 19–21, 51–6.
51 TsDAVO f. 34 op 1 sprava 4 no. 14–17.
52 TsDAVO f. 2 op 1 sprava 463 no. 35–7; idem, f. 178 op 8 sprava 39 no. 207–211. TsDAVO f. 182 op 1 sprava 2.
53 TsDAVO f. 166 op 1 sprava 720 no. 3–4. Idem,, sprava 728 no. 8. Kivshar, *Ukrainskyi knyzhkovyi rukh*, 160.
54 TaDAVO f. 34 op 3 sprava 1311 no. 29.
55 TsDAVO f. 3487 op 1 sprava 1 no. 4, 242. Between January and March of 1918 it produced 80 tons of cigarette paper. Idem, op 1 sprava 4 no. 93. TsDAVO f. 3585 op 1 sprava 1 no. 18.

56 TsDAVO f. 573 op 1 sprava 333 no. 43; idem, sprava 856 no. 1–5. Before they were evicted from Podillia in July 1920, they used stocks requisitioned from a local sugar refinery.

57 *Obzor deiatelnosti gubernskogo poligraficheskogo otdela za 1920 god* (Katerynoslav, 1924). *Tavricheskii golos* 2 (15) July 1920.

58 TsDAHO f. 1 op 20 sprava 757 no. 112. In another instance that April, Ukraine's Jewish Communist party (*Polaia Zion*) requested paper for a Mayday newssheet, adding that if Kharkiv could not supply it they would request it directly from Moscow. Idem, no. 25.

59 TsDAVO f. 166 op 2 sprava 28 no. 28. Rural medical centres apparently got nothing or little in 1920–1 and, consequently, could not compile statistics. A. G. Breznitskii, "Polozhenie vrachebno-sanitarnogo dela na sele," *Profilakticheskaia meditsina* no. 11–12 (1923) 132.

60 TsDAVO f. 3204 op 1 sprava 9 no. 29. The order was issued by the Standing Committee on the fight against Banditry (*Postoianna soveshchanniia po borbe s banditizmom*) headed by Rakovskii and established in February 1921 to coordinate anti-partisan operations.

61 TsDAVO f. 34 op 2 sprava 46 no. 8, 18, 33. Idem, op 3 sprava 1311 no. 30. Of the 15 paper factories under Bolshevik control in August, 4 were destroyed and the remainder had little or no fuel or raw materials. 4 of 5 pulp mills were also destroyed.

62 *Otchet po deialnosti Poltavskogo gubispolkoma i ego otdelov za 1920 god* (Poltava, 1921) 265. Another 38 tons was classified as rough paper.

63 While on the one hand, Moscow did send irregular supplies, on the other hand, Russian co-ops and local government agencies would buy-up en masse in Ukraine, for their own use, whatever office supplies they found, including paper. The medical directorate of the Kharkiv military district, which included half of Ukraine, in March 1920 complained office supplies had disappeared from markets because "big northern organizations, including entire provinces and various civilian and military organizations" could afford the astronomical prices and made bulk purchases. TsDAVO f. 342 op 1 sprava 73, no. 56.

64 TsDAVO f. 177 op 1 sprava 32 no. 43–4; idem, sprava 10 no. 10.

65 TsDAHO f. 1 op 20 sprava 370 no. 12–13. Promised less than one ton monthly by Moscow from stockpiles.

66 TsDAVO f. 1 op 20 sprava 762 no. 9, 19, 20, 53–4. Records do not reveal how the issue was resolved.

67 *Obzor deiatelnosti gubernskogo poligraficheskogo otdela za 1920 god* (Katerynoslav, 1921). Poltava province in 1920 had 33 printing shops (6 in Poltava), with 690 workers (312 in Poltava). *Otchet po deialnosti Poltavskogo gubispolkoma*, 60.

68 TsDAV0 f. 2 op 1 sprava 894 no. 48, 57–8; idem, f. 573 op 1 sprava 836 no. 48. The complaint echoed an earlier resolution of the 9th RCP conference. Dinershtein et al., *Izdatelskoe delo*, 70.

69 The British lifted their blockade after learning of Denikin's failure to take Moscow. Leaders concluded that the Bolsheviks would remain in power. The Bolsheviks paid from their hoard of more than 500 tons of gold and jewels sequestered, confiscated, or stolen from their subjects. S. McMeekan, *The Russian Revolution: A New History* (London, 2017), 302–3; P. Kenez, *The Birth of the Propaganda State: Soviet Methods of Mass Mobilization, 1917–1929* (Cambridge, 1986), 101.

70 TsDAVO f. 177 op 1 sprava 32 no. 37–42. He also complained that because few in his department knew anything about Ukraine or Ukrainian, only 20 per cent of books were in Ukrainian. That was tantamount to Russification and contrary to the decisions of 10th RCP congress of 1920.

71 TsDAHO f. 1 op 20 sprava 1460 no. 24–5.

72 Of these, 315 were typesetters. *Otchet o deialnosti Kievskogo gubotdela Vserossiiskogo soiuza rabochikh poligraf. proizvodstva* (Kyiv, 1923), 15. TsDAVO f. 573 op 1 sprava 847; idem, f. 34 op 3 sprava 1002 no. 5–13; idem, f. 34 op 3 sprava 962 no. 4; TsDAHO f. 1 op 20 sprava 638 no. 30. At least half of all print workers were typesetters.

73 *Otchet o deialnosti Kharkovskogo gubernskoho otdela Vserossiiskogo soiuza rabochikh poligraficheskogo proizvodstva za 1920 g.* (Kharkiv, 1921), 40–3, 73–9; *Otchet o deialnosti Poltavskogo gubernskogo otdela soiuza rabochikh poligraficheskogo proizvodstvo za 1920 god* (Poltava, 1921), 28–31.

74 N. Podvoisky, *Na Ukraine. Stati N. I. Podvoiskogo* (Kyiv, 1919), 21. This is confirmed by an August 1920 report that noted the central distribution organization did not actually control its network for the first six months of its existence. TsDAHO f. 1 op 20 sprava 370 no. 10–12.

75 Ia. Malyk, *Totalitaryzm Ukrainskomu seli. Persha sproba vprovadzhennia* (Lviv, 1996), 16–18.

76 TsDAHO f. 1 op 20 sprava 21 no. 2.

77 See TsDAVO f. 343 op 1 sprava 301 no. 8–53 for an example of wrangling over quotas among health, party, paper and press agencies. See also ibid., no. 122–55.

78 Leinwald, *Czerwonym mlotem w orla bialego. Propaganda sowiecka w wojnie z Polska*, 60–1. TsDAVO f. 342 op 1 sprava 177 no. 65, 135, 184, 225, 268–9, 293, 305.

79 Despite the Bolshevik paper-shortage, the agent reported that UNR printed propaganda was circulating. V. Kavennyk, ed., *Arkhiv Ukrainskoi Narodnoi Respubiky Ministerstvo Vnutrishnykh Sprav Zvity Departmetiv Derzhavnoi varty ta Politychnoi Informatsii (1918-1922)* (Kyiv, 2018) 287-89.

80 TsDAVO f. 166 op 1 sprava 728 no. 1–3. In May 1919 officials estimated they needed 100 railcars of paper monthly for all their publications.

81 TsDAVO f. 177 op 1 sprava 199 no. 31–33; idem, f. 177 op 1 sprava 215 no. 1–4.

82 TsDAVO f. 2 op 1 sprava 148 no. 4, 7, 13. They were in Polish, Romanian, and "Galician."
83 TsDAVO f. 4192 op 1 sprava 94 no. 8–10; idem, sprava 562 no. 40. Another set of figures compiled that same month shows 78 functioning locomotives and 2,255 functioning wagons. TsDAVO f. 340 op 1 sprava 2536 no. 35.
84 TsDAVO f. 340 op 1 sprava 2536 no. 10–14, 35. In May surveys of all Ukraine were compiled at least once if not twice weekly. Figures from 27 May and 21 June show that functioning wagons had declined from 44,501 to 39,302 and functioning locomotives from 1,616 to 1,475.
85 TsDAVO f. 4192 op 1 sprava 94 no. 8–10; idem, sprava 562 no. 40. UNR agents reported that nominally repaired locomotives normally had to be returned to repair shops after two weeks – where work was very slow because workers spent most of their time looking for food. TsDAVO f. 2297 op 1 sprava 30 no. 183.
86 TsDAVO f. 3205 op 1 sprava 11 no. 21.
87 TsDAVO f. 2 op 1 sprava 464 no. 116–17. Among the materials the Bolsheviks stripped from Ukraine in the spring of 1918 were more than 100 telegraph machines and 200 telephones from the Kharkiv region. It is unknown if these were ever returned. Ibid., f. 1 op 1 sprava 453 no. 6–7.
88 TsDAHO f. 1 op 20 sprava 29 no. 190–2; TsDAHO f. 1 op 20 sprava 29 no. 190–2. As of 1908, because train thieves cut telegraph lines to avoid capture, station guards had to either phone each other every five minutes, or telegraph each other between other messages, to ensure that lines were functional. Rudenko, *Diialnist ustanov poshty i telehrafu na Pravoberezhnyi Ukraini*, 88.
89 TsDAVO f. 2 op 1 sprava 849 no. 101–2, 132, 153. I found no references concerning the efficacy of repair work. TsDAVO f. 2579 op 1 sprava 72 no. 87.
90 TsDAVO f. 2 op 1 sprava 65 no. 8; ibid sprava 75 no. 84.
91 TsDAVO f. 34 op 3 sprava 882 no. 56.
92 B. Hud, *Zahybel Arkadii* (Lviv, 2006), 258–71. Unlike their counterparts in the Lithuanian provinces, with rare exceptions, Polish landowners met pre-1914 protests with repression instead of reform and thus never won sympathy from the surrounding peasant population. B. Hud, *Ukrainsko-Polski konflikty novitnoi doby. Etnosotsialnyi aspect* (Kharkiv, 2011), 235–7.
93 DNAB – "Down with Communes [*het kommunu*]," "GLORY TO FREE UKRAINE [*Slava vilnii Ukraini*]."
94 The Ukrainian sample here reviewed suggests that the rhetoric of unrestricted violence evident in leaders' correspondence and some newspaper articles figured little in their mass propaganda: J. Baberowski, *Scorched Earth. Stalin's Reign of Terror* (New Haven, 2016), 16, 41–51.

95 V.I. Lenin, *Collected Works* (Moscow, 1965), vol. 30: 291–7; Dmytrienko, *Lystivsky Bilshovytskykh orhanizatsii Ukrainy*, 144–68, 272–89.

96 TsDAVO f. 1738 op 1 sprava 31 no. 157. The Ukrainian national anthem was played alongside *L'Internationale* at the opening ceremonies, presumably thanks to Borotbists on the organizing committee.

97 There are no detailed membership statistics from before 1921. A random collection of fifty-two application forms from 1919 that asked not only for nationality but also for known languages gives some idea of Ukrainian representation in the party. Of the fifty-two rank-and-file applicants, thirteen indicated Ukrainian nationality and five knowledge of Ukrainian – of whom two were Jewish. TsDAHO f. 1 op 20 sprava 81.

98 V. Iurchuk et al., *Pervyi siezd kommunisticheskoi partii (bolshevikov) Ukrainy* (Kyiv, 1988), 126–37.

99 Descendents of Spanish settlers in Latin America seceded from the Spanish empire. Russians in Ukrainian provinces remained empire loyalists in 1917. L. Veracini, "Settler Colonialism and Decolonization," *Borderlands* 2 (2007), http://www.borderlands.net.au/vol6no2_2007/veracini_settler.htm.

100 Dutch radicals formed the Indonesian party but were only a tiny minority by the time it joined the Comintern – separate from the Dutch party. The Vietnamese party was separate from the French. The membership in Algeria was overwhelming settler/colonist. In 1935 the Algerian party separated from the French and only in 1956 called for independence. The Russians condemned the French in Algeria for opposing independence and backed the party's small pro-independent faction – the equivalent of the Ukrainian Communist Party they condemned in Ukraine. In 1922, when local communist leaders claimed that a Muslim revolution would mark a return to feudalism and that a French revolution was a precondition of an Algerian revolution, Trotsky condemned them as having a "slave-owner mentality." A. Drew, "Bolshevizing Communist Parties: The Algerian and South African Experiences," *International Review of Social History* 48 (August 2003): 181–9; E. Sivan, *Communisme et nationalisme en Algerie 1920–1962* (Paris, 1976).

101 V. Lenin, *Polnoe Sobranie Sochinennii*, 5th ed., 55 vols. (Moscow, 1958–70) 41: 433 This document was not published until 1942 and did not appear in the *Collected Works*. In 1900 Lenin supported the Boers, not the Zulus or Bantus.

102 N. Makhno, *Spovid anarkhista* (Kyiv, 2008), 375.

103 Lenin, *Collected Works*, vol. 28: 56.

104 F.M. Rudych, ed., *Vtoroi siezd Kommunisticheskoi partii* 7, 120–1, 169. He claimed that American and British imperialism, which was as bad as German imperialism, had turned the slogan of "the right to self-determination" into a counter-revolutionary attempt to break up all of

central Europe into small states. This idea was reaffirmed during the Third Party Congress of February 1919, where one speaker added that the idea of an "independent Ukraine" was "chauvinist." The UNR was a "rich peasant dictatorship" that had "inevitably" become an "imperialist counter-revolutionary dictatorship" used by Anglo-American imperialists as a tool against "the workers revolution in Ukraine." TsDAHO f. 1 op 1 sprava 15 no. 192–3.

105 V. Skorovstanskii [pseud. Shakhrai], *Revoliutsiia na Ukraine*, 2nd ed. (Saratov, 1918), xi. Iurkevych drew attention to this danger in his 1917 pamphlet *Russkie sotsial demokraty i natsionalnyi vopros*. English translations: M. Yurkevych, *Journal of Ukrainian Studies* (Spring 1982): 57–78. It is unknown whether Ukrainian Marxists knew of Kazimierz Kelles-Krauz, the Polish PPS theoretician who in the early years of the century also advocated linking national liberation to proletarian struggle.

106 NMIU – "To Peasants, workers and the entire population of Ukraine [*K krestianam, rabochim i vsemu naseleniiu Ukrainy*]." DNAB – "Proclamation to the citizens of Hadiach [*Vidozva do hromiadan mista Hadiacha*]." Arkhiv druku – "Red Mobilization Comrade Worker! [*Chervona mobylizatsiia tovaryshu robitnyche*]."

107 Originally published in *Izvestiia Iuga*, the article argued in support of the short-lived Krivyi Rih Republic: TsDAHO f. 5 op. 1 sprava 258 no. 237–41. Iurchuk et al., *Pervyi sized*, 152.

108 TsDAVO f. 1078 op 1 sprava 18 no. 23 v.

109 H. Efimenko, *Status USRR ta ii vzaemovidnosyny z RSFRR: dovhyi 1920 rik* (Kyiv, 2012), 143–52, 165, 199.

110 TsDAHO f. 1 op 20 sprava 162. Dated 12 June 1920, four days after the beginning of offensive against Poland.

111 TsDAHO f. 57 op 2 sprava 340 no. 31–2; idem, sprava 342 no. 50.

112 TsDAHO f. 57 op 2 sprava 453 no. 42–6, 53, 55, 62, 124, 131, 180, 208; idem, sprava 454 no. 261; idem, sprava 342 no. 49. Leinwand, *Czerwonym mlotem*, 164, 217, 279. In July 1920 leaflets referred to the "Communist Party of Galicia" that the Bolsheviks had appended to the CPU, whose leaders called themselves the "legal proprietor [*khozaiin*] of the Galician land." Yet they appealed to "Ukrainian Hutsuls." Propaganda during the Polish–Soviet war always used the form "Polish workers and peasants."

113 M.P. Donyi ed., *Bolshevistskie organizatsii Ukrainy (mart-noiabr 1917 gg.) Sbornik dokumentov i materialov* (Kyiv, 1957), 237–8. This was followed by a decision to publish in Ukrainian – something they had not done since their formation.

114 Lenin, *Collected Works*, vol. 25: 91; Donyi, ed., *Bolshevistskie organizatsii*, 321.

115 S.M. Korolivsky et al., *Grazhdanskaia voina na Ukraine 1918–1920* (Kyiv, 1967), I: 24. Two of the few Ukrainian Bolsheviks, Mykola Skrypnyk and Volodymyr Zatonsky, were instrumental in getting party leaders in April 1918 to drop the idea of incorporating Ukrainian lands into Russia as provinces, and to accept the permanence of what they had envisaged as a temporary Ukrainian republic on the grounds of political expediency. "A Ukrainian soviet federated republic within the [ethnic] borders of the [fourth] universal is necessary to counterpoise against the bourgeois Ukraine of the Central Rada." This permitted Bolshevik leaders to present a *de facto* foreign military invasion and occupation of what was a foreign territory as of November 1917, as part of a civil war. TsDAHO f. 57 op 2 sprava 487 no. 60–1.

116 "Tov. Zatonskii o vzaimootnosheniiakh Ukrainy i Velikorossii," *Izvestiia Kievskogo gubrevkoma*, 31 January 1920.

117 TsDAHO f. 57 op. 2 sprava 454 no. 193, 255; idem, sprava 453 no. 231. The leaflet also explained that Poland was the historical enemy of "the working people of Ukraine."

118 TsDAHO f. 57 op. 2 sprava 342 no. 62–5, 83, 104.

119 Lenin, *Polnoe sobranii*, 35: 116.

120 TsDAHO f. 1 op 1 sprava 15 no. 56; *Izvestiia* (Kyiv), 30 January 1918.

121 NMIU – "TO ALL CITIZENS OF KIEV [*Ko vsem grazhdanam g. Kieva*]."

122 Some Ukrainian Bolsheviks did use the term. A.A. and A.M. Plekhanov, eds., F.E. *Dzerzhinskii – predsedatel VChK-OGPU 1917–1926* (Moscow, 2007), 135, 188; S. Hurenko, ed., *Tretyi ziizd Komunistychnoï partiï (bilshovykiv) Ukraïny, 1–6 bereznia 1919 roku* (Kyiv, 2002), 43; Velychenko, *Painting Imperialism and Nationalism Red*, 74–6.

123 "Zavoeivateli ili osvoboditel," *Izvestiia* (Kyiv), 30 January 1918, explained that "northern armies" had come to liberate Ukraine from "false friends" and bring it the "spirit of revolution."

124 DNAB – "To all citizens of Kyiv [*Ko vsem grazhdanam g. Kieva*]." NMIU – "To Peasants, workers and the entire population [*K krestianam, rabochim i vsemu naseleniiu*]."

125 DNAB – "To all workers and cossacks of Kyiv [*Do vsikh robitnykiv ta kozakyv m. Kyiva*]."

126 TsDAHO f. 57 op. 2 sprava 342 no. 4–5, 8–19; NMIU l 1132. Ukrainians dominated in Ukrainian left-SR partisan units. Some were in partisan formations attached to the Red Army.

127 DNAB – "To the entire population of Ukraine [*Ko vsemu naseleniiu Ukrainy*]."

128 TsDAHO f. 57 op 2 sprava 347 no. 17; idem, sprava 453 no. 78–9. See also illus. 5.

129 NMIU – "To Peasants, workers and the entire population of Ukraine [*K krestianam, rabochim i vsemu naseleniiu Ukrainy*]." DNAB – "To all workers and cossacks of Kyiv [*Do vsikh robitnykiv ta kozakiv m. Kyiva*]."

130 TsDAHO f. 57 op. 2 sprava 342 no. 96, 131–6.

131 *Izvestiia* (Moscow), 3 January 1919.

132 DNAB – "'Ruskies' and 'Honks' [*'Katsap' i 'Khokhol'*]."

133 DNAB – "Who the communists (Bolsheviks) are [*Kto takie Kommunisty (Bolshevyky)*]."

134 DNAB – "The truth about the Bolsheviks [*Pravda o Bolshevikakh*]," "Why the Bolsheviks call themselves communists [*Pochemu bolsheviki nazyvaiut sebia kommunistami*]," "Whoever opposes the communists opposes soviet power [*Khto proty Kommunistiv toi proty Radianskoi Vlady*]," "Down with Communes [*Het Kommunu*]," "To the middle peasant [*Do seredniaka*]."

135 [Anon.], *'O Katsapakh'. Kak pomeshchiki i kulaki durachat krestian*, 3rd ed. (Kyiv, 1919).

136 TsDAHO f. 57 op 2 sprava 453 no. 231.

137 TsDAHO f. 57 op. 2 sprava 454 no. 56–57; idem, sprava 453 no. 231–2.

138 Nothing in the sample refers to Bukharin's "Theory of the Offensive," which justified the expansion of Bolshevik rule over foreign non-Russian territories by force of arms in the name of world revolution.Velychenko, *Painting Imperialism and Nationalism Red*, 85–6.

139 [N. Podvoiskii], *Oborona sotsialisticheskogo otechestva*.

140 [Anon.], *SLAVA PETLIURI (Na koho robyt Petliura)*; M. Kr., *Pravda pro Petliurivski brekhni*; idem, *Na Ukraine* is collection of articles explaining that no forces could triumph against the Bolsheviks because they represented the majority working poor. The Bolshevik task was difficult, however, insofar as it had to deal with the "general and political ignorance of the Ukrainian population" – the product of illiteracy resulting from Russification and tsarist rule.

141 TsDAHO f. 57 op. 2 sprava 453 no. 160–4.

142 TsDAHO f. 1 op. 20 sprava 369 no. 47–54.

143 TsDAHO f. 1 op 1 sprava 15 no. 194. P.P. Bachynsky et al., *Komunistychna partiia –natkhnennyk i orhanizator obiednavchoho rukhu Ukrainskoho narodu za stvorennia SRSR* (Kyiv, 1963), 94–5. See also *Kommunist* (Kharkiv), 30 January and 19 February 1919.

144 The article is reproduced in Vladimirov, ed., *Spravochnik prodovolstvennogo*, 6–7. Lenin, *Polnoe Sobranie*, vol. 38: 313.

145 Vladimirov, *Ukrainskie krestiane i prodovolstvennyi vopros*.

146 Iu. Kondufor, *Robitnychi prodovolchi zahony na Ukraini v 1919 rotsi* (Kharkiv, 1953), 55.

147 TsDAHO f. 57 op 2 sprava 454 no. 7–8, 138; TsDAHO f. 1 op 20 sprava 367 no. 86–8.

148 MNIU l 5677; TsDAHO f. 57 op 2 sprava 347 no. 20–4; idem, sprava 340 no. 143.

149 Vladimirov, *Ukrainskie Krestiane i prodovolstvennyi vopros;* TsDAHO f. 1 op. 1 sprava 15 no. 194.

150 DNAB – "CATCH THE THIEF [*Derzhy hrabizhnyka*]," "What Ukraine gave and received from Russia [*Shcho Ukraina dala i oderzhala vid Velikorosii*]." TsNB – "STOP THE THIEF." Arkhiv druku – "What is happening in the cities [*Shcho robytsia u misti*]."

151 TsDAHO f. 57 op 2 sprava 340 no. 140–8, 247; idem, sprava 342 no. 121–2, 142–3. One leaflet claimed that the CPU was "the only real proletarian party whose words never differed from deeds."

152 Lenin, *Polnoe Sobranie,* 28: 208–10; M. Agursky, *The Third Rome: National Bolshevism in the USSR* (London, 1987), 203–13, 215–20; I.V. Stalin, *Sochinenia* (Moscow, 1954), 4: 226.

153 *Chervonyi prapor,* 16 May and 11 July 1920; *Pravda,* 12 May 1920; Zinoviev and Bukharin condemned this exploitation of Russian imperialism. Bukharin, who saw no relationship between it and the new proletarian Soviet fatherland, called on Polish workers to support the first proletarian fatherland against their own capitalist fatherland. *Pravda,* 10 July 1920.

154 Leinwald, *Czerwonym mlotem w orla bialego,* 36–43, 101–3.

155 TsDAHO f. 57 op 2 sprava 453 no. 160–4. For incorrect use of "Ruskii," see also idem, sprava 342 no. 131. At the time, "Ruskii" in Ukrainian meant "Russian."

156 Arkhiv druku – "Who supports Petliura? [*Kto za Petliuru*]," "Bread and the Bayonet [*Khleb i shtyk*]," "Peasants! Who among you has not heard of the traitor Petliura [*Seliane. Kto iz vas ne slykhal o predatele Petliure*]." DNAB – "TO THE ENTIRE POPULATION OF RIGHT- BANK UKRAINE [*Ko vsemu naseleniu Pravoberezhnoi Ukrainy*]," "GLORY TO FREE UKRAINE [*Slava vilnii Ukraini*]," NMIU – "TO THE DEFENSE OF SOVIET UKRAINE [*Na zakhyst Nezalezhnoi Radianskoi Ukrainy*]."

157 NMIU – "THE COMMUNISTS ARE LIBERATING UKRAINE [*Kommunisty osvobozhdaiut Ukrainu*]."

158 DNAB – "FIRST HE SOLD YOU TO THE GERMANS [*Spershu vin prodav tebe Nimtsiam*]." Arkhiv druku – "An Appeal to Petliura's cossacks. Brother Cosssacks [*Vidozva do kozakiv Petliury*]," NMIU – "TO THE DEFENSE OF SOVIET UKRAINE [*Na zakhyst Nezalezhnoi Radianskoi Ukrainy*]." DNAB – "Letter to my native villagers [*Lyst do ridnykh selian*]."

159 Arkhiv druku – "I love my poor Ukraine [*Liubliu moiu Ukrainu ubohu*]."

160 TsDAHO f. 1. op 2 sprava 368 no. 142–5, 166–8. TsDAHO f. 57 op 2 sprava 453 no. 78–9. The first was signed by Hrinko, Education Commissar; the second was unsigned but from the same agency. While CPU leaders in leaflets called on the Red Army to "chase the Polish lords from our

historical lands," and wrote that eastern Galicia would be attached in some manner to Soviet Ukraine, Lenin and Trotsky announced it would be part of a Soviet Poland: S.M. Korolivsky et al., *Grazhdanskaia voina na Ukraine 1918–1920* (Kyiv, 1967), vol. 3: 293, 307–9.

161 TsDAHO f. 57 op. 2 sprava 347 no. 17; idem, sprava 453 no. 78–9, 131–3.

162 N.I. Faleev, *Za chto prolivala krov Ukraina?*

163 G. Zinoviev, *Kto nash glavnyi vrag na Ukraine?*

164 M. Pavlovich, *UKRAINA Kak obiekt mezhdunarodnoi kontr-revoliutsii*, 25.

165 Arkhiv druku – "Peasants Who among you has not heard of the traitor Petliura [*Seliane Khto iz vas ne slykhal o predatele Petliure*]," "An Appeal to Petliura's Cossacks [*Vidozva do kozakiv Petliury*]," DNAB – "FIRST HE SOLD YOU TO THE GERMANS [*Spershu vin prodav tebe Nimtsiam*]." Arkhiv druku – "An Appeal to Petilura's Cossacks. Brother Cosssacks" [*Vidozva do kozakiv Petliury*]. NMIU – "TO THE DEFENSE OF SOVIET UKRAINE [*Na zakhyst Nezalezhnoi Radianskoi Ukrainy*]." DNAB – "Letter to my native villagers [*Lyst do ridnykh selian*]."

166 DNAB – "Don't be Traitors [*Ne budte zradnykamy*]." TsDAHO – "Who Assisted the Polish Invasion? [*Khto dopomikh polskii navali*]." Arkhiv druku – "What does the Red Army do for Peasants [*Shcho robyt Chervona armiia dlia selian*]."

167 DNAB – "They sold Ukraine [*Prodaly Ukrainu*]."

168 DNAB – "A Reply to Mr. Hetman Petliura [*Otvet panu getmanu Petliure*]," "A REPLY TO BANDITS PETLIURA AND SOKOLOVSKY [*Vidpovid banditam petliuri ta sokolovskomu*]."

169 TsNB – "To the Pilots and Drivers in Petliura's Army [*Letchikam i motoristam petliurovskoi armii*]."

170 Arkhiv Druku – "To the workers and peasants of Eastern Galicia [*Do robitnykiv i selian Skhidnoi Halychyny*]," "Comrade Galician Sich Riflemen [*Tovaryshi Halytski Sichovi Striltsi*]," "Comrades workers and peasants of Eastern Galicia [*Tovaryshi robinyky ta seliane skhidnoi Halychyny*]," "Who is the real enemy of the Ukrainian language [*Khto spravzhnyi voroh Ukrainskoi movy?*]."

171 TsDAHO f. 1 op 20 sprava 333 no. 22–3.

172 M. Ravich-Cherkasskii, *Makhno i Makhnovshchina*; Ia. Selo, *Bandyty-'Sotisalisty'-Makhnovtsi*; G. Rakitov, *Pisma o Makhnovtsakh*. Kh. Rakovskii et al., *Doloi Makhnovshchinu*, included a section of statements allegedly from peasants, who described how they had suffered from requisitioning by Makhno's troops.

173 Arkhiv druku – "I'm for Makhno [*Ia za makhno*]," "Insurgents – Makhnovites! [*Povstantsy- Makhnovtsy*]," "Why Makhno opposes registration [*Pochemu Makhno protyv ucheta*]. " DNAB – "Bandits 'Insurgents' [*Bandity 'povstantsy'*]."

174 [Anon.], *Borba s Banditizmom (Tezisy-konspekt dlia lektorov).* A short list of sources contains a number of works by Rakovskii. Use of terror is not mentioned in the pamphlet, nor are Rakovskii's or Lenin's instructions to that effect. TsDAVO f. 2 op 1 sprava 232 no. 201. Lenin, *Polnoe sobranie,* 50: 245–6. Orders marked top secret to impose collective responsibility and destroy entire villages when necessary are reproduced in R. Krutsyk, ed., *Narodna viina 1917–1932* (Kyiv, 2011), 119. http://chtyvo.org.ua/authors/Krutsyk_Roman/Narodna_viina_1917-1932_Putivnykdo_ekspozytsii.

175 [Anon.], *Pravda o bolshevikakh;* D. Stonov (Vlodavskii), *Slovo Ukrainskim krestianam.*

176 DNAB – "Down with Communes [*Het Kommunu*]." Kharkivsky istorychnyi muzei – "Who is afraid of the communists? [*Komu strashni komunisty*]."

177 DNAB – "The Kulak, middle peasant and poor peasant [*Kulak, seredniak i bedniak*]," "In unity there is strength [*V hurti syla*]."

178 DNAB – "THEY ARE NOT DEFENDING THE FAITH [*Ne viru vony svoiu zakhyshchaiut*]."

179 TsDAHO f. 57 op 2 sprava 342 no. 138.

180 DNAB – "Down with the pretender [*Doloi samozvantsa*]," "The truth about communes [*Pravda o kommunakh*]," "DON'T BELIEVE FAIRY TALES ABOUT COMMUNES [*Ne verte skazkam o kommune*]." Kharkivsky istorychnyi muzei – "Why we need Committees of the Poor [*Nashcho nam potribni Komitety Bidnoty*]."

181 In Kharkiv province, local officials threatened to burn down the houses of those who refused to join communes and to not allocate them benefits or rations. The policy was changed in December 1919 when Lenin specifically condemned forcing peasants into communes. D. Mykhailychenko, "Polityka 'voiennoho komunizmu' i Ukrainske selianstvo (sichen–serpen 1919r.)," Kandydatska dysertatsiia, Kharkiv University (2002), 100.

182 DNAB – "Comrade peasants of Kyiv Province [*Tovaryshschi krestiane Kievshchiny*]." TsNB – "EVERYONE LIES IN THEIR OWN MANNER [*Kazhdyi vret po svoemu*]." DNAB –"25 OCTOBER [*25 Oktiabr*]." TsNB – "BROTHER COSSACKS! [*Braty kozaky*]." DNAB –"Order of the Revolutionary Military Council ... to the kozaks of the Petliura army [*Nakaz revoliutsiinoi Viiskovoi Rady ... Kazakam Petliurovskoi armii*]."

183 Panas Liukko, *Chy potribni nezamozhnomu selianynu ioho komitety.* TsDAHO f. 1 op. 20 spr. 21 no. 6.

184 Arkhiv druku – "To the Cossacks and officers of the Directory's Army [*Do kozakiv ta starshyn viisk Direktorii*]."

185 DNAB – "Its none of your business. Get lost [*Chyia-by korova mychala a vasha molchala*]." TsNB – "To Ukrainian Peasants duped by sovereignists [*Krestianam obmanutym ukrainskiami samostiinikami*]," "Concerning big

warlords and small bandit units [*Pro otamaniv velykykh ta malykh hrabizhnytskykh vataiah*," "ZELENY IS HELPING DENIKIN ESTABLISH SERFDOM [*Zeleny pomahaie Denikinu zavesty panshchynu*]," "HOW THEY DELUDE THE PEASANTS [*Iak vony duriat selian*]." DNAB –"TO DUPED PEASANTS AND WORKERS [*Do obdurenykh Selian i Robitnykiv*]," "EACH LIES IN THEIR OWN WAY [*Kozhen breshe po svoiomu*]."

186 TsNB – "STOP, PEASANT, AND THINK [*Ostanovys, krestianin, i podumai*]." DNAB – "A WORD TO THOSE DISSATISFIED WITH SOVIET POWER [*Slovo k nedovolnym sovetskoi vlastiu*]," "DOWN WITH HIRELINGS AND FOOLS [*Het pidnaimenykiv ta durystiv*]."

187 Reproduced in Ia. Storozhuk, *Pohliad suchasnyka v mynule* (Khmelnytsky, 2015), 103–5.

188 DNAB – "Dear Comrades, poor peasants of Kyiv province [*Dorohi Tovaryshi, Nezamozhnyky Kyivshchyny*]," "To the poor peasants of Kyiv province [*Do nezamozhnykh selian Kyivshchyny*]." TsDAHO – "We together defend ourselves from our enemies [*Spilno boronimosia vid nashykh vorohiv*]." DNAB – "Bandits 'Insurgents' [*Bandyty 'povstantsy'*]." Arkhiv druku – "We don't need the Makhno regime [*Ne treba nam Mokhnovshchyny*]," "What does the Red Army do for Peasants [*Shcho robyt Chervona armiia dlia selian*]."

189 Iu. Mordalevych, *Do Povstantsiv*. The last page includes a reproduction of the handwritten version of the first paragraph – presumably to demonstrate authenticity.

190 Arkhiv druku – "Comrade Peasants [*Tovaryshi seliane*]," "Iurko Mordalevych has come over to the Soviet side [*Iurko Mordalevych pereishov na bik Raianskoi Vlady*]." DNAB – "What ex petliurites say about the Petliura regime [*Shcho kazhut pro petliurovshchynu kolyshni petliurovtsi*]," "Letter to Bandits [*Lyst do Bandytiv*]." Kharkivsky istorychnyi muzei – "The Bandit – There is your enemy [*Bandyt. Os de nash voroh*]."

191 DNAB – "Letter to Bandits [*Lyst do Bandytiv*]." Kharkivsky istorychnyi muzei – "The Bandit - There is our enemy [*Bandyt- Os de nash voroh*]." "Insurgent Stop! Read carefully to the end [*Povstanets stii. Prochytai uvazhno do kintsia*]."

192 S. Vasylchenko, *Chervona Volia vilnoi Ukrainy*; Vasilchenko, *Kommunisticheskaia Partiia (bolsh.) na Ukraine. (Voprosy nashei raboty i taktiki)*.

193 [Anon.], *Dlia choho i iak kulaky tskuiut proty ievreiiv*; P. Eletskii, *O Ievreiiakh*.

194 Arkhiv druku – "Down with Traitors [*Doloi predatelei*]."

195 DNAB – "THAT THE PETLIURITES DO POGROMS [*Shcho Petliurovtsi robliat pohromy*]."

196 TsDAVO f. 343 op 1 sprava 308 no. 53, 204–5.

197 Detailed descriptions of requisitions, which included writing-paper and hair-clippers, and lists of what items and quantity of clothing and

dinnerware individuals were permitted to own legally in Poltava through 1919, are in the diary of Oleksandr Nesvitsky. Squads did night spot-checks. Items lost or damaged could not be replaced at the time. A pair of shoes that cost 25 roubles in 1914 cost 70,000 in 1919. *Poltava u dni revoliutsii ta v period smuti* (Poltava, 1995) 165–77, 195, *passim*.

198 Arkhiv druku – "Order No. 2 [*Nakaz ch.2*]," "ORDER No. 2 [*Prikaz No. 2.*]" DNAB – "Soviet Power and the Working Woman [*Radianska vlada i trudiashcha zhinka*]." TsNB – "ANOUNCEMENT Citizens! [*Vidozva. Hromadiane*]."

199 See the graphic, sometimes horrific, description of daily life that all except party members experienced in the provincial capital Chernihiv in 1919: D.V. Krainskii, *Zapiski tiuremnogo inspektora* (Moscow, 2016), https://coollib.com/b/377031/read.

200 DNAB – "Bandits "Insurgents [*Bandity 'povstantsy'*]." NMIU – "From the Executive Bureau of the Povit Soviet ... [*Ot Ispolnitelnago Biuro Uiezdnago Soveta*]."

201 Arkhiv druku – "Hunger that damned legacy of the old regime [*Golod – Eto prokliatoe nasledstvo ot starogo stroia*]."

202 Arkhiv druku – "Citizens! Stop and Think [*Hromadiane Stante i podumaite*]."

203 DNAB – "Obligatory ordinance [*Obiazatelnoe Postanovlenie*]," "Order no. 1 All Officers ... [*Prikaz No. 1. Vse ofitsery*]," "Order no. 1. The town of Big Tokmak [*Prikaz No. 1. Po mestechku B. Tokmaku*]," "Order no. 2 [*Prikaz No. 2*], "Announcement to the entire population of the town Tokmak [*Vozzvanie ko vsemu naseleniiu. m.b. Tokmaka*]." Arkhiv druku – "Order no 33 Volyn provincial Soviet Commissar of Food Supply [*Prikaz no. 33 Volynskago Gubernskago Sovetskago Komissara Prodovolstviia*]," "Order. Chief of Police 4th Zolotopolsyi region [*Prikaz Nachalnyka militsii 4go Zlatopolskogo raiona*]," "Order no. 11 [*Prikaz no. 11*]."

204 TsNB – "ANOUNCEMENT Citizens [*Vidozva. Hromadiane*]."

205 Ivanushchenko, *Ukrainska revoliutsiia 1917–1920 rr. v lystivkakh ta gazetakh*, 48–59.

206 Arkhiv druku – "Order no. 143 [*Prikaz No. 143*]," "Order No. 2 [*Nakaz ch 2*]."

207 Arkhiv druku –"ORDER No. [*Prikaz No. _*]."

208 DNAB – "Soviet Power and the Working Woman [*Radianska vlada i trudiashcha zhinka*]."

209 Arkhiv druku – "Ukrainian Red Youth [*Ukrainske Chervone Iunatstvo*]," "For all officials [*Dlia sluzhbovtsiv vsikh ustanov*]," "To all provincial Justice departments [*Vsim hub'vidiustam*]."

210 TsNB – "THE HYGIENE OF READING [*Gigiena chteniia*]," "THE TEN COMMANDMENTS OF THE RED ARMY READER [*Desiat zapovedei chitatelia-krasnoarmeitsa*]."

211 It is unknown if Lenin knew the Rada would declare independence. He did know the Germans were negotiating with the Ukrainians separately. The Congress's Resolution on the Russian Republic proceeded from the fallacious assumption that branches of the Russian Bolshevik party in non-Russian regions represented "the people" there and were not dependent on Bolshevik Russian troops. It read: "The Russian Socialist Soviet Republic is created on the basis of a voluntary union of the peoples of Russia in the form of a federation the soviet republics of these peoples." Lenin, *Polnoe Sobranie*, 35: 322. L. Hrynevych et al., *Istoriia Ukrainskoho viiska 1917–1995* (Kyiv, 1996), 68–71. Cited in E.H. Carr, *The Bolshevik Revolution 1917–1923*, vol. 1 (London, 1973), 133.

212 Emil Enno, the French representative, worked for French intelligence but had no delegated powers. His activities were disavowed by the foreign minister, Stephen Pichon. E. *Borschak*, "La *paix ukrainienne de Brest-Litovsk*," *Le Monde Slave*, no. 7 (1929), 63. Forged text and false claims: Korolivsky et al., *Grazhdanskaia voina na Ukraine* vol. 1: 554–5, 641–3.

213 I. Vyslotsky, *Spomyny rozvidchyka z chasiv pershoi svotovoi viiny* (Lviv, 2007), 185–95. Apparently local agents were supposed to distribute them in a specific order to build credibility. Distributed first were those mildly critical of the Bolshevik order. Bolshevik agents would also turn captured partisan-commanders into double-agents and, through them, issue leaflets with national rhetoric instructing followers to meet at specified times and places – where they would be shot or arrested. R. Koval, *Istorii Kholodnoiarskoi orhanizatsii* (Kyiv, 2016), 54–6.

214 *Novyny* (Zhmerynka), 25 February and 10 March 1919.

215 NMIU l 4185.

Conclusion

1 P. Hryhorenko, *Spohady* (Detroit, 1984), 50–1. The major non-Bolshevik groups there were the Whites and Makhno's anarchists.

2 I found one reference in Politburo protocols to "oral agitation." TsDAHO f. 1 op 6 sprava 1 no. 95. Whether this included spreading rumours is unknown.

3 Their correspondence and dispatches indicate Bolshevik leaders knew well the "enemy" were Ukrainians and that their power in Ukraine much depended on Russians–despite what they wrote in their propaganda. Velychenko, *Painting Imperialism and Nationalism Red*, 49–50.

4 TsDAHO f. 1 op 6 sprava 1 no. 94v. Bazhanov, *Vospominaniia byvshego sekretaria*, 123. Plekhanov, eds., *F.E. Dzerzhinskii – predsedatel VChK-OGPU*, 69. How Bolsheviks ensured Bolshevik majorities in *soviets* is described in E.A.

Sikorskii, *Iz istorii utverzhdeniia v Rossii diktatury Bolshevikov. (po materialam vserossiiskim i smolenskim)* (Smolensk, 2009), 150–61.

5 For a summary of the message imparted by the Ukrainian SR newspaper in 1917, see Skalsky, "Obraz tsentralnoi rady u svidomosti selian na pochatkovomu etapi Ukrainskoi revoliutsii," *Ukrainskyi istorchnyi zhurnal* no. 1 (2008), 53.

6 The warlord Semosenko on entering Proskuriv in February 1919 issued a leaflet forbidding pogroms. This was in accord with a Directory order to that effect dated 20 January. After crushing an attempted Bolshevik seizure of power, Semosenko gave a speech telling his men to kill Jews as they were Ukraine's worst enemies. A similar case of verbal exhortation is reported after Ukrainians thwarted a Bolshevik coup in Zhytomir in January 1919. L.B. Miliakova, ed., *Kniga pogromov* (Moscow, 2007), 48–51, 28–9, 87.

7 Miliakova, ed., *Kniga pogromov*, 492. The report noted that it was the armed men who killed and burned and that local civilians only looted.

8 Russian generals allowed their men to rape, loot, and abuse specific categories of civilians during the Galician campaign. Imperial army propaganda encouraged pogroms, as well as wartime spy mania, which further justified spontaneous violence against targeted civilians. The men who returned home were not resocialized into normal civilian values because the civil order that would have done that had broken down because of their absence. E. Lohr, *Nationalizing the Russian Empire: The Campaign against Enemy Aliens during World War I* (Cambridge, MA, 2003).

9 Cited in V. Morenets, ed., *Sim spohadiv Vyzvonoi viiny* (Kyiv, 2015), 92, 94–5.

10 I. Davydko, ed., *Evhen Chykalenko Shchodennyk* (1921) (Kyiv, 2015), 77–82, 121; S.P. Stehnyi, "Selianski povstannia v Pravoberezhnii chastyni USRR u 1921–1923 rr.," PhD diss., Kremenchuh National University (Kremenchuh, 2000); P.M. Isakov, "Selianski povstanskyi antykomunistychny rukh na Livoberezhnyi Ukraini (berezen 1919-lystopad 1921), PhD diss., Ukrainian Academy of Sciences, Institute of Ukrainian History (Kyiv, 2001). The idea appeared repeatedly in situation reports submitted to the government-in-exile through the first half of 1921. TsDAVO f. 1429 op 2 sprava 113 no. 61; idem, f. 3205 op 1 sprava 11 no. 10–25.

11 The Cheka had infiltrated the Ukrainian network. TsDAVO f. 3204 op 1 sprava 12 no. 38, 41a.

12 Patriotism, nationalism, imperialism, and monarchism were the last reasons British workers enlisted. J. Aulich and J. Hewitt, *Seduction or Instruction: First War Posters in Britain and France* (Manchester, 2007), 45; B. Zieman, *War Experiences in Rural Germany* (Oxford, 207), 137–41, 271.es

13 A. Watson, *Ring of Steel: Germany and Austria-Hungary in WW1* (London, 2014), 462–3, 487–8; O. Figes and B. Kolonitskii, *Interpreting the Russian Revolution:*

The Language and Symbols of 1917 (New Haven, 1999) 166, 175. German ideas were not only in front-line leaflets and pamphlets but also in Russian newspapers published in Berlin and Vienna and smuggled into Russia.

14 Their British rivals concluded that the Irish nationalists in 1919–20 had waged a very successful propaganda campaign. "In one department, namely publicity, it (Sian Fein) [*sic*] was unrivalled. This department was energetic, subtle and exceptionally skilful in mixing truth, falsehood and exaggeration and was perhaps the most powerful and the least fought arm of the Sian Fein forces." War Office, *Record of the Rebellion in Ireland and the part played by the Army in dealing with it* (London, 1922), II: 46.

15 C. Stuart, *Secrets of Crewe House: The Story of a Famous Campaign* (London, 1920), 93–4, 107–8. According to a German general, "what caused the most damage [to the army in the autumn of 1918] was the paper war waged by our enemies who daily flooded us with hundreds of thousands of leaflets extraordinarily well arranged and edited." Cited in G.G. Bruntz, *Allied Propaganda and the Collapse of the German Empire in 1918* (Stanford, 1938), 219. L. Sanders and P.M. Taylor, *British Propaganda during the First World War, 1914–18* (London, 1982), 250–9. For a survey of successes and failures of all sides on the Western Front, see C. Roetter, *Psychological Warfare* (London, 1974), 11–94.

16 I.V. Narskii, *Zhizn v katastrofe. Budni naseleniia Urala v 1917–1922 gg.* (Moscow, 2000), 300–13, 400. Other reports referred to shortages of material and agitators.

17 Surveys of soldiers' letters censored in the Kazan Military District, and letters to Petrograd's *soviet* and its *Izvestiia* newspaper from late 1917 and early 1918, confirm that Bolshevik propaganda during those months coincided with widespread attitudes. O.S. Porshneva, *Krestiane, rabochie i soldaty Rossii nakanune i v gody pervoi mirovoi voiny* (Moscow, 2004). National issues were inconsequential in this body of materials. Ukrainian historians have studied peasants' responses and attitudes, but there are no equivalent comprehensive surveys using analogous sources of popular attitudes in Ukraine. Some historians question how much congress resolutions by peasant delegates or intellectuals actually represented villagers' views. O.V. Mykhailiuk, *Selianstvo Ukrainy v pershi desiatylittia XX st.: Sotsiokulturni protsesy* (Dnipropetrovsk, 2007), 291–3. On Ukrainian peasants and the Central Rada, see V. Lozovy, *Ahrarna revoliutsiia v nadniprianskyi Ukraini: stavlennia selianstva do vlady v dobu tsentralnoi rady* (Kamianets-Podilskyi, 2008).

18 F.M. Rudych, ed., *Vtoroi siezd Kommunisticheskoi partii (bolshevikov) Ukrainy 17–22 oktiabria 1918 goda. Protokoly* (Kyiv, 1991), 59.

19 DNAB – "To the Ukrainian nation [*Do narodu Ukrainskoho*]." M. Shkilny, *Ukraina u borotbi za nezalezhnist* (Toronto, 1971), 73, 76, 106; I. Mazepa, *Ukraina v ohni i buri revoliutsii*, 3rd ed. (Kyiv, 2003), 48–9. M. Stakhiv,

Ukraina v dobi Dyrektorii UNR, 7 vols. (Toronto 1962–6), vol. 4: 218, claims that Ukrainian left-SR and left-SD propaganda undermined support for the UNR in 1919. V. Vynnychenko, *Vidrodzhennia natsii* (Vienna, 1920) pt II: 135, 154-9, claimed Ukrainian reality not Bolshevik propaganda explains why Ukrainian troops in late 1917 did not fight the Bolsheviks.

20 TsDAVO f. 182 op 7 sprava 5 no. 7–8; f. 1078 op 1 sprava 21 no. 4.

21 Lazarski, "White Propaganda Efforts in the South during the Russian Civil War 1918–1919," 692–5; TsDAHO f.1 op 20.

22 Malyk, *Totalitaryzm v Ukrainskomu seli. Persha sproba vprovadzhennia*, 30–5; P. Kenez, "Lenin and the Freedom of the Press," in A. Gleason et al., *Bolshevik Culture* (Bloomington, 1985), 144–8. Early 1920s surveys indicated that people read less than before 1917, and not only because of distribution issues. They either did not understand much of what was in print or found it uninteresting. J. Brooks, "Breakdown in Production," in A. Gleason et al., *Bolshevik Culture*, 165; M.S. Gus, *Iazyk gazety* (Moscow, 1926).

23 *Nova Hromada*, 11 January 1919. Any conclusive generalizations about the impact of propaganda would have to be based on a study of the experiences of individual units and incidents, to determine how many were turned by propaganda, as opposed to use or threat of force.

24 TsDAVO f. 2250 op 1 sprava 1 no. 65. Similar reports from 1917: Verstiuk et al., *Ukrainska tsentralna Rada*, 129.

25 Hud, *Zahybel Arkadii*, 280–3, 383.

26 TsDAVO f. 1115 op 1 sprava 20 no. 25.

27 TsDAVO f. 2 op 1 sprava 233 no. 90, 98.

28 P. V-K, "Volyn pid viiskovym zariadom Halychan 1919 r.," *Ukrainsky skytalets* no. 1 (1923), 47; no. 4, 23. D. Doroshenko, *Istoriia Ukrainy 1917–1923 rr. Tom 1* (New York, 1954), 225, 279, 337; Khrystiuk, *Zamitky i materialy do istorii Ukrainskoi revoliutsi*, II: 132, 135.

29 O. Nesmashny, "Lysty z Ukrainy," *Volia* (Vienna) (March 1921), 504.

30 TsDAVO f. 1092 op 2 sprava 73 no. 4–5.

31 M. Kovalchuk, *Nevidoma viina 1919 roku: Ukrainsko-bilohvardiiske zbroine protystovannia* (Kyiv, 2006), 363.

32 I. Zelenych, "Oznaiomlennia naselennia iz osoblyvostiamy vyborchoho zakonodavstva v 1917," *Problemy vyvchennia istorii Ukrainskoi revoliutsii 1917–1921 rr.* no. 10 (2014), 81; Basara, "Politychnyi sotsium ukrainskykh provintsiinykh mist za zvitamy instruktoriv Tsentralnoi Rady," in *Ukrainska Tsentralna Rada: postup natsiotvorennia ta derzhavobudivnytstva*, ed. V. Serhiichuk, 158–68.

33 M. Kovalevsky, *Pry dzherelakh borotby. Spomyny, vrazhennia refleksii* (Innsbruck, 1960), 255.

34 Verstiuk et al., *Ukrainskyi natsionalno-vyzvolnyi rukh*, 455; see also 365–7, 396–401, 491–5, 526–7, 605–9. TsDAVO f. 1115 op 1 sprava 44 no. 64–9

includes an extended account by an agitator of how local activists and his predecessor's incompetence in Sumy district had compromised Ukrainian issues there.

35 TsDAVO f. 1115 op 1 sprava 44 no. 126v, 134v.

36 N. Surovtsova, *Spohady* (Kyiv, 1996) 65; N. Myronets et al., *Ievhen Chykalenko Petro Stebnytsky. Lystuvannia 1901–1922 rokiv* (Kyiv, 2008), 505.

37 TsDAVO f. 1115 op 1 sprava 44 no. 83, 88–90; no. 49, 54–5. They also hung a portrait of Shevchenko in the county hall.

38 TsDAHO f. 5 op 1 sprava 17 no. 59; idem, f. 1 op 20 sprava 18 no. 63. In January 1921, at the last minute before their departures, the Central Committee sent a circular to all commissariats telling them to stop assigning bad agitators to propaganda trains and to choose competent and responsible people for the job. TsDAVO f. 348 op 1 sprava 109 no. 1.

39 TsDAVO f. 348 op 1 sprava 109 no. 1.

40 TsDAVO f. 2188 op 1 sprava 117 no. 72–3. O. Dotsenko, *Litopys Ukrainskoi revoliutsii: Materialy i dokumenty do istorii Ukrainskoi revoliutsii.* Reprint ed. (Philadelphia, 1988 [1923]) II: pt 4: 324. Tobacco is *tiutiun* in Ukrainian, *tabak* in Russian.

41 Ie. Chykalenko, *Uryvok z moïkh spomyniv za 1917 r.* (Prague, 1932); 30. Mykhailiuk, *Selianstvo*, 332.

42 *Arkhiv Russkoi Revoliutsii*, 22 vols. (Berlin, 1921–37), XVIII: 150–1. Just in case the Whites did win and the Hetman did return to power, fearful for their lives, former soldiers enriched local counterfeiters as they rushed to buy phoney medical-discharge certificates.

43 Malyk, *Totalitaryzm*, 20. TsDAHO f. 1 op 20 sprava 19 no. 20 v, 29, 57. Some inspectors were forthright in their assessments. In 1920, from Konotop in Chernihiv province, one wrote that the opposition stemmed from agents who were totally ignorant of Ukraine, and sometimes was a response to outright criminals in Bolshevik offices behaving beyond the limits of morality and law. TsDAHO f. 1 op 20 sprava 367 no. 122.

44 TsDAHO f. 1 op 20 sprava 44 no. 18, 26.

45 TsDAHO f. 57 op 2 sprava 281 no. 31, 45.

46 TsDAHO f. 1 op 20 sprava 358 no. 391. M. Kovalchuk, "Dokumenty z istorii antybilshovytskoho povstanskoho rukhu ...," in *Systemni zminy v Ukrainskomu suspilstvi pershoi polovyny XX stolittia: struktura dzherelnoi bazy doslizhennia*, ed. N. Myronets and V. Piskun (Kyiv, 2015), 59–70.

47 *Volia* (Vienna), no. 1 (June 1919), 15; Leinwald, *Czerwonym mlotem w orla bialego. Propaganda sowiecka w wojnie z Polska 1919–1920*, 54, 59. These reports claim that Polish propaganda was very effective.

48 TsDAVO, f. 2 op. 1 sprava 792 no. 3–6. The Jewish Section document has no date. TsDAHO f. 1. op 6 sprava 1 no. 23–7.

49 It was time-honoured practice in all empires to post foreigners among locals to enforce central rule. One historian has claimed that Dzerzhinskii

posted disproportionate numbers of Russified secular Jews to Ukraine, Armenians to his Georgian units, and Latvians to Russian units – few if any of whom spoke the local language. But there seem to be no published documents that would prove deliberate posting of Jews to provoke envisaged violent reactions against surrounding Jewish communities, to then justify repression of Ukrainians as "anti-Semites" – or "nationalists" or "counter-revolutionaries." G. Leggett, *The Cheka: Lenin's Political Police* (Oxford, 1981), 263. Maxim Gorky in 1922 believed that former members of the Black Hundreds who had gotten into the Cheka did what they could to appoint Jews to the most dangerous and unpleasant posts. A.M. Plekahnov, *Kto Vy "Zheleznnyi Feliks"?* (Moscow, 2013), 279; ibid, ed., *F.E. Dzerzhinskii – predsedatel VChK-OGPU*, 192.

50 Heifetz, *The Slaughter of the Jews*, 134; Cherikover, *Istoriia pogromnago dvizheniia na Ukraine*, 62, 133–6, notes that army agitators turned peasants against their Jewish neighbours.

51 TsDAVO, f. 1113 op. 2 sprava 213 no. 74; sprava 197 no. 184. See also the diary of the town of Talne's Jewish doctor, who noted that Ukrainians' hatred of secular Bolshevik Jews, who brought the Jewish ghetto's bad traits into offices, was unbounded. People accustomed to look at Jews as pariahs were shocked to find them at all levels of the administration, including the hated secret police and food supply organs. L. Bilinkis, "Hromadianska viina na Ukraini ta Evreii: Fragmenty," *Khronika 2000*, 21–2 (1998), 234–51.

52 *Arkhiv Russkoi Revoliutsii*, XVI: 206, 209.

53 N.P. Poletika, *Vidennoe i perezhitoe (Iz vospominaniy)* (Tel Aviv, 1982), 122–3. Heifetz, who sympathized with the Bolsheviks, specifically accused regular UNR troops of pogroms "organized by the Directory." *The Slaughter of the Jews*, 26–7, 53. Cherikover writes that government leaders at times equivocated or failed to condemn pogroms, which military hard-liners interpreted as consent to commit them. *Istoriia pogromnago dvizheniia* I: 77, 112, 124.

54 TsDAVO f. 1078 op 2 sprava 34 no. 1; A. Tagieff, *Protokoly sionskikh mudretsov. Falshivka i ee ispolzovanie* (Moscow, 2011), 64–5. For other instances of verbal incitement, see I. Nazhivin, *Zapiski o revoliutsii* (Vienna, 1921), 179, 196. Heifetz, *The Slaughter of the Jews, passim.*

55 The commandant of the town of Kytaihorod in 1919 told the assembled at a meeting: "it is time to kill all the Jews [*vyrizaty do ostiannoho*]." Cited in O.B. Komarnitsky and O.M. Zavalniuk, *Podilski mistechka v dobu Ukrainskoi revoliutsii* (Kamianets-Podilsky, 2005), 164, 167. Many Bolshevik situation reports that note leaflets or calls to begin pogroms or "beat the Jews" do not specify who issued them. TsDAVO f. 5 op 1 sprava 17 no. 32, 51v, 61.

56 Miliakova ed., *Kniga*, 87, 89, 96, 99, 103, 119, 167, 395, 437, 484. Of 391 recorded pogroms in Kyiv,Volyn, and Podillia provinces between 1918

and 1920, Ukrainian troops, usually in retreat and hungry and ragged, are identified as perpetrators in 68. A further 133 have no recorded perpetrators. Some soldiers were jailed or shot for participating in pogroms. Komarnitsky and Zavalniuk, *Podilski mistechka*, 171, 299–305; idem, *Mistechka Volyni ta Kyivshchyny u dobu Ukrainskoi revoliutsii 1917–1920 rr.* (Kamianets-Podilskyi, 2009), 289–94.

57 M. Lazarovych, "Deiaki aspekty borotby vlady druhoi UNR proty Ievreiskykh pohromiv," *Hrani* no. 6 (June 2012), 122–3. Jewish publishers often printed Ukrainian government leaflets. For an August 1919 contract between the Press Ministry and Simcha Kliger, see TsDAVO f. 1113 op 2 sprava 14 no. 41.

58 Goldshtein is not mentioned as a committee organizer in: L. Miliakova, "Le travail d'enquête des organisations juives sur les pogroms d'Ukraine, de Biélorussie et de Russie soviétique pendant la guerre civile (1918–1922)," *Le Mouvement Social* no. 222 (2008), 61–80.

59 Copies of the published trial transcripts are in the YIVO institute: Schwartzbard Papers, 39506. Parts are summarized in S.S. Friedman, *Pogromchik: The Assasination of Simon Petliura* (New York, 1976), 237–47. Freidmann and Goldstein assumed that the UNR controlled all the warlords and did not distinguish between critical opinions about Jews, ideological anti-Semitism, and incitement to commit violence. C. Gilley, "The Ukrainian Anti-Bolshevik Risings of Spring and Summer 1919," and "Beyond Petliura: The Ukrainian national movement and the 1919 pogroms," *East European Jewish Affairs* 1 (2017): 45–61, also fails to make this distinction. He misses the distinction between condemnation of some Jews and condemnation of all Jews, and he fails to examine the relationship between the empirical reality of the overrepresentation of secular apostate Jews in Bolshevik civil and party organizations and the "canard of Judeo-Bolshevism." On the overrepresentation of secular Russified Jews in the Bolshevik party and non-party Bolshevik government organizations, see Heifetz, *The Slaughter of the Jews*, 8–9; A. Gerrits, "Antisemitism and Anti-Communism: The Myth of 'Judeo-Communism' in Eastern Europe," *East European Jewish Affairs* 1 (1995): 49–72; S. Velychenko, *State Building in Revolutionary Ukraine* (Toronto, 2013), 191–4. Local Bolshevik officials were aware of the relationship: "agitation against the Jews comes from the passive white-collar workers [*intelligentsia*] and the bourgeoisie. The reason for this is the huge overflow [*bolshoe perepolnenie*] of Jews in city offices." TsDAVO f. 5 op 1 sprava 17 no. 64 v.

60 Nor are they supported by a recent study of Jewish-related subjects in two Ukrainian newspapers of the period, *Robitnycha hazeta* and *Ukraina*. O. Petrova, "The Jewish Question in the Ukrainian Revolution (1919–1920): A Reappraisal of Ukrainian-Jewish Relations Based on the Daily *Ukraina*,"

MA thesis, Central European University (Budapest, 2013). A collection of Jewish items from the Ukrainian press (December 1918 to March 1919) is held in YIVO.

61 TsDAVO f. 92 op. 2 sprava 76 no. 199; TsDAHO f. 8 op. 1 sprava 40 no. 61; Mykhailiuk, *Selianstvo Ukrainy*, 304–6.

62 TsDAHO f. 1. op 20 sprava 21 no. 6–10, 53; sprava 55 no. 23–5, 4–10; sprava 16 no. 70v.

63 TsDAVO f. 1092 op 2 sprava 73 no. 2–28; TsDAHO f. 1 op 20 sprava 55 no. 25.

64 TsDAVO f. 1429 op 2 sprava 113 no. 66v. The author claimed that Bolsheviks disguised their own men as bandits and sent them to raid and terrorize the populace into passivity.

65 A.K. Sokolov, *Golos naroda. Pisma i otkliki riadovykh sovetskikh grazhdan o sobytiiakh 1918–1932* (Moscow, 1998), 53.

66 TsDAVO f. 1429 op 2 sprava 113 no. 12.

67 *Volia* (Vienna), no. 2 (October 1920), 64–7.

68 K. Lavrynovych, "Povstanchyi rukh," *Volia* (Vienna), no. 1 (April 1921), 14; TsDAVO f. 2297 op 1 sprava 30 no. 183, 227.

69 E. Goldman, *My Disillusionment in Russia* (New York, 1923), 214; *Volia* (Vienna), no. 11 (March 1921), 498–506; *Volia* (Vienna), vol. 4 no. 2 (October 1920), 68.

70 Krainskii, *Zapiski tiuremnogo inspektora*. (no pagination): https://coollib.com/b/377031/read.

71 TsDAVO f. 3204 op 2 sprava 14 no. 12–13, 30, 39, 45.

72 TsDAVO f. 1492 op 2 sprava 113 no. 65. Apparently peasants were much concerned about religious issues that year, which is why the Bolsheviks resorted to this particular stratagem and why the peasants sought to confirm the claim. Idem, no. 62v, 98v, 143.

73 M. Frenkin, *Zakhvat vlasti Bolshevikami v Rossii i rol tylovykh garnizonov armii: Podgotovka i provedenie oktiabrskogo miatezha 1917–1918 gg*. (Jerusalem, 1982), 339–41; M. Kovalchuk, *Bytva dvokh revoliutsii. Persha viina Ukrainskoi Narodnoi Respubliky z Radianskoiu Rosieiu, 1917-1918 rr. Tom 1* (Kyiv, 2015), 286–92.

74 Zelenych, "Oznaiomlennia naselennia iz osoblyvostiamy vyborchoho zakonodavstva v 1917," 70, 90; Lozovyi, *Ahrarna revoliutsiia v Naddniprianskoii Ukraini: stavlennia selianstva do vlady v dobu Tsentralnoi rady*, 184.

75 TsDAVO f. 3204 op I sprava 11 no. 33. The observation was made by an unnamed Ukrainian professor who had worked for the Bolsheviks in 1920 in a job that involved travel. He fled in 1921 and filed his report in Berlin with the government-in-exile, from where a Bolshevik agent either stole or copied it.

76 TsDAVO f. 1429 op 2 sprava 113 no. 68. This observation was by a former UNR employee who had not fled with the Ukrainian-Polish armies in

1920. He travelled with a theatre company for five months through five hundred villages in the area west of the Dnipro.

77 As related by Antonenko-Davydovych: Tymoshenko ed., *Na shliakhakh i rozdorizhzhiakh:* http://chtyvo.org.ua/authors/Antonenko-Davydovych/Nashliakhakh_i_rozdorizhzhiakh/ > np.

78 Originally published in *Izvestiia Iuga* in an article supporting the short-lived Krivyi Rih Republic. TsDAHO f. 5 op 1 sprava 258 no. 237–41.

79 V.Zh. Tsvetkov, *Belye armii Iuga Rossii* (Moscow, 2000), 51–2; L. Hrynevych et al., *Istoriia Ukrainskoho viiska 1917–1995* (Kyiv, 1996), 245–7.

80 TsDAVO f. 2 op. 1 sprava 564 no. 32–3. Translated in part in S. Velychenko, *Painting Imperialism and Nationalism Red*, 212–14.

81 TsDAVO f. 1429 op 2 sprava 113 no. 63v; idem, no 23–4. The first report was by the above-cited UNR employee.

82 TsDAVO f. 3204 op 1 sprava 67 no. 36. V. Vasylenko, "Pidhotovka antybilshovytskoho povstannia v Ukraini u 1921 r. (za dokumentamy HAD Sluzhby bezpeky Ukrainy)," *Z arkhiviv VUChK-GPU-NKVD-KGB* 30–1(1–2) (2008) 138–97; idem, "Pivdenna hrupa viisk UNR u pidhotovtsi antybilshovyts'koho povstannia v Ukraini (1921 r.)," *Z arkhiviv VUChK-GPU-NKVD-KGB* 37(2) (2011), 94–125. I. Faizulin, "Iurko Tiutiunnyk i operatyvna rozrobka orhaniv DPU 'Sprava No. 39,'" in V.F. Verstiuk, ed., *Studii z istorii Ukrains'koi revoliutsii 1917–1921 rokiv: na poshanu Ruslana Iakovyshcha Pyroha. Zbirnyk naukovych prats* (Kyiv, 2011). D. Krasnosilsky, *Antybilshovytskyi rukh selian v pravoberezhnyi chastyni USRR*, 267–70.

83 TsDAHO f. 1 op 20 sprava 1457 no. 33–6, 46, 54, 60, 64.

84 TsDAHO f. 1 op 18 sprava 16 no. 50, 83; sprava 26 no. 16. Uman region peasants saw Petliura as their liberator from communism and could not imagine anyone except Jews being communists.

85 V. Popov, *Mizh vladoiu ta bezvladdiam. Naselennia Ukrainskykh mist u 1917–1920 rokakh* (Donetsk, 2013), 106, 147, 153–6, 176, 224, 568; Mykhailiuk, *Selianstvo*, 378–9.

86 The most recent extensive survey is T. Martin, *The Affirmative Action Empire: Nations and Nationalism in the Soviet Union, 1923–1939* (Ithaca, 2001), chs. 3, 6, 9.

87 Iu. Horlis-Horsky, *Spohady* (Lviv, 1935), 79–80. In Ukraine's large Russian-settlement towns in the southeast, such as Luhansk and Donets, anarchist and non-Bolshevik Russian party messages also faded.

88 V.A. Kravchenko, *I Chose Freedom* (New Brunswick, 1989), 31. See also Hryhorenko, *Spohady*, 59.

89 Mykhailiuk, *Selianstvo Ukrainy*, 263; L. Siegelbaum, *Soviet State and Society between Revolutions, 1918–1929* (Cambridge, 1992); V. Brovkin, *Russia after Lenin: Politics, Culture, and Society* (New York, 1998); V. Izmozik, "Voices from the Twenties: Private Correspondence Intercepted by the OGPU," *Russian*

Review (April, 1996): 287–308; S. Kulchytsky, ed., *Narysy povsiakdennoho zhyttia Radianskoi Ukrainy v dobu NEPU (1921-1928)* (Kyiv, 2010) I: 109–403.

90 V. Danylenko ed., *Ukrainska intelihentsiia i vlada. Zvedennia sekretnoho viddilu DPU USRR 1927–1929* (Kyiv, 2012), 117, 154, 164, 178, 293, 344, 417, 456, 483, 532. Reports noted support for Russian Menshevik and Russian SRs in cities.

Appendix

1 The 1920 census listed Ukraine's total population as approximately 4 million less than in 1917 – 1 million less urban population and 3 million less rural. *Naselenie Ukrainy po dannymy perepisi 1920 goda,* Statistika Ukrainy. No. 28 Seriia 1. Demografiia tom 1. Vypusk 11 (Kharkiv, 1922), Table 1. Table 2 gives population totals by district. L.S. Gaponenko and V.M. Kabuzan, "Materialy selskokhozaistvennykh perepisei 1916–1917 gg.," *Istoriia SSSR,* no. 6 (1961), 102, 114; I. Bruk and V.M. Kabuzan, "Chislennost i rasselenie Ukrainskogo etnosa v XVIII – nachale XX v.," *Sovetskaia etnografiia* no. 5 (1981), 23–4.

2 TsDAVO f. 34 op 3 sprava 896 no. 4.

3 TsDAVO f. 34 op 3 sprava 881 no. 52–3; idem, sprava 896 no. 4, 30–1. In Moscow five rotary presses, eleven lithographic presses, forty-three typesetting machines, and eleven of all other types of presses lay idle. The respective figures for Kyiv were thirteen, eight, and five. It is unclear whether the Kyiv survey included the old Iakovlev works.

4 TsDAVO f. 1184 op 1 sprava 11; *Volia* (Vienna) vol. 6 no. 2 (December 1919), 142.

5 E.G. Golomb and E.M. Fingerit, *Rasprostranie pechati v dorevoliutsionnoi Rossii i v Sovetskom Soiuze* (Moscow, 1967), 85.

6 Belov et al., *Iz istorii grazhdanskoi voiny*, II: 817–22; III: 316. Totals are not broken down for Ukraine. L.A. Molchanov, *Gazetnaia pressa Rossii v gody revoliutsii i grazhdanskoi voiny* (Moscow, 2002), 49, 137.

7 Fedoryshyn, *Presa*, 30.

8 TsDAHO f. 1 op. 30 sprava 333 no. 67.

9 V.M. Skachkov, ed., *Periodychni vydannia URSR: Gazety 1917–1960* (Kharkiv, 1965) 20; G.A. Belov et al., *Iz istorii grazhdanskoi voiny v SSSR* (Moscow, 1961) III: 301, 616; TsDAHO f. 1 op 20 sprava 318 no. 111; TsDAVO f. 34 op 2 sprava 132 no. 105. As of 1921 Kharkiv apparently had not got its lithographic press or a ration status for its printers. Idem, no. 105.

10 TsDAVO f. 177, op 1 sprava 41 no. 16–18. This figure does not include Crimea. The most newspapers (28) were in Kharkiv province. In some small towns papers were published in one or two hundred copies only. Not all papers appeared regularly.

11 TsDAHO f. 1 op 20 sprava 370 no. 16, 18. In July 1920, 488,992 copies of "all agitation literature" and 9,370 posters were distributed in all Ukraine.
12 TsDAHO f. 1 op 20 sprava 756 no. 167. *Kommunist* (Kharkiv) had the biggest press run – 25,000 copies.
13 TsDAVO f. 2 op 1 sprava 42 no. 8; idem, sprava 206 no. 4. For other provinces' details, idem, sprava 44.
14 TsDAVO f. 177 op. 1 sprava 41 no. 3, 4; idem, sprava 43 no. 33–4. It is not clear if there were two hundred copies each, or in total, for the Kharkiv newspapers. An undated chart, probably March 1921, indicates a per capita average distribution ratio in Donbass province (pop. 3,350,000) of 1: 82. TsDAVO f. 177 op 1 sprava 215 no. 97.
15 In an undated report from early 1919 the Central Distribution Agency estimated that Ukraine should have a minimal daily run of 350,000 copies. TsDAVO f. 2 op 1 sprava 17 no. 149.
16 TsDAHO f. 1 op 20 sprava 751 no. 2–3. The highest press run for a single paper was in Kharkiv (25,000). In all other provincial capitals the highest runs averaged 4,000 to 5,000.
17 TsDAHO f. 1 op 20 sprava 442 no. 5, 54, 56, 58, 65. Of the five where distribution did occur, Radomyshl district (1897 – 1,167,000 pop.) had the highest saturation with supposedly 66,055 copies of newspapers (1: 18), and 29,000 copies of leaflets and posters distributed during one month. Idem, no. 9, 29, 59, 52.
18 Population totals are from a 1920 All Ukrainian State Publishers (VUDV) report: TsDAVO f. 177 op 1 sprava 199 no. 31–3; TsDAVO f. 177 op 1 sprava 44 no. 14. This total counts approximately 1 million people more than the published 1920 census. In November 1920, 15 of Kyiv province's 31 newspapers (24 per cent of all printed copies), were imported from Russia. In 1921, 28 of Ukraine's 83 newspapers were published in Russia and imported.
19 TsDAVO f. 177 op 1 sprava 44 no. 57–62. R. Kuhn, *The Media in France* (London, 1995), 19.
20 Kivshar, *Ukrainskyi knyzhkovyi rukh iak istorychne iavyshche (1917-23 rr.)* 179.
21 *Otchet o deialnosti Kharkovskogo gubernskogo komiteta Kommunisticheskoi partii (bolshevikov) Ukrainy za vremia 22 dekabria 1919 g. po 1 marta 1920 g.* (Khariv, 1920), 23–4, 45.
22 All figures are rounded off. TsDAVO f. 5 op 4 sprava 10; idem, f. 2 op 1 sprava 463 no. 19–21. There are some minor differences between archival and published figures. A.A. Marinov, *V stroiu zashchitnikov oktiabria* (Moscow, 1982), 42–3; P.M. Popov, ed., *Knyhy i drukarstvo na Ukraini* (Kyiv, 1964), 212–23. Dmytrienko, *Lystivsky Bilshovytskykh orhanizatsii Ukrainy 1917–1920 iak istorychne dzherelo* 144–68, 288, 300–3. I; Zolotoverkhy,

Stanovlennia Ukrainskoi radianskoi kultury (1917–1920 rr.) (Kyiv, 1961), 188. A. Prykholko, "Knyzhkova produktsiia na Ukraini za chas revoliutsii," *Holos druku* no. 1 (1921), 30–1.

23 TsDAVO f. 177 op 1 sprava 196 no 2; idem, sprava 215 no 1, 4–5. It is unclear if the Ukraine totals also exclude Volyn and Podillia provinces. Six per cent of leaflets and 39 per cent of posters were imported from Russia. Another set of figures (idem, sprava 150 no. 21), gives 203,800 poster copies (41 per cent Ukr.).

24 TsDAVO f. 177 op 1 sprava 56 no. 29; idem, sprava 215 no. 18; idem, sprava 206 no. 14.

25 TsDAVO f. 177 op 1 sprava 32 no. 42.

26 Dmytrienko, *Lystivsky Bilshovytskykh orhanizatsii Ukrainy*, 120. V. Antonov-Ovsienko, *Zapiski o grazhdanskoi voine* (Moscow and Leningrad, 1924–35), III: 188.

27 M. Rubach, ed., *Radianske budivnytstvo na Ukraini v roky hromadianskoi viiny (November 1918–August 1919)* (Kyiv, 1962), 279. In 1920, in the Kamianets area, another train released either 6,000 to 7,500 copies of a two-page newspaper, or 15,000 copies of pamphlets, daily. TsDAVO f. 182 op 1 sprava 2.

28 TsDAHO f. 2 op 1 sprava 463 no 25. Unclear how much, if any, was in Ukrainian.

29 TsDAVO f. 573 op 1 sprava 855 no. 35–7, 69; idem, sprava 333 no. 173; TsDAVO f. 573 op 1 sprava 855 no. 197–8. All figures rounded off. Under normal conditions one rotary press used twenty-five tons of newsprint in eight hours. In 1920 it averaged seventeen tons.

30 *Kommunist* (Kyiv), 6 August 1919.

31 TsDAHO f. 1 op 20 sprava 358 no. 390.

32 TsDAVO f. 177 op 1 sprava 44 no. 13.

33 TsDAVO f. 177 op 1 sprava 215 no. 5.

34 TsDAHO f. 1 op 20 sprava 358 no. 50. The document also contains figures for Zhytomir district (no. 76) that are somewhat higher, but it is not clear if they refer to a two-week or one-month period.

35 TsDAHO f. 1 op 20 sprava 358 no. 390.

36 TsDAHO f. 1 op 20 sprava 358 no. 47, 78–9.

37 TsDAHO f. 1 op 20 sprava 360 no. 101–15. It is unclear in the reports if the local agent simply did not have the figures for these territories: 3,523 (2,930 Ukr.) copies of the Zvenyhorod newpaper were printed between 20 and 30 July.

38 "Stanovyshche na Ukraini," *Volia* (Vienna) (October, 1920), 64.

39 TsDAHO f. 1 op 20 sprava 364 no. 114–27. On average, 75 per cent of newspapers, but less than 50 per cent of pamphlets and leaflets, were in Ukrainian. Posters were apparently rare in villages.

40 TsDAHO f. 1. op 20 sprava 364 no. 30, 45, 62–4, 75–6.

41 TsDAHO f. 1. op 20 sprava 367 no. 25, 118, 253.

42 I.V. Narskii, *Zhizn v katastrofe. Budni naseleniia Urala v 1917-1922 gg.* (Moscow, 2000) 213.

43 Shafir, *Gazeta i derevnia,* 6–8, 17, 30, 36, 61, 90.

44 Surviving inventories and manifests indicate how many thousands of tons of paper and ink officials acquired, then printed, and distributed. For the year 1921, for example, TsDAVO f. 34 op 3 sprava 997.

45 M. Shendrovich, "Poligraficheskaia promeshlennost i perspektivy na 1921 god," *Pechat i revoliutsiia* no. 1 (May–July 1921), 31. Aulich and Hewitt, *Seduction or Instruction: First World War Posters in Britain and Europe,* 36.

46 Pedrini, *Propaganda, Persuasion, and the Great War,* 20, 60.

47 Siffer and Schnitzler, eds., *L'autre Guerre,* 16; R. Kuhn, *The Media in France* (London, 1995), 19; P. Albert, *La presse française* (Paris, 1998), 169. H.D. Fischer, ed. *Deutsche Zeitungen des 17. bis 20. Jahrhunderts* (Munich, 1972); A.P. Wadsworth, "Newspaper Circulation, 1800–1954," *Transactions of the Manchester Statistical Society,* Session 1954–5, 1–41.

Pamphlets

(Chronological order by issuing group)

Central Rada and UNR

Anon, *Iak i dlia choho treba orhanizuvatysia* (Poltava, 1917)
Anon, *Iakoho ladu nam treba* (Kyiv, 1917)
Baier M, *Zemelna reforma i osnovy zemelnoi polityky na Ukraini* (Kyiv, 1917).
– *Sotsiializatsiia chy zemelna vlasnist?* (Kyiv, 1918)
A. Boian, *Interesy robitnytstva ta natsionalne pytannia* (Kyiv, nd. 1917?)
V. Boiko, *Zemstvo i narodni upravy* (Kyiv, 1917)
M. Cherkavsky, *Do intellihentsii na Ukraini* (Zhytomir, 1917)
Hryhoriev nash [pseud. Nikifor Hryhoriiv], *Iakoi respubliky treba bidnym liudam?* (Kyiv, 1917)
V. Hryshchynsky, *Proletariat panuiuchykh ta pryhnichennykh natsii* (Katerynoslav, 1917)
M. Iakymenko, *Zemelna sprava na Ukraini* (np, 1917)
A. Khomyk, *Vserosiiski Ustanovchi zbory chy Vsesvitnyi Mizhnarodnyi Konhres?* (Fastiv, 1917)
Kh. Kolomeichenko, *Ekonomika i Ukraina* (np 1917)
S. Kulyk, "Iak Rossiia vyzyzkuie Ukrainu," *Pamiatkova knyzhka Soiuz Vyzvolennia Ukrainy i kalendar na 1917 rik* (Vienna, 1917)
I. Maievsky, *Chervonyi imperiialism. Po shliakhu kontr-revoliutsii* (Kyiv, 1917), reprinted in *Khronika 2000*, nos. 27–8 (1999): 286–96
P. Maltsiv, *Ukraina v derzhavnomu biudzheti Rossii* (Lubni, 1917)
A. Pilkevich, *Kto takie Ukrainsty i chego oni dobyvaiutsia* (Kyiv, 1917)
O. Pilch [Pylkevych], *Choho nas Ukrainstiv Katsapy prozvaly burzhuiamy* (np nd --1919?)
P. Syrotenko, *De povynna vyrishytysia zemelna sprava* (Poltava, 1917)

A. Ternychenko, *Kryvdy Ukrainskoho Khliboroba* (Lubni, 1917)
M. Zahirnia, *Pro derzhavnyi lad u vsiakykh narodiv*, (Kyiv, 1917)
B. Zaklynsky, *Katekhizm Ukrainstia*, 7th ed. (Lviv-Kyiv, 1918)
Anon, *Natsionale vidrozhennia i kooperatsiia (zbirnyk stattei)* (Kyiv, 1918)
Anon, *Cherez shcho Ukraina musila oddilytsia vid Rosii* (Kyiv, 1919)
Anon, *Choho my povynni borotys iz bolshovykamy-komunistamy* (np. 1919)
Anon, *Do robitnykiv i selian* (Kamianets-Podilsky, 1919)
Anon, *Federatsiia chy samostiinist?* (Vinnytsia, 1919)
Anon, *Shanuite narodniu intelihentsiiu* (Katerynoslav, 1919)
Anon, *Shcho tse za liude v avstriiskii formi idyt do nas?* (np. 1919)
Anon, *Shcho robyt pravyteltsvo Ukrainskoi respubliky dlia naroda?* (Vinnytsia, 1919)
Anon, *Pora vzhe buty nam svidomymy i korysnymy hromadianamy Ukrainskoi Narodnoi Respubliky* (np. 1919)
Anon, *Bezsovisnyi obman* (Kamianets-Podilsky, 1919)
Anon, *Ukraina v mizhnarodnii politytsi* (Kamianets, 1919)
Anon, *Svoia sorochka* (np, 1919)
Anon, *Pravdyve slovo pro bolshovykiv-komunistiv* (Kamianets-Podilsky, 1919)
Anon, *Cherez shcho chornosotentsi starorezhimnyky a vsiaki ynshi tsarsko-hetmanski prysluzhnyky tak nenavydiat i obbrikhuit Halychan* (Kamianets-Podilsky, 1919)
Anon, *Iak vony duriat* (Kyiv, 1919)
Anon, *Shaniute narodniu intelihentsiiu* (Katerynoslav, 1919)
Anon, *Do Halytskykh zhovniriv* (np, 1919)
Anon, "*Shcho to za Ukraina?*" (Kamianets-Podilsky, 1919)
Anon, *Lytsari* (np. 1919?)
Anon, *Do zbroii. Het Chervonykh imperialistiv* (np. 1919)
I. Iurkivsky, *Chomy my musimo borotys za samostiinu Ukrainsku Narodniu Respubliku* (Kamianets-Podilsky, 1919)
Io. Ivanovych, *Pro Derzhavu. Shcho take derzhava i derzhavne vlada, chy vony liudam potribni, ta iak povynni buty vlashtovani shchob trudovomu narodovi bulo dobre zhyty*, (Vinnytsia, 1919)
Nash H., *Vchimosia panuvaty* (Kyiv, 1919)
O. N[azaruk], *Za shcho my boremsia* (Kamianets, 1919)
S. Palyi-Fastivsky, *Pro te shcho bulo i bude, abo zhyv sobi sashka syva-semeriashka* (np, 1919)
V. Poliashchuk, *De-shcho pro orhanizatsiiu vlady* (Kamianets-Podilsky, 1919)

On Jews

Anon, *Ievrei ta Ukrainska Respublika* (Kamianets, 1919)
Hr. Hetmanets, *Do Strashnykh dniv u kyivi* (Kyiv-Lviv, 1919)

M. Hlushkivsky, *Sterezhitsia provokatsii* (Kamianets, 1919)
B Martos, *Do Ievreiskoho hromadianstva i robitnytstva na Ukraini* (Kamianets, 1919)
S. Zolotarenko, *Chomy sered Zhydivskykh robitnykiv ie bahato bolshevykiv?* (Kamianets, 1919)

Ukrainian Left-SRs and SDs

A.P., *Ukrainska partiia Sotsialistiv-Revoliutsioneriv i tymchasove Robitnyche-Selianskyi uriad Ukrainy* (Poltava, 1919)
V. Blakytnyi, *Iak prodavaly Ukrainu* (Kyiv, 1919)
V. Blakytny ed., *Vynnychenko proty Petliury* (np 1920)
Anon, *Do rozrishennia natsionalnoho pytannia* (Kyiv, 1920)
Anon, *Khto taki Kommunisty-Borotbysty* (Lubny, 1919; Kyiv 1920)
Iu, Chaikivsky, *Iak Halychan vtiahnuly v kontr-revoliutsiiu* (Kharkiv, 1920)
A. Richytsky, M. Tkachenko, *Proekt programy Ukrainskoi Kommunistychnoi Partii* (np. 1919)
A. Richytsky ed., *Nash Spir* (np., 1921)

Bolsheviks

Anon, *Gotuites rabochie i krestiany Ukrainy* (np. 1918)
Anon, *'O Katsapakh'. Kak pomeshchiki i kulaki durachat krestian* (3rd ed. Kyiv, 1919)
Anon, *Pravda o bolshevikakh* (Kyiv, 1919)
[N. Podvoiskii], *Oborona sotsialisticheskogo otechestva* (Kyiv, 1919)
idem, *Na Ukraine* (Kyiv 1919)
D. Stonov (Vlodavskii), *Slovo Ukrainskim krestianam* (Kremenchuh, 1919)
V. Zatonsky, *Otkrytoe pismo Tsentralnomu komitetu Ukrainskoi Kommunistycheskoi partii borotbistov* (np. 1919)
Anon, *Tezisy dlia sobesedovanii politrukov s krasnoarmeitsamy o znachenii Oktiabrskoi Revoliutsii* (np. 1920)
Anon, *Borba s banditizmom i kulatskoi vosstaniem na Ukraine* (np. 1920)
Anon, *SLAVA PETLIURI (Na koho robyt Petliura)* (np., 1920?)
Did Sokyrka, Nashe lykho, (abo shcho nam zavazhaie vstanovyty poriadok) , (Kharkiv, 1920)
N. I. Faleev, *Za chto prolivala krov Ukraina?* (Kharkiv, 1920)
Panas Liukko, *Chy potribni nezamozhnomu selianynu ioho komitety* (Kyiv, 1920)
M. Kr., *Pravda pro Petliurivski brekhni* (np.,1920?)
M. Pavlovich, *UKRAINA Kak obiekt mezhdunarodnoi kontr-revoliutsii* (Moscow, 1920)

G. Rakitov, *Pisma o Makhnovtsakh* (Katerynoslav, 1920)
Kh. Rakovskii et al, *Doloi Makhnovshchinu* (Kharkiv, 1920)
M. Ravich-Cherkasskii, *Makhno i Makhnovshchina* (Katerynoslav, 1920)
M. Riesner, *Cbto takoe sovetskaia vlast* (Pyriatyn, nd.)
Ia. Selo, *Bandyty-'Sotisalisty'- Makhnovtsi* (np. nd.)
S. Vasylchenko, *Chervona Volia vilnoi Ukrainy* (Kyiv, 1920)
S. Vasilchenko, *Kommunisticheskaia Partiia (bolsh.) na Ukraine. (Voprosy nashei raboty i taktiki* (Kyiv, 1920?)
M. Vladimirov, *Ukrainskie Krestiane i prodovolstvennyi vopros* (Katerynoslav, 1920)
Idem ed., *Spravochnik prodovostvennogo agenta Ukr. Sots. Sov. Respubliki. Vypusk 1 i 2* (Kharkiv, 1920)
G. Zinoviev, *Kto nash glavnyi vrag na Ukraine?* (Kharkiv, 1920)
Anon, V., *Zashchitu Sovetskoi Ukrainy. Sbornik Diplomaticheskikh dokumentov i istoricheskikh materialov* (Kharkiv, 1921)
Anon, *Borba s Banditizmom (Tezisy-konspekt dlia lektorov),* (Kharkiv, 1921)
Iu, Mordalevych, *Do Povstantsiv, Mii shliakh* (np. 1921)
G. Rakitov, *Pisma o Makhnovtsakh* (Katerynoslav, nd. – 1921?)

On Jews

Anon, *Dlia choho i iak kulaky tskuiut proty ievreiiv* (Odesa, 1920)
P. Eletskii, *O Ievreiiakh* (Chernihiv, 1919) .

Index

Page numbers in *italics* indicate images.

www.ingramcontent.com/pod-product-compliance
Lightning Source LLC
LaVergne TN
LVHW040151080826
844660LV00014B/926/J

* 9 7 8 1 4 8 7 5 0 4 6 8 7 *